HOME IMPROVEMENT COST GUIDE

SECOND EDITION

R.S. Means Company, Inc.

Consumers Union
Mount Vernon, New York

R.S. MEANS COMPANY, INC.

Publisher
William D. Mahoney

Senior Editors
Roger Grant
Charles Tringale
David Tringale

Contributing Editors
Allan Cleveland
Donald Denzer
Jeffrey Goldman
Dwayne Lehigh
Alan Lew
John Moylan
Kenneth Randall
Kornelis Smit
Edward Wetherill
Ernest Williams
Rory Woolsey
David Zuniga

Illustrations by
Carl Linde

ISBN: 0-89043-183-3

Consumers Union Edition

First printing, August 1989

Manufactured in the United States of America

Library of Congress Catalog Number 89-062814

Home Improvement Cost Guide (Second Edition) is a Consumer Reports Book published by Consumers Union, the nonprofit organization that publishes *Consumer Reports*, the monthly magazine of test reports, product Ratings, and buying guidance. Established in 1936, Consumers Union is chartered under the Not-For-Profit Corporation Law of the State of New York.

The purposes of Consumers Union, as stated in its charter, are to provide consumers with information and counsel on consumer goods and services, to give information on all matters relating to the expenditure of the family income, and to initiate and to cooperate with individual and group efforts seeking to create and maintain decent living standards.

Consumers Union derives its income solely from the sale of *Consumer Reports* and other publications. In addition, expenses of occasional public service efforts may be met, in part, by nonrestrictive, noncommercial contributions, grants, and fees. Consumers Union accepts no advertising or product samples and is not beholden in any way to any commercial interest. Its Ratings and reports are solely for the use of the readers of its publications. Neither the Ratings nor the reports nor any Consumers Union publications, including this book, may be used in advertising or for any commercial purpose. Consumers Union will take all steps open to it to prevent such uses of its material, its name, or the name of *Consumer Reports*.

FOREWORD TO THE CONSUMERS UNION EDITION

Since 1987, when we published the first edition of *Home Improvement Cost Guide*, Americans have increasingly stayed put and renovated, remodeled, or added on to their homes, largely because of climbing interest rates and inflated housing costs. According to the U.S. Census Bureau, Americans in 1986 spent $91.3 billion on residential maintenance and improvements, and by 1988 that figure had already climbed to $106 billion. During the same period, new home construction experienced a decline, the first such drop since the baby-boom housing expansion began in the early 1970s.

Without the rapid appreciation in property values to which most American homeowners had grown accustomed, homeowners have become increasingly conservative with their home improvement dollars. Among the many factors involved in deciding whether or not to make an improvement, cost is the primary consideration. And yet no other home improvement book we've seen covers costs in anything more than a cursory way. That's why *Home Improvement Cost Guide*, by the R. S. Means Company, remains a uniquely valuable consumer resource and tool.

Home improvement projects usually begin with a desired goal, sometimes vague or undefined, that somehow must translate into the final result: an updated bathroom, for instance, or a new bilevel deck. As the project progresses, questions of demolition, design, structural integrity, materials, special tools, licensed skills like plumbing and wiring, fixtures, and finished work may all come into play. The homeowner needs to determine not only who will do the work, but how much it should cost, how much he or she can afford, and how long it should take.

Home Improvement Cost Guide provides ready answers to these and many other questions, helping both the weekend home handyperson and the homeowner who wants to contract for the best skills and materials available. Written in clear, accessible language, the book details the costs, materials, labor, and time estimates for 74 popular home-improvement projects—interior and exterior—for nearly every part of the house likely to undergo renovation.

For the consumer looking to hire a contractor or tradesperson for the work, this guide provides a basis for evaluating and comparing bids, assessing how much of the quote is for materials, spotting hidden or unexpected charges, and determining construction quality standards to be observed. For the do-it-yourselfer, time requirements for each job are also discussed—from the beginner's level to professional skills. Some of the worst pitfalls of the home handyperson are thus side-stepped. Lack of skill or experience, insufficient tools, and underestimation of time required can, singly or collectively, make a do-it-yourself project more trouble and expense than it's worth; this book should help in avoiding all three.

In addition, *Home Improvement Cost Guide* notes the wide variation in both size and luxury for particular projects. For instance, five different kitchen plans are offered, each in a standard and deluxe model. Room additions range from 8 x 8 feet to 20 x 24 feet. While such a guide ideally would allow the homeowner to assemble a customized project component sheet to suit his or her individual needs, the number of variables affecting a particular job on a particular house are almost endless. Therefore, these 74 sample projects can only provide reference points for deciding what's feasible, what's affordable, what's reasonable to pay, and what's good building practice.

For additional guidance on the cost of basic materials as well as contractors' fees, the book contains an 81-page illustrated section on general building and replacement costs per linear or square foot for a variety of building practices, including excavations and foundations, exterior siding, roofing, and general mechanical and electrical work. Again, each entry pinpoints required materials and their unit costs, work hours, and contractors' fees. The appendix that follows, the Location Multiplier, allows you to adjust these average costs to your own area of the country by using price indexes provided for more than 500 American cities, plus 18 in Canada.

A number of changes have been incorporated into this edition of *Home Improvement Cost Guide* in an effort to make it even more current, authoritative, and accessible. The first and most important change is that *all* prices in the book have been thoroughly updated, so the information herein should be pertinent through the early 1990s. In addition, the estimate charts for

each of the 74 projects have been amended for greater clarity, and the figures are presented in such a way that both materials charges and man-hour charges are clear. Finally, each of the 74 projects in sections one and two now include cross-references to the corresponding pages in section three, and section three itself has been revised to make it more accessible.

The R. S. Means Company has published cost data for the construction industry for the past 44 years, and this book remains their only reference source for the consumer market. We welcome the availability of this valuable information and look forward to further updates of the material in future editions.

As is always the case when we publish a Consumers Union Edition of a book not of our own creation, the information and advice contained herein are those of the authors and not necessarily those of Consumers Union.

The Editors of Consumer Reports Books

TABLE OF CONTENTS

TABLE OF
CONTENTS Continued

TABLE OF CONTENTS Continued

FOREWORD

For the past 48 years, R.S. Means Company, Inc. has researched and published cost data for the building construction industry. *Home Improvement Cost Guide* applies that valuable experience to home projects. The book is designed and written to provide homeowners with professional information for the planning of residential improvements. Regardless of your own hands-on involvement in a particular project, the data in the book will acquaint you with the procedures, material costs, and contractor's charges required to complete it. Plans for 74 home improvement projects are presented, ranging from kitchen and bath renovations to greenhouse and skylight installations. Included in each of the model plans is a detailed, carefully-researched estimate of costs and installation times. There is also a description of the procedures required to build or install the facility. Pointers and precautions are provided to help you organize the project and assess the level of difficulty of its various operations. To help you determine the length of time required to complete the tasks, adjusted man-hours estimates are provided for do-it-yourselfers of three skill levels: beginners, handymen, and experts. Each model plan also includes a clearly labeled and accurately scaled illustration of the project, which identifies the material components and shows their relationship.

The book is divided into three sections. The first two, "Interiors" and "Exteriors", include all of the model projects. These sections are further divided into categories such as "Kitchens" and "Patios", each of which contains several different remodeling options. The third section is the "Details section", which supplements the first two parts of the book. It contains a handy reference guide to unit items and their prices and will help you to make adjustments in the model plans based on your individual requirements. Section Three will also enable you to estimate the cost of a project that you design completely on your own. Illustrations are provided in this section as well.

The purpose of the book is to inform you of not only the cost, but also the various factors which affect the planning process. This information will help you to determine which parts of the project you want to take on yourself, and which would be better undertaken by a contractor. When the planning and construction are accomplished with care, the lasting value of your home improvement will be assured; and your time and money will be soundly invested. With the right materials properly placed and in keeping with the design and style of your home, any of these remodeling projects will contribute comfort and convenience to your home life while adding value to your house. The cost of implementing your improvement plan may vary with the particular conditions of your project and your abilities as a do-it-yourselfer, but the benefits of good workmanship, materials, and organization will remain for years to come.

SECTION ONE INTERIORS

AND

SECTION TWO EXTERIORS

HOW TO USE SECTIONS ONE & TWO

The first two sections, "Interiors" and "Exteriors" provide descriptions and cost estimates for complete interior and exterior home improvement projects. Section Three, "Details," follows these two sections. This part of the book provides cost information for specific construction items. It can help you price the components for your individual projects. Tips for using Section Three can be found at the beginning of that section.

Each project plan presented in the "Interiors" and "Exteriors" sections contains three types of information to help you organize the job. The first is a detailed illustration, which shows the finished project and the relationship of its components. The second is a general description of the plan, which includes a review of the materials and the installation process. It also evaluates the level of difficulty of the project. The "What To

Watch Out For" section highlights ways to enhance the project or to cope with particularly difficult installation procedures. The third major element is a detailed project estimate chart, which lists the required materials and professional installation times and their corresponding costs. The components of this chart are described in detail below.

Key to Abbreviations
C.Y. - cubic yard
Ea. - each
L.F. - linear foot
Pr. - pair
Sq. - square (100 square feet of area)
S.F. - square foot
S.Y. - square yard
V.L.F. - vertical linear foot

Description of the materials used in the project.

Quantity of each material and its standard unit of measure is given in this figure. A key to the abbreviations can be found on this page.

Man-Hours represents the estimated time it takes a professional tradesman to perform each of the installations within the project. The total number of contractor's hours for a complete project is given at the bottom of this column.

Material cost estimated for each item in the "Description" column. This figure represents the price of a single unit, multiplied by the required number of units shown in the "Quantity" column. The prices reflect the national average of what you can expect to pay at a building supply retailer for the components used in the project. The material cost figure for the entire project can be found at the bottom of this column. (Sales tax has not been included in these figures and will have to be added for a more accurate total.) To tailor these prices to your specific area of the country, refer to the "Location Multipliers" in this book.

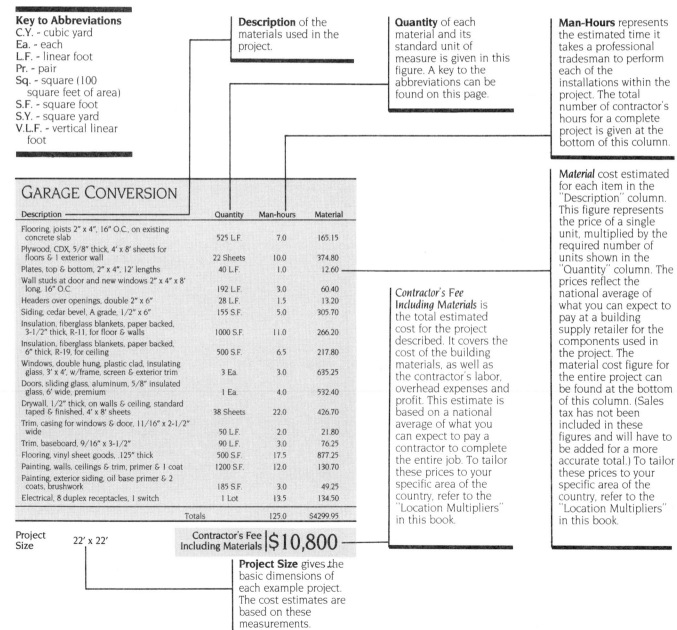

GARAGE CONVERSION

Description	Quantity	Man-hours	Material
Flooring, joists 2" x 4", 16" O.C., on existing concrete slab	525 L.F.	7.0	165.15
Plywood, CDX, 5/8" thick, 4' x 8' sheets for floors & 1 exterior wall	22 Sheets	10.0	374.80
Plates, top & bottom, 2" x 4", 12' lengths	40 L.F.	1.0	12.60
Wall studs at door and new windows 2" x 4" x 8' long, 16" O.C.	192 L.F.	3.0	60.40
Headers over openings, double 2" x 6"	28 L.F.	1.5	13.20
Siding, cedar bevel, A grade, 1/2" x 6"	155 S.F.	5.0	305.70
Insulation, fiberglass blankets, paper backed, 3-1/2" thick, R-11, for floor & walls	1000 S.F.	11.0	266.20
Insulation, fiberglass blankets, paper backed, 6" thick, R-19, for ceiling	500 S.F.	6.5	217.80
Windows, double hung, plastic clad, insulating glass, 3' x 4', w/frame, screen & exterior trim	3 Ea.	3.0	635.25
Doors, sliding glass, aluminum, 5/8" insulated glass, 6' wide, premium	1 Ea.	4.0	532.40
Drywall, 1/2" thick, on walls & ceiling, standard taped & finished, 4' x 8' sheets	38 Sheets	22.0	426.70
Trim, casing for windows & door, 11/16" x 2-1/2" wide	50 L.F.	2.0	21.80
Trim, baseboard, 9/16" x 3-1/2"	90 L.F.	3.0	76.25
Flooring, vinyl sheet goods, .125" thick	500 S.F.	17.5	877.25
Painting, walls, ceilings & trim, primer & 1 coat	1200 S.F.	12.0	130.70
Painting, exterior siding, oil base primer & 2 coats, brushwork	185 S.F.	3.0	49.25
Electrical, 8 duplex receptacles, 1 switch	1 Lot	13.5	134.50
Totals		125.0	$4299.95

Contractor's Fee Including Materials is the total estimated cost for the project described. It covers the cost of the building materials, as well as the contractor's labor, overhead expenses and profit. This estimate is based on a national average of what you can expect to pay a contractor to complete the entire job. To tailor these prices to your specific area of the country, refer to the "Location Multipliers" in this book.

Project Size	22' x 22'	Contractor's Fee Including Materials	$10,800

Project Size gives the basic dimensions of each example project. The cost estimates are based on these measurements.

SECTION ONE
INTERIORS

This section of the book is designed to inform you of the costs of various interior remodeling projects and to point out some practical concerns that will help to determine which parts of the job are appropriate for the do-it-yourselfer, and which are better left to the contractor. Cost is the primary consideration, with figures given for all materials required in a standard renovation. The estimated contractors' charges, also listed, should be weighed against the investment of the homeowner's time and willingness to tolerate the inconveniences which often accompany home remodeling.

The projects in this section share common features which apply specifically to interior remodeling. One is the degree of accuracy required in the layout of the improvement, and the measuring, cutting and assembly of materials. Because of these demands in interior work, do-it-yourselfers should not hesitate to call in contractors when needed. Although the cost of the project will increase with professional help, the long-term benefits of fine workmanship far outweigh the extra initial expense.

Preparation of the site is another factor which has special meaning in interior remodeling. Old fixtures may have to be removed, and floors, walls, and ceilings reconditioned and prepared to receive new coverings. Experienced do-it-yourselfers can handle many of these basic tasks, but beginners may have to spend some extra money for professional help. Correction of structural problems, particularly, should be left to qualified tradesmen and experts.

Heating, ventilating, plumbing and electrical work can also be a bit tricky in interior remodeling, especially in older houses where the heating system, piping or wiring is in questionable condition or inconveniently arranged. The example projects include the cost of basic plumbing and electrical work. Heating system modification costs have not been included. Should your project require changes to the heating and ventilating system, additional costs will be incurred. Refer to Section Three for help in determining these charges. Time is a major consideration, especially in kitchen and bathroom remodeling projects, where an expedient renovation can minimize the disruption borne by the household.

Another important consideration is the delivery and storage of materials for an interior project. The method of transporting the materials to the site and to the appropriate room in the house should be carefully planned. The size of entryways will have to be taken into account when moving large appliances or building components, and a location arranged for storage of materials, especially those which are not weather resistant.

All of the renovation projects covered in the "Interiors" section start with a space enclosed by walls and under the cover of a roof. If you are interested in building an addition to house your new room, there are cost guides and descriptions for these improvements in the "Exteriors" section of this book.

Remodeling the interior of your home presents some definite challenges, but it also promises rewards which are realized daily in the improved appearance, function, and value of your house. Being aware of what is involved in a project and knowing the costs in advance will help you to plan the best renovation.

HALF ATTIC

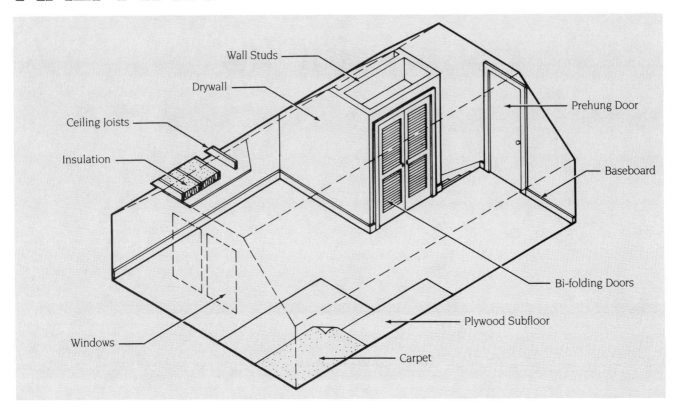

Wall Studs

Drywall

Ceiling Joists

Insulation

Prehung Door

Baseboard

Bi-folding Doors

Plywood Subfloor

Windows

Carpet

If space is limited in your attic, or if you want to continue using a portion of it for storage, then a partial renovation may accommodate your needs. Follow the same guidelines as in a full attic plan when you consider the feasibility of expanding a half attic space. The prime considerations are a large enough area, adequate head room, and accessibility.

MATERIALS

The materials used for a half attic renovation include the common interior construction components employed in most house systems. The framing members consist of construction grade 2" x 4"s for the walls and closet, and 2" x 6"s for ceiling joists. Conventional 1/2" sheetrock, taped and finished, paneling, or decorative veneers like barnboard may be installed at varying costs for the walls and ceilings. Care should be taken in selecting the R-value of the insulation material so that the attic room and the rest of the house are efficiently protected from heat loss and gain in the winter and summer.

You can save money by installing carpeting instead of hardwood floors, even though it requires installing 5/8" as opposed to 1/2" plywood subflooring. An alternative subfloor for the carpet, in cases where more strength is needed, consists of a layer of 1/2" sheathing plywood covered by a layer of 3/8" particleboard. Try to run the particleboard at right angles to the plywood and avoid coincidental seams of the two layers of material. This two-layer underlayment costs more and takes more time to install, but the extra money and effort will give your carpeting and the new floor a more even and durable surface.

The window unit used in this half attic is a metal-clad casement type, which is more expensive than a conventional all wood uninsulated window; but the extra initial cost will be returned over time in savings on fuel and maintenance. The door on the interior wall of the new room is a standard hollow-core lauan prehung unit, but you can purchase paneled and other solid or decorative doors at additional cost. The closet door used in this plan

is a bi-folding, louvered unit which provides total accessibility to the 4' closet opening.

The electrical materials include five receptacles, two light fixtures, and the wiring required to supply and connect the components. If you want to add to the electrical work, make sure that you plan ahead and do it before the sheetrock is installed. Also, check to see that your electric service has the capacity to allow for the new room's circuit. There is a good chance that the new supply wiring will have to be fished up from the service panel, so unless you are experienced in electrical work, call an electrician to perform this task.

Finishing the room can provide an excellent opportunity to gain some experience in the use of tools, even for novices. The cutting, staining or painting, and installation of trim boards may involve a few mistakes at first, but with a simple miter box, careful measuring, and some patience, you will catch on quickly. You can stain or paint the trim boards in your backyard or cellar before you install them, thus enabling you to paint the walls through to the finish coat. Any marks made during installation of the trim can be easily touched up in the final stage. Taping and finishing the sheetrock may take some time if you have never done it before; but the right tools, sound advice, and a quick lesson from a friend who has done it can give you professional results while saving you money.

LEVEL OF DIFFICULTY

Like a full attic conversion, a partial or half attic renovation project is a major challenge for homeowners, who are doing much of the work on their own. Although the project appears to be relatively routine, many different building skills are required to complete the job from framing through to the finish work. Beginnners should not jump into a project of this size without ample professional assistance and advice. If you are a beginner and want to tackle a half or full attic conversion, plan on adding 100% to the professional man-hours estimate. If you are acquainted with tools and have limited experience in building, add 50% to the professional time. Experts with extensive experience in building should anticipate an additional 15% above the professional time.

WHAT TO WATCH OUT FOR

The attic space of most old or new dwellings can be used for renovation if there is a minimum of 8' from the floor to the ridge board. If your attic does not have sufficient height and area to accommodate a livable room, then dormers may have to be constructed or other costly structural alterations may have to be made. Accessibility is another major consideration. Remember that a conventional staircase will take up precious living or storage space not only in the new attic room, but also in the floor below. Remember, too, that in most cases building materials will have to be carried to the second or third floor attic site, so carefully measure the stairway or other means of access to the work area to head off any materials access problems. It is also a good idea to check the floor joists in the attic for general condition and spacing. The ceiling joists in many older homes are spaced at odd intervals, rather than at 16", and, therefore, need additional strengthening to support the proposed living space above.

SUMMARY

If your house meets the basic height, space, and accessibility conditions, a half attic renovation may be an ideal way to convert often misused space to living area. It is the perfect solution if you need to expand, but would like to keep a portion of your attic for storage. Because this space is already under roof and protected from the elements, the construction of a new room can be accomplished easily and economically.

HALF ATTIC

Description	Quantity	Man-hours	Material
Flooring, underlayment grade plywood 4' x 8' sheets, 5/8" thick	9 Sheets	3.5	198.65
Ceiling joists, 2" x 6", 16" O.C., 7' long	17 Ea.	1.5	56.20
Plates, top & bottom, 2" x 4" 12' lengths	120 L.F.	2.5	37.75
Knee wall studs, 2" x 4", 16" O.C., 4' long	28 Ea.	2.0	35.25
Wall studs, 2" x 4", 16" O.C., 8' long	34 Ea.	4.5	85.55
Blocking, miscellaneous to wood construction, 2" x 4" x 8'	2 Ea.	0.5	5.00
Insulation, R-11, 3-1/2" thick, 15" wide foil-faced blanket 88 S.F. per roll	8 Rolls	3.5	230.00
Insulation, R-19, 6" thick, 15" wide foil-faced blanket 88 S.F. per roll	2 Rolls	1.0	83.05
Window, casement type, metal clad, double window, 4' x 4'	1 Ea.	2.0	355.75
Drywall, 1/2" thick plasterboard, taped and finished, 4' x 8' sheets	28 Sheets	16.0	271.05
Door, flush, hollow core, lauan finish, 2'-6" wide x 6'-8" high, prehung with casing and non-keyed lockset	1 Ea.	1.0	137.95
Closet door, bi-folding, louvered door 4' wide x 6'-8" high	1 Ea.	1.5	208.75
Trim, for closet jambs 1" x 6"	20 L.F.	1.0	13.30
Trim, casing, for window and closet door, pines, 11/16" x 2-1/2" wide	40 L.F.	1.5	17.40
Trim, for baseboard, pine, 9/16" x 3-1/2" wide	76 L.F.	2.5	64.40
Handrail, pine, 1-1/2" x 1-3/4", 2 pcs. @ 10' long	20 L.F.	1.0	23.75
Carpet, foam-backed, nylon, medium traffic	32 S.Y.	5.5	512.25
Painting, primer plus 1 coat, including walls & trim	1050 S.F.	10.5	114.35
Electrical, including switched hall and closet lights and 5 plugs	1 Lot	11.0	165.75
Totals		72.5	$2616.15

Project Size	16' x 20'	Contractor's Fee Including Materials	$5420

Key to Abbreviations
C.Y. - cubic yard   Ea. - each   L.F. - linear foot   Pr. - pair   Sq. - square (100 square feet of area)
S.F. - square foot   S.Y. - square yard   V.L.F. - vertical linear foot

FULL ATTIC

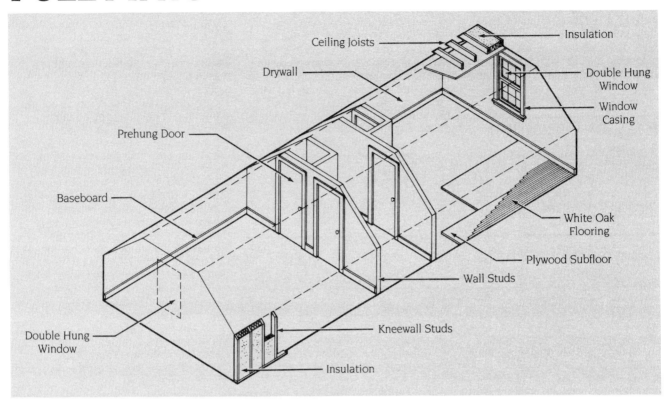

Ceiling Joists — Drywall — Insulation — Double Hung Window — Window Casing — Prehung Door — White Oak Flooring — Baseboard — Plywood Subfloor — Wall Studs — Kneewall Studs — Double Hung Window — Insulation

Expanding your home living space by using your attic requires careful consideration. Basic physical restrictions can cause problems or even prohibit attic renovation without major structural changes to the existing house. For example, inadequate head room results in the additional cost of adding dormers or raising the ridge and changing the roof line. Your attic should provide the minimum necessary head room for the area to be converted. If you have this capacity and can give up the floor area required for a staircase, then your attic can be converted into a comfortable, pleasant living area.

MATERIALS

The materials used for attic renovation are basically the same as those used for interior work anywhere in your home. One advantage of attic renovation, assuming that dormers or changes in the roof line are not required, is that the area is weather tight and protected at the start. Standard construction-grade framing

materials, including 2" x 4"s for wall studs and plates, and 2" x 6"s for ceiling joists, can be used to support 1/2" sheetrock. If you plan on installing wood floors, economical 1/2" sheathing plywood can be used for the subflooring. Insulation costs will vary according to recommended R-values for your area and preference for paperfaced, foilfaced, or unfaced fiberglass insulation. Windows for the gable ends of the attic room can be simple double-hung units or more expensive thermopaned casement models. Extra money invested at the time of construction for quality windows will be returned to you in energy savings and lower maintenance costs over the years.

The electrical materials used in the project include basic outlets, switches, lighting fixtures, and the wiring required to connect the various components. Make sure that you check local codes for proper installation if you are doing the electrical work on your own. Also, have the work inspected by a qualified person after you have installed it.

The finish work for your attic will vary according to your personal taste and the anticipated use of the living space. Taping and finishing the sheetrock and applying two coats of paint will finish the ceiling and walls. Hardwood flooring, carpeting, or other materials can be used for floor coverings. Basic prehung hollow-core lauan doors or more expensive paneled or louvre units can be used for the doorway and closets. For trim, ranch or colonial casing may be installed around doors, windows, and floors.

LEVEL OF DIFFICULTY

Major renovation of an attic is a challenging project for the most experienced handyman, even if dormers or other structural changes are not required. Accessibility alone can cause problems in getting materials to a second- or third-floor attic location. If you are to do some of the work alone, plan ahead as the project progresses and arrange to have someone assist you for an hour or two in carrying sheetrock, plywood, and other bulky items upstairs. Much of the work can be done by the homeowner, from easier jobs for beginners, like insulating and painting, to more skilled operations for experts, like framing, flooring, and window installation. Specialized work, especially electrical, should be left to the experts or contractors. If dormers are required, consider bringing in a professional contractor to build and close in the attic area. (See dormer construction project and costs in the "Exteriors" section.) As a general rule, beginners with little or no building experience should double the estimated man-hours for the project; handymen with some experience and skill in the use of tools should add an additional 50% to the man-hours estimate; and experts, about 20%. Beginners should seek professional help and advice throughout the various stages of the construction process.

WHAT TO WATCH OUT FOR

The primary considerations in any attic remodeling project are space and accessibility. Before you plan the renovation, check to see that the head clearance in your attic will allow for a 7'-6" or higher ceiling at the center of the room and that you have enough floor space to make the project worthwhile. Then, check on the accessibility of the attic. Consider the staircase in terms of additional cost as well as the reduction of living or storage area that it causes in the floor below. As a final preliminary check, make sure that the prospective floor joists for the attic room are sufficient to bear the added weight of the new living area. If they are not adequate, they will have to be strengthened at additional cost and time by adding floor joists before the project is begun.

SUMMARY

The use of attic space can be an efficient way to expand the living area of your home, especially when a steep-pitched roof provides enough room without the addition of dormers. If your house meets the requirements of area and accessibility, the attic can become an attractive source of new living space.

FULL ATTIC

Description	Quantity	Man-hours	Material
Flooring, underlayment grade plywood, 4' x 8' sheets, 1/2" thick	17 Sheets	6.0	302.80
Ceiling joists, 2" x 6", 16" O.C., 7' long	29 Ea.	3.0	95.80
Plates, top & bottom, 2" x 4", 12' lengths	252 L.F.	5.0	79.30
Kneewall studs, 2" x 4", 16" O.C., 4' long	58 Ea.	6.0	73.00
Wall studs, 2" x 4", 16" O.C., 8' long	44 Ea.	5.5	110.75
Blocking, miscellaneous to wood construction, 2" x 4" x 8'	5 Ea.	1.5	12.60
Insulation, R-11, 3-1/2" thick, 15" wide foil-faced blanket, 88 S.F. per roll	12 Rolls	5.5	345.00
Insulation, R-19, 6" thick, 15" wide foil-faced blanket, 88 S.F. per roll	3 Rolls	1.5	124.60
Windows, double hung, plastic clad, insulating, 3' x 4'	2 Ea.	2.0	423.50
Drywall, 1/2" thick plaster board, taped & finished, 4' x 8' sheets	60 Sheets	35.0	580.80
Doors, flush, hollow core, lauan finish, 2'-6" wide by 6'-8" high, prehung with casing	4 Ea.	3.5	367.85
Trim, casing for window, pine 11/16" x 2-1/2" wide	30 L.F.	1.0	13.10
Trim, for baseboard, pine, 9/16" x 3-1/2" wide	210 L.F.	7.0	177.90
Handrail, pine, 1-1/2" x 1-3/4", 2 pcs., 10' long	20 L.F.	2.0	23.70
Flooring, prefinished, white oak, prime grade 2-1/4" wide	550 S.F.	26.0	3327.50
Painting, primer plus 1 coat, including walls & trim	2100 S.F.	21.0	228.70
Lockset, residential, interior door, ordinary	4 Ea.	2.0	43.55
Electrical including hall light, two switched closet lights and 5 plugs per room	1 Lot	20.0	285.85
Totals		153.0	$6616.29

Project Size	16' x 36'	Contractor's Fee Including Materials	$14,510

STANDARD BASEMENT

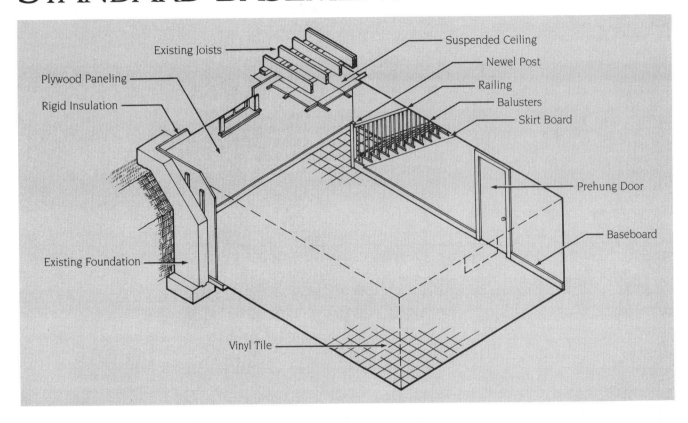

Existing Joists
Suspended Ceiling
Newel Post
Plywood Paneling
Rigid Insulation
Railing
Balusters
Skirt Board
Prehung Door
Existing Foundation
Baseboard
Vinyl Tile

Even if your basement is not constructed with a walk-out design, the area can be converted into efficient living space with a minimum of time, effort, and cost. The existing foundation walls provide a solid backing for a variety of finished wall materials; the floor joists for the room above are ready to support the new ceiling; and, in most cases, a concrete floor is in place to receive the new flooring. As long as the area is dry and the existing walls, ceiling, and floor are in good shape, a basement room is an efficient and cost effective place to expand your home's living space.

MATERIALS

With the house's foundation serving as a solid exterior wall system, a limited amount of partitioning is required to prepare the room for the finished walls. The area under the stairwell requires 2" x 4" framing members to back the paneling and to frame the understairs closet. In most cases, you will be able to use the existing cellar stair stringers, but if you have to construct the staircase from scratch, you can figure on extra cost

for the stringer material and other staircase support modifications. The concrete walls have to be prepared with 1" x 3" furring strips which are placed vertically at 16" on center and horizontally across the top and bottom of the wall. The furring strips can be fastened to the concrete with masonry nails or by firing special nails into the concrete with a stud gun. This procedure can be tricky and sometimes dangerous, so seek professional advice if you have not done it before. After you have completed all of the partitioning and prepared the walls to receive the paneling, the rough electrical work should be performed. Chances are, especially in new homes, that electrical circuits are readily available from the service panel in the basement. If you are unfamiliar with electrical installations, hire a professional to do the work or seek assistance from a qualified person. The styrofoam insulation material used on the exterior walls should match the thickness of the wall furring strips. You should also insulate the ceiling of the new room with fiberglass batts placed between the joists.

The finished walls, ceiling, and floor can be constructed from prefinished materials, all of them readily available from building supply outlets. The walls can be covered with an average grade prefinished paneling which can be nailed or glued to the furring strips. Cheaper grades of paneling are available, but the additional expense of a good quality paneling will make the finished product more attractive.

The ceiling consists of 2' x 4' prefinished fiber tiles which are suspended on a prepackaged system of hangers, carriers, and runners. These systems are usually accompanied by sample instructions and guidelines for installation by homeowners. The resilient tile flooring can be adhered directly to the concrete floor. Take some time to prepare the surface so that it is dry, clean, and smooth. If the concrete floor is sloped or in rough shape, then a subfloor may have to be constructed from 2" x 4" sleepers and sheathing. This installation requires some know-how and involves some extra cost, so get some advice and assistance if it has to be done.

Individual tiles or a variety of sheet goods are available for resilient flooring. Check with a flooring contractor or consult someone who has done this kind of work before you select the type of floor for your basement. Also, follow the manufacturers' instructions on the flooring material and adhesives to be used.

Finishing the basement will require extensive work on the staircase. It might be a good idea to hire a carpenter to place the risers, treads, bannisters, and handrail. Even if you are a fairly accomplished handyman, you might need assistance in this part of the project. The materials are expensive, and precision is required in calculations and cutting. For the door under the stairs, you can choose a modest prehung lauan unit, or a more expensive solid core or paneled design. Pine, colonial, or ranch design trim can be used for the facings

around the windows and doors and at the base of the walls. Inside and outside corner trim pieces are available at building supply outlets to finish the paneling.

LEVEL OF DIFFICULTY

The conversion of basement space to a comfortable living area requires a modest amount of skill and knowledge of remodeling. Except for the staircase and the electrical work, the project can be completed by most homeowners. If you are a beginner, seek the advice and assistance of professionals or experts as the building progresses. If you follow directions, work patiently, and learn from your mistakes, you should get very good results at a modest cost. Make sure that in following the professional man-hours estimates you add 80% to the time if you are a beginner or have very

limited building experience. If you are competent with tools and house projects, then add 40% to the estimated professional time. If you are an expert, an additional 10% should do it.

WHAT TO WATCH OUT FOR

One of the major problems with renovations of standard 75% below grade basements is moisture. Even though the basement may be dry and free from flooding or seepage during the wet times of year, ground moisture or condensation can be trapped in closed basements and cause dampness in your new room. If you sense that present or future moisture problems may affect the basement room, apply a sealer to the walls and floor as the first step in construction. If your basement is prone to occasional flooding, don't despair. Systems are available to correct the problem from both inside and outside the foundation. However, this procedure usually involves a significant expense. If your dwelling does have these problems, be sure to get professional advice and assistance before proceeding with the conversion.

SUMMARY

A dry basement which meets the height and accessibility requirements may be a source of new living area, and its renovation may help you to put this normally under-utilized space to better use. Because the rough walls, ceiling, and floor are already in place, the finishing of a basement room is a good way to expand your environment with a limited amount of cost and effort.

STANDARD BASEMENT

Description	Quantity	Man-hours	Material
Partition wall for stairway, 2" x 4" plates & studs, 16" O.C., 8' high	180 L.F.	3.0	56.60
Blocking, miscellaneous, nailers for walls	12 L.F.	0.5	5.65
Furring strips for walls, 1" x 3", 16" O.C.	665 L.F.	11.0	88.50
Insulation, rigid molded bead board, 1/2" thick	615 S.F.	6.5	126.50
Paneling, plywood, 1/4" thick, 4' x 8' sheets, birch faced, average grade	26 Sheets	38.0	855.70
Suspended ceiling system, 2' x 4' panels	440 S.F.	9.5	436.60
Door, flush, hollow core, lauan finish, 2'-6" wide x 6'-8" high, prehung	1 Ea.	1.0	91.95
Lockset, keyed, for flush door	1 Ea.	1.0	39.95
Stairway additions: skirt board, 1" x 10"	12 L.F.	2.0	21.05
Newel posts, 3'-4" wide, starting	1 Ea.	1.5	48.40
Balusters, turned, pine, 30" high	21 Ea.	6.0	88.95
Railing, oak, built-up	24 L.F.	3.5	123.40
Trim, jambs for doors & windows, 1" x 8" pine	16 L.F.	1.0	14.50
Trim, for baseboard, pine, 9/16" x 3-1/2" wide	96 L.F.	3.5	81.30
Trim, casing, pine, 11/16" x 2-1/2" wide	10 L.F.	0.5	4.80
Paint, trim, incl. puttying, primer & 1 coat	125 L.F.	2.5	7.85
Flooring, vinyl composition tile, 12" x 12", 1/16" thick	440 S.F.	11.0	266.20
Electrical, including 2 light fixtures w/wiring 2 switches & 6 duplex receptacles	1 Lot	13.5	180.65
Totals		115.5	$2538.56

Project Size	24' x 20'	Contractor's Fee Including Materials	$7420

Key to Abbreviations
C.Y. - cubic yard   Ea. - each   L.F. - linear foot   Pr. - pair   Sq. - square (100 square feet of area)
S.F. - square foot   S.Y. - square yard   V.L.F. - vertical linear foot

WALK-OUT BASEMENT

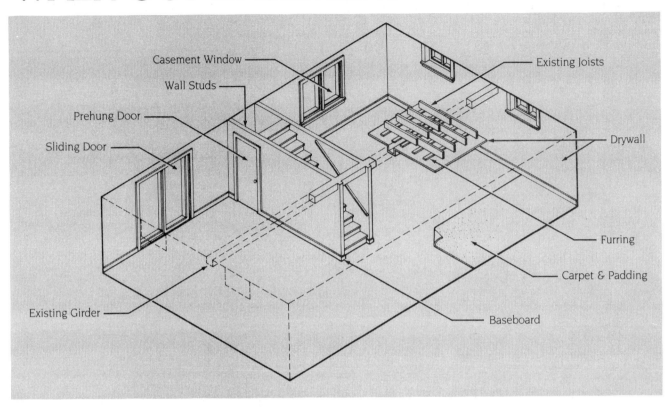

Casement Window

Wall Studs

Prehung Door

Sliding Door

Existing Girder

Existing Joists

Drywall

Furring

Carpet & Padding

Baseboard

Like attics, basements can also be economically converted to roomy, comfortable living areas. Basement renovation projects can turn under-utilized space into recreation, home office, or utility rooms. If your basement area is dry and already equipped with a walk-out doorway, a conversion can be easily undertaken, even if you have limited building experience.

MATERIALS

The materials used for a basement conversion are the same as those used in common home building construction. Because your foundation can serve as the rough wall system for the new room, 2" x 4" framing members are required only to enclose the entry staircase. Additional framing materials will be necessary at extra cost if you want to add a closet or storage area or to erect a partition for a second room. The support system for 1/2" drywall begins with 1" x 3" furring strips secured vertically at 16" on center to the existing foundation

wall. Consult someone who has experience in hammering concrete nails or firing specialized nails with a stud gun. If you plan to use 1/2" sheetrock on the ceiling, it might be a good idea to put the furring on the joists first to offset any settling or bowing that has occurred. The additional cost of this procedure is minimal, and the improvement in the appearance of your ceiling can make it worthwhile. Once the walls and ceiling have been furred, the rough electrical work can be done and the insulation and sheetrock put into place. If you are inexperienced in electrical installations, call a contractor or arrange to have a qualified person assist you in running the wires and installing the receptacles, switches, and fixtures. Drywalling a basement room is a challenging but reasonable undertaking for even inexperienced homeowners. You will need some help in bringing the sheetrock into the cellar and installing it on the ceiling; but with a little ingenuity, you can hang the sheets on the walls alone.

The taping and painting of the drywall can also be done on your own. If you have not worked with drywall before, seek some assistance and purchase or borrow the correct tools. Some good advice or instruction can head off much time-consuming sanding and finish work and enhance the appearance of the finished product.

If your foundation has been constructed to accommodate sliding doors and large window units, vinyl-clad, aluminum, or paintable wood door and window units can be installed after the old units have been removed. If, as in this example, concrete or block has to be removed in order to enlarge existing openings or to create new ones, you should consult a masonry contractor. When existing openings do not match the desired door and window design, you may choose to modify your plan somewhat for the sake of economy.

The cost of your project will vary according to the amount of professional assistance required. The door for the understairs closet or utility space can be an economical prehung hollow-core lauan model or a more expensive paneled or decorative unit. Pine boards in ranch or colonial trim are available for the jambs, casings, and interior facings of windows and doors. The baseboard can be obtained in the same styles and materials.

As for the carpet, a foam-backed type is used in this model, and can be installed directly on a clean, smooth concrete floor in a dry basement. If you have no experience in carpet laying, it might be a good idea to contact a professional.

LEVEL OF DIFFICULTY

A complete basement conversion requires a reasonable level of skill and a basic knowledge of tools and building, but many aspects of this project can be tackled by beginners. Except for the electrical work and the foundation preparation for windows and doors, most of the operations are relatively straightforward and uncomplicated. There is a limited amount of framing involved in the conversion, and, except for ceiling obstacles like existing plumbing and electrical fixtures, there are few problems to keep you from direct and rapid progress. If you are a beginner, double the estimated time for professional man-hours. Add about

40% to the man-hours estimate if you have had some experience with tools and renovation, and 10% if you are thoroughly skilled in these areas.

WHAT TO WATCH OUT FOR

Walk-out basements are usually accessible, but consider the size of your entranceways, as you will need to bring in some large materials. Also, double check the ceiling height to see that it meets your minimum requirements for head room. Remember that you will lose some height when you add furring to the joists, and more with a layer of sheetrock. Lighting fixtures installed in the ceiling also require safe clearance. If you have to box around low-hanging plumbing, you will lose some head room in those areas too. Lally columns which support the house's primary structural beams are another consideration. They can often be boxed in, but if they have to be removed or relocated, proper support systems must be installed to prevent expensive structural problems. These additional operations can affect remodeling costs significantly. It is best to check with a professional contractor before you make any changes that involve the structural support system.

SUMMARY

A dry and accessible walk-out basement is a good source of new living area. Because the space is already enclosed, much of the project can be accomplished by the do-it-yourselfer, for a modest investment.

WALK-OUT BASEMENT

Description	Quantity	Man-hours	Material
Partition wall for stairway, 2" x 4" plates & studs, 16" O.C., 8' High	312 L.F.	5.0	98.15
Blocking, miscellaneous, nailers for walls	24 L.F.	1.0	11.30
Cut masonry openings, 6' x 6'-8" and 4' x 4'	2 Ea.	35.0	0.00
Furring strips for ceiling & walls, 1" x 3", 16" O.C.	1400 L.F.	22.5	186.35
Insulation, rigid molded bead board, 1/2" thick, R-3.85	1020 S.F.	11.5	209.80
Drywall, 1/2" thick plasterboard, taped and finished, 4' x 8' sheets	74 Sheets	43.0	716.30
Windows, casement type, metal clad, double window, 4' x 4'	1 Ea.	2.0	474.30
Door, sliding, glass, wood, premium, 6' wide	1 Ea.	4.0	795.00
Door, flush, hollow core, lauan finish, 2'-6" wide x 6'-8" high, pre-hung	1 Ea.	1.0	91.95
Lockset, keyed, for flush door	1 Ea.	1.0	40.00
Trim, jambs for doors & windows, 1" x 8" pine	50 L.F.	2.0	45.35
Trim, for baseboard, pine, 9/16" x 3-1/2" wide	160 L.F.	5.5	135.55
Trim, casing for window, pine, 11/16" x 2-1/2" wide	48 L.F.	2.0	20.90
Railing, oak, built-up	24 L.F.	3.5	123.45
Paint, ceiling & walls, primer plus 1 coat	2370 S.F.	21.5	372.80
Paint, trim, wood, incl. puttying, primer and 1 coat	260 L.F.	5.0	15.75
Padding for carpet, sponge rubber cushion	910 S.F.	5.5	275.25
Carpet, nylon, 26 oz. medium traffic	910 S.F.	16.5	1893.90
Electrical including 2 light fixtures w/wiring and switches, and 10 duplex receptacles	1 Lot	19.0	240.20
Totals		206.5	$5746.30

Project Size	24' x 40'	Contractor's Fee Including Materials	$14,980

Key to Abbreviations
C.Y. - cubic yard   Ea. - each   L.F. - linear foot   Pr. - pair   Sq. - square (100 square feet of area)
S.F. - square foot   S.Y. - square yard   V.L.F. - vertical linear foot

HALF BATH, STANDARD

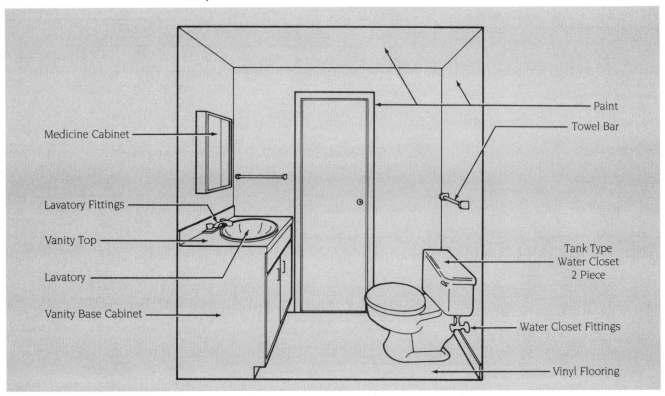

Medicine Cabinet

Lavatory Fittings

Vanity Top

Lavatory

Vanity Base Cabinet

Paint

Towel Bar

Tank Type
Water Closet
2 Piece

Water Closet Fittings

Vinyl Flooring

One of the most challenging, yet gratifying ways to improve your home is to remodel an existing bathroom facility. In some cases, the room has to be redone because of wear and age, but a renovation might also be undertaken to head off problems or simply to spruce it up. With today's fixtures and materials, remodeling a half bath may be easier and less expensive than you think, especially if you opt to do some or all of the work on your own.

MATERIALS

The plan for the standard half bath renovation includes the complete replacement of the basic plumbing fixtures, flooring, vanity cabinet, and accessories. The two primary plumbing fixtures in any half bath are the sink and the toilet. The size of the sink may

vary according to personal taste, but 18" round is a good, functional size for a porcelain-coated cast iron unit. A standard, two-piece, floor-mounted tank-type toilet, manufactured from vitreous china, is a basic stock item at any plumbing supply outlet. If you want colored fixtures rather than white, they will cost about 25% more. New chrome-plated fittings, including faucets and shut-off valves, complete the plumbing installation.

The flooring is a critical item in any room, but especially in a bathroom where water and moisture are ever-present. When you take up the old floor, make sure that you give the existing subflooring and floor joists a careful inspection for signs of rot and general deterioration. If the subfloor is solid and dry, leave it in place to be used as a base for the new floor. If the subfloor looks questionable, even if

only in one area, you should take the time to tear it up and replace it with new underlayment, comprised of 3/16" hardboard. The new finished floor of vinyl covering can be laid after the underlayment has been properly leveled and prepared to receive it. Before the new floor is put into place, you might want to clean and apply two coats of paint to the walls and ceiling. This makes the whole process easier, since you won't have to cover the floor when you paint. Wallpapering is another alternative, and while it may be slightly more expensive, it can go a long way to brighten a small room. Water-resistant, washable paper is available in a wide variety of patterns and colors.

A vanity cabinet to support the sink, a new medicine cabinet, and basic accessories add the finishing touches to the half bath. A 30" vanity with a laminated plastic (Formica) top provides some additional storage and shelf space. A basic, unlighted, metal medicine cabinet involves a modest investment that will be returned many times over in the convenience it provides. The stainless steel towel bars and tissue dispenser used in this example could be replaced by models made of other materials.

LEVEL OF DIFFICULTY

Even if you have only limited experience with plumbing installation, a small half bath renovation is a reasonable undertaking. Beginners might be better off leaving the actual installation and tying in of the fixtures and fittings to a professional, but the rest of the project, including the floor, involves manageable tasks that can be accomplished by novices with some professional advice and assistance. Beginners should plan on twice the estimated professional man-hours to complete the project. Even handymen and experts should tread carefully in the plumbing tasks, but the flooring, wall and accessories installations should pose no real problems. Handymen should add 50% to the professional man-hours estimate; experts, about 20%.

WHAT TO WATCH OUT FOR

One of the biggest problems in any bathroom renovation involves replacement of rotted and/or deteriorated subflooring and the structural members underneath or adjacent to it. In half baths, the problem occurs most frequently around the base of the toilet, where moisture from seepage or condensation collects and does not evaporate because of poor ventilation. If the rot or deterioration is extensive and joists or other structural elements have been affected, then a professional should be called in, at least to inspect the damage. Beginners, especially, should seek assistance if the situation requires correction. Handymen and experts should be able to handle the problem by removing the affected sections and adding replacement support. Insuring that the floor is solid and installing the new fixtures with care should keep future problems to a minimum.

SUMMARY

Renovating an existing half bath is a good way to improve the value and appearance of your home. It is an approachable project in that it does not tie up the only bath in the house and only two fixtures are involved. Beginners and handymen can add to their plumbing and remodeling experience by tackling this project, but they should seek professional advice along the way.

HALF BATH, STANDARD

Description	Quantity	Man-hours	Material
Rough in frame for medicine cabinet, 2" x 4" stock	8 L.F.	0.5	2.25
Flooring, underlayment grade, hardboard, 3/16" thick, 4' x 4' sheets	2 Sheets	0.5	10.10
Painting, ceiling, walls & door, primer & 1 coat	162 S.F.	1.5	17.65
Medicine cabinet, with mirror, stock, 16" x 22" unlighted	1 Ea.	1.0	52.00
Vanity base cabinet, 2 door, 30" wide	1 Ea.	2.0	199.65
Vanity top, plastic laminated, basic	1 Ea.	1.0	18.20
Lavatory, with trim, porcelain enamel on cast iron, 18" round	1 Ea.	2.5	117.35
Fittings for lavatory	1 Set	8.5	65.85
Towel bars, stainless steel, 18" long	2 Ea.	1.0	41.40
Toilet tissue dispenser, surface mounted, stainless steel	1 Ea.	0.5	21.20
Flooring, vinyl sheet goods, backed, 0.093" thick	20 S.F.	0.5	30.25
Toilet, tank type, vitreous china, floor mounted, 2 piece, white	1 Ea.	3.0	139.15
Fittings for toilet	1 Set	8.5	100.75
Totals		31.0	$815.80

Project Size	4' x 6'	Contractor's Fee Including Materials	$2210

HALF BATH, DELUXE

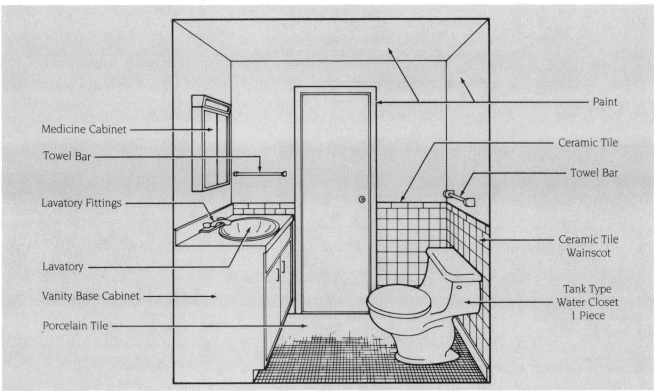

Medicine Cabinet

Towel Bar

Lavatory Fittings

Lavatory

Vanity Base Cabinet

Porcelain Tile

Paint

Ceramic Tile

Towel Bar

Ceramic Tile
Wainscot

Tank Type
Water Closet
1 Piece

Often a half bath is located in an area of your home where more decorative and deluxe features are desired - perhaps off a recreation room or a room where you do most of your entertaining. A deluxe half bath may also be in order simply because you want to upgrade the facility in keeping with other improvements throughout your dwelling.

MATERIALS

The materials used in the deluxe half bath include the same basic plumbing and decorating items of a standard half bath, but they have been upgraded to create a more decorative and deluxe facility. The toilet is a floor-mounted, one-piece unit of colored vitreous china. The lavatory is

a trimmed 18" round porcelain on cast iron model, also in color. If you want white fixtures, you can deduct about 30% of the estimated cost of the toilet and 25% from the price of the sink. Chrome-plated fittings have been selected for the sink and toilet in this model.

The deluxe half bath also features ceramic tile on both the floor and the lower part of the wall. Working with ceramic floor and wall materials requires some skill and the right tools, but with some advice and assistance at the start, beginners can produce pleasing results. Ceramic floor tile is more durable and easily maintained than vinyl and most other floor coverings. Ceramic wainscoting has the same benefits and also gives the room a neat look. The ceiling, upper part of walls, and door can be finished with a primer and finish coat of paint.

Washable wallpaper can also enhance the room's appearance.

The choice of the vanity and other accessories for the deluxe half bath should suit your personal taste and coordinate with the style of the room. A deluxe 30" two-door vanity with plastic laminate top provides extra storage space, and the high quality hardwood cabinet offers an attractive support for the sink. A lighted medicine cabinet with a built-in mirror is another feature. Stainless steel towel bars and tissue dispenser are one option, but other accessories are available in a variety of materials and costs.

LEVEL OF DIFFICULTY

The deluxe half bath is a fairly demanding project for even experienced do-it-yourselfers. The two most difficult tasks involved in the renovation are the plumbing procedures and the floor and wall ceramic tile installations. Both of these jobs require specialized skills and a considerable degree of expertise. Beginners can handle the ceramic work, but only if they are given ample instruction beforehand and guidance during the installation. If you have not done any plumbing work in the past, you should leave the fixture installations to professionals, even if you are an accomplished do-it-yourselfer. Handymen and experts should be able to complete a great deal of this project, including tile installation, but they will need to obtain the specialized tools for ceramic work and seek some instruction at the start. In using the professional man-hour estimates, add 100% to the time if you are a beginner, 50% if you are an experienced handyman, and 20% if you are an expert.

WHAT TO WATCH OUT FOR

Ceramic tile, like any other wall or floor covering, requires a dry and clean surface for mounting. Be sure to check the condition of the floor underlayment and the sheetrock before laying the tile. The rough floor surface must be cleaned, leveled, and smoothed out before the tile flooring sections are laid. The sheetrock on the walls must be clean, dry, and solid to provide adequate backing for the wall tiles. Bathrooms are notorious collectors of moisture, and the adhesives used in ceramic tile installations will not bond effectively to damp or moist surfaces. The extra cost involved in preparing or replacing the existing floor or walls is money well spent to ensure a quality installation.

SUMMARY

Upgrading a basic half bath to deluxe standards can enhance the value and overall appearance of your home. Because a half bath is not the major facility in a house, its renovation does not involve as much inconvenience as that of a full bath. As a result, you may be able to perform much of this project yourself to make it a more economical undertaking.

HALF BATH, DELUXE

Description	Quantity	Man-hours	Material
Rough in frame for medicine cabinet, 2" x 4" stock	8 L.F.	0.5	2.25
Painting, ceiling walls & door, primer & 1 coat	142 S.F.	1.0	15.45
Medicine cabinet, with mirror, stock, 16" x 22", lighted	1 Ea.	1.5	101.65
Deluxe vanity base cabinet, 2 door, 30" wide	1 Ea.	2.0	186.35
Vanity top, plastic laminated, maximum	1 Ea.	1.0	41.45
Lavatory, with trim, porcelain enamel on cast iron, 18" round, in color	1 Ea.	2.5	146.70
Fittings for lavatory	1 Set	8.5	66.00
Towel bars, stainless steel, 18" long	2 Ea.	1.0	41.40
Toilet tissue dispenser, surface mounted, stainless steel	1 Ea.	0.5	21.20
Walls, ceramic tile wainscoting, thin set, 4-1/4" x 4-1/4" tile	20 S.F.	4.0	31.45
Flooring, porcelain type, 1 color, color group 2, 1" x 1" tile	20 S.F.	4.0	45.75
Toilet, tank type, vitreous china, floor mounted, 1 piece, in color	1 Ea.	3.0	566.30
Fittings for toilet	1 Set	8.5	100.75
Totals		38.5	$1366.70

Project Size	4' x 6'	Contractor's Fee Including Materials	$3100

Key to Abbreviations
C.Y. - cubic yard   Ea. - each   L.F. - linear foot   Pr. - pair   Sq. - square (100 square feet of area)
S.F. - square foot   S.Y. - square yard   V.L.F. - vertical linear foot

FULL BATH, STANDARD

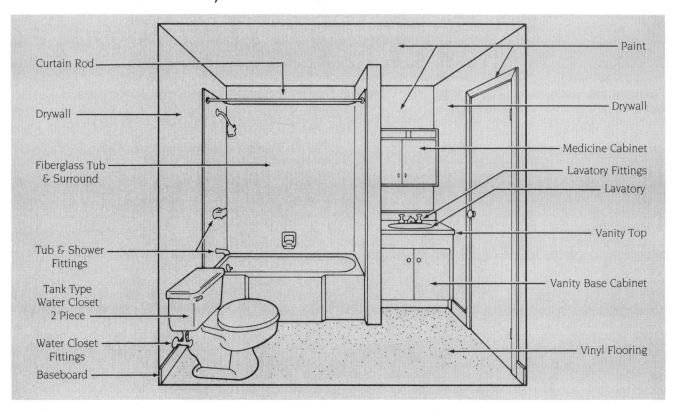

Curtain Rod

Drywall

Fiberglass Tub & Surround

Tub & Shower Fittings

Tank Type Water Closet 2 Piece

Water Closet Fittings

Baseboard

Paint

Drywall

Medicine Cabinet

Lavatory Fittings

Lavatory

Vanity Top

Vanity Base Cabinet

Vinyl Flooring

Even though the renovation of a full bath involves adding only one more fixture than that of a half bath, the full bath project is a significantly more costly, time consuming, and challenging undertaking. If your house has just one bathroom, expediency in the plumbing installation becomes especially critical. Despite the inconvenience caused while the work is carried out, a modernizing or remodeling project like this can result in a more attractive, low-maintenance bathroom for years to come.

MATERIALS

The materials employed in the complete renovation and remodeling of a standard full bath consist of the three basic plumbing fixtures, the flooring, wall and ceiling coverings, and the vanity and various accessories common to most bathrooms. The plumbing fixtures consist of replacement sink, toilet, and shower

and tub unit. For the sink, you probably should stay with a standard-sized porcelain-on-cast iron unit, with an 18" round bowl and appropriate trim. If you want the sink to be colored instead of white, add about 25% to the estimated cost of the fixture. The two-piece floor-mounted toilet also costs about 25-30% more for color than the estimated unit price. The fiberglass bathtub and modular shower surround come as a ready-to-assemble unit which can provide years of trouble-free service when properly installed and maintained. The fixture costs for the sink and tub units listed in the chart include the faucets, control, and shower head. The various fittings required to tie in the plumbing fixtures to the water supply and drainage systems are listed separately and include such items as the shut-off valves and rough plumbing. Beginners should definitely hire a plumber to install the fixtures, and even

handymen should consider professional assistance in taking out the old fixtures and installing the new ones.

The installation of the floor, wall and ceiling materials should be manageable tasks for most homeowners. In any bathroom remodeling project, the floor is a critical concern because it is exposed to splashed water and other forms of moisture. The condition of the subfloor and its supports should be carefully determined, particularly in the area around the tub and toilet. Take a few minutes after you have removed the old tub and toilet to poke the underlayment, subfloor, and floor joists with a screwdriver or awl to locate any soft spots, wet areas, or decay. If you find places where the flooring or joists are in questionable condition, they will have to be replaced at additional cost. If the problem is extensive, seek professional assistance before going ahead, even if you are a reasonably experienced handyman. After the new underlayment has been placed, vinyl sheet flooring can be laid either by a specialty contractor or on your own if you have done this before.

A small framing job is required if no partition exists between the foot of the tub and the vanity. Beginners should seek some assistance here. The cavity surrounding the tub and shower module should be walled with 1/2" water-resistant drywall which must be taped and finished after the shower module is placed. The other walls, ceiling, and door can be painted with a primer and finish coat of durable, washable paint.

The conventional bathroom accessories, vanity, and medicine cabinet provide options of varying costs for the homeowner. A standard two-door, 30" vanity with a durable Formica-type top serves as a support for the sink while providing necessary storage. The medicine cabinet should also be large enough to accommodate the needs of your family. If you want a cabinet with built-in lighting, the cost is higher than the estimate given.

LEVEL OF DIFFICULTY

Tackling a full bath renovation is a big job for even experienced and competent handymen. A full range of building skills is required, from simple tasks like painting, to specialized plumbing work. Even the most

experienced do-it-yourselfers should think twice about carrying out the plumbing installations, especially if old fixtures have to be removed before the new ones are installed. Beginners should not attempt the extensive plumbing required in the project, especially the installation of the tub and shower fixtures. They should double the estimated man-hours for other tasks in the project. Handymen and experts should add about 50% and 20%, respectively, to the professional time estimates throughout.

WHAT TO WATCH OUT FOR

If you plan to install the fiberglass tub and shower module on your own, take some time to read up on the intricacies of the task and seek some assistance from a qualified person. Even small discrepancies in alignment, caused by a settled floor or an out-of-plumb wall, can create major obstacles during installation, and they should be allowed for or corrected beforehand. Routine jobs like cutting the openings for the rough plumbing for the shower valve and tub fill can become difficult if the overall alignment of the unit is not true. Make sure that the manufacturer's guidelines and instructions are followed closely during the installation. The size of the tub is also a factor to consider, especially in terms of doorway clearances within the house. If accessibility does turn out to be a problem, you might want to look into a collapsible model.

SUMMARY

A standard full bath renovation or installation is a major project, but with the right materials and plumbing fixtures, it is an undertaking that can be at least partially completed by most experienced home handymen. When the job is done properly, it will add value to your home and provide years of dependable service.

FULL BATH, STANDARD

Description	Quantity	Man-hours	Material
Partition wall, between vanity & tub, 2" x 4" plates & studs, 16" O.C., 8' high	64 L.F.	1.0	20.15
Rough in frame for medicine cabinet, 2" x 4" stock	10 L.F.	0.5	3.15
Drywall, 1/2" thick, on walls, water resistant, taped & finished, 4' x 8' sheets	2 Sheets	1.5	27.10
Flooring, underlayment grade, hardboard, 3/16" thick 4' x 4' sheets	4 Sheets	1.0	21.70
Painting, ceiling, walls & door, primer & 1 coat	310 S.F.	1.5	33.75
Vanity base cabinet, 2 door, 30" wide	1 Ea.	2.0	199.65
Vanity top, plastic laminated, basic	1 Ea.	1.5	45.40
Lavatory, with trim, porcelain enamel on cast iron, 18" round	1 Ea.	2.5	127.05
Fittings for lavatory	1 Set	8.5	73.30
Bathtub, module & shower wall surround, molded fiberglass, 5' long	1 Ea.	4.0	617.10
Fittings for tub & shower	1 Set	9.5	85.40
Curtain rod, stainless steel, 5' long, 1" diameter	1 Ea.	1.0	24.20
Medicine cabinet, sliding mirror doors, 34" x 21", unlighted	1 Ea.	1.5	185.10
Flooring, vinyl sheet goods, backed 0.093" thick	36 S.F.	1.0	54.45
Toilet, tank type, vitreous china, floor mounted, 2 piece, white	1 Ea.	3.0	139.15
Fittings for toilet	1 Set	8.5	101.60
Toilet tissue dispenser, surface mounted, stainless steel	1 Ea.	0.5	23.00
Towel bar, stainless steel, 30" long	1 Ea.	0.5	21.80
Trim, baseboard, 9/16" x 3-1/2" wide, pine	12 L.F.	0.5	10.15
	Totals	50.0	$1813.21

Project Size	7' x 8'	Contractor's Fee Including Materials	$4330

Key to Abbreviations
C.Y. - cubic yard   Ea. - each   L.F. - linear foot   Pr. - pair   Sq. - square (100 square feet of area)
S.F. - square foot   S.Y. - square yard   V.L.F. - vertical linear foot

FULL BATH, DELUXE

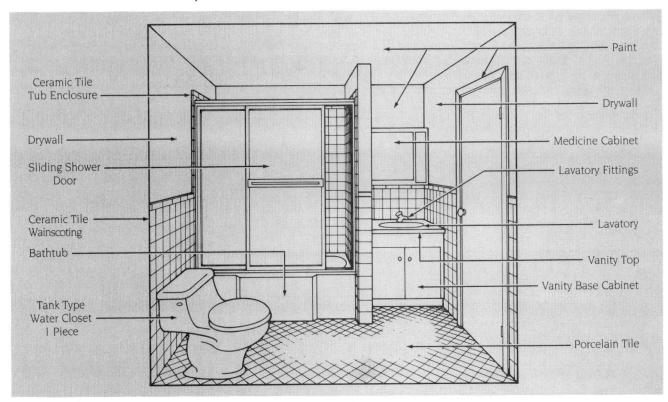

Paint

Ceramic Tile Tub Enclosure

Drywall

Drywall

Medicine Cabinet

Sliding Shower Door

Lavatory Fittings

Ceramic Tile Wainscoting

Lavatory

Bathtub

Vanity Top

Tank Type Water Closet 1 Piece

Vanity Base Cabinet

Porcelain Tile

The deluxe full bath includes the amenities and upgraded fixtures to provide an attractive and durable addition to any home. For the additional expense of deluxe features like a one-piece toilet, a sliding shower door, and ceramic tile, this bath offers first quality materials for a relatively modest investment, especially if you opt to do most of the work on your own.

MATERIALS

The deluxe full bath features top-of-the-line fixtures, durable ceramic wall and floor tiling, and quality accessories. The fixtures used in the bath include matching colored 18" lavatory, single-piece floor-mounted toilet, and porcelain enamel on cast iron recessed tub with a non-skid mat bottom. Complementing the fixtures and included in the estimated cost are quality faucets, valves and diverters, and shower head. The fittings for the fixtures, including the minimum rough

plumbing and supply valves, are listed as a separate cost which may vary according to the amount of rearranging and plumbing modifications made for the particular facility. If you're considering doing the deluxe bath remodeling project on your own, you may want to hire a plumber for the removal and installation of the primary fixtures, especially the tub and shower which require thorough plumbing skills.

The wall and flooring systems of the deluxe bath feature ceramic tile. Although the wall area looks relatively small in comparison to, say, a bedroom, don't let it fool you. And even though the ceramic tile covers only the lower portion of the walls outside of the tub area, there is quite a bit of effort and expense involved in tiling this room. If you haven't done tile work before, check with an experienced person for advice; also, get the right tools for the job. The grouting process alone requires some know-how and patience. Give

particular attention to the ceramic work around the tub and shower. As for the floor, the ceramic installation is a little easier and faster because the material comes in sections, usually 1' x 1', which can be trimmed and cut where necessary as the floor is laid. The partition between the tub and vanity is constructed of 2" x 4"s and should be carefully plumbed and set precisely at a right angle to the line of the tub. If it is out of plumb even slightly, the ensuing drywall and, particularly, ceramic tile installations become more difficult. The upper part of the walls and the ceiling require two coats of paint (one primer and one finish coat) to complete the job correctly. The door and any trim work should also be refinished with paint, or stained and then sealed with two coats of polyurethane.

The vanity and other accessory items for the deluxe bath can vary with individual taste, but a 30" two-door deluxe vanity cabinet with a first quality top adds an attractive and functional support for the lavatory. The medicine cabinet can include a built-in lighting fixture and twin sliding mirror doors at reasonable cost. The towel bar and tissue dispenser can be of conventional design, and selected from various materials such as stainless steel, chrome and ceramic. Instead of a basic shower curtain and support rod, the deluxe bath also includes a sliding shower door made from tempered glass.

LEVEL OF DIFFICULTY

The deluxe full bath project poses certain challenges, and expediency is a prime consideration, especially if your home has just one bathroom facility. For all but the expert level of do-it-yourselfers, a plumber should be hired to do the fixture installations. Beginners should also hire someone to do the tile work for this project. In time, a poor tiling job will cost you many times over the installer's fee in leakage and water problems around the tub and shower. Beginners can figure on 150% added to the man-hours estimate on other parts of the project. They are advised to seek professional assistance along the way. Handymen should contract the plumbing and add 70% to the man-hours estimate for all other operations involved in the renovation. Experts who can handle the plumbing should be able to complete the entire project with about 30% added to the professional time estimate.

WHAT TO WATCH OUT FOR

There are many critical parts to any bathroom renovation, but perhaps the most important task outside of the actual plumbing work is the drywalling and ceramic work in the tub and shower area. Be sure to install 1/2" water resistant sheetrock for the tile backing and then tape and finish it thoroughly to eliminate moisture penetration at the seams. Thoroughly taping and finishing the drywall seams and nail or screw head indentations also provides a flush, continuously flat surface for the ceramic tile. Install the tile carefully, following the adhesive manufacturer's instructions and recommendations. After the tile has been installed, grout it thoroughly, paying careful attention to the vertical corner nearest the shower head to make sure that no voids or open spaces exist in the line of grout. If you've included a ceramic soap dish or handle fixture in the tub and shower enclosure, then grout around it carefully as well. A bead of flexible caulking or tub sealer along the seam at the top of the tub will add further protection against water penetration and subsequent damage to the floor and wall in the tub area. Even though these preventive measures may take a little extra time and add a bit to the cost of the project, they will save you considerable expense and aggravation in years of trouble-free use of the tub and shower facility.

SUMMARY

Whether you are modernizing an old bath or constructing a new one, the value and comfort of your home will be enhanced. You can save on labor costs while learning and doing some of the work on your own, and the investment of your time and money will be returned in future years.

FULL BATH, DELUXE

Description	Quantity	Man-hours	Material
Partition wall between vanity and tub, 2" x 4" plates and studs, 16" O.C., 8' high	64 L.F.	1.0	20.10
Rough-in frame for medicine cabinet, using 2" x 4" stock	10 L.F.	0.5	3.15
Drywall, 1/2" thick, on walls, water resistant, taped and finished, 4' x 8' sheets	2 Sheets	1.5	27.10
Painting, ceiling, walls, and door, primer and 1 coat	230 S.F.	2.5	25.05
Vanity base cabinet, deluxe, 2 door, 30" wide	1 Ea.	2.0	279.50
Vanity top, Formica covered	1 Ea.	1.0	136.10
Lavatory, with trim, porcelain enamel on cast iron, 18" round, color	1 Ea.	2.5	158.80
Fittings for lavatory	1 Set	8.5	73.30
Bathtub, recessed, porcelain enamel on cast iron, w/trim, mat bottom, 5' long, color	1 Ea.	4.0	317.05
Fittings for tub and shower	1 Set	9.5	85.40
Sliding shower door, deluxe, tempered glass	1 Ea.	2.0	320.65
Medicine cabinet, sliding mirror doors, 34" x 21", lighted	1 Ea.	1.5	242.00
Walls, ceramic tile, shower enclosure and wainscoting, thinset, 4-1/4" x 4-1/4"	140 S.F.	12.5	728.40
Flooring, porcelain tile, 1 color, 1" x 1" tiles	36 S.F.	4.0	135.00
Toilet, tank type, vitreous china, floor mounted, 1 piece, color	1 Ea.	3.0	597.75
Fittings for toilet	1 Set	8.5	100.75
Toilet tissue dispenser, surface mounted, stainless steel	1 Ea.	0.5	23.00
Towel bar, stainless steel, 30" long	1 Ea.	0.5	21.80
Totals		65.5	$3294.90

Project Size	7' x 8'	Contractor's Fee Including Materials	$6980

Key to Abbreviations
C.Y. - cubic yard Ea. - each L.F. - linear foot Pr. - pair Sq. - square (100 square feet of area)
S.F. - square foot S.Y. - square yard V.L.F. - vertical linear foot

MASTER BATH, STANDARD

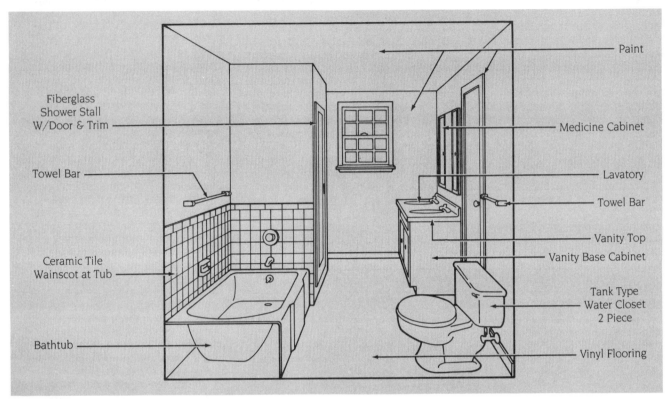

Paint

Fiberglass
Shower Stall
W/Door & Trim

Medicine Cabinet

Towel Bar

Lavatory

Towel Bar

Vanity Top

Vanity Base Cabinet

Ceramic Tile
Wainscot at Tub

Tank Type
Water Closet
2 Piece

Bathtub

Vinyl Flooring

A standard master bath includes the three basic plumbing fixtures of most standard full baths and adds a fourth fixture in the form of a separate shower unit. The 8' x 10' master bath is designed for large homes that provide the space for such a facility off the master suite. The addition of the fourth plumbing fixture and the larger size of the master bath make this remodeling project that much more time-consuming and costly than the renovation of a standard half or full bath. In short, it is a bigger job, but the installation methods are basically the same as those for other bathrooms.

MATERIALS

The materials used in the master bath include the four primary plumbing fixtures, typical bathroom floor and wall coverings, and the amenities and accessories found in most baths. The lavatories are standard porcelain-on-cast iron units in white with 18" bowls, and the toilet is a common two-piece,

floor-mounted vitreous china model, also in white. Add about 30% to the estimated cost of these fixtures, as well as to the price of the tub, if you want them in color. The tub is a standard 5' recessed porcelain enamel-on-cast iron unit. The head of the tub backs to a partition which separates it from a one-piece fiberglass shower stall. It is important to note that backing the tub to the shower creates savings in the rough plumbing cost and installation time for these fixtures. The rough plumbing for both fixtures fits easily into the 2" x 4" partition which separates the two units.

The flooring, wall and ceiling coverings for the master bath are available in many options and varying price ranges. If you choose to economize, you can install a quality grade of low-maintenance vinyl flooring and place a limited amount of ceramic tile around the tub area. Both of these materials require some knowledge and skill in their respective installations; but

because they are relatively small flooring and tiling jobs, handymen and advanced beginners can accomplish them with some advice, guidance, and the right tools. The ceramic work involves just two half-wall sections at the side and head of the tub; the flooring installation requires only two cut outs, one for the vanity and one for the toilet flange. As with other bathroom flooring jobs, make sure that the subflooring and its supports are in good shape before you begin laying the new underlayment and vinyl finish material. If you neglect moisture problems at the time of installation, you will wind up paying for them in aggravation and premature replacement costs.

The vanity, medicine cabinet, and other accessories should be in keeping with the decor of a master bath. A full 72" vanity with matching formica top provides ample storage and counter space around the sink. A smaller, more economical medicine cabinet can be installed, but the recommended two-cabinet model is commensurate with master bath standards. You can also select, at varying costs, tissue dispensers and towel bars in several designs and of several different materials.

LEVEL OF DIFFICULTY

Like the other three or four-fixture baths, the standard master bath requires significant remodeling skills and competence with tools. Beginners and handymen should not tackle the extensive plumbing required in installing the four fixtures. If the rough plumbing is already in place and functioning properly, the fixture installation will be easier, but still challenging. In situations where relocation of the fixtures or new rough plumbing is called for, a plumber should do the work. Even skilled or expert do-it-yourselfers should consider professional help for fixture relocations. For all tasks involved in this bathroom project, exclusive of the plumbing, beginners should add 100% to the man-hour estimates, handymen should add an additional 50%, and experts about 20%.

MASTER BATH, STANDARD

Description	Quantity	Man-hours	Material
Partition wall for shower stall, 2" x 4" plates & studs, 16" O.C., 8' high	152 L.F.	2.5	47.80
Rough-in-frame for medicine cabinet, 2" x 4" stock	16 L.F.	0.5	5.00
Drywall, 1/2" thick on shower stall walls, water resistant, taped & finished 4' x 8' sheets	3 Sheets	2.0	27.10
Flooring, underlayment grade, hardboard 3/16" thick 4' x 4' sheets	4 Sheets	1.0	32.50
Painting, ceiling, walls & door, primed & 1 finish coat	330 S.F.	3.0	19.95
Vanity base cabinet, 2 door, 72" wide	1 Ea.	2.0	447.70
Vanity top, plastic laminate	1 Ea.	2.0	254.10
Lavatory with trim & faucet, porcelain enamel on cast iron, 18" round, white	2 Ea.	5.0	254.10
Fittings for lavatory	2 Ea.	16.5	146.60
Shower stall with door and trim, fiberglass 1 piece, 3 walls, 32" x 32"	1 Ea.	7.0	284.35
Bathtub, recessed, porcelain enamel on cast iron, w/trim, mat bottom, 5' long	1 Ea.	4.0	317.05
Fittings for tub and shower	1 Set	9.5	85.40
Medicine cabinet, center mirror, 2 end cabinets, 72" long	1 Ea.	2.0	266.20
Walls, ceramic tile at tub, thinset, 4-1/4" x 4-1/4"	12 S.F.	1.5	62.45
Flooring, vinyl sheet goods, backed, .093" thick	50 S.F.	2.0	75.65
Toilet, tank type, vitreous china, floor mounted, 2 piece	1 Ea.	3.0	139.15
Fittings for toilet	1 Set	8.5	101.60
Towel bar, stainless steel - 30" long	2 Ea.	1.0	43.55
Toilet tissue dispenser, surface mounted, stainless steel	1 Ea.	0.5	23.00
Trim, baseboard, 9/16" x 3-1/2" wide, pine	16 L.F.	0.5	13.55
Totals		74.0	$2646.85

Project Size	8' x 10'	Contractor's Fee Including Materials	$6640

Key to Abbreviations
C.Y. - cubic yard Ea. - each L.F. - linear foot Pr. - pair Sq. - square (100 square feet of area)
S.F. - square foot S.Y. - square yard V.L.F. - vertical linear foot

WHAT TO WATCH OUT FOR

Installing sheet flooring requires knowledge of the vinyl material, several important tools, and an awareness of several "tricks of the trade." However, with a few suggestions and advice, most handymen and advanced beginners can complete the finished flooring work for the standard master bath project for the cost of the material, adhesive, and incidental expenses. First, make sure that the underlayment is thoroughly nailed, dry and clean. All seams and indentations should be filled and sanded to surface level with a floor leveler. The next step involves making a template for the floor area from building paper (felt roofing paper, etc.), with the cutouts and precise edge cuts included. Strips of the felt paper attached to the large pieces of the template with masking tape provide a precise replica of the entire floor area, including all irregularities along the edges. After the design of the template has been transferred by tracing onto the vinyl, it can be carefully cut with a good pair of scissors or a sharp utility knife. Before spreading the adhesive with a grooved trowel, double check the fit of the new cut piece by laying it on the bathroom floor and pressing it into corners and along the edges. Follow the directions of the adhesive manufacturer for spreading the material and laying the floor. Use a borrowed or rented floor roller to complete the installation. This method of placing the vinyl applies to a one-piece installation; a two-piece job requires more expertise and several additional steps.

SUMMARY

If the value and size of your home justify installing or renovating a master bath, you can approach the project knowing that your investment will be returned. Carrying out this enterprise can be a major undertaking for even skilled handymen, but you can complete much of the work on your own if you have the time and seek advice as you proceed.

MASTER BATH, DELUXE

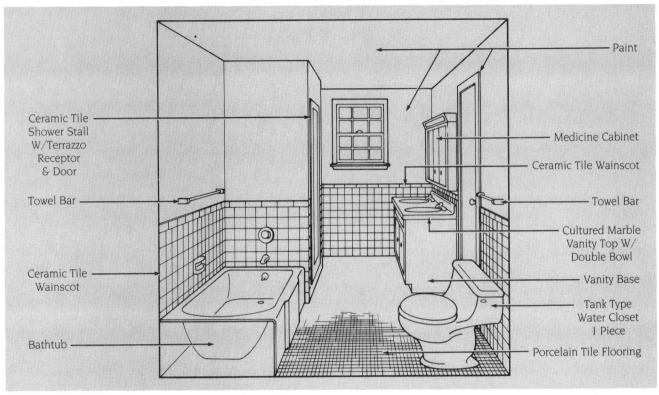

Ceramic Tile Shower Stall W/Terrazzo Receptor & Door

Towel Bar

Ceramic Tile Wainscot

Bathtub

Paint

Medicine Cabinet

Ceramic Tile Wainscot

Towel Bar

Cultured Marble Vanity Top W/ Double Bowl

Vanity Base

Tank Type Water Closet 1 Piece

Porcelain Tile Flooring

The extra accessories and amenities offered in this deluxe master bath are designed to reflect the quality of larger, more expensive homes. The four-fixture project offered in this plan involves a considerable commitment of both money and time. If you plan to accomplish some or all of this renovation on your own, don't hesitate to seek the assistance of knowledgeable people. Good advice can save you money and prevent damage to quality fixtures and materials.

MATERIALS

The fixtures and accessories selected for this room are first quality and appropriate for a deluxe bathroom facility. The four plumbing fixtures include a porcelain-on-cast iron recessed tub with a non-skid mat bottom and a separate shower stall with a terrazzo receptor. The toilet is a quality one-piece floor-mounted unit made from vitreous china. Both the tub and toilet are available in white or colored styles, with the colored fixtures costing about 25% to 30%

more than the white units. The basic rough-in for these fixtures may cost more than the estimated price if relocation or replacement of the existing plumbing is required. Only expert do-it-yourselfers and plumbers should tackle the plumbing tasks encountered in this project.

Ceramic tile is the primary wall and floor covering throughout the deluxe master bath. If you are considering doing the tiling in this bath, then be prepared to make a major commitment to the task. All of the walls are wainscoted to a height of about 4', and the shower stall above the terrazzo receptor is completely tiled. If you haven't done any tile work before, you should hire a tilesetter to do the job. A poor tiling job will not only harm the appearance of the bathroom, but also invite major problems from water penetration later on. The shower stall and tub area, in particular, require precise tile installation if they are to remain watertight for a long period of time.

Placing the ceramic flooring is a bit easier than installing the ceramic wall tile, but it also requires patience and a reasonable level of skill. Like any other flooring job, one of your first and most important concerns should be the thorough inspection and proper reconditioning and preparation of the subfloor.

The accessories and amenities included in the plan for the deluxe master bath can be altered or changed within a wide range of options. Basic items like the tissue dispenser and towel bar, for example, are available in ceramic, chrome, wood, and stainless steel. Different styles of deluxe and standard vanity cabinets can also be purchased at varying costs to suit the decor of your bath. The oversized medicine cabinet unit may be replaced with a half-wall mirror and decorative lighting fixtures.

LEVEL OF DIFFICULTY

Installing this bathroom is a major job for even the accomplished remodeler. The extensive tile work and complexity of the plumbing fixtures dictate that even the most experienced worker will need some advice from a professional. In this case, we suggest that the expert add 25% to the man-hours given. The home handyman should have the plumbing contracted and get assistance on the tile work. Jobs like constructing the partition at the head of the tub and drywalling and finishing the shower stall are well within the realm of most experienced do-it-yourselfers. Handymen should add 60% to the man-hours for these and the other remaining tasks. Beginners could attempt the medicine cabinet, towel bars, and toilet accessories installation, and can also save on labor costs by painting the walls, ceiling, door, and trim. They should add 100% to the man-hours for these items and leave the rest of the work to professional contractors.

WHAT TO WATCH OUT FOR

The deluxe master bath includes some specialized items that require careful treatment during installation. Two of these are the cultured marble vanity top and the terrazzo receptor for the shower stall. Both units will provide years of service when properly installed. They are, however, prone to cracking and chipping if they are not handled carefully during placement or if they are improperly supported or fastened. The marble top should be carefully placed and then leveled on the vanity cabinet. Follow the adhesive manufacturer's instructions when securing the top. The terrazzo receptor, or pan for the base of the shower, should be carefully aligned and leveled at the base of the pre-framed shower stall before the drain is permanently set and secured.

SUMMARY

Renovating a master bath or expanding a full bath to a four-fixture deluxe facility improves the value of your home as well as its comfort. If this plan is in keeping with the size and style of your home, it can be a rewarding remodeling project.

MASTER BATH, DELUXE

Description	Quantity	Man-hours	Material
Partition wall for shower stall, 2" x 4" plates & studs, 16" O.C., 8' high	152 L.F.	2.5	47.80
Rough in frame for medicine cabinet, 2" x 4" stock	16 L.F.	0.5	5.00
Drywall, 1/2" thick on shower stall walls, water resistant, taped & finished, 4' x 8' sheets	5 Sheets	3.0	67.75
Painting, ceiling, walls & door, primer & 1 coat	330 S.F.	1.5	35.95
Deluxe vanity base cabinet, 2 door, 72" wide	1 Ea.	4.0	626.75
Vanity top, cultured marble, 73" x 22" double bowl	1 Ea.	3.0	210.55
Fittings for lavatory	2 Sets	16.0	146.60
Shower stall, terrazzo receptor, 36" x 36"	1 Ea.	8.0	611.05
Shower door, tempered glass, deluxe	1 Ea.	2.0	183.90
Bathtub, recessed, porcelain enamel on cast iron, w/trim, mat bottom, 5' long, color	1 Ea.	4.0	317.05
Fittings for tub & shower	1 Set	9.5	85.40
Medicine cabinet, center mirror, 2 end cabinets 72" long, lighted	1 Ea.	2.0	266.20
Walls, ceramic tile, shower stall & wainscoting, thin set, 4-1/4" x 4-1/4"	170 S.F.	15.5	884.50
Flooring, porcelain tile, 1 color, color group 2, 1" x 1"	40 S.F.	3.5	208.10
Toilet, tank type, vitreous china, floor mounted, 1 piece, color	1 Ea.	3.0	597.75
Fittings for toilet	1 Set	8.5	101.60
Towel bar, stainless steel, 30" long	2 Ea.	1.0	43.55
Toilet tissue dispenser, surface mounted, stainless steel	1 Ea.	0.5	23.00
Totals		88.0	$4462.50

Project Size	8' x 10'	Contractor's Fee Including Materials	$9100

Key to Abbreviations
C.Y. - cubic yard   Ea. - each   L.F. - linear foot   Pr. - pair   Sq. - square (100 square feet of area)
S.F. - square foot   S.Y. - square yard   V.L.F. - vertical linear foot

DELUXE BATH

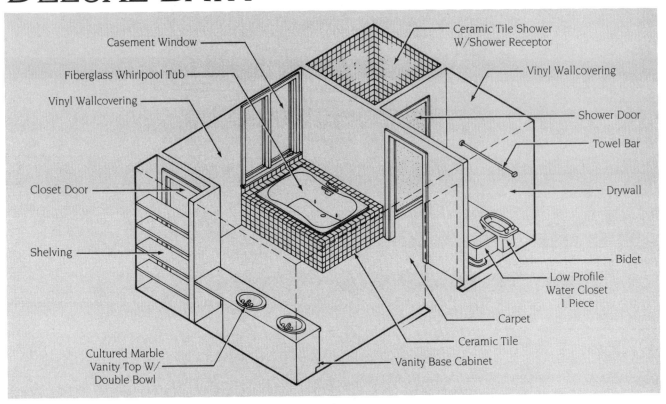

Casement Window

Fiberglass Whirlpool Tub

Vinyl Wallcovering

Closet Door

Shelving

Cultured Marble
Vanity Top W/
Double Bowl

Ceramic Tile Shower
W/Shower Receptor

Vinyl Wallcovering

Shower Door

Towel Bar

Drywall

Bidet

Low Profile
Water Closet
1 Piece

Carpet

Ceramic Tile

Vanity Base Cabinet

If your home has the space to accommodate a deluxe bath, or if you are building an addition large enough for such a room, this remodeling plan will help you in selecting materials and designing the facility. The project is a costly one, as only top-of-the-line fixtures and materials are recommended to complement the size and intended comfort and luxury of this room. Many different layouts are possible in the design of a five-fixture deluxe bathroom, as long as the available floor area allows for them and for the various amenities and accessories. If your house or addition is not large enough to accommodate the facility or if you do not have the minimum 12' x 18' area recommended for a deluxe bath, then you might reconsider doing the project or arrange, at added expense, to alter the floor plan in the area where the facility is to be located. A deluxe bath requires adequate floor space, and cramming the fixtures into too small an area or reducing the bath's open space will only detract from its intended luxury. Because of the magnitude of the project and the high cost of the fixtures and materials, do-it-yourselfers are advised to take a realistic look at the renovation and seriously consider hiring a contractor to install the facility.

MATERIALS

The materials included in the deluxe bath are of the highest available quality short of custom-made items. The five plumbing fixtures include a one-piece, low-profile, colored toilet and matching bidet, a double-bowl lavatory cast into the cultured marble vanity top, a 5' x 5' ceramic shower stall, and a 46" x 56" molded fiberglass tub with whirlpool. The estimated cost of these fixtures includes the appropriate trim like faucets, valves, diverters, and shower head. Additional expense may be added to the estimated cost of the fittings if the rough plumbing is not in place or requires relocation. Added expense will also be incurred if the deluxe bath project is a renovation of an existing facility and old fixtures have to be removed.

The floor, ceiling, and walls of the deluxe bath also incorporate the best available structural materials and finish coverings. The floor is comprised of 1/2" underlayment-grade plywood over the subfloor and then covered with a high quality wool carpet and pad. If the deluxe bath is a brand new installation or part of a larger renovation project, the ceiling should be leveled and covered with 1/2" drywall. After it is taped and finished, it should be painted with a primer and a finish coat of high quality paint. The walls should also be covered with 1/2" sheetrock. Be sure to use 1/2" water resistant drywall on the wall areas near the tub, on the tub support, and around the shower stall. After the walls have been taped and finished, they can be painted or covered with a washable vinyl wallpaper. Ceramic tile should be installed on all walls in the shower stall and on the tub support. The partition between the shower and tub compartments and the framing for the storage closet, shower stall, and the tub support should be built of construction grade 2" x 4"s. If you are doing some or all of the floor, ceiling, and wall installations yourself, it's best to take the time to do them thoroughly, and seek advice along the way. The deluxe quality of the fixtures and materials should be backed up by solid workmanship in the installation process. Beginners and less experienced handymen should hire a contractor to perform most of these tasks.

The window, door, and vanity installations also include first quality materials. The exterior wall can be enhanced with a plastic-clad thermopane casement or sliding window unit. Six-panel or other decorative solid doors between compartments and on the closet maintain the deluxe character of the facility. Louvered units are also available if more ventilation is desired

within the bath and the closet. The prefinished shelving for the closet and the deluxe vanity cabinet offer functional and attractive amenities to the facility. A large mirror on the wall area above the lavatory and vanity unit provides a practical substitute for a mirrored medicine cabinet while contributing to the feeling of spaciousness of the bath.

LEVEL OF DIFFICULTY

As noted in the introduction to the plan for this remodeling project, the deluxe bath is a luxurious facility comprised of expensive plumbing fixtures and other costly building materials. If these fixtures and amenities are within your budget and you have a home large enough to accommodate them, you might find it most expedient to hire a contractor to do the installations. Tasks like the painting and wallpapering can be completed by the homeowner to cut

some of the cost, and beginners can accomplish these jobs without much difficulty. Handymen and expert do-it-yourselfers who want to have a hand in constructing the facility should leave the plumbing, ceramic, and carpeting installations to the professionals, but they should be able to complete most of the other jobs involved in the project. Experts should add about 30% to the professional time estimates for those tasks which they intend to do; handymen, about 70%.

WHAT TO WATCH OUT FOR

The finish materials applied to the floor, ceiling, and walls of any bath should be durable, water and moisture-resistant, and easy to maintain. For these reasons, ceramic tile has proven to be one of the most effective coverings for bathroom installations. The portions of walls, ceilings, and trim which require painting should be carefully prepared, primed, and then finish-coated with a high quality paint. Gloss or semi-gloss finishes generally hold up better than flat finishes and are easier to clean. If you prefer wallpaper, select a product that is labeled as washable. Even though vinyl wallcoverings, for example, may cost more than conventional wallpaper, they are worth the extra initial expense because of their durability and low maintenance. Carpeting can be used as a bathroom floor covering, but it has to be cleaned more often than the carpeting in other locations in your home. Also, if it gets wet constantly and is not given a chance to dry, it is prone to mildew and, under prolonged wet conditions, deterioration. For regular bathroom use, ceramic and resilient floor coverings are more practical but certainly less comfortable under foot than carpeting.

DELUXE BATH

Description	Quantity	Man-hours	Material
Partition walls, 2" x 4" plates and studs, 16" O.C., 8' high	400 L.F.	6.0	125.85
Framing around tub, 2" x 4" stock	80 L.F.	3.0	25.20
Drywall, 1/2" thick on walls & ceilings, water resistant, taped & finished, 4' x 8' sheets	32 Sheets	18.5	433.65
Sub-flooring underlayment grade, plywood, 1/2" thick, 4' x 8' sheets	6 Sheets	2.5	65.05
Vanity, deluxe base cabinet, 4 doors, 21" x 76"	1 Ea.	4.0	711.50
Vanity top, including basins, cultured marble	1 Ea.	5.0	392.05
Fittings for lavatory	2 Sets	16.5	146.40
Tub, whirlpool, molded fiberglass, 56" x 46"	1 Ea.	16.0	2662.00
Fittings for bathtub	1 Set	9.5	85.40
Shower receptor & fittings	1 Ea.	11.0	297.15
Shower door, tempered glass, deluxe	1 Ea.	2.0	320.65
Window, 4' x 4'-6", plastic clad, casement type	1 Ea.	2.0	469.50
Doors, 6 panel pine doors, 2'-6" wide x 6'-8" high	2 Ea.	2.0	348.50
Trim for doors, window & baseboard, 9/16" x 3-1/2" wide	180 L.F.	6.0	152.45
Painting, ceiling & trim, primer & 1 coat	800 S.F.	3.5	87.15
Tile, ceramic, shower & tub, 4-1/4" x 4-1/4"	210 S.F.	19.0	1092.65
Wallpaper, vinyl, fabric backed, medium weight	560 S.F.	9.5	420.10
Shelving, 10" wide, prefinished, 4' long	4 Ea.	2.0	111.30
Toilet, one piece, low profile	1 Ea.	3.0	732.05
Fittings for toilet	1 Set	8.5	101.60
Bidet, vitreous china, white trim	1 Ea.	3.5	338.80
Fittings for bidet	1 Set	8.5	101.60
Carpet, wool, including pad	24 S.Y.	5.5	828.50
Mirror over vanity, plate glass, 6' x 4'	1 Ea.	1.0	158.25
Totals		168.0	$10,207.35

Project Size	12' x 18'	Contractor's Fee Including Materials	$21,040

Key to Abbreviations
C.Y. - cubic yard   Ea. - each   L.F. - linear foot   Pr. - pair   Sq. - square (100 square feet of area)
S.F. - square foot   S.Y. - square yard   V.L.F. - vertical linear foot

SUMMARY

Adding or remodeling a bath to deluxe standards is a way to increase your comfort while boosting the overall value and atmosphere of your house. If a deluxe bathroom fits in with your lifestyle and your home is spacious enough to accommodate it, this project can pay dividends in the coming years.

FREESTANDING FIREPLACE

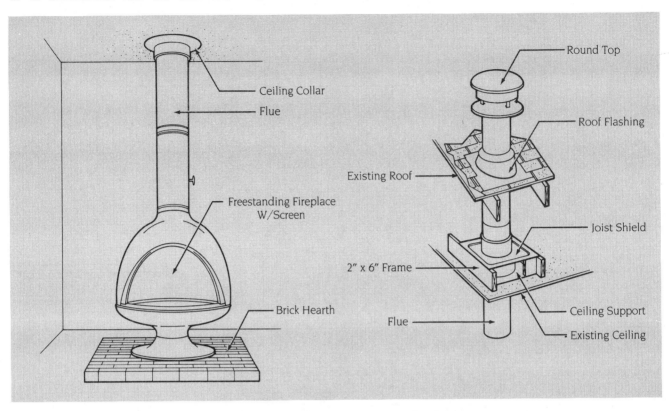

Ceiling Collar

Flue

Freestanding Fireplace W/Screen

Brick Hearth

Round Top

Roof Flashing

Existing Roof

2" x 6" Frame

Flue

Joist Shield

Ceiling Support

Existing Ceiling

An alternative to conventional masonry or preconstructed,built-in fireplaces is the freestanding, prefabricated model. These units can be installed economically by the experienced do-it-yourselfer. The hearth in this plan is brick masonry, but prefabricated hearths are also available. Because the fixture stands away from the walls, expensive and time-consuming room preparations are usually not required. Sometimes the walls will need to be treated with fire-proofing materials because of their proximity to the fireplace.

MATERIALS

Very few conventional building materials are required for this project, as the installation of a freestanding fireplace involves limited preparation. Besides the fireplace itself, a hearth must be placed under and around the base of the unit, and the flue pipe must be installed with appropriate fittings. The fireplace is available as a preassembled unit or in sections that

require assembly before being installed. Many different styles and designs can be purchased at varying costs, but most of the units have a base with a hood to divert smoke and the by-products of combustion into the flue. The base of some models comes factory-equipped with a heat resistant liner, while others require the application of a protective substance or recommend that sand or heat resistant tiles to be used to protect the metal base from damage caused by overheating. Some of the units are enclosed except for an access and viewing opening in one section; other designs feature 360° of heat resistant glass between the hood and base. One of the advantages of freestanding fireplace units is that they are capable of radiating heat in all directions, and, therefore, surpass conventional wall fireplaces in heating efficiency.

A fire-resistant hearth is a vital part of a freestanding stove installation. This plan recommends the use of standard

new or used brick placed on a mortar bed and then grouted to form the hearth, but a wide variety of tiles may also be used. An economical hearth can be built with stone fragments or other loose non-combustible materials, placed 2" to 3" deep within a framed circular, oval, or square perimeter. Regardless of the type of material and the design used, make sure that you follow the manufacturer's recommendations and local code regulations for safe surface and depth dimensions of the hearth.

The materials used for the flue pipe assembly are normally included as part of the fireplace kit. If they are not included, then check with your retailer or the manufacturer of the unit and purchase approved insulated chimney pipe, high quality stove pipe, and similarly safe and durable fittings and flashings. Make sure that the pipe matches the fireplace unit, as it is one of the bigger investments in this project and replacing it would be costly. Unlike prefabricated built-in fireplace installations, the section of flue pipe which runs from the top of the free-standing fireplace to just below the ceiling does not have to be made of insulated materials. In fact, it is to your advantage to run uninsulated stove pipe in this section because it radiates precious heat. Above this section, from just below the ceiling through to the top of the flue, you should use the recommended insulated chimney pipe material.

LEVEL OF DIFFICULTY

The installation of a free-standing fireplace does not require a high level of ability in the use of tools. Beginners, with help, can handle some of the tasks required to complete the installation. The most difficult operation involves cutting the openings in the ceiling and roof for the flue. Beginners should hire a qualified professional to do this part of the installation and to place the chimney pipe, the flashing unit, the joist shield, and the ceiling support fittings. Handymen should be able to accomplish this entire installation, but they should get some advice and instruction before cutting the openings if they are inexperienced in this task. Experts should be able to complete all parts of the project in 10% additional time over the man-hours estimate. Handymen should add 30% to the estimated time, and slightly more for the hole-cutting and roof flashing installation. Beginners should add 75% to 100% to the professional time for the fireplace unit and hearth installations and hire a professional for the rest of the job.

WHAT TO WATCH OUT FOR

One of the problems encountered when installing flue pipe is keeping the line of pipe straight and plumb from the top of the fireplace through to the roof. Because the sections of insulated chimney pipe interlock precisely, they cannot be bent or angled without damaging the connection and creating a fire hazard. It is important, therefore, that you take the time to align the centers of the proposed openings before you make the cuts. After you have determined where the ceiling opening is to be located (midway between joists directly above the location of the fireplace) use a plumb bob to find the center point of the roof opening. Double check your marks and then make your cuts slightly oversize to allow for easier placement of the preassembled chimney pipe.

SUMMARY

Freestanding fireplaces provide an economical alternative to conventional and prefabricated built-in fireplaces. They are easier to install and offer the advantages of greater heating efficiency than most built-in installations. With all these features, plus a choice of available styles, these units can fit harmoniously into many homes.

FREESTANDING FIREPLACE

Description	Quantity	Man-hours	Material
Cut ceiling & roof opening for flue	2 Ea.	4.0	0.00
Frame through ceiling and roof, 2" x 6"	16 L.F.	0.5	7.55
Fittings, ceiling support, 10" diam.	1 Ea.	1.0	72.60
Fittings, joist shield, 10" diam.	1 Ea.	1.0	41.15
Hearth, 5' x 5', standard size brick	1 Ea.	8.0	108.90
Fireplace, prefab, freestanding, with hood, screen & flue	1 Ea.	6.0	726.00
Flue, 10" diam., additional height needed	5 V.L.F.	5.0	344.85
Fittings, roof flashing, 6" diam.	1 Ea.	0.5	30.55
Fittings, round top, 10" diam.	1 Ea.	1.0	83.50
Totals		27.0	$1415.10

Project Size	5' x 5' x 13'	Contractor's Fee Including Materials	$2980

Key to Abbreviations
C.Y. - cubic yard   Ea. - each   L.F. - linear foot   Pr. - pair   Sq. - square (100 square feet of area)
S.F. - square foot   S.Y. - square yard   V.L.F. - vertical linear foot

BUILT-IN FIREPLACE

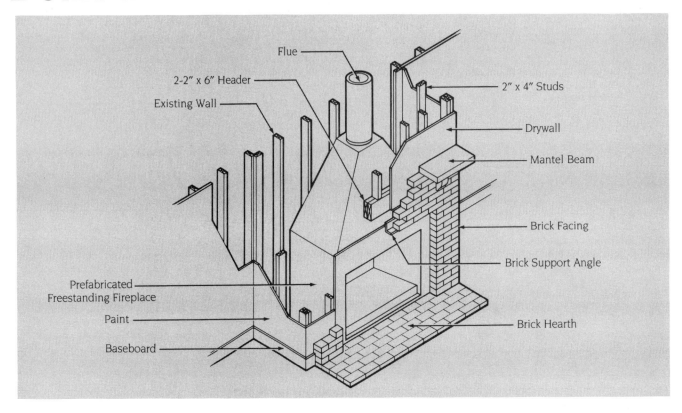

Flue

2-2" x 6" Header

Existing Wall

2" x 4" Studs

Drywall

Mantel Beam

Brick Facing

Brick Support Angle

Prefabricated Freestanding Fireplace

Paint

Baseboard

Brick Hearth

With careful planning and appropriate design, a new fireplace can make a drab room come alive with atmosphere. Conventional fireplaces made of brick and/or other masonry materials are difficult to install in an existing house, but other options are available which involve less work and expense. One of the most popular alternatives is a prefabricated fireplace unit that comes from the supplier ready for installation, complete with flue pipe and accessories. Before placing the unit, the area where it is to be located has to be framed and prepared to receive it. The extent of preliminary work depends on many variables, such as the floor level where it is to be placed, whether it is to be installed on an interior or exterior wall, and, especially in old houses, the amount of leveling and reconditioning required for the support floor surface. If the floor is not level or its support system is inadequate, the materials cost estimate of this project will be higher. Homeowners who are skilled with tools should be able to do most of the work on this job.

MATERIALS

The materials required to complete the installation include the prefabricated freestanding fireplace unit, its flue, related accessories, a simulated brick chimney top, brick and masonry materials for the facing, and conventional framing and wall supplies. The heart of the project is the prefabricated fireplace, which is an efficient and economical alternative to standard brick and mortar installations. Many different manufacturers produce these units, usually from sheet steel. The structure may look heavy, but it is lightweight enough to be carried and placed by two people. Also, most prefabricated fireplaces do not require additional floor support, as they weigh about as much as a heavy piece of furniture. Make sure that you purchase a unit that complies with the standards of stove and freestanding fireplace approval agencies. Also, follow carefully the manufacturer's instructions and precautions during installation of the fireplace and its flue assembly.

Before the unit is placed, the cavity or wall area where it will sit permanently has to be framed with 2" x 4"s. The cost of the framing materials for this operation will depend on the particular location of the fireplace. For example, if the unit is to extend outside of the house, the exterior wall will have to be built, at more expense, to enclose the fireplace unit and the flue. If the installation is to be located inside the room (as in this example) and backed to an existing partition or wall, the materials cost will be lower. Remember that if the fireplace unit is located in the room, it will take up considerable floor space. The exterior placement may cost you more, but the extra expense may be worth it to save floor space. After the fireplace has been put into position and the flue pipe safely tied in, the new framing should be covered with 1/2" fire resistant drywall which is then taped, finished, and painted or wallpapered to suit the room's decor.

The brick hearth and facing recommended in this plan can enhance the fireplace opening. Other noncombustible veneers provide viable options at varying costs. The laminated hardwood mantel is one of many alternatives available for dressing up the opening. The design and choice of materials for the facing, hearth, and mantel should be given careful consideration before the selections are made. Brick, marble, and stone are among the materials that can be used. Some extra expense may be worthwhile, as the aesthetic appeal of the fireplace is important.

Take care in cutting the openings for the flue pipe and be sure to use high quality fittings and flashing where necessary. Joist shields should also be installed where needed for safety. A simulated brick chimney top is a feature which adds to the appearance of the job by hiding the top of the insulated piping. If the pipe extends from a rear-facing or hidden section of your roof or if you are not fussy about the exposed pipe, then omit the simulated chimney as a decorative extra and deduct its cost from the project.

LEVEL OF DIFFICULTY

Although the installation of a prefabricated fireplace may appear to be a major undertaking, with the right conditions it can be a fairly uncomplicated project for the capable do-it-yourselfer. The masonry tasks demand specialized skills and should be completed by a professional if you have not had experience in laying stone or brick. Remember that attractive brick work on the hearth and facing are important, so even experts may consider hiring a professional mason. Most of the other tasks, including cutting the ceiling and roof openings, can be completed by handymen and experts. Get some advice from a knowledgeable person if you have not cut ceilings or roof holes before. Beginners should limit themselves to the finish work, the framing, and drywalling. If you are a beginner, seek some help before you attempt any task that you have not done before. Beginners should also leave the actual fireplace and flue installation to a competent contractor. Experts should add about 10% to the man-hours estimate and more for the

masonry operations. Handymen should tack on about 40% to the time for the framing, drywalling, and finish work, excluding the masonry. They should increase the time for hole-cutting and fireplace and flue installation by 100% if they have not had prior experience with these tasks. Beginners should double the time estimate for any jobs they intend to complete.

WHAT TO WATCH OUT FOR

Two aspects of this project should be noted as critical, one affecting materials and labor costs and the other, safety. The expense for both materials and labor will vary significantly from the plan's estimate if the prefabricated fireplace unit will be used as a replacement for an existing fireplace facility or if extensive demolition and alteration of the site are required before the new fireplace is installed. The materials cost will also be increased considerably if an exterior chase has to be built to house the fireplace and flue pipe, especially if the fireplace is to be located on the first floor of a two-story house. Safety is another aspect of this project which has to be monitored carefully throughout the installation process. Follow the manufacturer's safety recommendations closely and observe local building codes which deal with fireplace or woodburning stove regulations. Most communities require approval of all new fireplace and stove installations, so arrange to have the inspection before you drywall the fireplace enclosure.

SUMMARY

A new fireplace is one way to give your family room, living room, or den new life and atmosphere and some extra heat during the cooler months. With the installation of a prefabricated fireplace unit, you can save on material costs and also labor by doing much of the work on your own.

BUILT-IN FIREPLACE

Description	Quantity	Man-hours	Material
Framing, fireplace enclosure, 2" x 4" studs & plates, 16" O.C.	14 L.F.	2.5	50.00
Header over opening, 2" x 6"	12 L.F.	0.5	5.65
Cut ceiling & roof opening for flue	2 Ea.	3.0	0.00
Frame, through ceiling & roof, 2" x 6"	16 L.F.	0.5	7.55
Fittings, ceiling support, 10" diam.	1 Ea.	1.0	72.60
Fittings, joist shield, 10" diam.	1 Ea.	1.0	47.20
Drywall, 1/2" thick on walls, fire resistant, taped & finished, 4' x 8' sheets	4 Sheets	2.5	44.90
Fireplace, prefab, built-in, with hood, screen & flue	1 Ea.	9.0	762.30
Facing, 6' x 5', standard size brick	30 S.F.	11.0	66.15
Hearth, 3' x 6', standard size brick	1 Ea.	8.0	108.90
Mantel beam, laminated hardwood, 2-1/4" x 10-1/2" x 6'	1 Ea.	2.0	102.85
Simulated brick chimney top, 3' high, 16" x 16"	1 Ea.	1.0	151.25
Fittings, roof flashing, 6" diam.	1 Ea.	0.5	30.55
Trim, baseboard, 9/16" x 3-1/2"	10 L.F.	0.5	8.45
Painting, walls & trim, primer & 1 coat	90 S.F.	1.0	98.00
Totals		44.0	$1556.35

Project Size	5' x 6' x 13'	Contractor's Fee Including Materials	**$3780**

Key to Abbreviations
C.Y. - cubic yard   Ea. - each   L.F. - linear foot   Pr. - pair   Sq. - square (100 square feet of area)
S.F. - square foot   S.Y. - square yard   V.L.F. - vertical linear foot

MASONRY FIREPLACE

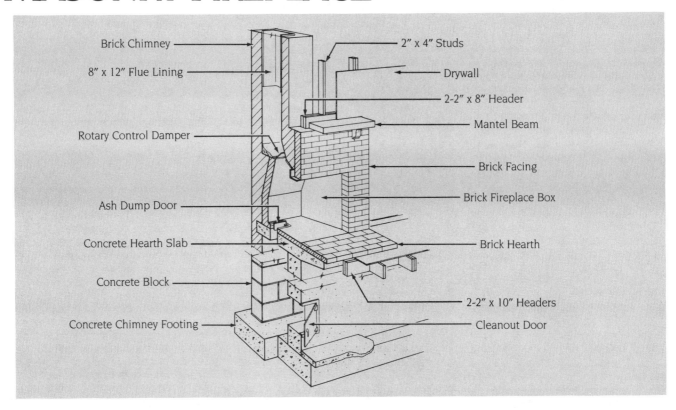

Brick Chimney

8" x 12" Flue Lining

Rotary Control Damper

Ash Dump Door

Concrete Hearth Slab

Concrete Block

Concrete Chimney Footing

2" x 4" Studs

Drywall

2-2" x 8" Header

Mantel Beam

Brick Facing

Brick Fireplace Box

Brick Hearth

2-2" x 10" Headers

Cleanout Door

Although the construction of a masonry fireplace involves considerable time, inconvenience, and expense, it is a durable fixture which contributes to the appearance and atmosphere of a room. Both of these features make it a good investment. Masonry work does require some specialized skills and tools, however, and do-it-yourselfers should be cautioned about tackling this project if they do not have any experience in this area. The site preparation, actual construction of the fireplace and chimney, and inside and outside finishing operations should all be carefully planned in the proper sequence so that inconvenience can be kept to a minimum. If you have not done masonry work before, seek advice from a qualified person before you start, and do some reading on the subject. When you begin the project, plan to work slowly and patiently with a gradual increase in productivity as you acquire skill in the masonry operations. The rewards of personal satisfaction, savings on construction costs, and added value to your home can make your efforts worthwhile.

MATERIALS

The materials used in the installation of a masonry fireplace include conventional masonry products, as well as framing lumber for alternations that need to be made to accommodate the new structure. There are also some incidental materials associated with the fireplace, chimney, and flue. The total cost of these items will vary with each installation, depending on the amount of required site preparation, the height of the chimney, and the extent of finish work needed to receive the new chimney on the side and roof of the house. Costs for materials will also vary with the type of masonry veneer selected for the facing of the fireplace, hearth, and chimney. Before the fireplace and chimney can be put into position, extensive site work is required on the inside and, usually, on the outside of the house. The estimates given in this plan will help you to determine the cost for this work. On the inside of the house, framing materials are required to maintain the floor and exterior wall

support system when the openings are cut for the hearth and fireplace. Before cutting the wall opening and installing the headers, be sure to provide temporary ceiling support, as the outside wall may be a load bearing structure. The same precaution should be taken before cutting the floor joists for the hearth. The materials for these temporary 2" x 4" support partitions have not been included in the estimate, but the same lumber used for the ceiling support can be reused for floor support and, possibly, elsewhere in the installation where 2" x 4"s are required. If you have not performed framing and support operations before, get some advice before you tackle them, as mistakes and poor workmanship can cause serious structural damage to the house.

Outside of the house, the site must be prepared for the construction of a foundation to bear the weight of the chimney. Because this foundation should extend to the full depth of the house's foundation, a considerable amount of excavating has to be done.

This excavation usually has to be done by hand because of its proximity to the structure and finished landscaping. Machine excavation can sometimes be done at extra cost. After the excavation has been completed, a footing is placed; and later, concrete blocks are laid to serve as the foundation for the fireplace and chimney. Additional labor costs also have to be included for removing the siding and preparing the rake boards or eaves to receive the new chimney.

The masonry materials used in this plan include bricks, concrete blocks, flue liner, and mortar. These items are readily available from most building and masonry supply outlets, but it pays to shop around for them. Here are a few suggestions to assist you in the purchase. First, try to buy all of the materials from the same retailer. By consolidating your order, you will get a better price. Second, have the materials delivered to your property, with the delivery charge included in the bill at the time of purchase. Unless the materials have to be transported an excessive distance, most retailers will not charge you for delivery of an order of this size. Third, select the veneer material carefully, as conventional red brick is only one of many options. Field stone, quarry-prepared stone, and cobblestone are other choices that function well and give a different appearance. The costs for these alternative materials will vary, depending on the required preparation of the stone, its quality, and its availability. Concrete block with stucco veneer is an attractive, yet economical option for chimney design.

The appropriate fittings, prefabricated firebox, and roof flashing should be selected with the aid of a mason and/or a reputable retailer if you are unfamiliar with these specialty items. Make sure, for example, that you match the size of the cast iron damper unit and firebox and that you install appropriately sized clean-out fittings. The flashing required to join chimney and roof must be carefully installed to assure that the structure is weather-tight. If the new chimney is placed on the gutter side of the roof, a cricket (a sort of diverter) will have to be constructed at extra cost. Additional expense will also be incurred if a chimney cap is needed to avert downdrafts in your fireplace. The rental of staging or scaffolding is one more cost to figure in for work on the chimney construction.

LEVEL OF DIFFICULTY

As noted at the outset of this project description, a significant amount of skill and experience in masonry work is required to take on the building of this fireplace. If you are accomplished in the use of tools, but have not worked with masonry materials before, you should do some reading on the subject, seek advice from a mason, and even complete a trial project like an outdoor barbeque or a small brick and block retaining wall. Experts and some experienced handymen should be able to complete the framing tasks, the excavation and leave the remainder of the project to a professional. Handymen and experts should add about 60% and 30% respectively, to the man-hours estimates for the framing and site preparation operations. If you plan to do the masonry work, and are inexperienced in bricklaying, then double or even triple the professional time, even if you are an expert in other remodeling skills. Plan to work very slowly at first, with a gradual increase in productivity as you gain experience and the project progresses.

WHAT TO WATCH OUT FOR

One of the most important elements of any fireplace is the firebox. Inaccurate alignment or incorrect sizing of this component can adversely affect the fireplace's operation by causing inefficient draft. Seek advice from a mason before you construct the firebox, as his experience and knowledge can help prevent the incorrect or ineffective placement of this vital fireplace component. It may be worth the expense of hiring a mason for this task if you do not have the skill and know-how to complete it on your own.

SUMMARY

Installing a conventional masonry fireplace in your home is a major remodeling project, but one which can be tackled, at least in part, by do-it-yourselfers. It is a fairly involved project, but will result in a pleasing and practical addition to your home.

MASONRY FIREPLACE

Description	Quantity	Man-hours	Material
Excavating by hand, heavy soil, for chimney foundation	9 C.Y.	18.0	0.00
Concrete chimney footing	0.5 C.Y.	2.0	62.00
Concrete block, 8" thick, for foundation wall, 32" x 60" x 8'	85 S.F.	8.0	140.00
Concrete block, 8" thick, for chimney, 32" x 40" x 8'	70 S.F.	6.5	127.05
Framing, joists, 2" x 10", fireplace foundation opening	30 L.F.	1.0	24.00
Cleanout door & frame, cast iron, 8" x 8"	1 Ea.	1.0	14.50
Framing, walls, header over fireplace opening, 2" x 8" & 2" x 4"	20 L.F.	1.0	13.80
Fireplace box, complete	1 Ea.	8.0	133.10
Damper, rotary control, cast iron, 30" opening	1 Ea.	1.5	54.00
Facing, 6' x 5', standard size brick	30 S.F.	11.0	55.00
Hearth, 3' x 6', standard size brick	1 Ea.	8.0	200.00
Mantel beam, rough texture wood, 4" x 8" x 6'	6 L.F.	1.5	25.00
Demolition, remove siding, cut roof	1 Ea.	8.0	0.00
Chimney, 16" x 20" x 12", standard size brick, 8" x 12" flue	12 V.L.F.	12.0	240.75
Flashing at siding & roof	30 S.F.	2.0	49.00
Totals		89.5	$1102.20

Project Size	6' x 6' x 20'	Contractor's Fee Including Materials	$4190

Key to Abbreviations
C.Y. - cubic yard   Ea. - each   L.F. - linear foot   Pr. - pair   Sq. - square (100 square feet of area)
S.F. - square foot   S.Y. - square yard   V.L.F. - vertical linear foot

GARAGE CONVERSION

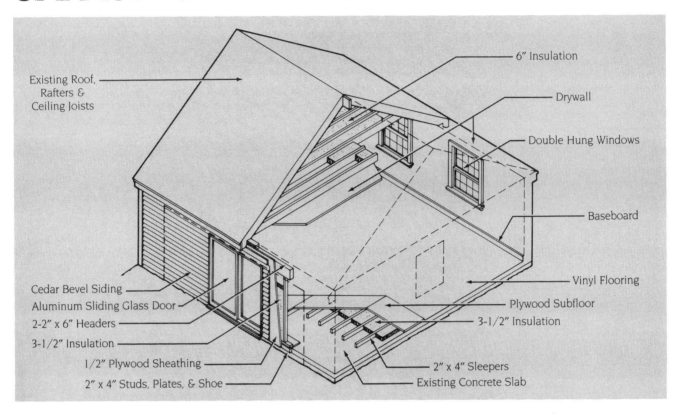

Existing Roof, Rafters & Ceiling Joists

6" Insulation

Drywall

Double Hung Windows

Baseboard

Cedar Bevel Siding
Aluminum Sliding Glass Door
2-2" x 6" Headers
3-1/2" Insulation
1/2" Plywood Sheathing
2" x 4" Studs, Plates, & Shoe

Vinyl Flooring
Plywood Subfloor
3-1/2" Insulation
2" x 4" Sleepers
Existing Concrete Slab

Like unfinished attic and basement areas, garages can be economically converted to living, work, or studio space, especially if the garage is attached as an integral part of the existing house. Because the expenses for excavation, foundation work, framing, and closing in the new living area have already been taken care of, your only concerns will be the costs of preparing the interior, adding the windows and a door, and closing in, when necessary, portions of the exterior walls. If you are doing the work on your own, plan on a challenging project, but one that includes the benefits of accessibility and a convenient location.

MATERIALS

The primary materials used for the garage conversion consist of framing lumber, various sheet goods for the floor, walls, and ceiling, several windows, sliding glass doors, and the finish materials for the inside and the outside of the exterior walls.

Insulation, electrical materials, and various incidentals are also required and will vary in type, amount, and size, depending on such factors as the geographical area of your home and the particular location of the garage in relation to the main structure.

The minimum framing and structural lumber required in the garage conversion includes 2" x 4"s and a few 2" x 8"s. The 2" x 4"s used as sleepers for the support system of the new floor should be treated with wood preservative before they are placed. Although it is more expensive, pressure-treated wood can also be used for superior quality sleepers. Conventional 2" x 4"s are used as studs in the exterior walls to frame in the new windows and sliding glass door unit and to frame the new wall that fills the old garage door opening. Sheathing plywood, 5/8" in thickness, serves as the rough covering for the sleepers and the exterior of the new wall framing. Be sure to insulate the floor and place a vapor barrier on top of the 2" x 4" floor sleepers before

laying the plywood. Additional framing may be required at extra cost if the floor of the new room has to be raised or the ceiling lowered for aesthetic or practical reasons.

The wall studs and ceiling joists of the new room can be covered with various types of materials, such as drywall or wood paneling. An economical choice is 1/2" drywall. If the garage is already drywalled, but not insulated, hire an insulating contractor to blow insulation into the walls, and, if necessary, the ceiling. If your garage is situated under the living area of your house, it may already be insulated. While the walls are open, the rough electrical work should also be installed. As for the exterior, these walls should be finished with matching siding around the new window and door installations and in the wall space which fills the void left by the garage door. Make sure that you lace the new siding into the old, prime all of the new materials, and then put a uniform finish coat on all three sides of the new room's exterior.

The windows and door selected for the new room should match or complement the style and design of other units in your house. The type of windows suggested in the plan are of standard size and design, but many other styles and sizes are available at varying costs. The sliding glass door unit, too, is a standard item, but many other options in both sliding and conventional door styles can be purchased over a wide price range. One general rule to follow when purchasing window and door units is that quality products will usually return the homeowner's investment in energy savings, durability, and low maintenance costs over the life of the unit.

The finish work in the new room should reflect its anticipated use. The trim for the windows and door, as well as the baseboard, can be painted, stained, or left natural and finished with a clear sealer. A wide range of flooring materials can be installed, from hardwood to carpeting or, as in this plan, durable vinyl sheet goods. Make sure that you vent the subflooring support system so that it can breathe. Also, if you plan to use vinyl or carpeting for the finished floor, it might be worth the additional expense and time to install a layer of 3/8" particle board underlayment over the sheathing plywood. Not only will the surface material look and wear better, but the floor will be stronger, more even, quieter, and warmer.

LEVEL OF DIFFICULTY

The conversion of a garage into living space is a major undertaking; but because of the convenient location and accessibility of the work site, it is the type of project that can be done in stages, over a longer period of time than other remodeling jobs. Many of the tasks involved in the final stages of the project can be accomplished by beginners who seek advice and assistance from knowledgeable people. Novices, however, should leave the window, door, and filler framing jobs to a professional. The installation of the floor sleepers, too, can be a tricky job, especially in garages with sloped or uneven concrete floors. Shimming is necessary in constructing the support frame, and often the 2" x 4" sleepers have to be ripped to size so that they can be set on the sloped concrete. These operations demand skill in the use of tools and the basic know-how of someone who has done this work before. Beginners and most handymen should leave the electrical work to a competent tradesman. As a general rule, if you are a beginner, add 90% to the man-hours estimate for those tasks which you feel you can handle. If you are a reasonably skilled handyman, add 40% to the estimate and more if you plan to lay the sleeper support system and to rough in the windows, sliding doors, and fill in the garage door opening. Experts should add about 10% to all tasks involved in the conversion.

WHAT TO WATCH OUT FOR

Problems with the floor and ceiling heights can be corrected with careful design and planning. Garage floors, for example, are often located below grade level or are pitched dramatically for drainage. Take stock of the existing floor's location and slope before you determine the level of the new floor and the design for its support. You should also make provisions to divert surface water via drains or other means so that run-off or icing won't penetrate under the floor of the new room and cause damage. Garage ceilings, too, vary in height, so plan on some additional expense if new ceiling joists have to be installed to decrease the height, or if other modifications have to be made to raise it.

SUMMARY

A garage conversion is another way in which you can use an existing sheltered area to create new living space in your home. This often underutilized area can be conveniently remodeled to become a comfortable and functional room.

GARAGE CONVERSION

Description	Quantity	Man-hours	Material
Flooring, joists 2" x 4", 16" O.C., on existing concrete slab	525 L.F.	7.0	165.15
Plywood, CDX, 5/8" thick, 4' x 8' sheets for floors & exterior wall	22 Sheets	10.0	374.80
Plates, top & bottom, 2" x 4", 12' lengths	40 L.F.	1.0	12.60
Wall studs at door and new windows 2" x 4" x 8' long, 16" O.C.	192 L.F.	3.0	60.40
Headers over openings, double 2" x 6"	28 L.F.	1.5	13.20
Siding, cedar bevel, A grade, 1/2" x 6"	155 S.F.	5.0	305.70
Insulation, fiberglass blankets, paper backed, 3-1/2" thick, R-11, for floor & walls	1000 S.F.	11.0	266.20
Insulation, fiberglass blankets, paper backed, 6" thick, R-19, for ceiling	500 S.F.	6.5	217.80
Windows, double hung, plastic clad, insulating glass, 3' x 4', w/frame, screen & exterior trim	3 Ea.	3.0	635.25
Doors, sliding glass, aluminum, 5/8" insulated glass, 6' wide, premium	1 Ea.	4.0	532.40
Drywall, 1/2" thick, on walls & ceiling, standard taped & finished, 4' x 8' sheets	38 Sheets	22.0	426.70
Trim, casing for windows & door, 11/16" x 2-1/2" wide	50 L.F.	2.0	21.80
Trim, baseboard, 9/16" x 3-1/2"	90 L.F.	3.0	76.25
Flooring, vinyl sheet goods, .125" thick	500 S.F.	17.5	877.25
Painting, walls, ceilings & trim, primer & 1 coat	1200 S.F.	12.0	130.70
Painting, exterior siding, oil base primer & 2 coats, brushwork	185 S.F.	3.0	49.25
Electrical, 8 duplex receptacles, 1 switch	1 Lot	13.5	134.50
Totals		125.0	$4299.95

Project Size   22' x 22'

Contractor's Fee Including Materials **$10,800**

Key to Abbreviations
C.Y. - cubic yard   Ea. - each   L.F. - linear foot   Pr. - pair   Sq. - square (100 square feet of area)
S.F. - square foot   S.Y. - square yard   V.L.F. - vertical linear foot

STRAIGHT WALL KITCHEN, STANDARD

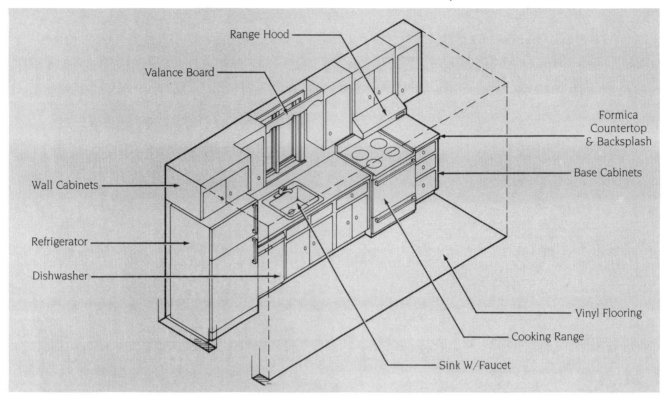

Range Hood

Valance Board

Formica Countertop & Backsplash

Base Cabinets

Wall Cabinets

Refrigerator

Dishwasher

Vinyl Flooring

Cooking Range

Sink W/Faucet

Because of limited floor or wall area, particularly in smaller houses, kitchen facilities must sometimes be confined to a single wall. Often, as with corridor-style kitchens, the components must be cleverly arranged to meet a pressing need for space. It is important in these cases, therefore, that the homeowner select the cabinets, appliances, and other materials with efficient use of space as one of the primary guidelines. If the size or shape of the room is not a problem, and the straight wall kitchen design is a matter of personal preference, then the homeowner has greater flexibility in making these decisions. Remember that you should weigh the various costs of kitchen materials against their long-term use, convenience, and appearance. Even a relatively basic kitchen renovation like this straight wall facility requires careful planning and selection of materials to fit the particular area, food preparation needs, and budget of the homeowner.

MATERIALS

When compared to larger facilities, this standard straight wall kitchen plan is limited in floor, counter, and cabinet area, but it maintains an efficient arrangement, nevertheless. The use of standard-grade products keeps the materials costs to a modest level, yet the result of the project should be an attractive new facility that will function well for many years. For most do-it-yourselfers, this project is challenging, but more manageable than larger kitchen renovations. If you choose to do some of the work on your own, the cost for this installation can be reduced considerably.

As in most kitchen renovations, the greatest single expenditure is for the cabinets and the cost of their installation. Although the standard grade cabinets included in this plan lack the deluxe paneled features of more expensive models, they are comparable in all other aspects. They are made of quality hardwoods, include durable hardware, and come completely finished from the factory or shop. Before you purchase the

cabinets for your new kitchen, do some research, shop extensively, and know precisely what you are buying. Be wary of products that are suspiciously low in price; examine sample units to determine their materials and construction, and find out if auxiliary items like sufficient shelving and durable hardware are included in the quoted price. If you plan to install the cabinets on your own, get some advice before you start the job and work slowly during the placement of the units. Beginners should leave the cabinet installation to a professional, but experts and moderately skilled handymen should be able to handle this single wall placement if they are given some professional advice before starting.

The surface coverings used in this kitchen project are economical materials which have proven to be attractive, durable, and easily maintained in kitchen use. The countertop is covered with heat and water resistant Formica applied to particleboard. You can purchase the countertop as a prefabricated unit from the cabinet retailer or from suppliers who specialize in counter-top manufacture. You might save some money by making the counter-top on your own, but it is a difficult procedure involving materials which are not easy to work with. If you decide to do the countertop on your own, hold up on cutting the opening for the sink until you have conferred with your plumber. He may prefer to do the entire sink installation, including the cutting of the opening, at one time. The vinyl flooring material is also a proven product for kitchen use. Many decorative options are available in both sheet and tile format. Sheet goods cost slightly more; and because they must be laid in single or several large pieces, they require more skill to install than tiles. The materials are comparable in durability, but the fact that sheet flooring is seamless makes it less prone to water penetration. Experts can lay the floor in this kitchen, and amply skilled handymen can do the same if they are given professional guidance.

The appliances for this standard straight wall kitchen have been selected with economy in mind. If space is not a problem, a standard-sized refrigerator and range should be placed at a workable distance from one another along the run of the facility. Undersized appliances are available for situations where space is a critical concern, but they are usually special order units and cost more. If you can fit standard-sized appliances into the new facility, you should do so whenever possible. Be sure to allow for the extra cost of new electrical or plumbing rough-in necessitated by relocation or reconditioning of the old lines. The estimate for this plan includes plumbing rough-in for a double-bowl sink, but it does not allow for additional plumbing for relocation of the fixture. A smaller single-bowl sink can be installed in place of the double-bowl unit. By making this change in the plan, you would add space to the counter area while reducing the cost.

LEVEL OF DIFFICULTY

Because of its basic one-wall layout and its limited number of components, this kitchen remodeling project can be accomplished by all experts and those handymen who are advanced in their building skills. Many different construction operations are required to complete the project, and all do-it-yourselfers should proceed slowly and seek advice before starting unfamiliar tasks. The installation of cabinets, countertop, and flooring, as well as plumbing and electrical work requires knowledge, special skills and tools, and careful work. Evaluate your abilities and attempt only those tasks which you feel you can manage. Taking on more than you can handle may result in costly damage to materials and the additional expense of hiring a contractor to correct faulty installations. Beginners should not attempt the cabinet or countertop placement, but they may be able to handle the other jobs, including the flooring, if they seek guidance along the way. They should add 100% to the professional time for the basic tasks, and more for the flooring work. Experts and handymen should add 20% and 50%, respectively, to the time estimates for all tasks, except the cabinet placement. They should add 50% and 100%, respectively, for that operation, to allow for slower, more careful work.

WHAT TO WATCH OUT FOR

One way to save money on this and other kitchen remodeling projects is to remove the old facility on your own. The job may appear to be routine, but it does require skill in the use of tools and knowledge of fundamental building practices. Be especially careful in dismantling the old cabinets, and avoid doing careless damage to the walls and ceiling in the process. Take the necessary precautions of shutting off water and electrical supply lines to the kitchen before removing the sink, range hood, and other appliances. If you are unfamiliar with plumbing and electrical work, call a professional to do the disconnecting before you start the removal. Make arrangements for the hauling away of old materials and for any help you might need to remove or transport them.

SUMMARY

This remodeling project demonstrates how an efficient and economical kitchen facility can be installed on a single wall. Its basic, space-saving layout and modest cost make it a practical design for smaller homes and an approachable undertaking for do-it-yourselfers.

STRAIGHT WALL KITCHEN, STANDARD

Description	Quantity	Man-hours	Material
Blocking, for mounting cabinets, 2" x 4" stock	18 L.F.	1.0	5.65
Plywood, underlayment grade, 3/8" thick, 4' x 8' sheets	4 Sheets	1.5	63.50
Flooring, vinyl composition tile, 12" x 12" x 1/16", plain	65 S.F.	2.0	93.60
Wall cabinets, 12" deep, hardwood	9.5 L.F.	3.0	363.95
Base cabinets, 24" deep, hardwood	6.5 L.F.	4.0	599.90
Countertop, 1-1/4" thick Formica, w/backsplash	8.5 L.F.	2.5	51.45
Valance board over sink	4 L.F.	0.5	29.05
Trim, crown molding, stock pine 9/16" x 3-5/8"	28 L.F.	1.0	37.30
Paint, ceiling & walls, primer & 1 coat	285 L.F.	2.5	31.05
Paint, cornice trim, puttying, primer & 1 coat	28 L.F.	0.5	1.70
Cooking range, free-standing, 30" wide, one oven	1 Ea	2.0	314.60
Hood for range, 2-speed, 30" wide	1 Ea.	3.5	96.80
Refrigerator, no frost, 19 C.F.	1 Ea.	2.0	726.00
Dishwasher, built-in, 2 cycle	1 Ea.	4.0	471.90
Sink w/faucets & drain, stainless steel, self-rimming, 32" x 22", double bowl	1 Ea.	6.5	371.45
Rough-in, supply, waste & vent for sink & dishwasher	1 Ea.	9.0	79.70
Totals		45.5	$3337.60

Project Size	6'-6" x 14'	Contractor's Fee Including Materials	$6350

Key to Abbreviations
C.Y. - cubic yard   Ea. - each   L.F. - linear foot   Pr. - pair   Sq. - square (100 square feet of area)
S.F. - square foot   S.Y. - square yard   V.L.F. - vertical linear foot

STRAIGHT WALL KITCHEN, DELUXE

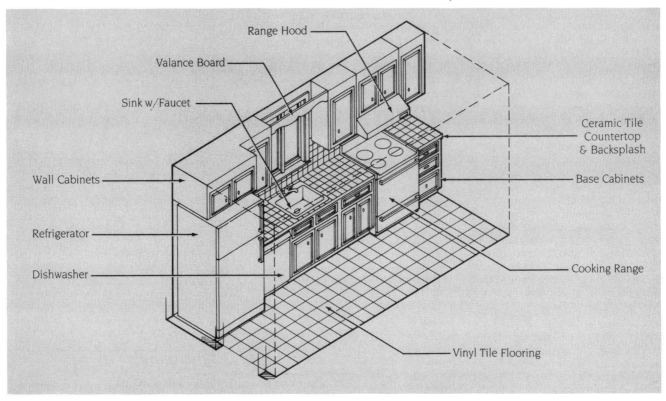

The deluxe features of this straight wall kitchen facility enhance its appearance and convenience while maintaining the efficiency and durability standards required of all kitchens. This plan might be appropriate for those who prefer the features of the deluxe projects and whose kitchens are a highly visible area in their homes. Although this plan presents a small and relatively simple renovation design, its materials are expensive, and do-it-yourselfers should use discretion in determining which tasks they will undertake.

MATERIALS

The materials used in this deluxe kitchen design are top-of-the-line products which will enhance the appearance of the facility and provide many years of reliable service. Some substitutions can be used, but these modifications should be made with discretion and thought given to their aesthetic impact on the kitchen's appearance. Remember that kitchen

products are in place for a long time and economizing with lower-grade substitutes may lead to problems in the future. If you feel that you need guidance, consult a professional kitchen planner. The cost of such a service may save you unnecessary expense in materials and improve the efficiency of the facility.

The cabinets in this plan are hardwood units with paneled cabinet doors. Because the cabinets establish the decor of the room, they are its main feature and are worthy of some advance planning and research. Since much of the expense of the new facility is incurred in the cost of the cabinets, you will want to buy units of high quality materials and construction. If you are installing the cabinets on your own, follow accepted carpentry methods and work slowly and carefully. Rushing this operation can result in misaligned components and, worse, damage to expensive prefinished cabinets.

The ceramic tile used for the counter-top and the vinyl tile used for the floor provide durable, easily maintained, and attractive surfaces. The ceramic tiles are available in many colors and designs which can be highlighted with colored epoxy grout to create an attractive and functional work surface and backsplash. If you plan to do the tile work on your own, be sure to fasten the plywood subsurface firmly to the base cabinets, as movement of this support surface subsequent to the tile installation can cause the grout to crack and, eventually, the tiles to loosen. Also, make sure that the plywood surface is clean, dry, and level before the tiles are placed. The vinyl flooring for the facility can be comprised of sheet goods or individual tiles as determined by personal preference or the aesthetic mandates of color, design, and surface texture. Remember that the flooring should be installed after all other kitchen components, except the refrigerator and free-standing stove, have been placed. The vinyl material should cover the floor surface under the plug-in appliances, but not the area under the cabinets.

The appliances for this straight wall facility should be placed in locations which will make them conveniently accessible during their use. Before purchasing the refrigerator, for example, determine which design features of the appliance will best suit its location. Size, left- or right-hand door opening, side-by-side or upper and lower freezer/refrigerator layout are all important considerations, especially in smaller kitchens. If a built-in range is utilized, special cabinet and countertop planning is required, whereas a freestanding unit requires only a standard opening, so plan accordingly. A change from built-in to freestanding range, or vice versa, after the cabinets have been purchased, will require a costly alteration. A dishwasher is a modern convenience, but in a single wall kitchen, it will take up 30" of already precious base cabinet space. Therefore, you may wish to forego this feature. If you do intend to install the dishwasher as a new or relocated facility, remember that it requires both plumbing and electrical rough-in and hook-ups at an increase in the cost of the installation.

LEVEL OF DIFFICULTY

Like the standard straight wall kitchen, this remodeling project provides the opportunity for do-it-yourselfers to accomplish a significant amount of the work on their own. Although the undertaking is challenging because of the wide variety of skills required to complete the installation, its single wall layout and small area make it a reasonable project for experts and competent handymen. Remember that precise measurement, tight fits, and accurate alignment are required in all interior finish operations, especially kitchen cabinet, countertop, and flooring placement. Also, bear in mind that you are working with deluxe materials that are expensive to replace or repair if you damage them with poor workmanship and carelessness. As a general rule, beginners should not attempt the cabinet installation and should double the estimated professional time for basic tasks. Experts and handymen should add 20% and 50%, respectively to the man-hours estimates for the basic operation, and 50% and 100% for the

cabinet placement. Specialized jobs like the tiling, flooring, electrical installation and plumbing should be attempted only by individuals experienced in these areas of construction, or by accomplished do-it-yourselfers.

WHAT TO WATCH OUT FOR

Because the cabinet system for this kitchen project is basic in its single wall design and limited in the number of units, its installation is a manageable undertaking for skilled do-it-yourselfers. If you follow a few basic guidelines, work patiently, and seek advice before you start and when any problems develop, your efforts can produce professional results and considerable savings in labor costs.

Here are a few suggestions to get you started. Thoroughly prepare the walls and floor in the cabinet area by making sure that they are solid, free from voids and obstructions, and reasonably plumb and level. Install the wall units first, making all fastenings temporary as you keep a constant check on tight abutments and the alignment of facings. Maintain plumb and level as you proceed, using shims and spacers where needed. Follow the same process for the base cabinets, giving special attention to irregularities or slope of the floor. Make all permanent fastenings with heavy wood screws or lag bolts after the entire system has been placed. Install the valance and trim after the wall units have been permanently placed. At least two workers are needed for the cabinet installation, so plan accordingly.

SUMMARY

This straight wall kitchen plan demonstrates how a small facility can take on an elegant appearance as deluxe products are incorporated into its construction. The additional expense of its top quality materials will be returned in many years of pleasant, practical, and dependable use.

STRAIGHT WALL KITCHEN, DELUXE

Description	Quantity	Man-hours	Material
Blocking, for mounting cabinets, 2" x 4" stock	18 L.F.	1.0	5.65
Plywood, underlayment grade, 3/8" thick 4' x 8' sheets	4 Sheets	1.5	63.50
Flooring, vinyl sheet goods, .0125" thick	65 S.F.	2.0	93.60
Wall cabinets, 12" deep, hardwood, deluxe	9.5 L.F.	3.0	509.60
Base cabinets, 24" deep, hardwood, deluxe	6.5 L.F.	4.0	839.85
Plywood sub-base for countertop, 1/2" x 4' x 8' sheets	1 Sheet	0.5	17.80
Ceramic tile for countertop and backsplash	30 S.F.	3.0	174.25
Valance board over sink	4 L.F.	0.5	29.05
Trim, crown molding, stock pine, 9/16" x 3-5/8"	28 L.F.	1.0	37.25
Paint, ceiling & walls, primer & 1 coat	185 S.F.	1.5	20.15
Paint, cornice, trim, puttying, primer & 1 coat	28 L.F.	0.5	1.70
Cooking range, built-in, 30" wide, one oven	1 Ea.	8.0	968.00
Hood for range, 2-speed, 30" wide	1 Ea.	5.5	290.40
Refrigerator, no frost, 19 C.F.	1 Ea.	4.0	1331.00
Sink w/faucets & drain, stainless steel, self-rimming, 32" x 22", double bowl	1 Ea.	6.5	371.45
Dishwasher, built-in	1 Ea.	8.0	471.90
Rough-in, supply, waste & vent for sink & dishwasher	2 Ea.	17.5	159.35
Totals		68.0	$5384.50

Project Size	6'-6" x 14'	Contractor's Fee Including Materials	$10,170

Key to Abbreviations
C.Y. - cubic yard   Ea. - each   L.F. - linear foot   Pr. - pair   Sq. - square (100 square feet of area)
S.F. - square foot   S.Y. - square yard   V.L.F. - vertical linear foot

CORRIDOR KITCHEN, STANDARD

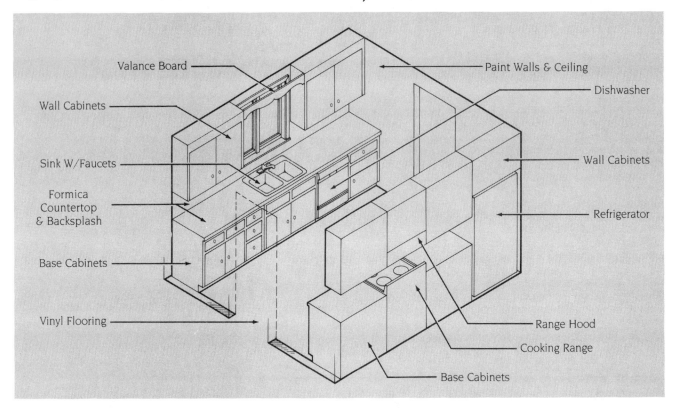

Valance Board

Wall Cabinets

Sink W/Faucets

Formica Countertop & Backsplash

Base Cabinets

Vinyl Flooring

Paint Walls & Ceiling

Dishwasher

Wall Cabinets

Refrigerator

Range Hood

Cooking Range

Base Cabinets

With the specialized materials and products that are available, an efficient kitchen facility can be installed in a remarkably small area. An appropriate selection of decorative components and clever placement of appliances and cabinets can provide a surprising sense of spaciousness to offset the limited square footage. This standard corridor kitchen project demonstrates how limitations of size can be overcome to create an efficient and attractive facility at a reasonable cost. As in all kitchen projects, many remodeling and building skills are required to complete the renovation. Carpentry, electrical, and plumbing tasks are all involved. Also, because the kitchen area of any home performs a vital function, expediency in completing the project is an important consideration. A long period of renovation work translates into an extended interruption of the routine of home life. If you plan to complete the project on your own, you might want to set a block of time aside to complete most of the work in a concentrated week's effort rather than spreading it out over several weekends.

MATERIALS

The materials used in this kitchen plan are standard grade items, readily available from kitchen suppliers and building supply retailers. To remodel an existing kitchen completely, you may have to modify some of the suggested cabinet and appliance selections to suit your space limitations. Also, your choice of cabinets and appliances should be carefully determined, since the major costs for any kitchen facility are focused on these components. Wise selection of these items can help you to meet your food preparation needs and decorative standards without sacrificing quality. Because the corridor kitchen layout allows for only two walls of work space, the design and arrangement of the cabinet system must be efficient. This plan recommends standard-sized wall and base units with depths of 12″ and 24″, respectively. These depths should be maintained wherever possible because other kitchen plumbing fixtures and appliances are designed around these standard dimensions. Altering the base cabinet depth, particularly, will cost you more money for custom or

special order units and can cause additional expense and aggravation in selecting appliances, sinks, and other kitchen fixtures. If your kitchen area is too narrow to accommodate the 24″ deep base cabinets on both walls, seek advice and suggestions from a professional contractor before you begin the project. When making the choice between giving up floor space and giving up cabinet space, in most cases you will be better off with diminished floor space and standard sized cabinets. The countertop, like the cabinets, should also be designed with efficiency in mind so as to produce a maximum amount of surface area on the two walls. Formica-type counter coverings are durable, easy to clean, and economical, but other more expensive materials like ceramic tile can serve as attractive and functional substitutes. The trim work for the cabinets, including the valance board over the sink and the molding at the top of the wall units, should be selected on the recommendation of the cabinet manufacturer. The valance is usually available as a factory or shop-made part of the cabinet assembly.

Before the cabinets are installed, the ceiling, floor, and walls of the kitchen area have to be reconditioned and prepared. The expense incurred in this step of the project will depend largely on the amount of fundamental restoration required. Tearing out old cabinets and stripping the floors of old linoleum or tile are difficult jobs that take time and require some know-how. Be sure to correct any structural or cosmetic deficiencies in the walls and floor. Any straightening or smoothing of existing rough ceiling, wall, or floor surfaces done at this stage of the project will expedite the rest of the installation. Remember too, that if you plan to continue to use your kitchen during the period of the remodeling work, you will have to move appliances and temporarily rearrange the facility as the job progresses. If you are doing work on your own, plan to have someone available to lend assistance. Like cabinet systems, appliances vary significantly in quality and cost. The price estimates provided in this plan are based on medium priced appliances with a limited number of operational accessories and convenience options. Because the recommended range and refrigerator are free-standing models, just about any standard-sized unit can be installed. The two-speed, 30" wide, hood and exhaust fan unit is also a common item which can be purchased at most kitchen, electric, or building supply outlets. If possible, duct the exhaust vent to the outside. Remember that the cost for appliance installation will vary if the new unit is to be placed in a different location. Electric or gas ranges, for example, require special supply connections that should be installed by qualified tradesmen.

LEVEL OF DIFFICULTY

Kitchen remodeling demands knowledge of and skill in many different building operations. Cabinet installation, plumbing, electrical work, and flooring placement are just some of the tasks that the handyman has to contend with during the revovation process. Most beginners can handle the basic jobs like the ceiling, wall and floor preparation, and the painting and staining; but they should leave the specialized work to the carpenter, plumber, or electrician. Even moderately skilled handymen should hire a professional to install the cabinets and countertop. Because kitchen cabinets involve substantial expense and specialized knowledge of installation procedures, even expert do-it-yourselfers might consider hiring a professional for this job. Handymen and experts should add about 50% and 20%, respectively, to the professional time estimate for all tasks, except the cabinet installation and plumbing work. If they intend to perform these operations, they should add to the man-hours. Beginners should attempt only those tasks mentioned earlier and plan to double the professional time for their work.

WHAT TO WATCH OUT FOR

If new underlayment cannot be placed directly on the existing floor, the difficult chore of stripping the old resilient floor will have to be accomplished. You can use several methods in performing this task, depending on the amount, type, and condition of the covering to be removed. If the area is relatively small, the old material can be peeled and chipped by hand with a flat bar or other blade-type instrument. If the old material has a backing, and some of it stays on the floor, hand or power sanding may be needed to get it up. Larger floors can be stripped in the same way, but you might look into renting a floor grinder if the job looks too big to do by hand. Before the new covering is laid, be sure that the old underlayment is fastened thoroughly and that all seams and voids have been filled with floor leveler and sanded smooth.

CORRIDOR KITCHEN, STANDARD

Description	Quantity	Man-hours	Material
Blocking, for mounting cabinets, 2" x 4", stock	38 L.F.	1.5	11.95
Plywood, underlayment grade, 1/2" thick, 4' x 8' sheets	4 Sheets	1.5	71.25
Flooring, vinyl sheet goods 0.125" thick	96 S.F.	3.5	377.55
Wall cabinets, hardwood, 12" deep	18.5 L.F.	4.5	708.70
Base cabinets, hardwood, 24" deep	18 L.F.	6.5	1270.45
Countertop, 1-1/4" thick Formica, w/backsplash	18 L.F.	5.0	108.90
Valance board over sink	4 L.F.	0.5	29.05
Trim, crown molding, stock pine 9/16" x 3-5/8"	42 L.F.	1.0	55.90
Paint, Primer and 1 coat, ceiling & walls	425 S.F.	3.5	46.30
Paint, trim, puttying, primer & 1 coat	42 L.F.	1.0	2.55
Cooking range, free-standing, 30" wide, one oven	1 Ea.	2.0	314.60
Hood for range, 2-speed, 30" wide, vented	1 Ea.	3.0	36.30
Refrigerator, no frost, 19 C.F.	1 Ea.	2.0	726.00
Dishwasher, built-in, 2 cycle	1 Ea.	6.5	471.90
Sink w/faucets & drain, stainless steel, self-rimming, 33" x 22", double bowl	1 Ea.	6.5	371.45
Rough-in, supply, waste & vent for sink & dishwasher	1 Ea.	9.0	79.70
Totals		57.5	$4682.56

Project Size	11' x 11'-6"	Contractor's Fee Including Materials	$8810

SUMMARY

Corridor kitchens, because of their two-wall cabinet layout, require both imagination and careful planning in a remodeling design. With the thoughtful arrangement of cabinets and appliances, a stylish and efficient facility can be created.

CORRIDOR KITCHEN, DELUXE

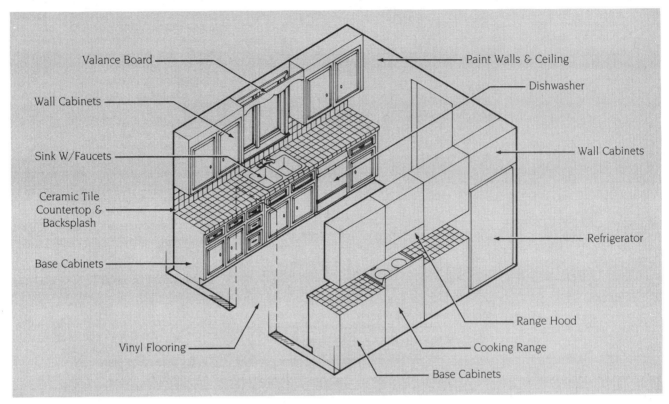

Valance Board

Wall Cabinets

Sink W/Faucets

Ceramic Tile
Countertop &
Backsplash

Base Cabinets

Vinyl Flooring

Paint Walls & Ceiling

Dishwasher

Wall Cabinets

Refrigerator

Range Hood

Cooking Range

Base Cabinets

The arrangement of walk-through or corridor kitchens provides the opportunity for the homeowner to install deluxe cabinets, appliances, and finish materials in a two-wall format. This remodeling plan utilizes upgraded appliances, decorative cabinet work, and other amenities, like a ceramic tile countertop, to enhance the appearance and overall quality of the facility. The deluxe corridor kitchen renovation can make better use of the given space while adding value to your home.

MATERIALS

The materials used in the deluxe corridor kitchen plan consist of the fundamental appliances, cabinet system, plumbing fixtures, and finish materials found in most kitchen installations. As in the standard corridor kitchen plan, this two-wall kitchen design presents the challenge of limited space to the homeowner. For this reason, the materials have to be wisely chosen to ensure efficient use of both floor and work area.

The cabinets are the single most important item installed in any kitchen. Those chosen for this plan are top quality units with raised panel doors on both the wall and base systems. In addition to the superior quality hardwood used in their manufacture, this deluxe cabinet system also features roller drawer slides and other durable hardware fittings. The cost of this cabinet system will vary according to the choice of wood and modifications in its layout. If you are doing the job on your own, double check all of your measurements before you order the cabinets, as miscalculations when dealing with expensive hardwood units like these can be disastrous. In fact, unless you are a skilled do-it-yourselfer, hire a professional to do the entire cabinet installation, including the preorder measuring.

The countertop and backsplash for this deluxe corridor kitchen are covered with ceramic tile instead of the more commonly used Formica.

This addition to the deluxe facility adds both durability and elegance to the the work surface, but it costs more and requires some know-how in its installation. Even if you have worked with ceramic tile before, you will find that kitchen counter tiling requires unique methods of placement and grouting. Many different designs, surface textures, and sizes of tile are available at varying costs. There are also options of color and grouting materials.

In preparing the ceiling, floor, and walls to receive the new materials, follow accepted construction techiques and avoid any tendency to cut corners. Check the subfloor and its support system and the condition of the ceiling and walls after the old cabinets, appliances, and flooring have been removed. If you see the need to recondition the existing ceiling, floor, or wall, make the repairs then, even if it means adding an unexpected expense for drywall or plywood. Doing the job thoroughly may boost the cost a bit, but will save you money and headaches in the long run. Plan to paint the ceiling and walls as soon as possible after the preparation of the kitchen area has been been completed. The painting job will go faster if it is done before the installation of the new appliances, cabinets, and floor.

The appliances included in this kitchen plan complement the high quality cabinets, countertop, and floor covering. Two of the appliances, the range and the dishwasher, require special provision in the cabinet design because they are built-in units. The installation of both of these appliances should be performed by professionals, and extra costs should be figured in for the additional hook-ups. The range hood is another item that should be professionally installed. The expense for rough-in of the double-bowl sink has been included in the plan, but this cost will exceed the estimate if you plan to move the sink from its old location.

LEVEL OF DIFFICULTY

The remodeling of a deluxe kitchen demands the same levels of expertise and versatility as those involved in a standard kitchen project, but the installer has the added responsibility of working with more expensive materials. Tearing out the old facility, preparing the ceiling, floor, and walls, and painting are all tasks within the reach of beginners and handymen. It is a good idea to seek advice, however, before attempting unfamiliar jobs. Removing the old cabinets and countertop, for example, can pose a challenge if these fixtures are tied into the walls, ceiling, or floor. Cabinets in many older dwellings are not constructed in the contemporary modular design, and may be difficult to dismantle, often leaving holes and large voids which must be repaired before the new cabinets are installed. The ceramic tile installation, flooring, and routine plumbing and electrical work can be accomplished by experts who are familiar with the correct procedures. The cabinet installation should only be undertaken by a carpenter or an expert do-it-yourselfer

with experience in this area. The risk of damaging or misaligning a very costly system can prove too great for the inexperienced worker. Beginners should add 100% to the estimated time for all tasks which they have done before, and more if the job is new to them. Handymen should add 50% to the man-hours for the removal of the old facility, site reconditioning, placing the underlayment, and the painting. Experts should seek advice in the cabinet installation and should add 20% to the professional time for the rough work and the painting. If they tackle the ceramic tile installation, they should add 50% to the estimated time to allow for a slow, methodical operation. All plumbing and electrical tasks should be done by a qualified tradesman, unless the homeowner is an expert with a substantial amount of experience in these areas.

WHAT TO WATCH OUT FOR

The ceramic kitchen countertop tiling materials are available in kits complete with inside and outside corner pieces. You may have to compromise on your choice of design, color, or texture if you choose one of the kits, but the advantage of easy installation may make the compromise worthwhile. Be sure to follow the tile manufacturer's guidelines for the installation, particularly for the recommended adhesive and grout. Before you begin the tiling operation, make sure that the plywood subsurface is properly fastened, leveled, and prepared to the tile manufacturer's standards.

SUMMARY

The deluxe corridor kitchen, with its amenities and top-of-the-line appliances and materials, raises the quality and enhances the decor of a standard corridor kitchen. If your home warrants this improvement and if the deluxe additions are within your budget, you will benefit from the investment in the convenience, appearance, and durability of the facility.

CORRIDOR KITCHEN, DELUXE

Description	Quantity	Man-hours	Material
Blocking, for mounting cabinets, 2" x 4" stock	38 L.F.	1.0	11.95
Plywood, underlayment grade, 1/2" thick, 4' x 8' sheets	4 sheets	1.5	71.25
Flooring, vinyl sheet goods 0.125" thick	96 S.F.	3.5	377.50
Wall cabinets, deluxe, hardwood, 12" deep	18.5 L.F.	4.5	992.35
Base cabinets, deluxe, hardwood, 24" deep	18 L.F.	6.5	1778.55
Plywood sub-base for countertop, 1/2" x 4' x 8' sheets	2 sheets	1.0	35.60
Ceramic tile for countertop and backsplash	65 S.F.	6.0	377.50
Valance board over sink	4 L.F.	1.0	29.05
Trim, crown molding, stock pine, 9/16" x 3-5/8"	42 L.F.	1.5	55.90
Paint, primer and 1 coat, ceiling & walls	300 S.F.	2.5	32.70
Paint, cornice trim, puttying, primer & 1 coat	42 L.F.	1.0	2.55
Cooking range, built-in, 30" wide, one oven	1 Ea.	8.0	968.00
Hood for range, 2-speed, 30" wide, vented	1 Ea	5.5	290.40
Refrigerator, no frost, 19 C.F.	1 Ea.	4.0	1331.00
Sink w/faucets & drain, stainless steel, self-rimming, 33" x 22", double bowl	1 Ea.	6.0	371.45
Dishwasher, built-in, 2 cycle	1 Ea.	8.0	471.90
Rough-in, supply, waste & vent for sink	2 Ea.	17.0	159.35
Totals		78.5	$7357.00

Project Size	11' x 11'-6"	Contractor's Fee Including Materials	$13,560

Key to Abbreviations
C.Y. - cubic yard   Ea. - each   L.F. - linear foot   Pr. - pair   Sq. - square (100 square feet of area)
S.F. - square foot   S.Y. - square yard   V.L.F. - vertical linear foot

L-SHAPED KITCHEN, STANDARD

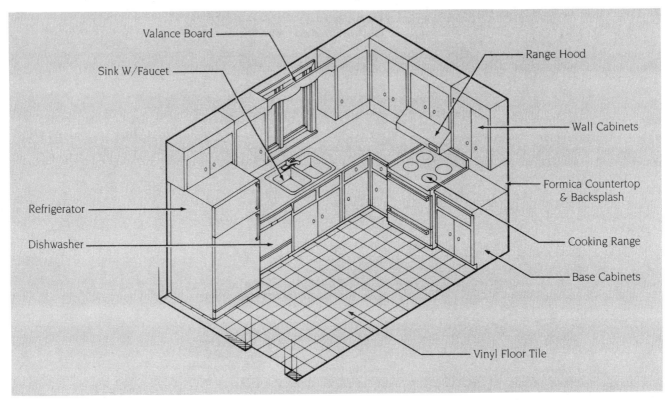

Valance Board

Sink W/Faucet

Range Hood

Wall Cabinets

Formica Countertop & Backsplash

Refrigerator

Cooking Range

Dishwasher

Base Cabinets

Vinyl Floor Tile

Many kitchens are formed by two perpendicular walls in an L-shape. This type of corner layout consolidates the kitchen's work and appliance area into two walls and opens up floor space for either an eating area or an unobstructed entryway into an informal dining or living area. Like corridor kitchens, L-shaped facilities also require an efficient layout to make the best use of a limited space. This standard L-shaped kitchen plan demonstrates how you can turn a less spacious kitchen into a convenient and comfortable facility for a modest price.

MATERIALS

The materials included in this plan have been selected for their economy, durability, practicality, and attractive appearance. The cabinets are constructed of hardwood and contain quality hardware. Birch, maple, and similar hardwoods are commonly used in cabinet manufacture, but more economical materials are also available. Pine and other softwoods make cabinets that are pleasing to the

eye, although they may prove less durable. Formica-veneered units can also serve as a practical alternative to hardwood cabinets. They are durable, low in maintenance, and attractive; but, depending on your selection, they may be more expensive. Be sure to investigate all of the options before purchasing the cabinets, as there is a wide choice in price and quality. After you have decided on the price range, design, and preferred material, get the facts about the construction of the specific models under consideration. Quality cabinets will last longer and will also bring some immediate rewards in terms of their prominent effect on the appearance of the kitchen.

The coverings for the countertop, backsplash, and floor in the kitchen are conventional and popular materials. Formica and other plastic laminates make ideal kitchen counter-tops because they are durable, heat and water resistant, and easy to clean and maintain. They are also available in a wide variety of textures and colors. The flooring material suggested

in the plan consists of 12" x 12" vinyl tiles, but other resilient tile and sheet flooring materials can be installed at varying costs. If you plan to do the flooring for the project, you will find the tiles easier to lay than sheet flooring. Be sure that the subfloor is in good condition and that the underlayment is adequately prepared before you begin the tile placement. Follow carefully the adhesive manufacturer's guidelines and recommendations during the installation process. Also, remember that the finished floor should be laid under all appliances, but not under the cabinets. If the floor of the L-shaped kitchen terminates at the opening of the entryway, make provisions, whenever possible, to avoid a height discrepancy between the edges of the abutting floors.

The appliances in this kitchen plan include a standard, mid-priced cooking range, a 19 cubic foot refrigerator, and a standard, 2-cycle dishwasher. The range and refrigerator are freestanding models which can be purchased at the homeowner's convenience and put into place after the remodeling work is finished. However, if the range is a gas model, it should be professionally installed. Because the dishwasher is built-in and needs professional electical and plumbing hook-ups, it should be installed during the construction process, after the countertop has been put in place. Additional expense will have to be figured in for the electrical and/or plumbing rough-in if the range hood or sink have to be relocated.

LEVEL OF DIFFICULTY

This kitchen plan is a manageable project for expert do-it-yourselfers, but it is still too far advanced for most beginners and handymen. Like any other kitchen renovation, the critical task of installing the cabinets is the most difficult undertaking. Since this kitchen involves two relatively short runs of cabinet units, installation is simplified; however, the alignment of the inside corner cabinets requires precise and skillful workmanship. The plumbing and electrical tasks, especially rough-in relocations or new hook-ups, should be performed by a professional, unless you have a good deal of experience in these areas. Experts should add 20% - 30% to the

professional time for all of the aspects of this project which they are prepared to undertake. Handymen with limited remodeling experience should plan on an additional 50% for any rough work, like the wall and ceiling reconditioning and painting and the placing of underlayment. If they tackle the tile floor installation, they should double the professional time estimate. Beginners should not attempt the cabinets, countertop, plumbing, and electrical installations, and they should add 100% to the estimated man-hours for all other tasks, except the finished flooring. They should triple the estimated time for this job and seek professional instruction and advice before starting.

WHAT TO WATCH OUT FOR

One of the most neglected components of kitchen installations is the range hood and its accompanying exhaust fan and filtering system. If at all possible, the unit should vent to the outside of the house to rid the kitchen area of cooking odors, smoke, and moisture. If the hood and fan are located on an outside wall, the venting is easily accomplished directly through the wall. Most range hoods come with standard fittings for this type of installation, including a weathertight external port. If the hood is located on an interior wall, duct work should be run to the closest or most accessible outside wall. You may have to use some ingenuity to hide the duct in the wall cabinets or in the back of a closet on the opposite side of the partition, but it can be done. Remember that the labor and materials costs will be higher, though, for this extra work. If external venting cannot be accomplished, then make sure that the hood is equipped with the correct filters for a non-vented model.

"L"-SHAPED KITCHEN, STANDARD

Description	Quantity	Man-hours	Material
Blocking, for mounting cabinets, 2" x 4", stock	32 L.F.	1.5	10.05
Plywood, underlayment grade, 1/2" thick, 4' x 8' sheets	3 Sheets	1.5	53.45
Floor tile, 12" x 12" x 1/8" thick, vinyl, solid color	72 S.F.	2.0	174.25
Wall cabinets, hardwood, 12" deep	16 L.F.	4.0	612.95
Base cabinets, hardwood, 24" deep	12 L.F.	4.0	846.95
Countertop, 1-1/4" thick Formica, w/backsplash	13 L.F.	3.5	78.65
Valance board over sink	4 L.F.	0.5	29.05
Trim, cornice molding, stock pine 9/16" x 1-3/4"	20 L.F.	0.5	9.90
Paint, primer & 1 coat, ceiling & walls	250 S.F.	2.0	27.25
Paint, cornice trim, puttying, primer & 1 coat	20 L.F.	0.5	1.20
Cooking range, free-standing, 30" wide one oven	1 Ea.	2.0	314.60
Hood for range, 2-speed, 30" wide, vented	1 Ea.	3.0	36.30
Refrigerator, no frost, 19 C.F.	1 Ea.	2.0	726.00
Dishwasher, built-in, 2 cycle	1 Ea.	4.0	325.00
Sink w/faucets & drain, stainless steel, self-rimming, 43" x 22", double bowl	1 Ea.	6.0	371.45
Rough-in, supply, waste & vent for sink & dishwasher	1 Ea.	8.5	79.70
Totals		49.5	$3843.65

Project Size	8' x 12'	Contractor's Fee Including Materials	$7890

Key to Abbreviations
C.Y. - cubic yard   Ea. - each   L.F. - linear foot   Pr. - pair   Sq. - square (100 square feet of area)
S.F. - square foot   S.Y. - square yard   V.L.F. - vertical linear foot

SUMMARY

A more efficient use of space is the primary goal of this standard L-shaped kitchen renovation. At the same time, it incorporates various components which improve the appearance and convenience of your kitchen and add value to your home. Because some of the work can be done by the homeowner, this project can also be economical.

L-SHAPED KITCHEN, DELUXE

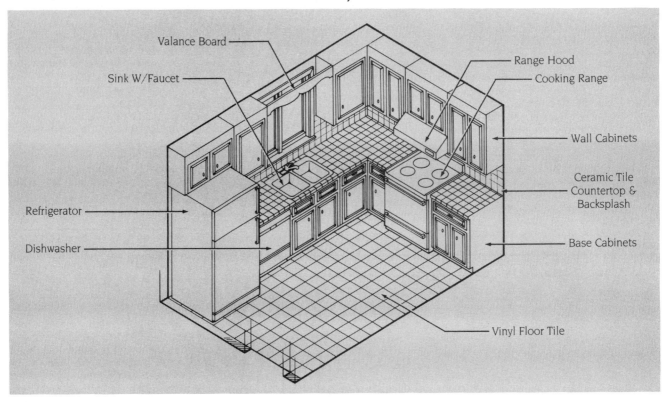

Valance Board

Sink W/Faucet

Range Hood

Cooking Range

Wall Cabinets

Ceramic Tile
Countertop &
Backsplash

Refrigerator

Dishwasher

Base Cabinets

Vinyl Floor Tile

Corner, or L-shaped, kitchen arrangements are often used in situations where the food preparation area is adjacent to or clearly visible from the eating area. For example, in some cases, the open floor area of the kitchen itself is occupied by a table and chairs; in other situations, one or both of the vacant walls may be open to a remote eating or living area. Because of the visibility of the cabinets and appliances, attractive, deluxe products may be chosen to enhance the kitchen's appearance. This kitchen plan demonstrates how a conventional corner or L-shaped facility can be upgraded to deluxe standards.

MATERIALS

Like other deluxe kitchen plans included in this section, the L-shaped model utilizes top-of-the-line products in place of economical, standard-grade components. The homeowner's choice of these top-quality cabinets, appliances, and finish materials should be based on several factors, including budget, the

decor and furnishings of other rooms in the house, and personal preference. There is room for compromise, which is to say that a kitchen facility does not have to be exclusively standard or deluxe. However, be sure to make any substitutions carefully so as not to disturb the aesthetic balance.

This L-shaped kitchen plan includes top quality hardwood wall and base cabinets. Paneled doors and drawer facings are common in deluxe cabinet systems, but other options are also available. Formica and other brand name plastic laminates, for example, provide durable, easily-maintained surface coverings for quality cabinets. Remember that kitchen cabinets are permanent installations that you will use daily for many years, so do some research and see what is available before you buy. After you have purchased the cabinets, it is best to have them installed by a professional. Only expert do-it-yourselfers who have done extensive cabinet work should consider tackling this part of the project.

The flooring and countertop surface coverings also involve some important decisions on the part of the homeowner. Like the cabinets, these surfaces require materials which are functional, attractive, and complementary to the color and design of the rest of the kitchen. Many quality resilient flooring materials are available at varying costs, including vinyl tiles and sheet goods and other composition products. The kitchen floor requires more upkeep than any other floor in the house, so keep maintenance and durability in mind when you make your choice. If you plan to lay the floor on your own, and you have a choice between vinyl tiles and vinyl sheet goods in the same pattern, you will find the tile installation the easier of the two. Generally, sheet flooring requires more skill to place, particularly in situations where scribing of the material is needed along skewed or bowed walls in older homes. Ceramic tile provides a deluxe alternative to the commonly-used Formica countertop and backsplash material. Like Formica, it is durable, low in maintenance, and attractive. With the right color grout, ceramic tile gives the countertop a neat, up-to-date appearance. Remember that because tiled counter-tops must be fabricated on the site, the charge for their installation is significantly more than for shop-prepared Formica units.

The appliances included in the deluxe L-shaped kitchen include a top-of-the-line refrigerator, dishwasher, and built-in range. Many options are available in the selection of these items, depending on the size of the kitchen area and personal preference. Be sure to allow for the additional expense of appliance installations which require relocation of rough-in or new hook ups. Call in a plumber or electrician for all major plumbing or electrical tasks.

LEVEL OF DIFFICULTY

Because of the high cost of the deluxe appliances and other expensive materials used in this kitchen, most beginners and handymen should hire a remodeling specialist or general contractor to do the better part of the work. Removing the old cabinets, stripping the floor, and preparing the walls and ceiling are jobs that the homeowner can accomplish to save on labor costs, but even these tasks require knowledge of tools and some remodeling experience. Get some advice from a professional or an experienced do-it-yourselfer before you attempt any operations that are new to you. Also, removal of the old cabinets and appliances usually requires two workers, so plan accordingly and line up some help well in advance of the start of the project. The cabinet and countertop installations for this renovation should be left to experienced tradesmen. Even accomplished do-it-yourselfers should consider restricting their efforts to tasks other than these. As a general rule, beginners should add at least 100% to the man-hours estimates for the jobs which they tackle; handymen, 50%-70%; and experts, 20%.

WHAT TO WATCH OUT FOR

Corner cabinets can waste considerable space if built and installed in the conventional manner. There are several ways to reclaim some or all of this often wasted cabinet area. One is to install a "lazy susan" or rotating cabinet fixture, to provide shelf and storage space that is immediately accessible. These are commonly installed in base corner units, but they are a special order item and will add to the cost of the cabinets.

SUMMARY

If the value of your home is in keeping with this project and the renovation suits your budget, this plan is a good way to increase the efficiency and to improve the appearance of your L-shaped kitchen. The cost of top quality components and professional installation is an investment in a highly visible and heavily utilized area of your home.

L-SHAPED KITCHEN, DELUXE

Description	Quantity	Man-hours	Material
Blocking, for mounting cabinets, 2" x 4" stock	32 L.F.	1.0	10.10
Plywood, underlayment grade, 1/2" thick, 4' x 8' sheets	3 Sheets	2.5	53.45
Floor tile, 12" x 12" x 1/8" thick, patterned vinyl	72 S.F.	2.0	261.35
Wall cabinets, 12" deep, hardwood, deluxe	16 L.F.	5.0	858.25
Base cabinets, 24" deep, hardwood, deluxe	12 L.F.	4.0	1185.70
Plywood, sub-base for countertop 1/2" x 4' x 8' sheets	1 Sheet	0.5	17.85
Ceramic tile for countertops and backsplash	53 S.F.	5.0	307.85
Valance board over sink	4 L.F.	0.5	29.05
Trim, cornice molding, stock pine 9/16" x 2-1/4"	20 L.F.	0.5	9.95
Paint, primer & 1 coat, ceiling	96 S.F.	1.0	10.45
Paint cornice trim, puttying, primer & 2 coats	20 L.F.	0.5	1.25
Cooking range, built-in, 30" wide, one oven	1 Ea.	8.0	968.00
Hood for range, 2-speed, 30" wide	1 Ea.	5.5	290.40
Refrigerator, no frost, 19 C.F.	1 Ea.	4.0	1331.00
Sink w/faucets & drain, stainless steel self-rimming, 43" x 22", double bowl	1 Ea.	6.5	423.50
Dishwasher, built-in, 2 cycle	1 Ea.	8.0	471.90
Rough-in, supply, waste & vent for sink & dishwasher	2 Ea.	17.5	159.35
Totals		72.0	$6389.40

Project Size	8' x 12'	Contractor's Fee Including Materials	$11,800

Key to Abbreviations
C.Y. - cubic yard   Ea. - each   L.F. - linear foot   Pr. - pair   Sq. - square (100 square feet of area)
S.F. - square foot   S.Y. - square yard   V.L.F. - vertical linear foot

U-SHAPED KITCHEN, STANDARD

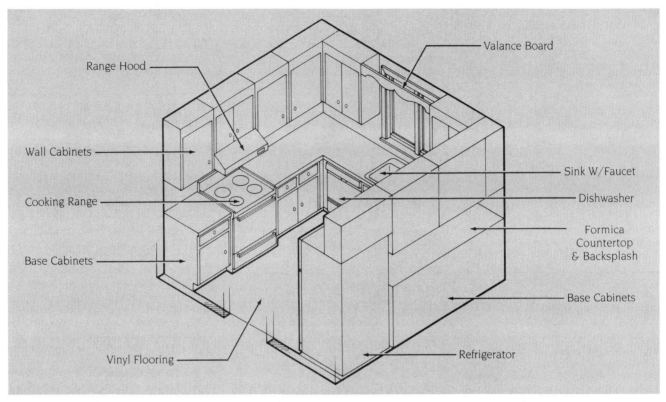

Range Hood

Wall Cabinets

Cooking Range

Base Cabinets

Vinyl Flooring

Valance Board

Sink W/Faucet

Dishwasher

Formica Countertop & Backsplash

Base Cabinets

Refrigerator

One of the most efficient layouts for kitchen design is the three wall, or U-shaped kitchen. Like the island and peninsula plans, it is a challenging remodeling project for the do-it-yourselfer because of its size and extensive cabinet and countertop system. All three walls of the facility are equipped with upper and lower cabinet units, with the range, sink, and refrigerator each on separate walls. This triangular setup of the three primary kitchen components is often recommended by experts as one of the best operational layouts for the kitchen, providing that there are not more than 7 or 8 feet between them. If your kitchen area has the necessary space and shape requirements, this U-shaped layout can be a most efficient arrangement.

MATERIALS

The U-shaped kitchen presented in this model offers an economical plan to install an attractive facility with durable and easily maintained products. Although the suggested components are not as elaborate as

those found in deluxe kitchens, they are comparable in most respects and will last just as long.

The cabinet system in this kitchen plan is comprised of hardwood wall and base units complete with valance and appropriate trim. Because many cabinet options are open to the homeowner, it pays to do some research and to shop for a system that meets decorative and durability standards, while remaining within budget limitations. Look into the fine points of the cabinet units, including the quality of their construction, type of hardware, quality of finish, and the cost of installing them. If the retailer does not provide an installation service, a qualified carpenter or kitchen remodeler can do the work. If you plan to install them on your own, consider the expense of the materials and the skillful placement required for this job, and work slowly and patiently. Do-it-yourselfers who are not experienced in cabinet work should get professional advice before they start. Asking the right person at the right time can save you money by heading off installation problems.

The Formica countertop, vinyl flooring, and painted ceiling and wall surfaces are conventional kitchen finish coverings which will provide years of service. Be sure to coordinate the design and color of these surface materials with the cabinets and appliances before the project starts. Following a master plan, which includes the specific complementary colors and designs for all components, ensures uniformity of appearance and predictable materials costs before the work begins. Selecting and buying as you go can cause piecemeal results as well as unanticipated fluctuations in the expense of materials. Whenever possible, do the painting of the ceiling and walls before the cabinets, counter-top, and floor are in place. Painting at the end of the project will take longer and require more brushwork, covering, and taping around the finished surfaces. Be sure that the subfloor has been thoroughly reconditioned before the underlayment and vinyl flooring are placed. If the existing underlayment is in good condition after the old surface flooring has been removed, leave it in place and prepare it for the new vinyl. You will save on the cost of the underlayment material and avoid floor level discrepancies at doorways. If the existing underlayment is not in good condition, you will have to tear up some or all of it and replace it. Double check the thickness of the old underlayment before you purchase the new material. The appliances in this standard U-shaped kitchen include a free-standing range, standard-sized refrigerator, and built-in dishwasher. The estimated prices for these items are based on white-finish models in the middle of the price spectrum. If you want the range and refrigerator in color, plan on an additional 10% over the standard models. Before selecting colored models, check to see that the dishwasher panel is available in the same color. If the panel has to be special ordered in the appropriate color, you will have to add to the cost for this extra. Expenses for the basic

plumbing rough-in and sink trim are included in the estimate, but relocation costs, whether plumbing or electrical, have not been figured in. Any major electrical and plumbing work should be done by qualified professionals.

LEVEL OF DIFFICULTY

Remodeling a U-shaped kitchen is a big undertaking for the most experienced do-it-yourselfers. Planning the new facility, removing the old one, reconditioning the site, and installing the new materials require many different remodeling skills. The various steps in the renovation process should be carefully coordinated in a sequence that will minimize delays and inconvenience. The most challenging task in the project is the cabinet planning and installation. Accurately measuring the linear footage of your

space and determining the correct number of standard-sized cabinets are critical tasks at the outset. The subsequent installation of the system requires thorough carpentry know-how, and thus, only experts should tackle this job. Even they should consider hiring a professional if they are inexperienced in cabinet placement. Experts should add 50% to the estimated man-hours for the countertop, cabinets, and flooring operations and tack on 20% for all other jobs. Handymen and beginners should use discretion in attempting any tasks which are unfamiliar to them and add 50% and 100%, respectively, to basic work like reconditioning the site and painting.

WHAT TO WATCH OUT FOR

The ceiling height for this kitchen plan is the standard 7'6" found in most modern homes. Older homes, and even some newer ones, often have higher ceilings that require the placement of a soffit to finish the space between the top of the cabinets and the ceiling. This element is often overlooked when planning the cabinet system and may become an expensive extra if it has not been included in the plan and installation agreement with the retailer. Be sure to clarify this issue before you finalize the cabinet and installation contracts.

SUMMARY

The standard U-shaped kitchen is a functional, attractive, and economical food preparation facility. Remodeling or rearranging an old three wall kitchen with new products can provide years of dependable and enjoyable use while adding value to your home.

U-SHAPED KITCHEN, STANDARD

Description	Quantity	Man-hours	Material
Blocking, for mounting cabinets, 2" x 4" stock	50 L.F.	2.0	15.75
Plywood, underlayment grade, 1/2" thick, 4' x 8' sheets	4 Sheets	1.5	71.25
Flooring, vinyl sheet goods, 0.093" thick	85 S.F.	3.0	241.70
Wall cabinets, 12" deep, hardwood	21 L.F.	5.0	804.50
Base cabinets, 24" deep, hardwood	14 L.F.	5.0	988.15
Countertop, 1-1/4" thick Formica w/backsplash	21 L.F.	6.0	559.05
Valance board over sink	4 L.F.	0.5	29.05
Trim, cornice molding, stock pine, 9/16" x 2-1/4"	30 L.F.	1.0	14.90
Paint, ceiling & walls, primer & 1 coat	320 S.F.	3.0	34.85
Paint, cornice trim, puttying, primer & 1 coat	30 L.F.	0.5	1.85
Cooking range, free-standing, 30" wide, one oven	1 Ea.	2.0	314.60
Hood for range, 2-speed, 30" wide	1 Ea.	3.5	60.50
Refrigerator, no frost, 19 C.F.	1 Ea.	2.0	726.00
Sink w/faucets & drain, stainless steel, self-rimming, 43" x 22", double bowl	1 Ea.	6.5	371.50
Dishwasher, built-in, 2 cycle	1 Ea.	4.0	314.60
Rough-in, supply, waste & vent for sink & dishwasher	2 Ea.	17.5	159.40
Totals		63.0	$4707.65

Project Size	9'-6" x 10'-6"	Contractor's Fee Including Materials	$9620

Key to Abbreviations
C.Y. - cubic yard   Ea. - each   L.F. - linear foot   Pr. - pair   Sq. - square (100 square feet of area)
S.F. - square foot   S.Y. - square yard   V.L.F. - vertical linear foot

U-SHAPED KITCHEN, DELUXE

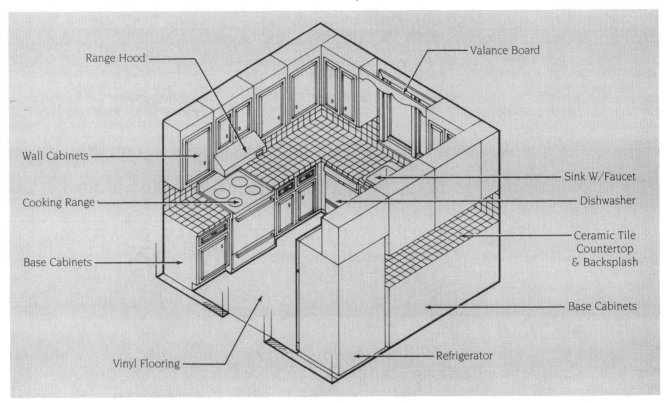

Range Hood · Valance Board · Wall Cabinets · Cooking Range · Base Cabinets · Vinyl Flooring · Sink W/Faucet · Dishwasher · Ceramic Tile Countertop & Backsplash · Base Cabinets · Refrigerator

The deluxe facility presented in this plan demonstrates how a basic three wall kitchen layout can take on an elegant appearance while meeting the practical demands of the kitchen. Amenities like a premium-quality range and ceramic tile countertop add to the cost of the renovation, but they return to the homeowner benefits of appearance and efficiency, while increasing the value of the home. Although this kitchen is more expensive to install than a standard facility of comparable size, homeowners can reduce the costs by doing some of the work on their own. Knowing their limits as handymen and taking on the appropriate tasks are the keys to success.

MATERIALS

The materials and fixtures in this deluxe facility are the highest quality of ready-made components. The cabinet system, surface coverings, and appliances are available in designs and colors that will complement any decor. Consistency in the kitchen's

appearance should be one of the foremost considerations, so take your time and shop wisely before you begin the project. If you need assistance, seek the advice of a kitchen expert who can suggest the best combinations of materials and save you unnecessary expense and frustration.

The selection of materials for the kitchen should begin with the cabinets, since they serve as the focal point of the new room. Deluxe kitchens usually include paneled or decorative hardwood cabinets that are durably constructed and carefully finished, but Formica and softwoods are also commonly installed at varying costs. When shopping for the cabinet systems, be sure to get several estimates on identical or similar units. By reducing the number of variables, you will be able to compare prices more accurately. Be sure to get an itemized written agreement which includes the basic units and all of the auxiliary cabinet materials, like the trim pieces and valance. If installation of the cabinets is part of the contract,

be sure to include in the agreement the labor cost for installing any trim items. Unless you are an expert do-it-yourselfer, the cabinets for the U-shaped kitchen should be placed by a professional.

The kitchen floor and countertop should match the deluxe quality of the cabinet system. Vinyl flooring is available in a wide range of colors, designs, and surface textures and provides the durability and low maintenance of a proven product. Ceramic and poured composition floors can also be used in deluxe facilities, but they cost more and require specialized installation skills. The countertop material suggested in this plan is ceramic tile, but Formica is an attractive, less expensive substitute. Remember that the ceramic tiling has to be done on the site after the cabinets are placed and before the sink is installed, so plan the timing carefully to avoid delays. If you are doing the ceramic work on your own, figure on a time-consuming job to cover the three wall surface layout and its backsplash. Selecting the color and design of the tile is an important decision, but you will also want to make sure that the color of the grouting coordinates well with the tile and the room. The preparation and painting of the ceiling and walls should be completed before any other finish materials are placed. Doing these tasks first makes them faster and easier and contributes to a neater end result.

Many different appliance options are open to the homeowner who is planning a deluxe kitchen, including a wide selection of built-in ranges and ovens. Remember that if you are upgrading the present facility from standard to deluxe, additional electrical and, possibly, plumbing work will be required at extra cost. Also, electric-to-gas, and gas-to-electric range conversions involve considerable work by qualified tradesmen, so plan accordingly. The refrigerator and dishwasher should not require additional installation costs, providing that they are not relocated and the rough-in and hook-ups are already in place, The addition of an ice

maker or cold water option for a deluxe refrigerator requires extra plumbing to connect the water supply tubing. The conventional range hood can be replaced by an under-counter exhaust and vent system. These units are an expensive option on some built-in ranges, but they work more efficiently than conventional hoods and open up more wall cabinet space above the range. Because all of these appliances demand professional quality installations, do-it-yourselfers who are not experienced in electrical and plumbing work should hire capable people to perform the necessary tasks.

LEVEL OF DIFFICULTY

This three wall kitchen project involves a major commitment of both time and money, so tread carefully if you are inclined to do the job on your own. The basic tasks of removing the old facility, reconditioning and preparing the site for the new products, and applying paint and stain can be

accomplished by beginners if they are given ample guidance as they proceed with these operations. They should add 100% to the professional time estimates for these jobs. Handymen should add 50% to the man-hours for the same tasks and plan on doubling the professional time for the flooring, if vinyl tile is the chosen material. The installation of vinyl sheet flooring, ceramic tile, and cabinets should be left to experts and tradesmen. Experts should add 50% to the estimated man-hours for the flooring and ceramic work, at least 75% for the cabinet installation, and 20% for the more basic operations. Except in the case of experts who have had had extensive remodeling experience, the plumbing and electrical work should be performed by professionals.

WHAT TO WATCH OUT FOR

Ceramic tile provides a durable, attractive, and easily maintained surface for kitchen countertops, but it does have its drawbacks. One is that the material itself is more expensive than Formica and other plastic laminates. Also, because each countertop has to be constructed at the site, the labor costs are higher than shop-fabricated Formica tops. Although ceramic tiles are heat and water resistant, they are prone to chipping and cracking when they are struck by hard objects. The grouting, too, has to be inspected periodically, and repaired, if necessary, to correct cracking that may have developed. Despite these shortcomings, ceramic tile has a neat and elegant appearance which contributes to the overall atmosphere of the deluxe kitchen.

SUMMARY

Upgrading a U-shaped kitchen to deluxe standards is a challenging undertaking which requires a considerable commitment of both time and money by the homeowner. With some do-it-yourself cost-cutting, however, the renovation can be completed with professional results and at reduced expense.

U-SHAPED KITCHEN, DELUXE

Description	Quantity	Man-hours	Material
Blocking, for mounting cabinets, 2" x 4" stock	50 L.F.	1.5	15.75
Plywood, underlayment grade, 1/2" thick, 4' x 8' sheets	4 Sheets	1.5	71.25
Flooring, vinyl sheet goods, 0.093" thick	85 S.F.	3.5	241.70
Wall cabinets, 12" deep, hardwood, deluxe	21 L.F.	5.0	1126.43
Base cabinets, 24" deep, hardwood, deluxe	14 L.F.	5.0	1383.30
Plywood sub-base for counter-top, 1/2" x 4' x 8' sheets	2 Sheets	1.0	35.60
Ceramic tile for countertops and backsplash	83 S.F.	7.5	482.05
Valance board over sink	4 L.F.	0.5	29.05
Trim, cornice molding, stock pine, 9/16" x 2-1/4"	30 L.F.	1.0	14.85
Paint, ceiling, primer & 1 coat	100 S.F.	1.0	10.90
Paint, cornice trim, puttying, primer & 1 coat	30 L.F.	0.5	1.85
Cooking range, built-in, 30" wide one oven	1 Ea.	8.0	968.00
Hood for range, 2-speed, 30" wide	1 Ea.	5.5	290.40
Refrigerator, no frost, 19 C.F.	1 Ea.	4.0	1331.00
Sink w/faucets & drain, stainless steel, self-rimming, 43" x 22", double bowl	1 Ea.	6.0	423.50
Dishwasher, built-in	1 Ea.	8.0	471.90
Rough-in, supply, waste & vent for sink & dishwasher	2 Ea.	17.5	159.35
Totals		77.0	$7056.85

Project Size	9'-6" x 10'-6"	Contractor's Fee Including Materials	$15,110

PENINSULA KITCHEN, STANDARD

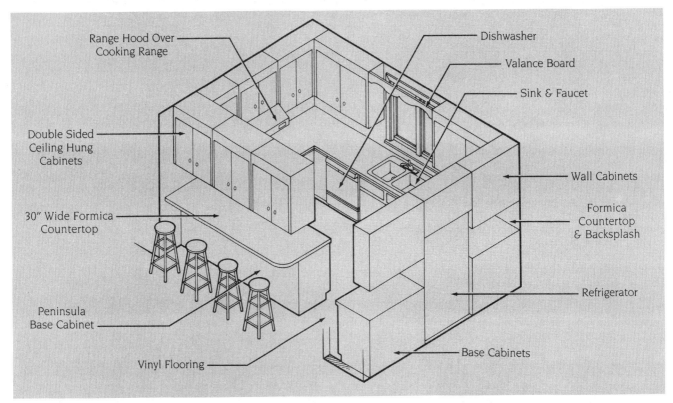

Range Hood Over Cooking Range

Double Sided Ceiling Hung Cabinets

30" Wide Formica Countertop

Peninsula Base Cabinet

Vinyl Flooring

Dishwasher

Valance Board

Sink & Faucet

Wall Cabinets

Formica Countertop & Backsplash

Refrigerator

Base Cabinets

A peninsula kitchen design offers an attractive and functional alternative to conventional layouts. Although it requires more floor space, cabinets, and countertop area, this configuration pays off in terms of its efficiency and the bonus of a built-in eating or serving area. This model is economically equipped and should return many years of enjoyable and trouble-free use.

MATERIALS

Even though this kitchen plan features standard grade components, it is still an expensive project because all four sides of the kitchen are being equipped with new materials. Whether you are redoing an old peninsula area, or creating a new one from a U-shaped kitchen, the practicality and convenience of this layout can make the extra investment worthwhile.

The cabinet system included in this plan is one of the most extensive installations found in the various kitchens outlined in this section. The design of the cabinets on the three walls of the "U" follows the basic layout of 12" deep wall units and 24" deep base cabinets, with standard cutouts for the various appliances and windows. The peninsula area provides the opportunity for some extra options in cabinet planning. While these modifications might boost your investment at the start, they are far easier to install at this stage than they would be later. The overhead peninsula cabinets, for example, can be designed with doors opening to both sides of the divider. The base peninsula cabinet can also be cleverly designed to provide for the greatest degree of utility. The side facing away from the kitchen is generally left solid but the side facing the kitchen can be

imaginatively designed with many possible combinations of drawers and storage cabinets. These peninsula cabinet extras do increase the cost of the unit significantly, but the convenience they add to the kitchen area may be worth it. Before you determine the design, materials, and specific layout of the cabinets for this kitchen plan, compile a list of the features that you want in the cabinet system and make a rough drawing. Then, sit down with a kitchen specialist and plan the system. Because the cabinet work for this kitchen is so complex, it's best not to attempt the plan entirely on your own.

The choice of countertop and floor coverings should also be given careful consideration. Formica is still one of the best and most economical kitchen countertop materials because of its water and heat-resistant properties, easy maintenance, and durability. The color and design of the floor should complement that of the countertop and cabinets. Although it is a relatively small area in this kitchen, the aesthetic impact of the floor is still important. Vinyl tiles or sheet goods are a good choice, as they come in a wide range of designs and colors and are reasonably priced. Before the finished floor is laid, make sure that the subfloor and its supports are in good condition. The area under the peninsula should be carefully checked for strength, and the subflooring around the sink should be examined for signs of wetness and rot. If either of these areas needs attention, repairs should be made before any new installations are performed; the extra cost will have to be figured in for materials and/or a contractor's fees.

The appliances for the standard peninsula kitchen consist of a mid-priced, free-standing electric cooking range and a 19 cubic foot refrigerator. Both of these units can be installed by the homeowner or delivery person, as long as the electrical hook-ups are in place. The range hood should be installed by an electrician because the unit has to be direct-wired to the supply cable. The double-bowl sink should also be tied in by a qualified tradesman, particularly if a new rough-in is required. If additional electrical or plumbing rough-in is needed, it should be completed before the finish materials are placed. These jobs take less time when the walls, ceiling, and floor are unfinished and accessible to the worker. As a result, they will cost you less if they are done beforehand.

LEVEL OF DIFFICULTY

The peninsula kitchen is a very demanding remodeling project which requires building skills and expertise in the use of tools. If you are a beginner, you should limit your efforts to the basic tasks like preparing and painting the walls and ceiling and installing the underlayment for the floor. Handymen should restrict their involvement to these basic tasks, but might also try the removal of the old cabinets if they have had some remodeling experience. Experts might want to stop short of the cabinet installation, but they should be able to handle most of the other tasks, providing that they have had some experience in those areas. Beginners ought to double the professional time estimate for the basic tasks, and handymen should add 50-70%, depending on their level of ability. Experts should add about 20% to the man-hours for basic jobs, like painting and installing the underlayment, and 50%-75% for specialized tasks, like flooring, plumbing, and cabinetwork.

WHAT TO WATCH OUT FOR

Major remodeling projects like kitchen renovations often provide the opportunity to check the existing electrical system in a house. If you hire a professional to do the electrical work on your new kitchen, it might be worth the extra expense to have him inspect the existing kitchen wiring and the electrical service throughout your house. This may give you the chance to have any needed repairs made at a convenient time.

SUMMARY

The standard peninsula kitchen plan can be an economical source of new convenience and a more pleasant atmosphere, providing it fits into your available kitchen space and suits your lifestyle. It does require some professional installations, but with good planning, the do-it-yourselfer can save money by performing some of the other tasks.

PENINSULA KITCHEN, STANDARD

Description	Quantity	Man-hours	Material
Blocking, for mounting cabinets, 2" x 4" stock	72 L.F.	2.0	92.35
Plywood, underlayment grade, 1/2" thick, 4' x 8' sheets	4 Sheets	1.5	71.25
Flooring, vinyl sheet goods, 0.125" thick	100 S.F.	3.5	393.25
Wall cabinets, 12" deep, hardwood	34 L.F.	8.0	1302.50
Base cabinets, 24" deep, hardwood	20 L.F.	7.0	1411.60
Peninsula base cabinet, custom-built 24" deep x 9' long	9 L.F.	4.5	1089.00
Countertop, 1-1/4" thick Formica, with backsplash	23 L.F.	6.0	139.15
Countertop for peninsula, 1-1/4" thick Formica, 30" wide	9 L.F.	2.5	190.60
Valance board over sink	4 L.F.	0.5	29.05
Trim, cornice molding, stock pine, 9/16" x 2-1/4"	46 L.F.	1.0	22.85
Paint, ceiling & walls, primer & 1 coat	600 S.F.	5.0	65.35
Paint, cornice trim, puttying, primer & 1 coat	46 L.F.	1.0	2.80
Cooking range, built-in, 30" wide, one oven	1 Ea.	4.0	423.50
Hood for range, 2-speed, 30" wide, vented	1 Ea.	3.5	36.30
Refrigerator, no frost, 19 C.F.	1 Ea.	2.0	726.00
Sink w/faucets & drain, stainless steel, self-rimming, 33" x 22", double bowl	1 Ea.	8.0	471.90
Dishwasher, built-in, 2 cycle	1 Ea.	6.5	371.45
Rough-in, supply, waste & vent for sink & dishwasher	1 Ea.	9.0	79.70
Totals		76.0	$6918.60

Project Size	9'-6" x 13'	Contractor's Fee Including Materials	$12,850

Key to Abbreviations
C.Y. - cubic yard   Ea. - each   L.F. - linear foot   Pr. - pair   Sq. - square (100 square feet of area)
S.F. - square foot   S.Y. - square yard   V.L.F. - vertical linear foot

PENINSULA KITCHEN, DELUXE

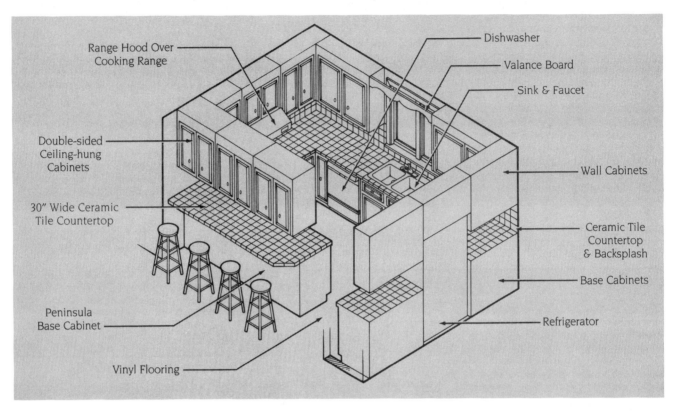

Range Hood Over Cooking Range

Double-sided Ceiling-hung Cabinets

30" Wide Ceramic Tile Countertop

Peninsula Base Cabinet

Vinyl Flooring

Dishwasher

Valance Board

Sink & Faucet

Wall Cabinets

Ceramic Tile Countertop & Backsplash

Base Cabinets

Refrigerator

The layout of the peninsula kitchen lends itself to being a social and activity center in the home as well as the primary eating and food preparation area. As a result, the installation of deluxe products can be a good investment in an attractive facility. Top quality cabinets, appliances, and surface coverings can turn an old kitchen into a delightful eating and gathering place for family and guests. This model can be used to renovate an existing peninsula design, or to improve a conventional U-shaped layout by adding the peninsula unit. Whatever the case, this plan outlines a remodeling project that is first-rate in appearance, efficiency, and durability. Because of the size of the facility and the high cost of its components, most do-it-yourselfers should use discretion in tackling the specialized tasks.

MATERIALS

The materials included in the deluxe peninsula kitchen are standard products that have been upgraded.

Substitutions of comparable deluxe products are readily available to meet the particular needs and to satisfy the personal taste of the homeowner. Some advance planning and research will get you started. A qualified kitchen expert can help you select the cabinets, surface coverings, and appliances from a range of deluxe components. The large number of cabinets used in the peninsula kitchen and the complexity of their layout make them the most important element of the facility. To maintain deluxe standards, the cabinets should be made of quality hard or softwood with paneled or other decorative features on the doors and drawer facings. Included in the cost of the cabinets in this plan are high quality hardware and the custom features of the peninsula unit. However, the cost for any other cabinet amenities and specialized units must be tacked on to the estimate. A "lazy-susan", for example, is a useful device for gaining easier access to the dead storage space found in the corners of both the wall and base units. Cabinet extras

like this one are usually expensive, but they complement the other deluxe products in the kitchen and add to its operational convenience. The peninsula cabinets can also be imaginatively and attractively customized. Although these modifications may cost more initially, the investment will be returned in the benefits of convenient, personalized use for many years to come. Even if you plan to do some of the work in this kitchen renovation, you should leave the cabinet installation to a professional, unless you are an expert in home remodeling. The cost and magnitude of a four-wall system demand precise installation by a skilled worker.

Like the cabinets, the choice for flooring in this kitchen is top quality. Various options are available, but vinyl tile and sheet goods are among the most popular kitchen floor materials because of their appearance, low maintenance, and durability. Also, because they are manufactured in so many colors, surface textures, and designs, vinyl floor coverings are relatively easy to coordinate with the counter top, cabinets, and appliances.

The surface of the countertop for this deluxe kitchen may be covered with a high quality ceramic tile or appropriate Formica veneer. Both of these products are heat and water resistant, durable, and attractive. Although ceramic tile adds to the deluxe appearance of the facility, it is more expensive than Formica and harder to install. If you plan to do this part of the project on your own, be sure to get some advice and installation tips from a knowledgeable person. Also, before you choose tile for the peninsula countertop, consider the intended use of this area. For example, if it is to be used as a writing as well as an eating surface, ceramic tiling might not be a good choice. Formica or even hardwood could be used instead for the peninsula unit surface, and you could still put ceramic tile on the other countertops in the kitchen. Before the cabinets, countertop, flooring, and

appliances have been installed, recondition the ceiling and walls and then roll them with a primer and a finish coat of paint.

The appliances for the deluxe peninsula kitchen should also complement the other quality products used in the facility. Remember that additional electrical work may have to be completed before the built-in range, dishwasher, and range hood are installed. The sink and dishwasher will also require new plumbing rough-in if they are being relocated. These tasks should be accomplished by qualified professionals or by expert handymen who have considerable electrical and plumbing experience.

LEVEL OF DIFFICULTY

Most of the tasks involved in remodeling a peninsula kitchen are highly specialized and require considerable ability in the use of tools. Experts who have extensive remodeling experience should be able to handle most of the work, but they

should proceed slowly on highly demanding jobs like hanging the cabinets and installing the ceramic tile. If they plan to complete these tasks, they should allow ample time - perhaps double the professional time estimate - as the materials are expensive and quality workmanship is called for. Experts should add 20% to the man-hours estimate for all other tasks and, depending on the amount of their experience, more for the flooring, plumbing, and electrical work. Handymen and beginners should restrict their involvement to the basic tasks like the removal of the old kitchen, reconditioning of the site, and painting. They should add 50% and 100%, respectively, to the professional time for all of these tasks.

WHAT TO WATCH OUT FOR

As noted earlier, the peninsula unit provides the homeowner with the opportunity to design an attractive and practical eating and utility area. One way to enhance both its appearance and function is to add electrical conveniences and lighting fixtures. There are many possibilities; for example, install one or several duplex outlets in convenient locations on and around the unit, or build direct or indirect lighting into the underside of the overhead unit. Both of these electrical improvements can be done for a reasonable cost, yet they provide a lot of convenience. A warming plate can also be installed in the surface of the base unit, but this electrical amenity will add significantly to the cost. Be sure to have the wiring capacity for the existing kitchen circuits checked before you add these or other new electrical fixtures. These items should be carefully planned in advance, as spur-of-the-moment modifications will cost more for installation after the finished materials are in place.

SUMMARY

The deluxe peninsula kitchen is an expensive and complex remodeling project which can enhance the quality of life in your home. The high grade of its components can add value to your dwelling, while improving its appearance and versatility.

PENINSULA KITCHEN, DELUXE

Description	Quantity	Man-hours	Material
Blocking, for mounting cabinets, 2" x 4" stock	72 L.F.	2.5	22.65
Plywood, underlayment grade, 1/2" thick, 4' x 8' sheets	4 Sheets	1.5	71.25
Flooring, vinyl sheet goods, 0.125" thick	100 S.F.	3.0	393.25
Wall cabinets, 12" deep, hardwood, deluxe	34 L.F.	8.0	1823.75
Base cabinets, 24" deep, hardwood, deluxe	20 L.F.	7.0	1976.20
Peninsula base cabinet, custom-built, 24" deep x 9' long	9 L.F.	4.5	1089.00
Plywood sub-base for counter-top, 1/2" x 4' x 8' sheets	3 Sheets	1.0	53.45
Ceramic tile for countertop and backsplash	106 S.F.	9.5	615.65
Valance board over sink	4 L.F.	0.5	29.05
Trim, cornice molding, stock pine, 9/16" x 2-1/4"	46 L.F.	1.5	22.85
Paint, ceiling, primer & 1 coat	125 S.F.	1.0	13.60
Paint, cornice trim, puttying, primer & 1 coat	46 L.F.	1.0	2.80
Cooking range, built-in, 30" wide, one oven	1 Ea.	8.0	968.00
Hood for range, 2-speed, 30" wide, vented	1 Ea.	5.5	290.40
Refrigerator, no frost, 19 C.F.	1 Ea.	4.0	1331.00
Sink w/faucets & drain, stainless steel self-rimming, 33" x 22", double bowl	1 Ea.	6.0	371.45
Dishwasher, built-in	1 Ea.	8.0	471.90
Rough-in, supply, waste & vent for sink & dishwasher	2 Ea.	17.5	159.35
Totals		91.0	$9705.60

Project Size	9'-6" x 13'	Contractor's Fee Including Materials	$17,740

Key to Abbreviations
C.Y. - cubic yard   Ea. - each   L.F. - linear foot   Pr. - pair   Sq. - square (100 square feet of area)
S.F. - square foot   S.Y. - square yard   V.L.F. - vertical linear foot

ISLAND KITCHEN, STANDARD

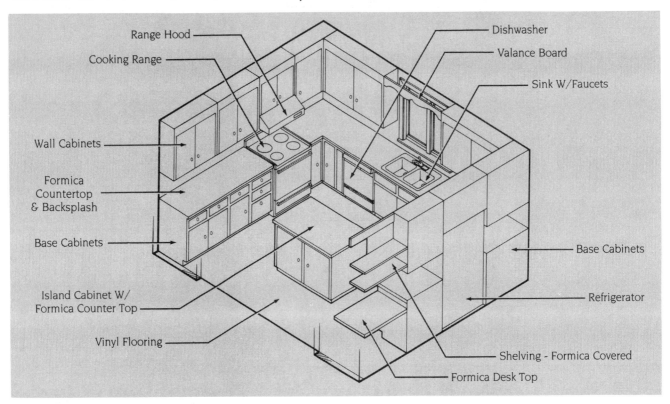

Range Hood

Cooking Range

Dishwasher

Valance Board

Sink W/Faucets

Wall Cabinets

Formica Countertop & Backsplash

Base Cabinets

Base Cabinets

Island Cabinet W/ Formica Counter Top

Refrigerator

Vinyl Flooring

Shelving - Formica Covered

Formica Desk Top

Based on square footage, the kitchen is one of the most expensive rooms in your home to renovate, primarily because of the cost of the specialized appliances, cabinets and flooring systems used. It is also one of the most challenging rooms for the handyman to tackle for a variety of reasons. Because the kitchen's function is vital to the routine of home life, a long and drawn-out remodeling project can only add to the inconvenience during the renovation process. Professional remodelers can do the job faster and with less aggravation and disturbance of the household routine. Also, kitchen renovations demand a wide range of construction tasks, some of them too specialized for the average handyman to undertake. Despite the costs, inconvenience and challenges, the benefits returned in both home life and the increased value of the house make the effort worthwhile.

MATERIALS

The kitchen, more than any room in your house, contains materials and appliances that vary greatly in quality and, therefore, cost. Cabinets alone constitute an area of kitchen materials that run the gamut from economical mass-produced particleboard units to custom-made soft or hardwood designs with raised panels or other decorative features.

The standard island kitchen attempts to strike a happy medium in terms of cost without sacrificing quality. The floor and walls of the kitchen include standard materials that can be installed by most handymen. Make sure that you carefully check the existing subflooring for rot before laying the new underlayment and vinyl tiling. Also keep in mind that the vinyl flooring surface should extend under appliances, but not under the cabinets in the new kitchen. The walls and ceiling should be coated with a quality primer and finish coat before the floor, cabinets, and appliances are installed.

Applying the paint first saves time because you don't have to worry about masking the cabinets and covering the appliances and floor while rolling the ceiling or doing brush work.

The plumbing and electrical work required in this kitchen renovation will vary, depending on the extent to which appliances and the sink are moved from their old locations. If your remodeling project includes relocation of the sink to another wall, then you'll have to allow for more roughing materials, time, and expense. The same type of cost variables will also be included in the relocation of a gas or electric range or a dishwasher. Careful consideration should be given to the amount of plumbing and electrical work to be attempted by the homeowner, particularly in kitchen installations. Beginners should leave all of the plumbing and electrical work to professionals; handymen should do the same, unless they have had extensive experience in these areas.

Installing and relocating rough plumbing for a double-bowl sink, for example, is a job that should be undertaken only by an expert do-it-yourselfer or a qualified plumber.

The cabinet work in this standard island kitchen involves a complete set of top and bottom units on the three sides of the room's perimeter surrounding the island unit. A custom Formica countertop ties the lower units together to form a versatile, continuous work surface. Custom shelving for a bookcase and desk area is also included. The quality of the cabinet materials, as well as the design of the cabinet door and drawer facings, significantly affects their cost. Quality prefabricated units, for example, generally cost less than similar quality, custom-made units. If you are doing the work yourself and have not had experience with cabinet installation, seek some assistance. Seemingly small problems like a wall corner slightly out of plumb or out of square can raise havoc with the alignment of the cabinet facings and counter top. Skilled handymen and experts should be able to perform the cabinet installation, but beginners and even reasonably experienced do-it-yourselfers should leave this part of the project to a professional.

The appliances for any kitchen renovation, like the cabinets, can raise or lower the cost of the job significantly, depending on the quality of the item and the number of extra features you require in the appliance. If you want to stay in the middle of the price spectrum, a basic one-oven, four-burner range will meet most of your cooking needs. Refrigerators vary greatly in capacity and optional functions, but a standard 19 cubic foot frost-free unit with freezer above generally fulfills a family's needs. A basic two-cycle dishwasher is considered a necessity today. If you're doing the electrical and plumbing work on your own, remember that the dishwasher will require both plumbing and electrical connections.

LEVEL OF DIFFICULTY

A complete kitchen renovation is a demanding remodeling job, but one that a handyman can tackle. Tearing out the old kitchen, reconditioning the site and installing the new components are jobs that take time, effort and an extensive knowledge of tools and building skills. Beginners should be able to accomplish some of the easier tasks like the laying of subflooring and the painting, but should get some professional assistance before starting tasks which are new to them. The more sophisticated jobs involved in the project, such as plumbing, electrical, and cabinet and countertop installations, should be left to the expert do-it-yourselfers or professional contractors. Beginners should double or triple the estimated man-hours, even for the basic tasks. Handymen should add about 75% to the estimated times of those tasks which they feel they can accomplish. Experts should tack on about 40% to 50% to the man-hours estimates throughout the project.

WHAT TO WATCH OUT FOR

Renovating the kitchen in an older home often presents the challenges of sagging or sloped floors, bowed or out-of-plumb walls, and other problems which can test even professional builders. The problems become magnified for the handyman, because he simply has not had experience in dealing with them. Don't hesitate to seek advice from a qualified person who knows, for example, how to scribe a countertop into a skewed wall or how to make adjustments to allow for a dip or bulge in the floor. Asking the right person at the right time can save you aggravation and money in the long run.

SUMMARY

Modernizing and rearranging an old kitchen is an exciting way to improve your home. A project like this adds considerable value to your house and improves the overall quality of living for your family.

ISLAND KITCHEN, STANDARD

Description	Quantity	Man-hours	Material
Blocking, for mounting cabinets, 2" x 4", stock	68 L.F.	2.0	21.40
Plywood, underlayment grade, 1/2" thick, 4' x 8' sheets	6 Sheets	2.5	106.90
Floor tile, 12" x 12" x 1/16" thick, vinyl composition	125 S.F.	3.0	98.30
Wall cabinets, hardwood, 12" deep	26 L.F.	6.0	996.00
Base cabinets, hardwood, 24" deep	30 L.F.	10.5	2117.40
Island cabinet, 30" x 48" base	1 Ea.	2.0	484.00
Countertop, 1-1/4" thick, Formica, including backsplash	24 L.F.	6.5	145.20
Island top, 1-1/4" thick, 32" x 50", Formica	1 Ea.	1.0	24.20
Valance boards over sink and book shelf	8 L.F.	0.5	58.10
Desk top, 1-1/4" thick, Formica covered	1 Ea.	1.0	20.00
Shelving, 3/4" thick, Formica covered	8 L.F.	1.0	49.85
Trim, cornice molding, stock pine 9/16" x 2-1/4"	36 L.F.	1.0	17.85
Paint, primer and 1 coat, ceiling and walls	450 S.F.	3.5	49.00
Paint, cornice trim, puttying, primer and 1 coat	36 L.F.	0.5	2.20
Cooking range, built-in, 30" wide, one oven	1 Ea.	4.0	423.50
Hood for range, 2 speed, vented, 30" wide	1 Ea.	3.0	36.30
Refrigerator, no frost, 19 C.F.	1 Ea.	2.0	726.00
Sink with faucets and drain, stainless steel, self rimming, 43" x 22", double bowl	1 Ea.	6.0	423.50
Dishwasher, built-in, 2 cycle	1 Each	4.0	278.30
Rough-in supply, waste and vent for sink and dishwasher	2 Ea.	17.5	159.35
Totals		77.5	$6237.35

Project Size	11'-6" x 14'-6"	Contractor's Fee Including Materials	$11,770

Key to Abbreviations
C.Y. - cubic yard   Ea. - each   L.F. - linear foot   Pr. - pair   Sq. - square (100 square feet of area)
S.F. - square foot   S.Y. - square yard   V.L.F. - vertical linear foot

ISLAND KITCHEN, DELUXE

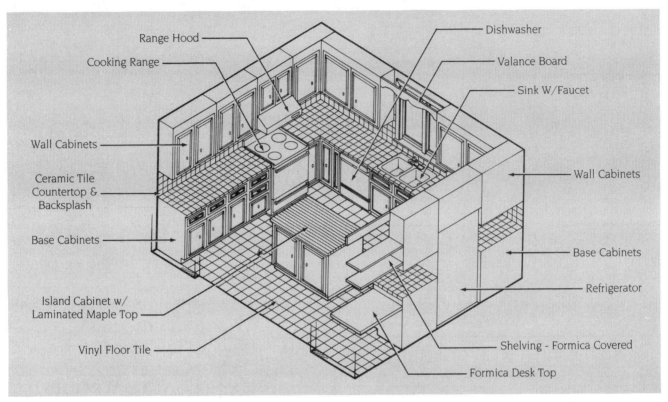

Range Hood
Cooking Range
Dishwasher
Valance Board
Sink W/Faucet
Wall Cabinets
Ceramic Tile Countertop & Backsplash
Base Cabinets
Wall Cabinets
Base Cabinets
Refrigerator
Island Cabinet w/ Laminated Maple Top
Vinyl Floor Tile
Shelving - Formica Covered
Formica Desk Top

Like the other deluxe kitchens presented in this section, this facility features the upgrading of standard kitchen materials to top-of-the-line products. If it is within your budget and fits in with your home and lifestyle, a deluxe island kitchen may be the appropriate remodeling design to follow. This plan outlines a luxurious alternative to simpler, more standard arrangements. Good planning and professional workmanship will be rewarded with a beautiful, durable, and functional kitchen area.

MATERIALS

Because this kitchen plan involves deluxe appliances, cabinets, and other materials, its cost is substantially higher than that of a standard facility of the same size. All of the basic components of the kitchen can be replaced by less expensive items, and substitutions can be made to reduce the cost to a compromise level somewhere between that of a standard facility and this one. Remember,

though, that any replacements should be made with discretion, as the aesthetic balance of the kitchen's appearance is important. Your personal taste and the decor of your home should serve as your guides when determining the materials for the new facility.

One of the most pleasing features of this kitchen plan is the "U"-shaped cabinet layout with a convenience island located in the center of the room. This layout requires a fairly large kitchen area to ensure enough floor and counter space without cramming its design and creating a closed-in feeling. The island cabinet puts normally wasted floor space to practical use as a food preparation or utility work surface. Depending on the intended function of the island, a variety of surface materials can be used, from laminated hardwoods in butcher-block design, to stone, ceramic tile, or Formica-type coverings. The wall and base cabinets which border the island cabinet can be

constructed from a variety of hard or soft woods with paneled or decorative drawer and door facings. The valance boards, desk top, and shelving should be included in the design and manufacture of the cabinet system.

The materials used for the floor and countertop of the new kitchen are products which complement the elegance of the cabinets. This plan includes durable vinyl tiles for the floor surface, but sheet goods are also available at varying costs. The ceramic tiling on the countertop and backsplash provide a durable and attractive alternative to plastic laminate coverings.

The design and capacity of the appliances to be included in the deluxe island kitchen should be determined by such variables as the size of your family, extent of anticipated use of the kitchen, and food preparation methods. Such considerations as preference for gas or electric range, refrigerator and freezer capacity, and general use of appliances should be carefully weighed before you select the fixtures and decide on their location in the new kitchen. Conversion from an electric to gas range, for example, requires significant rough-in preparation which should be built into both the design and the cost of the overall kitchen plan before the work begins. Other appliance, plumbing and electrical relocations should be similarly planned and incorporated into the cost of the facility before you begin the renovation. Changing your mind on such matters after the work has begun will usually cost you more money and aggravation.

LEVEL OF DIFFICULTY

The kitchen is a challenging room for the handyman to remodel because carpentry, plumbing, electrical, flooring, and other specialized building skills are required. Also, most of the materials used in kitchen construction are expensive, and many are difficult to install. For example, the planning, measuring, and placing of the cabinet and counter top systems in this plan involve three walls totaling 30 linear feet, with appropriate allowances for a window, sink, under-counter dishwasher, refrigerator, built-in range, oven and hood, as well as the island unit. Overseeing and accomplishing this cabinet installation requires the skill of a professional. Experts should have prior experience with cabinet installation and tile work if they plan to tackle the project. Beginners and handymen can save on labor costs by removing the old facility, placing the underlayment, and reconditioning and finishing the walls and ceiling, but they should leave the cabinet and appliance installation and the tile work to professionals. They should add 100% and 50% respectively, to the professional time for laying the plywood and painting. Experts should add 20% to the time estimates for these tasks and 50% to 100% to the time for the more specialized jobs within the kitchen.

WHAT TO WATCH OUT FOR

If you plan to do some or all of the work on this remodeling project, take stock of your building skills and the amount of free time available in your personal schedule. Kitchens, like baths, are difficult facilities to remodel because their operation is vital to the daily routine of home life. Disturbing their function can cause considerable inconvenience, especially if the interruption is prolonged and the work done piecemeal on weekends, evenings, and holidays. In most cases, a concentrated and limited period of remodeling is desirable for kitchen projects. Make plans ahead of time to arrange for alternative meal preparation and to allow for the inconvenience. If you are doing the work on your own, build in some extra time for those hidden problems that always surface.

SUMMARY

The deluxe island kitchen provides an attractive and functional design. If the plan is in keeping with your lifestyle and fits into your available space, this project will increase the value of your house while making the kitchen more functional, attractive, and convenient. The renovation is a major undertaking requiring the skills of a contractor, yet you can still do some of the work so long as you plan carefully and get good advice.

ISLAND KITCHEN, DELUXE

Description	Quantity	Man-hours	Material
Blocking, for mounting cabinets, 2" x 4" stock	68 L.F.	2.5	21.40
Plywood, underlayment grade, 1/2" thick, 4' x 8' sheets	6 sheets	2.5	106.90
Floor tile, 12" x 12" x 1/16" thick, embossed vinyl composition	125 S.F.	3.0	98.30
Wall cabinets, deluxe, hardwood, 12" deep	28 L.F.	6.0	1394.60
Base cabinets, deluxe, hardwood, 24" deep	23 L.F.	10.5	2964.25
Island cabinet, 30" x 48" base	1 Ea.	2.0	726.00
Plywood sub-base for countertops 1/2" x 4' x 8' sheets	3 Sheets	0.5	35.65
Ceramic tile for countertops and backsplash	105 S.F.	9.0	609.85
Island Top, maple, solid laminated 1-1/2" thick	24 L.F.	7.0	871.20
Valance boards over sink & bookshelf	8 L.F.	0.5	58.10
Desk-top, 1-1/4" thick, Formica-covered	1 Ea.	1.0	18.40
Shelving, 3/4" thick, Formica-covered	8 L.F.	1.0	49.35
Trim, cornice molding, stock pine, 9/16" x 2-1/4"	36 L.F.	1.0	17.85
Paint, primer & 1 coat, ceiling & walls	170 S.F.	1.5	18.50
Paint, primer & 1 coat, cornice trim, puttying	36 L.F.	0.5	2.20
Cooking range, built-in, 30" wide, one oven	1 Ea.	8.0	968.00
Hood for range, 2-speed, 30" wide	1 Ea.	5.5	290.40
Refrigerator, no frost, 19 C.F.	1 Ea.	4.0	1331.00
Sink w/faucets & drain, stainless steel, self-rimming, 43" x 22", double bowl	1 Ea.	6.0	371.45
Dishwasher, built-in, 2 cycle	1 Ea.	8.0	471.90
Rough-in, supply, waste & vent for sink and dishwasher	2 Ea.	17.5	159.35
Totals		97.5	$10,584.65

Project Size	11'-6" x 14'-6"

Contractor's Fee Including Materials	$19,060

Key to Abbreviations
C.Y. - cubic yard   Ea. - each   L.F. - linear foot   Pr. - pair   Sq. - square (100 square feet of area)
S.F. - square foot   S.Y. - square yard   V.L.F. - vertical linear foot

Stairway, Disappearing

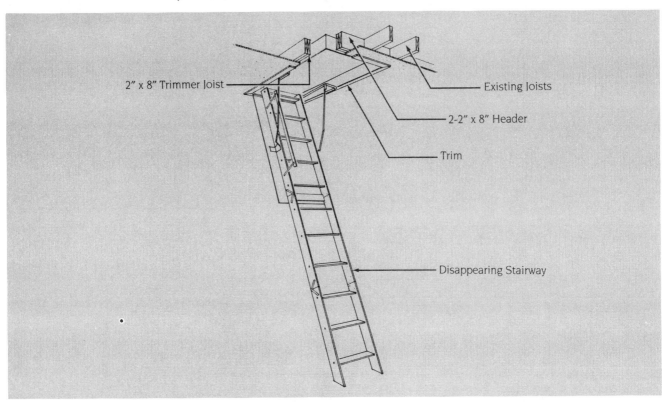

2" x 8" Trimmer Joist —

— Existing Joists

— 2-2" x 8" Header

— Trim

— Disappearing Stairway

The disappearing or fold-down stairway can solve attic and storage area access problems without wasting valuable floor space. The prefabricated fold-down units literally disappear into the ceiling after use, leaving the area below, usually a hallway or bedroom, open for normal use. The installation of the unit is a moderately difficult operation, but one that advanced beginners could tackle and complete as a weekend project. It must be done to professional standards, however, as it can otherwise become dangerous. The various fittings, screws, nuts, and bolts also tend to loosen and require periodic tightening to keep the structure strong and safe. Because the stairway is very steep with narrow treads, it is really more like a convenient ladder than a set of stairs. On account of these drawbacks, a disappearing stairway should not be installed as an economical substitute for a permanently placed staircase, and it should be used only for its intended temporary, make-do purpose.

Materials

The list of materials needed for the disappearing stairway installation begins with the factory-prepared unit. Conventional framing and support lumber will also be needed to restore the ceiling bracings that are weakened when room is made for the stairway. The unit comes from the supplier fully assembled and with complete instructions and guidelines for the installation procedure. As noted earlier, several manufacturers produce the stairway units in varying levels of quality and cost. Shop around and purchase the one which best suits your needs. Before you place and secure the stairway in its permanent position, check it over carefully by examining the condition of the wood and the tightness of the fittings and fasteners. The treads, rails, and supports should be solid and free of cracks or imperfections. Some of the units come with a built-in handrail, but others require installation of an

accompanying safety rail during the stairway's placement. If your stairway is the latter type, make sure that you take the time to attach the handrail carefully, as it is an essential safety item. Regardless of the quality or design of the disappearing stairway which you have selected, follow precisely the manufacturer's installation instructions and guidelines.

The framing and support materials used to strengthen the ceiling opening for the stairway unit are basically the same as those included for the circular stairway project. A general rule is that the joist materials should match the dimensions of the existing joists on the floor of your attic or storage room. In most newer homes, the joists or stringers are 2" x 8"s or 2" x 6"s depending on the structural design of the house and location of the area accessed by the stairway. If the disappearing stairway is to be placed near a supporting wall or partition, the required amount of support lumber may be reduced. However, if the unit has to be placed in the middle of the ceiling, away from partition or wall support, additional joists and blocking may be needed for adequate support. Galvanized joist hangers should also be used where needed for the headers and trimmer joists. The trim pieces used to face the unit should match the design of the trim work in the room or hallway where the stairway is placed. After the unit is installed and trimmed, it can be painted to blend in with the ceiling.

LEVEL OF DIFFICULTY

This project places moderate demands on the skill level of the handyman. With some advice and instruction from a professional, advanced beginners can handle most of the tasks. The biggest challenge involved in the installation process is the cutting of the opening and subsequent joist support placement. These are moderately difficult procedures because of the awkward ceiling location and the cutting by power or hand tools overhead or in a stooped position from the attic floor. If you don't have skill with tools, especially the use of a circular or saber saw overhead, then hire a contractor to do the cutting and joist work. Most handymen should be able to complete this project if they have had experience with cutting joists beforehand. If you are reasonably skilled in the use of tools, but have not performed these specific tasks before, then seek some advice before you start the project. Experts should have no trouble in completing all tasks required to install the stairway and should add about 10% to the estimated professional time. Handymen should add about 30% to the man-hours if they are experienced in cutting and joist support work, and about 50% if they are not. Beginners should not attempt the cutting and joist support operations unless they are advanced enough to use tools in the awkward positions required for this installation. Regardless of your level of remodeling skill, bear in mind that the installation of a disappearing stairway is a two-man job, so plan accordingly.

WHAT TO WATCH OUT FOR

The prefabricated disappearing stairway unit is ready to be placed in the prepared opening as soon as it is uncrated; but it should be handled carefully, because it is heavy and can be put out of square if dropped or mishandled. Take some time to make up temporary guides out of strapping or other scrap lumber, and tack them to the ceiling side of the unit. These guides help to keep the face of the unit flush with the ceiling and can double as temporary supports while the stairway unit is fastened from above. You can also make up a "T" to hold the assembly in place while it is being fastened. If you plan to refinish the ceiling below, you can tack two pieces of strapping across the opening and place the unit on them from above. Two workers are required for the placement of the unit, one above to do the fastening, and one below to position the stairway and to man the temporary supports. When fastening the unit, use shims to keep it square and to avoid bowing of the side pieces of the frame. Before seating the fasteners, double check the stairway box to see that it is square. If it is not, the unit will not seat properly in the fold-up position, and the ends of the stair rails will not sit evenly on the floor when the unit is in fold-down position. Follow the manufacturer's recommendations for trimming the stair rails at the correct length and angle.

SUMMARY

A disappearing staircase is one way of solving access problems to an attic or storage area. The prefabricated unit is moderately difficult to install, but the job can be completed within a workday by most handymen and experts.

STAIRWAY, DISAPPEARING

Description	Quantity	Man-hours	Material
Cut opening for stairway, 30" x 60"	1 Ea.	2.0	0.00
Rough in opening for stairway, headers, double 2" x 8" stock	12 L.F.	1.0	8.30
Trimmer, joists, fastened to existing joists, 2" x 8" stock	28 L.F.	0.5	13.20
Hangers for headers & joists, 18 ga. galv. for 2" x 8" joists	4 Ea.	0.5	2.65
Blocking, miscellaneous to joists, 2" x 8" stock	8 L.F.	0.5	5.35
Stairway, disappearing, custom grade, pine, 8'-6" ceiling	1 Ea.	2.5	121.00
Trim, casing, 11/16" x 2'-2"	16 L.F.	1.0	7.00
	Totals	8.0	$157.50

Contractor's Fee Including Materials	$440

Key to Abbreviations
C.Y. - cubic yard   Ea. - each   L.F. - linear foot   Pr. - pair   Sq. - square (100 square feet of area)
S.F. - square foot   S.Y. - square yard   V.L.F. - vertical linear foot

STAIRWAY, CIRCULAR

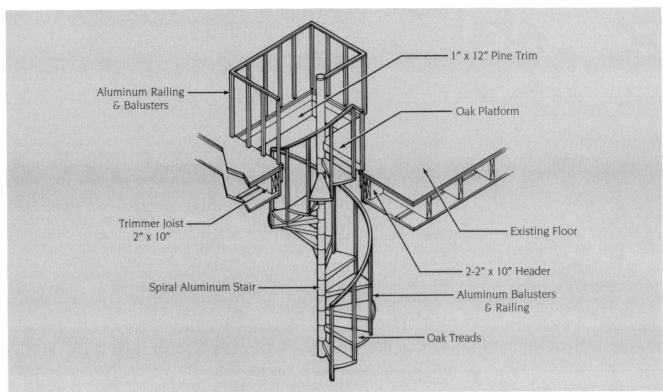

Aluminum Railing & Balusters

1" x 12" Pine Trim

Oak Platform

Trimmer Joist 2" x 10"

Existing Floor

2-2" x 10" Header

Spiral Aluminum Stair

Aluminum Balusters & Railing

Oak Treads

While conventional staircases take up a significant area on two levels, circular stairways can be an efficient alternative, particularly in smaller dwellings where space is at a premium. A prefabricated model can simplify the project and provide a new or more efficient stairway between levels of the house.

MATERIALS

The materials used for this project include the factory-made circular stairway unit and the framing and support materials required to maintain the floor and ceiling strength. The stairway itself is spiral in design, consisting of a heavy aluminum or steel center support pole and triangular treads which fan outward from it. Several other tread materials are available at varying costs, including steel and cast iron.

The stairway comes from the supplier in a prepackaged kit with instructions and guidelines for installation. After the ceiling opening has been cut to the dimensions specified by the manufacturer, it should be framed. The stairway is then assembled in place by sections, and plumbed, leveled, and fastened in its final location.

After the first step, which involves cutting out the required ceiling and floor spaces, the exposed joists will need to be boxed off and framed. The lumber used for the trimmer joists and headers should match the existing joists, which are usually 2" x 10"s. Additional 2" x 10"s may be required for blocking near the opening. These and any joist hangers that are needed will add some extra cost to the project.

Because much of the load of the stairway is concentrated on the base plate, additional support should be provided beneath the floor on which the stairway stands. Usually, doubling the existing 2" x 10"s in the area directly under the unit and adding supplementary blocking is enough. Plan on spending some extra time and money for this operation if you have to cut into a finished ceiling below to install these additional floor support members. If you are inexperienced in these tasks, then seek assistance or hire a professional to do the work. Inadequate placement of these structural components can cost you more in the long run because of repairs needed to correct sagging ceilings or floors.

The materials used to finish the ceiling cut out should match the trim work in the room below. The rough 2" x 10" box should first be faced with pine boards and then finished with one of several available types of trim. Care should be taken at the start in cutting the stairway opening to avoid the extra expense of patching the ceiling material around it later.

LEVEL OF DIFFICULTY

The installation of a circular stairway may at first appear to be a routine project, but the consequences of doing the work incorrectly make it a job for accomplished handymen. Beginners may be able to assemble the stairway and do the finish work, but they should hire a professional contractor to cut the opening and reinforce the joists. Experts and handymen who

have experience in framing should be able to accomplish most of the work on this project. Handymen without experience in structural carpentry should get some help and guidance before attempting those tasks. Beginners should add 150% to the estimated professional time if they plan to assemble the stairway and secure the permanent installation. They should also seek professional assistance on the task before they tackle it. Handymen should add 90% to the man-hours estimate for the actual stairway installation and 75% to the time for cutting and framing work if they have some experience with these kinds of tasks. They should double the time for the cutting and joist work if they have not performed this task before. Experts should add 20% - 30% to the man-hours estimates throughout the project.

WHAT TO WATCH OUT FOR

There are several considerations that can save you time and money on this project. One is selecting the right location for the new stairway if the choice is open to you. A position near a corner or wall is desirable because it normally involves less reinforcing work. Remember that you have to be aware of head room requirements at the top of the stairway, particularly if it leads to an attic or room with sloped ceilings. If the stairway leads to a second or third story room with a finished floor, extra materials and labor may be required to trim the floor area around the opening. Exercise care when cutting the opening; try to avoid damage to the existing ceiling and floor, as this can add needless cost and time to the finish work on the project.

SUMMARY

If you are cramped for space and in need of a stairway to the attic or next floor in your house, a circular staircase may provide the solution to your problem. The installation requires only as much floor area as a circle 4' to 5' in diameter, and as long as care is taken in the cutting and framing, the result should be a sturdy and functional stairway.

STAIRWAY, CIRCULAR

Description	Quantity	Man-hours	Material
Cut opening for stairway, 5' x 5'	1 Ea.	4.0	0.00
Rough in opening for stairway, headers, double 2" x 10" stock	40 L.F.	2.0	27.60
Trimmer joists, double, 2" x 10" stock	40 L.F.	1.0	18.90
Blocking, miscellaneous to joists, 2" x 10" stock	12 L.F.	0.5	11.35
Reinforcement of first floor, double existing joists, 2" x 10" joists	40 L.F.	1.0	37.75
Hangers for headers & joists, 18 ga galv., 2" x 10" joists	4 Ea.	0.5	2.65
Stairs, spiral aluminum, stack unit, 5' diam. oak treads, 14 treads & platform	1 Ea.	10.5	2631.75
Trim, casing at opening, 11/16" x 2 -1/2"	22 L.F.	1.0	9.60
Trim, pine, 1" x 12" at stair opening	22 L.F.	3.5	43.90
Totals		24.0	$2783.50

Project Size	5' diam. x 13 risers	Contractor's Fee Including Materials	$4990

Key to Abbreviations
C.Y. - cubic yard   Ea. - each   L.F. - linear foot   Pr. - pair   Sq. - square (100 square feet of area)
S.F. - square foot   S.Y. - square yard   V.L.F. - vertical linear foot

STAIRWAY, STANDARD

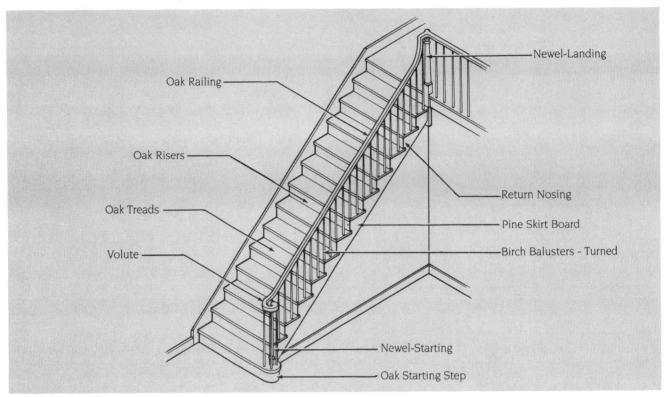

Oak Railing

Oak Risers

Oak Treads

Volute

Newel-Landing

Return Nosing

Pine Skirt Board

Birch Balusters - Turned

Newel-Starting

Oak Starting Step

Renovating an existing stairway requires a substantial level of carpentry skill and knowledge. For this reason, beginners and handymen with limited experience in this area should plan to hire a carpenter for much of the work in this project. There are many reasons why stairway installations demand specialized building skills, but foremost among them is the precise cutting and fitting of hardwood treads, risers, railings, bannisters, and other milled stairway materials. Despite these very demanding aspects, there are other tasks within this project that the do-it-yourselfer can accomplish. The expense and time put into the renovation, whether the work is done by the homeowner or a professional, will result in a refreshing improvement in your home. Because a stairway is often the focal point of the entryway, hallway, or room that it enters, select your materials with both appearance and function in mind.

MATERIALS

This remodeling project has been planned around the renovation of an existing flight of stairs, measuring 4' in width and rising to a height of 8'-6". The installation is typical of those found in many two-story dwellings, but variations in such factors as stairway design, height, width, and tread-to-riser proportion are as numerous as the dwellings themselves. The best course of action for the homeowner is to duplicate as closely as possible the existing stairway. Significantly altering the design, size, or direction of the staircase or attempting to match exactly a plan that differs from the original structure will add to the time and cost of the project.

The materials used in this plan consist primarily of milled wood products typical to most house stairway systems. Oak is the featured wood, but

other hard or soft woods may be installed at varying costs. Under normal conditions, it is best to duplicate the material of the existing staircase as well as its design. Oak has been chosen for this plan because it is the most commonly used material for treads. It is durable, pleasing in appearance, relatively economical, and is readily available in most areas of the country. The risers in this stairway plan are also made from oak, but soft woods like fir and pine can function adequately in its place. If you are looking for a cost-cutting measure, or if the stairway is to be carpeted, the use of softwood treads and risers in place of oak will reduce your materials expense considerably. In addition to the treads and risers, a special starting step and tread nosing will be needed to complete the stairway.

The materials used for the handrail and its support are also constructed of woods milled specifically for stairways. The homeowner has a wide choice of variously priced materials, from economical soft wood bannisters to expensive and ornate hardwood rails, newels, and rail starters. If you want to spruce up or change the design of your stairway, this is the place to do it, as structural alterations usually are not required to modify the stairway's railing system.

In addition to these milled woods, some rough lumber may also be required to replace damaged or warped stringers and other stairway supports. When removing the old stairs, try to avoid chipping or cracking the existing stringers. If they are straight, level, and sound, then leave them in place and save yourself the time and cost of replacement. If you are not sure about their condition, then have a knowledgeable person check them.

LEVEL OF DIFFICULTY

As noted in the description of this project, the renovation of a stairway demands a considerable level of carpentry skill and know-how. The finish tasks, particularly the cutting and fitting of the risers and treads and the setting of the railings, newel, and bannisters, require precise planning and mastery of woodworking skills. Near perfect accuracy of measurement in all aspects of the project is also necessary to assure quality of appearance and safety in the use of the new stairway. Beginners, therefore, should not attempt any of these advanced carpentry tasks and should restrict their efforts to the removal of the old stairway and finish work, such as the staining or sealing of the stairs. Handymen might be able to accomplish some of the finished carpentry on the stairs, but only if they have worked with hardwoods and have had some experience in finish carpentry. Handymen should stop short of the newel, railing, and bannister installations. Experts should be able to install the treads, risers, and various trim pieces; but they, too, should leave the railing work to a carpenter unless they have the know-how, skill, and correct tools to tackle this part of the installation. Generally, beginners should double the professional time for the removal of the existing stairway and any finish work, like painting and staining.

Handymen who want to install the treads, risers, and trim on the stairs should plan to work slowly and deliberately. They should triple the professional time for these tasks and should add 50% to the man-hours estimate for the removal of the old stairway. Experts, unless they are accomplished carpenters or woodworkers, should double the professional time for the installation of the treads and risers and leave the placement of the newels, railings, and bannisters to a professional.

WHAT TO WATCH OUT FOR

Very often the stairways in older homes bow, twist, or sag out of alignment because of settling. It is important, therefore, to check the condition and alignment of the stringers and other supporting members under the stairway after you have removed the old treads and risers. Before you install any of the new materials, you must correct any problems which will cause the new stairway to tilt, sag, or become poorly aligned. Failure to correct these kinds of problems make the installation more difficult and harm the appearance of the new stairs.

SUMMARY

A stairway often occupies a central place in the house, and thus its improvement can enhance the overall appearance and comfort of the home. The services of a contractor may be required for this job, as the types of skills involved are not often in the do-it-yourselfer's range of experience. Nevertheless, this project has valuable benefits in terms of added safety and aesthetic appeal.

STAIRWAY, STANDARD

Description	Quantity	Man-hours	Material
Removal of existing stairway	1 Ea.	8.0	0.00
Rough stringers, three 2" x 12", 14' long	54 L.F.	4.0	42.70
Treads, oak, 1-1/16" x 9-1/2" wide, 4' long	12 Ea.	6.0	361.80
Risers, oak, 3/4" x 7-1/2" wide, 4' long	13 Ea.	6.0	214.90
Single end starting step, oak	1 Ea.	1.0	35.85
Balusters, turned, 42" high, birch	27 Ea.	7.0	196.05
Newels, 3-1/4" wide, starting and landing	2 Ea.	4.0	235.95
Balusters, turned, 30" high, birch, at landing	6 Ea.	2.0	36.30
Railings, oak, built-up, stair & landing, incl. volute	20 L.F.	3.0	102.85
Skirt board, pine, 1" x 12"	14 L.F.	2.5	29.65
Totals		43.5	$1256.05

Project Size	4' wide x 13 risers	Contractor's Fee Including Materials	$3090

Key to Abbreviations
C.Y. - cubic yard   Ea. - each   L.F. - linear foot   Pr. - pair   Sq. - square (100 square feet of area)
S.F. - square foot   S.Y. - square yard   V.L.F. - vertical linear foot

SECTION TWO
EXTERIORS

This section of the book deals with remodeling projects which take place on the outside or apart from the main structure of your home. As in the "Interiors" section, the goal is to inform you of the costs involved and to point out various factors which affect the planning process. Figures are given for the materials, man-hours, and contractor's fees required for the renovation. With this information, you can determine which tasks within the project you want to accomplish yourself and which ones to leave to a contractor. The example projects make suggestions for materials, but other possibilities also exist. The prices for many alternative products can be found in Section Three.

Exterior remodeling has its own set of challenges, but also offers certain advantages over interior projects. Because you are working primarily on the outside of a structure, you generally will have better access to the work area. Carpentry, and especially framing skills, play an important role in erecting the support system of the new structure. The more complicated framing jobs should probably be handled by a contractor. The electrical and plumbing work is more approachable to the do-it-yourselfer because the walls are open for rough-in work. However, if you are inexperienced in these areas, hiring a professional is advised. General precautions should be taken whenever the exterior of the existing house is penetrated. Extra care during the project will head off the expense of repairing damaged finished walls or support members.

The materials required for outdoor projects tend to be of a quantity and size that require delivery by the supplier. Storage is also a consideration. Another point to keep in mind is the availability of building products. Because some components may have to be ordered in advance, arrangements should be made as soon as possible. Exterior projects sometimes require extra cost for the rental or purchase of special equipment. For the major renovations, it may be best to subcontract the foundation work and framing to a professional who is properly equipped.

Almost all of the projects should have a master plan drawn up in advance. A detailed floor plan will suffice for many of the projects, but a larger scale structure, such as an addition or garage might require side elevations as well. If this drawing cannot be accomplished by the homeowner, a professional can be hired at extra cost. The benefits can be well worth the investment. Another matter which should be taken care of at the beginning is the application for required building permits and an investigation into zoning regulations.

In figuring your total costs, you may need to include extra expenses for such items as a heating system for the additions. Some of the projects may incur extra costs for related procedures, such as adding a driveway for a new garage, or removing one for a garage conversion. Difficult sites and poor soil conditions can also increase your costs. Keep in mind the fact that modifications may need to be made on the model plans and that the costs will change from those listed according to your special requirements.

The projects in this "Exteriors" section are, for the most part, large scale. Some require considerable planning and involve factors different from those in interior remodeling. Knowing in advance both the costs and the work that are involved should prepare you to make the best choices for your exterior improvements.

FINISHED BREEZEWAY, WITH SCREENS

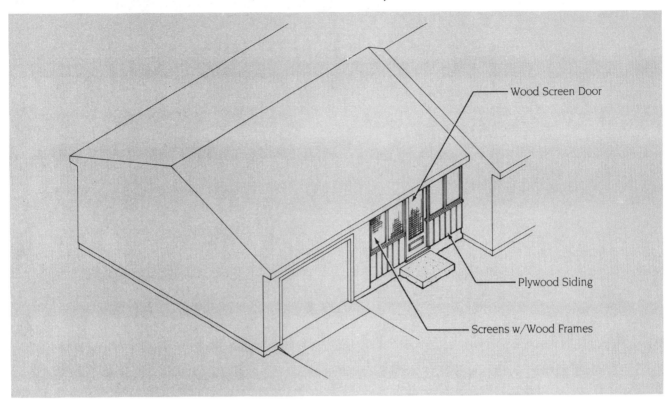

Wood Screen Door

Plywood Siding

Screens w/Wood Frames

A screened-in sitting or eating area can add pleasure and comfort to any home. Such a facility can be created without building a separate structure if an existing breezeway is used. Because the roof, side walls, and floor are already in place, the cost of remodeling a breezeway is considerably less than that of a new addition. Also, because breezeways are generally at the first floor level, the project site is easily accessible and can usually be framed and screened with few logistical problems. Like deck projects, breezeway conversions normally cause little or no disruption to the home's routine, and, therefore, can be completed at a slower pace. For these reasons, this project provides an excellent opportunity for the homeowner to cut costs by accomplishing most of the work on his own. If you are willing to seek advice and work patiently, this screened-in breezeway plan can be installed for a modest price.

MATERIALS

The materials needed to complete this breezeway remodeling project include standard 2" x 4"s to frame the knee wall and door opening, 2" x 6"s for the rafters, appropriate coverings for the knee wall, ceiling, and floor, and the screen panels and door. All of these materials are readily available from building supply outlets, so it pays to compare prices from several different retailers. The screen panels are specialty items which have to be custom fitted to the opening created by the knee wall frame. If you hire a contractor to build the panels, it might be a good idea to have him install them as well. If you intend to build the panels on your own, develop a master plan for all of the screening to determine the most cost-effective width for the individual panels, and then base the order for the screening and wood frame on that factor. Plan to include delivery as a part of the

purchase order for all of the materials, as the lumber needed to frame the enclosure, the knee wall, and ceiling coverings is cumbersome and will have to be trucked.

Precise framing is required for the knee wall, as it serves as the primary support for the screen panels. If it is not level and plumb, the panels will not seat correctly and openings will result along the abutting edges. If the existing wood or concrete floor of the breezeway is uneven or slanted, you will have to shim or angle the bottom of the knee wall frame to attain a level surface on the top. Do-it-yourselfers who are inexperienced in framing procedures should get some assistance before or during the knee wall construction, as its placement must be correct for the rest of the job to go smoothly. After the knee wall is in place and the doorway has been framed, rough-sawn plywood siding is applied to the exterior.

In this enclosure, the ceiling is prepared with 2" x 6" joists, spaced 24" on center. Although 16" spacing is the accepted standard in other types of construction, 24" spacing is adequate for this project. This plan includes 3/8" rough-sawn fir plywood for the ceiling surface, but other materials can be installed at varying costs. The price of indoor/outdoor carpeting is also included, though other types of floor materials, such as weather resistant tiling and exterior floor paint, can also be used. The inside of the knee wall is covered with fir plywood in this model, but once again, other choices are available. Be sure to include additional expense for any electrical work, such as a ceiling light fixture, door lamp, and watertight duplex outlets. Especially if you plan to use the enclosure at night, some provision for lighting should be made in the master plan before construction begins. If you wait until the new materials are in place, the labor cost for electrical work will be higher than if you have it done beforehand.

Particular care should be exercised in the planning, building, and installation of the screen panels. A prefabricated type is included in this estimate, but do-it-yourselfers may consider making their own. Be aware, however, that they are tricky to make and require the proper tools and know-how. Fiberglass and aluminum screening are available in different grades and at varying costs, so shop carefully if you are making the screens yourself. Even tension of the screening is important for both the appearance and longevity of the panels, so get some instruction from a knowledgeable person on the ins and outs of screen panel manufacture before you start. You might consider installing them in such a way that they can be conveniently removed for periodic cleaning, painting, and storage during the off season. Prefabricated aluminum screen panels can also be used as an alternative to the suggested wood-framed units, but they have to be custom made and, therefore, cost more.

LEVEL OF DIFFICULTY

This project is a manageable undertaking for most do-it-yourselfers who have a basic knowledge of carpentry and experience in the use of tools. The most challenging task is the planning, building, and installation of the screen panels. As noted earlier, this part of the project should be left to professionals or expert do-it-yourselfers. The hanging of the screen door also requires advanced carpentry skills. Generally, beginners should not attempt the frame, rafter, door, carpeting, and screening tasks; and they should double the professional time estimates for all other jobs. They should seek professional help on unfamiliar tasks. Handymen should stop short of the screen panel fabrication and carpeting; but they should be able to complete the rest of the project with the addition of about 40% to the man-hours estimates. Experts should allow an additional 10% in time for all tasks, and more for the screen panels if they have no experience in this operation.

WHAT TO WATCH OUT FOR

The details of the wood-framed screen panel installation will vary according to the desired finish appearance of the enclosure. In a basic installation, the panels can be secured at the top and bottom to the interior or exterior face of the new wall. In a more finished installation, the panels can be placed within the framed opening and secured with stops made from trim material, such as quarter-round moulding or 1" x 1" pine strips.

Brass or galvanized wood screws can then be used as fasteners to allow for easy removal of the panels for maintenance or storage during the off season. This type of finished installation will require additional materials and more time to accomplish; but the extra cost and effort may prove worthwhile.

FINISHED BREEZEWAY, WITH SCREENS

Description	Quantity	Man-hours	Material
Framing for knee wall, plates 2" x 4" stock	96 L.F.	2.0	30.20
Framing for knee wall, studs, 2" x 4" x 3'	60 L.F.	1.5	14.50
Framing for doorways, 2" x 4" x 8'	72 L.F.	1.5	22.65
Ceiling joists, 2" x 6" x 24', 24" O.C.	240 L.F.	3.5	113.25
Ceiling, rough sawn cedar, plywood, 3/8" thick, pre-stained	9 Sheets	7.0	372.87
Siding for knee wall, both sides rough sawn cedar, 5/8" thick, pre-stained	2 Sheets	1.5	82.86
Wood screens, 1-1/8" frames	200 S.F.	9.0	605.00
Screen door, wood, 2'-8" x 6'-9"	2 Ea.	2.5	382.35
Painting, inside wall & trim, primer and 2 coats	200 S.F.	2.5	29.05
Indoor/outdoor carpet, 3/8" thick	32 S.Y.	12.0	818.93
	Totals	43.0	$2471.65

Project Size	24' x 12'	Contractor's Fee Including Materials	$5840

Key to Abbreviations
C.Y. - cubic yard   Ea. - each   L.F. - linear foot   Pr. - pair   Sq. - square (100 square feet of area)
S.F. - square foot   S.Y. - square yard   V.L.F. - vertical linear foot

SUMMARY

An existing breezeway already has the basic requirements of a roof and two walls that make it easily convertible to a screened-in porch. It is in a convenient work location, and many of the tasks are within reach of do-it-yourselfers. The costs can be kept down because of the relatively small quantities of materials required and the potential savings on labor.

FINISHED BREEZEWAY, WITH WINDOWS

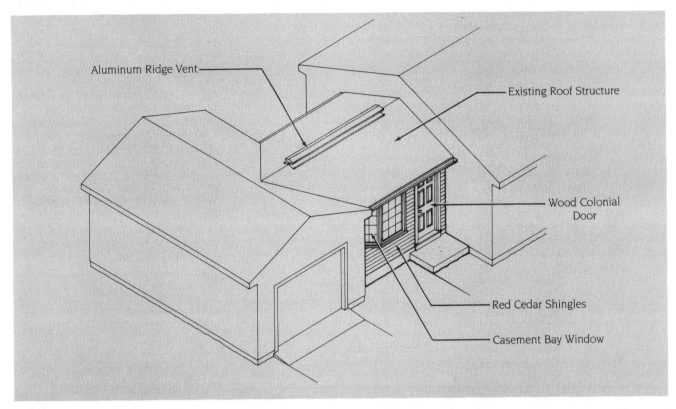

Aluminum Ridge Vent

Existing Roof Structure

Wood Colonial Door

Red Cedar Shingles

Casement Bay Window

Breezeways can be readily converted to interior living space because two walls, the roof, floor, and support structure are already in place. The project requires framing the two open sides and all of the tasks necessary to finish the exterior of the two new walls, including the installation of a door and windows. After the breezeway has been closed in, the necessary interior finish work is completed, as in other types of conversion projects. Because the breezeway is usually located on the first floor with immediate accessibility from the yard and garage, the logistics of materials storage and transport are minimal. This plan demonstrates how a 12' x 12' breezeway can be converted to interior living space at reasonable cost. With some or all of the work done by the homeowner, the price of the improvement can be reduced substantially. Beginners and less-skilled handymen should not attempt to complete the entire project, but they can accomplish most of it.

MATERIALS

The materials included in this plan consist of standard construction products available at building supply outlets and lumber yards. First of all, framing materials will be needed for the two open walls. Exterior and interior sheathing is also required, along with a door, windows, and insulation. Floor coverings, trim work, and a minimal electrical installation complete the list of supplies for the interior work.

The framing for the two open walls is constructed from 2" x 4"s set 16" on center with a single bottom and a doubled top plate. The door and window rough openings should be built into the partition using jack studs and 2" x 8" headers. After the framing is in place, 1/2" plywood sheathing is placed on the outside. When the door and windows have been installed, the siding is put on. Try to match closely the siding on the new room to that of the rest of the house by using the

same material, following existing course lines, and painting and finishing it in the same style. Additional cost can be anticipated for the matching of expensive sidings and for any special installation techniques required to install them.

The door and window units included in the plan can be altered to meet the style and design of the house. The three-lite bay unit, for example, is an attractive and practical window, but two double-hung windows may be more appropriate. As a general rule, a quality window product is a worthwhile investment. Years of energy efficiency, easy operation, and low maintenance will return the extra initial expense. The same rule holds for the selection of the exterior door unit. Before you attempt to install the door and windows, line up a helper, because these items are heavy, can be awkward to manipulate, and are expensive to repair if they are dropped or mishandled.

The materials used in the interior of the remodeled breezeway include new 2" x 6" ceiling joists (if none are in place, strapping, insulation and drywall for the ceiling and walls, and carpeting for the floor. As in other interior remodeling projects, many alternative materials are available at varying costs to suit your personal tastes and home decor. Remember that if portions of the exterior house and garage walls are included in the new room, they must be stripped of their exterior siding and drywalled or covered with suitable interior wall material. The garage wall may also have to be insulated and the garage doorway dressed up or relocated. All of these operations will add cost and time to the job.

Before the interior wall and ceiling coverings are installed, the rough electrical wiring and boxes have to be in place. This plan includes the basic electrical service of four wall outlets and a switch box. If you want to put in an overhead fixture, recessed or track lighting, a door lamp, or other electrical facilities, the cost for the project will increase. Hire a qualified electrician to do the work if you are unfamiliar with electrical installation procedures. Do-it-yourselfers should not attempt to tie in the new wiring to the panel, even if they are experienced enough to do all other parts of the electrical installation.

LEVEL OF DIFFICULTY

Handymen with a command of basic carpentry and remodeling skills and experts should be able to complete most of this project. The site is convenient, the extent of remodeling is fairly limited, and the tasks are routine, with the exception of the electrical and carpeting installations. Specialty contractors should be hired to perform these operations in most cases. Even experts should weigh the savings of doing these jobs on their own against the benefits of fast, high-quality professional work. For all tasks, except the electrical and flooring work, handymen should add 40% to the professional time, and experts 10%. Beginners should hire a contractor to do all of the exterior work, including the window and door installations. With some instruction and guidance, they can perform some of the insulating, drywalling, painting, and trim work. They should, however, leave the placement of the ceiling joists, electrical installation, and carpeting to professionals. For the interior jobs which they do take on, beginners should add 80% to the professional time estimate.

WHAT TO WATCH OUT FOR

Although this breezeway project presents an economical means of converting exterior space to interior living area, it contains some potential problems that may add to its cost and increase the installation time. The doorway into the house will require attention, because it should be converted into an interior opening and trimmed with the same materials used in the new room. If the doorway is one step above the new floor level, a suitable interior step should be built. The old door from this location can be used for the new exterior installation as a cost-cutting measure.

SUMMARY

Because a breezeway already has a floor, roof, and two walls, it is a practical, convenient source of new interior living space. The tasks involved in its conversion are within the realm of many do-it-yourselfers, and this aspect of the project can make it an economical undertaking as well.

FINISHED BREEZEWAY, WITH WINDOWS

Description	Quantity	Man-hours	Material
Wall framing: studs, 2"x 4", 16" O.C., 8' long	240 L.F.	4.0	75.50
Plates, single bottom, double top, 2" x 4"	80 L.F.	2.0	25.20
Headers, over windows & door, 2" x 8"	30 L.F.	1.5	20.70
Sheeting, plywood, 1/2" thick, 4' x 8' sheets	6 Sheets	3.0	95.25
Ceiling joists, 2" x 6", 16" O.C. 12' long	12 Ea.	2.0	67.95
Ceiling furring 1" x 3" strapping, 16" O.C.	150 L.F.	3.5	18.15
Insulation, ceiling, 6" thick, R-19, paperbacked	150 S.F.	1.0	65.35
Insulation, walls, 3-1/2" thick, R-11, paperbacked	200 S.F.	1.0	53.25
Sheetrock, walls & ceilings, 1/2" thick, 4' x 8' sheets taped & finished	18 Sheets	10.0	175.00
Door, exterior, 2 lite, colonial, 2'-8" x 6'-8"	1 Ea.	1.0	296.45
Window, 3 lite bay window, casement type, plastic clad, premium	1 Ea.	2.0	1210.00
Window, 2 lite casement window, plastic clad, premium	2 Ea.	2.0	484.00
Siding, No. 1 red cedar shingles, 7-1/2" exposure	190 S.F.	7.5	183.90
Roof vent, ridge type	12 L.F.	1.0	31.50
Trim, colonial casing, windows, door & base	120 L.F.	4.5	106.00
Paint, walls, ceiling and trim, primer and 2 coats	575 S.F.	7.0	90.45
Carpet, nylon antistatic	16 S.Y.	3.0	296.20
Pad, sponge rubber	16 S.Y.	1.0	43.55
Electrical work, 1 switch, 4 plugs	1 Lot	3.0	74.95
	Totals	60.0	$3413.35

Project Size	12' x 12'	Contractor's Fee Including Materials	$7080

Key to Abbreviations
C.Y. - cubic yard   Ea. - each   L.F. - linear foot   Pr. - pair   Sq. - square (100 square feet of area)
S.F. - square foot   S.Y. - square yard   V.L.F. - vertical linear foot

BREEZEWAY, NEW CONSTRUCTION

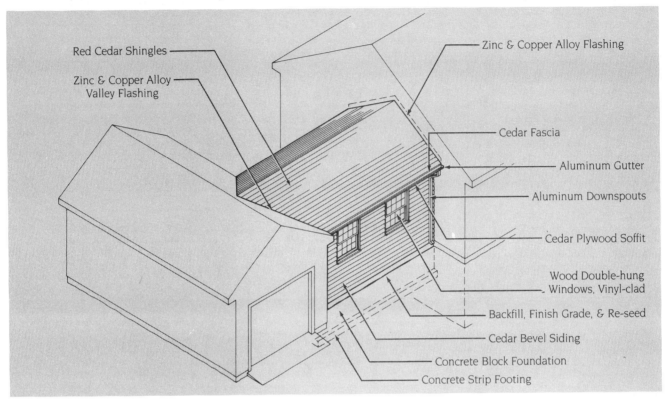

Red Cedar Shingles

Zinc & Copper Alloy
Valley Flashing

Zinc & Copper Alloy Flashing

Cedar Fascia

Aluminum Gutter

Aluminum Downspouts

Cedar Plywood Soffit

Wood Double-hung
Windows, Vinyl-clad

Backfill, Finish Grade, & Re-seed

Cedar Bevel Siding

Concrete Block Foundation

Concrete Strip Footing

This plan demonstrates how the area between a detached garage and house can be converted to living space. As detailed here, the new structure is connected to the end wall of the house and the side wall of the garage. Depending on the configuration of the existing structures, alternative designs and/or alignments may be required, with accompanying variations in cost. Because the breezeway room has to be constructed within established boundaries, it is a challenging project for do-it-yourselfers, but one that can be completed by those who have a reasonable level of remodeling skill. The results of the project will enhance your home's appearance and value and add considerably to its living area.

MATERIALS

The exterior components of this breezeway room are essentially the same as those used to construct the shell of a complete house. A foundation is required to support the load of the new structure, and framing, wall, and roof materials are employed

to complete the shell and make it weathertight. Materials for finishing the interior have not been listed in the plan, but you can get accurate estimates of their cost and installation time from the breezeway conversion plan in this section.

The foundation materials consist of a concrete footing and concrete block wall. Before the footing and wall are placed, excavation of the site is required to make room for the new foundation. Because of the close quarters between the existing structures, much of the digging will probably have to be done by hand, so plan accordingly and allow plenty of time for the job. After the foundation wall is in place, 2" x 8" joists and plywood decking are placed to frame the rough floor of the new room. Before installing the joists, cover the area with a vapor barrier, then insulate between the joists before laying the subfloor. The foundation and floor must be correctly installed to ensure a firm and level starting point for the rest of the project.

The walls of the breeezeway room are constructed from standard materials, including 2" x 4"s, sheathing, windows, a sliding glass door, and finished siding. Before the framing begins, allow some time to prepare the adjacent walls of the house and garage to receive the new materials. The siding must be stripped and, in some cases, a door or window may have to be removed or relocated if it will interfere with the framing process. The new partitions should be carefully laid out, since they must be erected to a predetermined height and length as established by the existing garage and house. This plan suggests 25/32" wood fiberboard for sheathing, but 5/8" CDX plywood can also be used at a slight increase in cost. Make sure that the wall framing is even with the face of the concrete to allow the siding to extend over the lip of the foundation for proper weather protection.

When the rough walls have been erected, the 2" x 6" ceiling joists should be installed to keep the new walls in place before the roof is framed. The placing of the rafters is the most challenging part of the project, and advanced framing skills and know-how are required to do the job, so get help if you have not done it before. Be sure that you check the condition of the garage shingles, support, and sheathing before you begin the framing for the new roof. Do not proceed with the installation of the new roof until any deficiencies have been corrected. Additional cost and time will be required if you are careless in stripping the old roofing, so work slowly and remove only as much as you have to. After 1/2" plywood has been placed on the rafters, the roofing material is installed to make the new structure weathertight. The cost for the roofing material and the time to install it will vary with different products. Because roofing is a specialty trade, even accomplished handymen might consider subcontracting this part of

the job. In most cases, a qualified tradesman will do this work faster and more effectively than even expert do-it-yourselfers.

After the roof and soffit are in place, the door and windows can be installed and the exterior walls sided. This plan suggests a high-quality vinyl-clad sliding glass door unit and four matching thermopane windows. Both of these products feature the advantages of low maintenance, neat design, and energy savings. Costs will vary considerably with the choice of alternative door and window products, so shop wisely and select quality units which will fit your design standards and budget. Like the roofing, the siding material for the new room should also match or complement the material on the house and garage, and it should be appropriately finished with paint or stain to blend with the existing structures. Gutters and downspouts are an integral part of the weatherproofing of the shell, so don't cut corners by leaving them out of the exterior finishing.

LEVEL OF DIFFICULTY

Building this breezeway project poses a major challenge to all do-it-yourselfers; however, it can serve as an excellent opportunity to advance your building skills. All of the basic operations in exterior house construction are required to complete the job, from foundation work and framing to exterior finish work like siding and gutter installations. Because the foundation involves specialized know-how, inexperienced do-it-yourselfers should consider hiring a qualified tradesman for this part of the project. Beginners should add 100% to the professional time for the basic tasks they take on, such as excavation, installing the sheathing, painting, and landscaping. Handymen should add 40% to the time for the basic tasks and wall framing, and 60% for roof framing. They should seriously consider hiring a tradesman for the foundation and roofing operations if they are inexperienced in these areas. Experts should add 10% to the professional time for all tasks, except the foundation work and roofing. The time increase for these jobs should be gaged according to the amount of experience they have in these areas.

WHAT TO WATCH OUT FOR

Hiring specialty contractors often makes sense even if you have experience and skill enough to complete the job on your own. The roofing for this project is a good example. A capable roofer can close in this structure quickly and thoroughly, even though there is a considerable amount of flashing involved. The correct installation of the valley is particularly important to prevent leaking and major water damage to the interior later on. A professional roofing job ensures that such problems won't arise.

SUMMARY

This breezeway plan demonstrates how the space between the house and garage can be converted to a comfortable interior living area. If your property is laid out in the appropriate way, much of the work can be done by do-it-yourselfers, with considerable savings in labor costs.

BREEZEWAY, NEW CONSTRUCTION

Description	Quantity	Man-hours	Material
Excavate by hand for footing, 4' wide, 4' deep	19 C.Y.	19.0	0.00
Footings, 8" thick x 16" wide x 32'	2 C.Y.	5.5	167.00
Foundation, 8" concrete block, 3'-4" high	120 Block	10.5	181.50
Floor framing, sill plate, 2" x 6"	32 L.F.	1.0	15.10
Joists, 2" x 8" x 10', 16" O.C.,	160 L.F.	2.5	110.35
Insulation, 6" thick, R-19	160 S.F.	1.0	75.50
Subfloor, 5/8" x 4' x 8' plywood	5 Sheets	2.5	85.20
Wall framing, 2" x 4" x 8', 16" O.C. studs and plates	32 L.F.	5.0	99.10
Headers over openings, 2" x 8"	48 L.F.	2.5	33.10
Sheathing for walls, wood fiberboard, 25/32" thick, 4' x 8' sheets	8 Sheets	3.5	92.95
Roof framing, joists, 2" x 6" x 10', 16" O.C.	130 L.F.	2.0	61.35
Ridge board, 1" x 8" x 12',	24 L.F.	1.0	8.15
Rafters, 2" x 6" x 12', 16" O.C.	312 L.F.	5.0	147.25
Valleys rafters, 2" x 6"	32 L.F.	1.0	15.10
Sub-fascia, 2" x 8" x 16'	32 L.F.	2.5	22.05
Sheathing for roof, 1/2" thick, 4' x 8' sheets	15 Sheets	5.5	238.15
Felt paper, 15 lb.	500 S.F.	1.0	16.95
Shingles, #1 red cedar, 5-1/2" exposure, on roof	5 Sq.	16.0	665.50
Flashing, zinc & copper alloy, .020" thick	140 S.F.	7.5	296.45
Fascia, 1" x 8" rough-sawn cedar	32 L.F.	1.0	26.35
Soffit, 3/8" rough-sawn cedar plywood, stained	48 S.F.	1.5	62.15
Gutters & downspouts, aluminum	52 L.F.	3.5	52.25
Windows, wood, plastic-clad, insulated 3' x 4'	4 Ea.	4.0	847.00
Sliding glass door, wood, vinyl-clad, 6' x 6'-10"	1 Ea	4.0	844.60
Siding, cedar-beveled, rough-sawn, stained	220 S.F.	7.5	516.45
Backfill, finish grade & re-seed	1 Lot	13.0	12.10
Totals		129.0	$4691.65

Project Size	10' x 16'	Contractor's Fee Including Materials	$11,200

Key to Abbreviations
C.Y. - cubic yard   Ea. - each   L.F. - linear foot   Pr. - pair   Sq. - square (100 square feet of area)
S.F. - square foot   S.Y. - square yard   V.L.F. - vertical linear foot

SINGLE CARPORT, ATTACHED

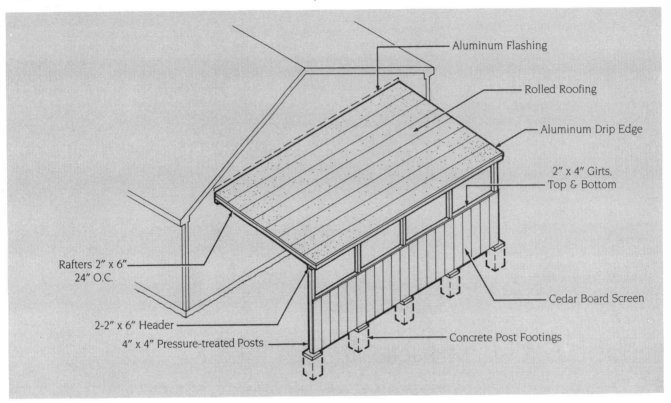

Aluminum Flashing

Rolled Roofing

Aluminum Drip Edge

2" x 4" Girts,
Top & Bottom

Rafters 2" x 6"
24" O.C.

Cedar Board Screen

2-2" x 6" Header

4" x 4" Pressure-treated Posts

Concrete Post Footings

Carports offer a simple and economical alternative to the more costly framing and finish work required for conventional garages. In addition to requiring less material, carports are also easier to build than garages. Their uncomplicated design and structure offer the opportunity for do-it-yourselfers to do all or much of the work on their own. Free-standing carports require considerably more skill and know-how to erect than those that are attached to the house, but both projects can be completed by handymen who have basic construction skills and knowledge. This plan demonstrates how a one-car facility can be built for modest expense. Many do-it-yourselfers can complete the job for the cost of the materials.

MATERIALS

The components of this carport project are standard construction materials that can be purchased at building supply outlets. Try to buy all of the

materials at the same place, and be sure to make arrangements for curb delivery as part of the purchase price. Because the carport is attached to the house on one side and open at either end, materials are needed only for the side opposite the house and the roof. Both of these sections are basic in their design and thus, are fairly easy to build, providing that you lay them out correctly, follow good carpentry practices, and work slowly on tasks that are new to you.

The side of the structure serves two purposes: providing the support for one end of the roof and supporting the girts to which the siding is fastened. Because the roof structure is large and heavy, the five 4" x 4" posts which support it must be set in concrete footings at least 3' deep. Precise placement of the posts is important, so take time to space them at even intervals, align them with a stringline, and plumb them with a

level. If you place the 4" x 4"s in concrete, be sure to use pressure-treated lumber as recommended in the plan. Standard grade 4" x 4"s can also be used at reduced cost, but they should not be set in concrete and require fastening to anchors preset in the footings.

After the posts have been placed, the roof can be framed with 2" x 6"s, set 24" on center, and doubled headers. This roof framing task is the trickiest operation in the project, so get some help if you have not done it before. Be sure to cut the joists at the correct angle on the house end and at the reverse angle on the other end. Also, prepare the house wall to receive the roof assembly by cutting back the siding to the sheathing and arranging for the roof flashing. The method of installing the flashing will depend on the type of siding, so costs may vary for this operation. At the other end of the roof frame, temporary support should be provided for the first few joists before the headers are positioned and fastened. Be sure to square the frame before laying the 1/2" plywood roof sheathing and to stagger the termination seams of the plywood as you are placing it. Rolled roofing material should be used in place of asphalt shingles, because of the flat pitch of the shed roof. The installation of this type of roofing can go quickly with the right methods and equipment. With a little advice and instruction beforehand, and the right tools, most handymen can undertake the job, even if they have no prior experience with rolled roofing. Be sure to place the drip edge on all open sides of the roof before you apply the roofing material and to install flashing on the house side.

Once the roof is completed, the girts can be placed between the posts, and then a 5' high screen attached to them to make up the side of the carport. This plan suggests rough-sawn 1" x 12" cedar siding boards, but many options are available to suit the style and decor of the house, including various wood sheet goods, and fiberglass and metal panels. The cost of these products varies widely, as does their installation time.

No consideration has been given in the plan for the cost of the floor surface within the carport because it is assumed that a driveway is already in place. If a floor surface is needed, the cost of asphalt pavement, concrete, or gravel, and the time to install it, will have to be added to the project estimate.

LEVEL OF DIFFICULTY

This carport plan is a manageable exterior project for most handymen, including beginners who have the time to work slowly and are willing to learn as they go. Some of the tasks involved in the building process require knowledge that beginners may not have, but the required skills can be learned by trial and error and proper guidance from an experienced builder. Two of the jobs within this project are critical: the precise setting and leveling of the support posts and accurate layout and placement of the roof frame. If these two installations are correct, the rest of the job should go smoothly. If you are a beginner, be sure to get some assistance, particularly on these and other unfamiliar tasks. Handymen and experts should be able to handle all of the tasks required in the project, but may need to learn the details of roll-roofing installation before they begin that part of the job. Generally, beginners should double the professional time for all tasks; handymen should add 40%; and experts, about 10%.

SINGLE CARPORT, ATTACHED

Description	Quantity	Man-hours	Material
Excavate post holes, incl. layout	5 Ea.	7.5	0.00
Concrete, field mix, 1 C.F. per bag, for posts	5 Bags	2.5	15.30
Posts, pressure-treated, 4" x 4" x 10'	50 L.F.	2.0	56.90
Headers, 2" x 6", doubled	96 L.F.	3.5	59.25
Joists/rafters, 2" x 6" x 12', 24" O.C.	132 L.F.	4.5	81.45
Sheathing, 5/8" plywood, 4' x 8' sheets	288 S.F.	3.5	153.35
Roofing, rolled, 30 lb., asphalt-coated felt	3 Sq.	2.5	93.90
Drip edge, aluminum, 5"	48 L.F.	1.0	8.70
Girts, 2" x 4", for screening panel	40 L.F.	1.5	16.45
Siding boards, cedar, rough-sawn, 1" x 12", board on board	110 S.F.	3.5	150.40
Paint, primer & 2 coats, all exposed wood	625 S.F.	12.0	151.25
	Totals	44.0	$786.95

Project Size	11' x 21'	Contractor's Fee Including Materials	$2380

Key to Abbreviations
C.Y. - cubic yard   Ea. - each   L.F. - linear foot   Pr. - pair   Sq. - square (100 square feet of area)
S.F. - square foot   S.Y. - square yard   V.L.F. - vertical linear foot

WHAT TO WATCH OUT FOR

With the investment of a little more time and money, carports can be made to double as screened-in sitting and eating enclosures. Once the carport structure, as described in this plan, has been completed, screen panels can be made up to fit the open areas in the rear end and side of the enclosure. The front end of the carport can be fitted with roll-down screening that can be raised when the facility is used to shelter the car. These modifications will increase the cost of the project, but they can be done at any time after the carport itself is finished and will add considerably to the practical use of the enclosure.

SUMMARY

A carport can serve as a practical alternative to a full garage at a fraction of the cost for both materials and labor. Because of the basic design of this project, most handymen can complete this home improvement for only the cost of the materials.

DOUBLE CARPORT, FREESTANDING

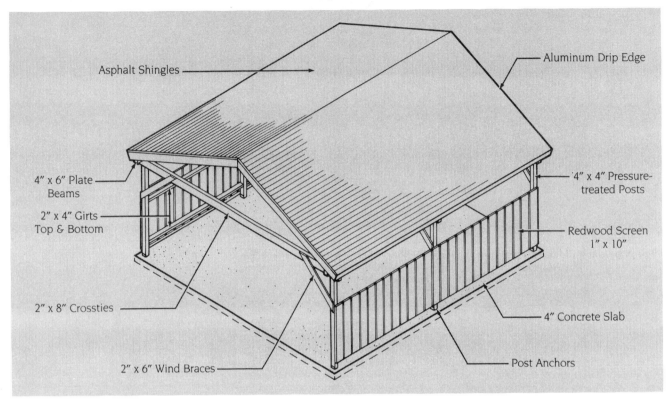

Asphalt Shingles

Aluminum Drip Edge

4" x 6" Plate Beams

2" x 4" Girts Top & Bottom

2" x 8" Crossties

4" x 4" Pressure-treated Posts

Redwood Screen 1" x 10"

4" Concrete Slab

2" x 6" Wind Braces

Post Anchors

Carports can be relatively small, simple enclosures, like the one-car, attached model on the previous pages, or they can be constructed on a larger scale in freestanding design. This plan demonstrates how a two-car facility can be economically built by using post-and-beam construction methods. Although the carport in this plan is large in size, with over 400 square feet of floor area, the simplicity of its design makes it a reasonable undertaking for handymen who are experienced in the use of tools and have a fundamental knowledge of carpentry. Because of the size of this structure, beginners should leave much of the post-and-beam support installation and roof framing to the professional, but they are encouraged to tackle some of the other tasks in the project. Generally, skilled handymen and experts can complete the entire project, with the exception of the concrete floor.

MATERIALS

The materials used in this project start with ready-mixed concrete for the floor

and the conventional components of post-and-beam construction, including 4" x 6"s and 4" x 8"s (or doubled 2" x 8"s). Standard grade 2" x 6" rafters, plywood sheathing, and asphalt shingles are needed for the roofing, and siding material is required for screening. All of these products, except the ready-mixed concrete, are readily available at lumber yards and building supply outlets, so do some comparison-shopping before you buy. Also before you finalize the purchase agreement, make sure that arrangements have been made for curb delivery. Although this structure is simple in design, the materials used in its construction are heavy and require trucking.

The preparation for the wood structure begins with the excavation for and placement of the concrete floor. There are several important aspects in this procedure which, when closely monitored, can help the rest of the project go smoothly. The first is to double check the square and level of the 2" x 6" form before the concrete is placed. The second is to be sure that the post anchors for the 4" x 6"s are set in precise position and alignment as

they are embedded in the concrete. Remember that the wood structure will be supported by the slab and aligned according to the position of the anchors, so measure and square the layout carefully. If you are unfamiliar with this type of concrete placement, get some assistance from an experienced person or subcontract this part of the project to a professional.

The post-and-beam construction of the roof support requires basic carpentry know-how and some engineering skills as well. The three post and crosstie assemblies can be laid out and fabricated on the slab before being raised and positioned on the anchors and temporarily braced. Be sure that they are plumb, level, and square before the 4" x 6" plate beams are placed and fastened. Some skilled handymen and experts can tackle this operation, but beginners and handymen with limited building skills should seek the help of a more experienced friend or hire a professional for this procedure.

The roof frame is constructed of 2" x 6" rafters, set 24" on center, and a 2" x 8" ridge board. Like the post-and-beam support system, the roof framing requires a fundamental knowledge of carpentry and advanced building skills. If you are unfamiliar with the process of cutting and setting rafters, get some instruction beforehand, and be sure to have some helpers available. Remember, too, that you will be working 8' to 12' off the ground when placing the rafters, so make arrangements to rent or borrow some staging, tressel ladders and planks, or other means of working safely and efficiently at the 12' ridge board height. An alternative to installing the rafters is to purchase manufactured 2" x 4" trusses and place them 24" on center. The cost for materials will be higher, but the roof will go up faster.

The 1/2" plywood sheathing is placed on the rafters after the roof frame has been squared and fastened. The aluminum drip edge, which is installed before the roofing is laid, is an inexpensive but important item, as it provides run-off clearance for rain water and creates a straight, neat, finished edge for the roofing. Experts and most handymen should be able to handle this roofing job, as it consists of straight runs with no valleys, flashing, or other challenging obstacles.

Because the finished sides of the carport should conform to the style and decor of your house, you can select from many different materials, including plywood products, siding boards, and metal and fiberglass panels. This plan suggests that the 1" x 10" redwood tongue-and-groove siding be placed on the 2" x 4" girts as screening and then stained or painted. The post-and-beam supports, girts, rafters, underside of the roof deck, and the fascia board are also covered with two coats of stain or paint.

LEVEL OF DIFFICULTY

This carport plan calls for a moderate to advanced level of building expertise and carpentry skills. In addition, the size of the structure and the post-and-beam layout requirements involve complex planning that may put parts of the project out of reach for beginners and many handymen.

After the supports and roof frame are in place, most handymen can finish the job, including the installation of the roof sheathing and shingles. Be sure to get some instruction in the roofing process if you have not laid shingles before. Straight roofs are not that hard to install, and a good start can make it a fairly simple operation.

Beginners and handymen with no related experience should hire a professional for the concrete slab installation. Experts and handymen should allow extra time for a careful layout of the forms and should arrange to have several helpers on hand when the concrete is placed. Accomplished handymen and experts should add 100% and 50%, respectively, to the professional time for the slab installation, including the form work. They should add 40% and 10%, respectively, for all other tasks. Beginners should not attempt the slab, post-and-beam support, or roof-framing jobs. They should double the professional time for all other tasks, providing they are given ample instruction before they start. They should be aware that power tools are required for some parts of this project and plan accordingly.

WHAT TO WATCH OUT FOR

The concrete surface that serves as the floor of the carport is an important feature of the structure and must be correctly placed. If you are installing it on your own, be sure to set the forms accurately so that the edges of the slab are level and square. Metal-rod or wire reinforcement, a sub-base of granular material, and a plastic vapor barrier are also necessary for correct installation. Remember, too, that provisions for surface-water drainage should be made by crowning the slab. Wind-driven rain or snow, and water from wet or snow-covered vehicles can collect and puddle in low spots on the surface, but these problems can be avoided with proper finishing of the floor. Seek help from a cement mason or concrete contractor if you are inexperienced and need assistance in placing the slab.

SUMMARY

Although this double carport is fairly basic in design, it is a challenging undertaking for most do-it-yourselfers. It is not out of reach, however, with help and guidance. This project is a good way to gain experience while creating a practical addition to your home.

DOUBLE CARPORT, FREESTANDING

Description	Quantity	Man-hours	Material
Grading, by hand, for slab area	53 S.Y.	2.0	0.00
Edge forms for floor slab	86 L.F.	5.0	20.80
Concrete floor slab, 4" thick, 3000 psi complete	460 S.F.	14.5	879.45
Post anchors, embedded in slab	6 Ea.	0.5	2.45
Posts, pressure-treated, 4" x 6" x 8'	48 L.F.	2.5	81.90
Crossties, 2" x 8" x 22'	132 L.F.	5.0	116.60
Plate beams, 4" x 6" x 12'	48 L.F.	2.0	81.90
Ridge board, 2" x 8", x 12'	24 L.F.	1.0	21.20
Fascia board, 2" x 8" x 12'	48 L.F.	2.0	42.40
Rafters, 2" x 6" x 12', 24" O.C.	288 L.F.	9.5	177.75
Sheathing, 1/2" plywood, 4' x 8' sheets	544 S.F.	6.0	269.90
Drip edge, aluminum, 5"	96 L.F.	2.0	17.45
Shingles, asphalt, 235 lb. per square	6 Sq.	9.0	218.90
Braces, 2" x 6" x 4'	40 L.F.	1.5	24.70
Girts, 2" x 4" for screening panels	84 L.F.	2.5	34.55
Screening, redwood channel siding, 1" x 10"	210 S.F.	6.0	304.90
Paint, primer & 2 coats	1100 S.F.	21.0	266.20
Stain, 2 coats, brushwork on screen	420 S.F.	5.0	81.30
Totals		97.0	$2642.35

Project Size	20' x 21'	Contractor's Fee Including Materials	$7200

Key to Abbreviations
C.Y. - cubic yard   Ea. - each   L.F. - linear foot   Pr. - pair   Sq. - square (100 square feet of area)
S.F. - square foot   S.Y. - square yard   V.L.F. - vertical linear foot

GROUND LEVEL DECK

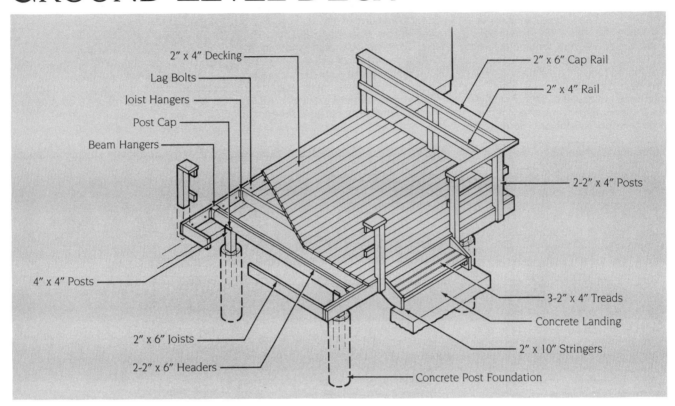

2" x 4" Decking
Lag Bolts
Joist Hangers
Post Cap
Beam Hangers
4" x 4" Posts
2" x 6" Joists
2-2" x 6" Headers

2" x 6" Cap Rail
2" x 4" Rail
2-2" x 4" Posts
3-2" x 4" Treads
Concrete Landing
2" x 10" Stringers
Concrete Post Foundation

The addition of a deck is one of the easiest and most economical ways to improve the exterior of your home. Basic single-level decks are usually uncomplicated in their construction and are, therefore, manageable undertakings for homeowners who have limited building experience. This deck plan demonstrates how an attractive and functional facility can be constructed for a modest investment of both time and money. Because the deck is relatively small in area and built at ground level, it is an ideal project for beginners and handymen to gain experience in home improvement.

MATERIALS

Most decks built at foundation or ground level are comprised of the same basic components. These vary in size and number, according to the method of installation, the dimensions of the structure, its height above grade, and the complexity of its design. The materials used are basic

decking products available at most building supply outlets, but they vary in quality and price, so do some comparison shopping before you buy. When you purchase the materials, select them yourself, if possible, looking for straight deck boards and sound support members. You should also clarify the conditions of delivery at the time of the purchase, since most suppliers will make curb deliveries free of charge for a complete deck order.

All of the wood products for this deck are specially designed for use in exterior structures which are exposed to the elements. Pressure-treated deck materials are more costly than conventional, untreated components, but they are a much better choice. The additional expense for pressure-treated wood is well worth the investment to guarantee the deck's longevity.

The support system for this 8' x 10' ground-level deck consists of footings, 4" x 4" posts, and the frame, which is comprised of 2" x 6" joists and

headers. Before you begin the excavation for the footings, lay out their locations accurately to ensure a square and level support system for the rest of the structure. Several methods can be employed to establish the location of the support posts and their footings, but one of the most accurate is to approximate the layout with batter boards at the four corners, and then establish, by the use of stringlines, equal diagonals. Failure to place the footings and posts precisely at square with each other and with the side of your house will adversely affect the rest of the project. Double check the post locations before you set them in concrete and be sure to use cylindrical "tube" forms for the foundations. These are available at most building supply yards and are well worth the price. Review the layout of the 2" x 6" frame as well, to be sure that the doubled joists are correctly aligned with the 4" x 4" supports.

The decking suggested in this plan consists of 2" x 4"s laid across the frame and fastened with galvanized nails. However, decking materials of another thickness, width, or edge type can also be installed. Remember that the decking itself is the most visible component of the structure, so additional expense for aesthetic reasons may be a worthwhile investment. This deck plan includes a basic post-and-rail design for the railing system. It is one of the simplest railing designs to install, and it creates an attractive border with a 2" x 6" cap, which can double as a convenience shelf or a support for planters. More elaborate railings are also possible, but most of them require more materials and installation time. The system in this plan is very economical and basic in its design, but it is not child-proof. Safer, more expensive railings should be installed in decks that are high enough to create a safety hazard for small children. Stairway railings are not included in this plan because of its one-step access, but they should be installed at extra cost on deck stairways of more than one step. The posts for the railings should be constructed from 4" x 4"s which are mortised into the frame and then fastened with lag bolts. Although the fitting of the posts takes a little longer and the lag bolts are more expensive than nails, the finished installation looks better, is more secure, and will last longer.

GROUND LEVEL DECK

Description	Quantity	Man-hours	Material
Layout, excavate post holes	4 Ea.	4.0	0.00
Concrete, field mix, 1 C.F. per bag, for posts, incl. 8" dia. forms	4 Bag	7.0	102.90
Deck material, pressure treated lumber,			
Posts, 4" x 4" x 4'	16 L.F.	1.0	18.20
Headers, 2" x 6" x 10'	40 L.F.	1.5	24.70
Joists, 2" x 6" x 8'	72 L.F.	2.5	44.45
Decking, 2" x 4" x 10'	280 L.F.	8.5	115.20
Stair material, stringers, 2" x 10" x 3'	6 L.F.	0.5	7.10
Treads, 2" x 4" x 3'-6", 3 per tread	12 L.F.	0.5	4.95
Landing, precast concrete, 14" wide	4 L.F.	1.0	32.90
Railing material, posts, 2" x 4" x 3'	30 L.F.	1.0	12.35
Railings, 2" x 4" stock	52 L.F.	1.5	21.40
Cap rail, 2" x 6" stock	26 L.F.	1.0	16.05
Joist hangers, 18 ga. galvanized	7 Ea.	0.5	4.65
Nails, #10d galvanized	8 LB.	0.0	6.80
Bolts, 3/8" lag bolts, long	18 Ea.	0.0	17.20
Totals		30.5	$428.85

Project Size	8' x 10'	Contractor's Fee Including Materials	$1560

Key to Abbreviations
C.Y. - cubic yard   Ea. - each   L.F. - linear foot   Pr. - pair   Sq. - square (100 square feet of area)
S.F. - square foot   S.Y. - square yard   V.L.F. - vertical linear foot

LEVEL OF DIFFICULTY

Because this deck plan is basic in its design and constructed at ground level, it is an approachable project for beginners and less skilled handymen. A few basic carpentry skills, along with some experience in measuring, plumbing, and leveling, are required. Beginners should seek advice before they start and as the project progresses, and should double the professional time for all tasks involved in this project. Handymen and experts should add 30% and 10% respectively, to the estimated man-hours for the installation process.

WHAT TO WATCH OUT FOR

Because this deck is built at ground level with limited access to the terrain underneath, precautions should be taken to restrict unwanted vegetation from growing in this area. Some weeds and hardy grasses can establish themselves under the deck, eventually restricting ventilation and creating an eyesore. Decks which are built in sunny locations are particularly susceptible to this problem. To prevent this unwanted growth, remove about 3" to 4" of topsoil from the area to be covered by the deck and then cover it with a layer of polyethylene. Place enough gravel over the plastic to bring the entire area to grade level. This procedure will increase the cost of the job, but it will prevent a problem that is difficult to correct after the deck is in place.

SUMMARY

This basic deck project provides an excellent opportunity for inexperienced do-it-yourselfers to improve their construction skills. With some advice and instruction, they can complete this deck for the cost of materials, while adding an attractive, functional, and valuable addition to their homes.

ELEVATED DECK

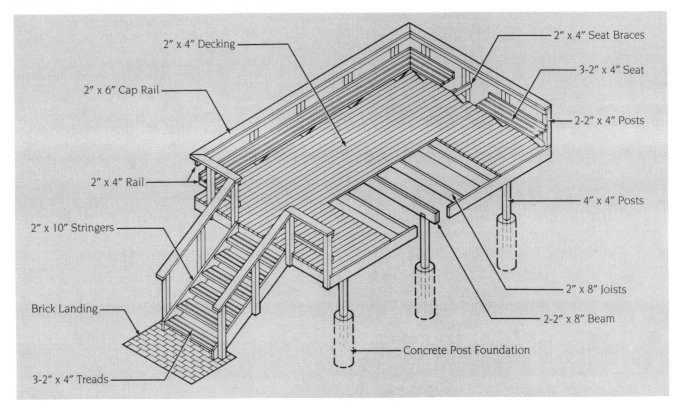

2" x 4" Decking

2" x 6" Cap Rail

2" x 4" Rail

2" x 10" Stringers

Brick Landing

3-2" x 4" Treads

2" x 4" Seat Braces

3-2" x 4" Seat

2-2" x 4" Posts

4" x 4" Posts

2" x 8" Joists

2-2" x 8" Beam

Concrete Post Foundation

As in any other exterior home improvement, a deck's size and design should be determined by its intended use, the type and size of the house to which it will be attached, and budget limitations. Sometimes a large deck is most suitable for the needs and style of the house, but the cost of professional installation is prohibitive. This plan demonstrates how a 10' x 16' deck, complete with stairway and two-sided bench-railing, can be constructed for a reasonable cost by the do-it-yourselfer. Because the deck is only 4' above grade, it is still a manageable project for handymen who do not have extensive building skills.

MATERIALS

The durability and ecomomy of pressure-treated lumber has helped to make decks a popular home improvement in recent years. The components of this deck are all constructed from pressure-treated products which are readily available at most building supply outlets. Shop

around for the materials, both for quality and price. In making your selection, try to stay away from boards with excessive knots, voids, twisting, warping, or cupping. Make sure that you arrange delivery, as lumber for this size deck does require trucking. Such a purchase will probably warrant free curb delivery, providing the site is a reasonable distance from the supplier.

The support system and frame for this deck plan consist of six 4" x 4" posts set in 3' concrete footings. The 2" x 8" joists are spaced 2' on center, with doubled support joists at 6' intervals, and doubled 16' headers. It is most important that you lay out the footing and post locations accurately, since the rest of the structure depends on their alignment. If you are inexperienced with the placement of footings and setting of support posts, do some research or seek professional help. Errant placement of the posts is difficult to correct once the concrete footing has set, so double check all measurements as you go and be sure

to use 8" diameter "tube" forms for the foundations. Before you begin construction of the frame, review the layout template to be sure that the doubled support joists will be correctly aligned when they are placed. The frame for this deck, like that of the redwood deck, can be partially constructed on level ground and then raised into position to be finished. Be sure to square all corners and tie them with strapping before you lag the inside headers into the sill and start laying the deck.

Because 2" x 4" decking is used in this plan, fewer joists are required than for thinner deck boards. If you intend to use 1" boards, however, the spacing of the joists will have to be reduced to 16", their number increased, and the layout of the doubled joists changed accordingly. All of these modifications will affect the cost as will changing the pattern of the decking. Designs, like diagonal decking, create attractive surfaces, but they waste material and demand more installation time. If you placing the decking in the conventional manner, be sure to measure accurately and make precise saw cuts; the cut-off pieces will be used later to fill out the courses. Use a spacer to keep the opening between courses at about 1/8" or slightly wider. This space is an important feature of the surface, as it allows for the drainage of rainwater, helps to ventilate the structure, and prevents the build-up of moisture-laden matter between the deck boards. Take time to align the nail heads by snapping chalklines before you fasten the surface, as they are one of the most visible features on the deck.

There are many options for the railing, bench, and stairway design. Standard 4" x 4" posts and 2" x 4" rails are used for the most economical railing system, but 2" x 2" balusters can also be installed at more expense to enhance the railing design or to make it child-safe. Costs can be cut by eliminating the bench altogether, or by reducing its length and limiting it to one side of the deck. Seek assistance from a qualified person if you have not installed a stairway before. Even though this one consists of only six steps, its assembly does require some skill and know-how. Safety is a primary consideration for any set of stairs, and consistent vertical spacing from tread to tread is one way of ensuring it. Proper support and correct placement of stringers and stairway railings are also critical safety considerations. Get some help when it comes time to accomplish these important carpentry tasks.

LEVEL OF DIFFICULTY

This deck can be built by most handymen who have a reasonable level of skill in home improvement projects. Its 10' x 16' size makes it a major project, but the work time can be spread out because of the convenience of the location. A basic knowledge of carpentry is needed for the installation of all of the deck's components. If you are willing to work slowly and seek guidance as you progress, many of these skills can be acquired and developed as you go. In short, it is an excellent project for learning more about carpentry and building. Beginners can tackle this deck, but only if they are given thorough instruction before they start and plenty of guidance during the construction. They should plan on tripling the estimated times, even with professional assistance. Handymen should add 40% to the professional time for the framing and decking tasks and 75% for the footing, post, railing, bench, and stairway installations. Experts should add 10% to the estimated man-hours for all parts this project.

WHAT TO WATCH OUT FOR

No cost has been included in the estimate for the painting, staining, or finishing of the deck because none is required. The factory coloring of the pressure-treated lumber will gradually change to a natural wood color over several years' time. If you want to finish the deck, transparent stain looks good and requires little upkeep. Pressure-treated wood can be painted or coated with heavy-bodied stain, but regular maintenance will be needed to preserve its appearance. If you plan to finish the deck with any of these coverings, consider pre-painting or pre-staining the material with a base coat before construction, and a finish coat after the deck is in place. Decks are surprisingly difficult to paint and this method assures at least basic coverage of hard-to-get-at places like the edges of the decking, and the undersides of the bench, railings, and stair treads.

SUMMARY

Although this deck project involves a large-sized structure, it can be built by most handymen who are willing to invest the time, get help in starting out, and seek guidance as they go. By doing the work on your own, you can produce an attractive and functional home improvement for the cost of the material.

ELEVATED DECK

Description	Quantity	Man-hours	Material
Layout, excavate post holes	6 Ea.	6.0	0.00
Concrete, field mix, 1 C.F. per bag, for posts, incl. 8" dia. forms	6 Bags	10.5	154.35
Deck material, pressure treated lumber			
posts, 4" x 4" x 7'	48 L.F.	2.0	54.60
Headers, 2" x 8" x 16'	64 L.F.	2.5	39.50
Joists, 2" x 8" x 10'	120 L.F.	4.5	74.05
Decking, 2" x 4" x 12'	576 L.F.	17.0	236.95
Stair material, stringers 2" x 10" x 10'	20 L.F.	1.0	23.75
Treads, 2" x 4" x 3'-6", 3 per tread	70 L.F.	2.0	28.80
Landing brick on sand, no mortar	16 S.F.	3.0	131.65
Railing material, posts, 4" x 4" x 3'	48 L.F.	2.5	19.75
Railings, 2" x 4" stock	96 L.F.	5.0	39.50
Cap rail, 2" x 6" stock	48 L.F.	1.5	29.65
Bench material, seat braces, 2" x 4"	108 L.F.	3.0	44.45
Joist hangers, 18 ga. galvanized	12 Ea.	1.0	8.00
Nails, #10d galvanized	15 LB.	0.0	12.70
Bolts, 3/8" lag bolts, long	28 Ea.	0.0	26.75
	Totals	61.5	$924.45

Project Size	10' x 16'	Contractor's Fee Including Materials	$3250

Key to Abbreviations
C.Y. - cubic yard   Ea. - each   L.F. - linear foot   Pr. - pair   Sq. - square (100 square feet of area)
S.F. - square foot   S.Y. - square yard   V.L.F. - vertical linear foot

ELEVATED DECK, REDWOOD,

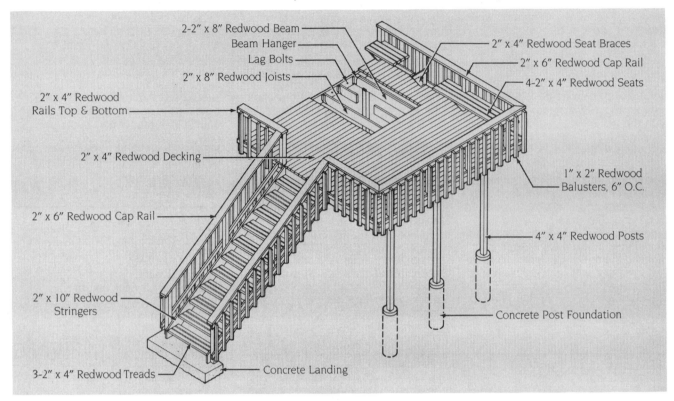

2-2" x 8" Redwood Beam
Beam Hanger
Lag Bolts
2" x 8" Redwood Joists

2" x 4" Redwood Seat Braces
2" x 6" Redwood Cap Rail
4-2" x 4" Redwood Seats

2" x 4" Redwood Rails Top & Bottom

2" x 4" Redwood Decking

2" x 6" Redwood Cap Rail

1" x 2" Redwood Balusters, 6" O.C.

4" x 4" Redwood Posts

2" x 10" Redwood Stringers

Concrete Post Foundation

3-2" x 4" Redwood Treads

Concrete Landing

Because of its attractive grain and coloring and its ability to resist rot and deterioration, redwood has been popularly used as a deck material for many years. However, it is more costly than standard deck lumber and may be difficult to get, except by special order, in some areas of the country. This plan presents a deluxe 12' x 12' redwood deck with a built-in perimeter bench and bannistered safety railing. Although it is more expensive and has a more complex design than some of the other decks in this section, it is an improvement that will add beauty, comfort, and value to your home. Skilled handymen and experts should be able to handle the construction of this deck, but beginners and those with limited carpentry skills should hire a contractor to do much of the work. Because of the high cost of the material and the advanced construction skills required to install the stairway and bench-railing system, do-it-yourselfers should use discretion in tackling this project.

MATERIALS

The materials used in this plan consist of the basic deck components in redwood, including 4" x 4" support posts, 2" x 8" joists and headers for the frame, 2" x 4" decking, and 2" stock in varying widths for the bench, railing, and stairway. Galvanized joist supports, 10d nails, and 3/8" lag bolts are also included in the design of the deck to ensure sturdy fastening, safety, and durability of the structure. Many other types of galvanized brackets, fittings, and fasteners are also available at reasonable extra cost if needed for special conditions or additions to this design.

Because this deck measures 12' in length, six footings and support posts must be installed. Be sure to square the four corners before locating the post positons . Also, make sure that you follow the plan and include six, not four, supports for this deck.

Economizing by eliminating structural components, even for a deck, will cost you more money and aggravation in the long run because of sagging, loosening of the structure, and other conditions which require repair.

As with any deck, but especially because this one is located 8' above ground, it is important that the deck frame be plumb, level, and square. Before fastening the joists, review the accuracy of the layout to be sure that the doubled joists are precisely aligned with the 4" x 4" support posts. This alignment must be exact to ensure safe bearing of the load of the structure. Before laying the decking, double check the frame for level and square. Then tie the outside corners temporarily to hold them at right angles while you place the surface material.

The 2" x 4" decking suggested in this plan provides an attractive and durable surface, but redwood boards of other widths can also be used. The deck boards may also be laid diagonally to add a different design feature to the surface. There is more waste of materials when the decking is installed in this way, so plan on about 25% in additional cost for the deck boards if you want them laid at 45 degrees. As you place the decking, allow proper spacing between courses, place the cupped side of the boards down, and use enough nails. To keep the rows of nail heads straight, lay the entire deck with minimum fastenings, and then complete the nailing by following chalk lines.

The built-in railing bench included in this deck plan can be altered to suit personal taste and the practical needs of the structure. The railing consists of 2" x 2" balusters set 6" on center, 2" x 4" rails and 4" x 4" fitted and lagged posts. The balusters take time to install and add considerably to the materials cost, but they are an important safety feature in any deck set this high off the ground. Check local ordinances for deck railing standards before you design the railing systems. Note that the stairway also includes balustered railings and

wide treads for safe access. Skill and time is required to cut and install standard stringers. Risers can also be added for safety, but they will boost the cost and may conflict with the open and airy motif desired in most deck designs. If you are inexperienced in any of the finish carpentry tasks required in the project, especially the stairs, balustered railing, and bench, seek professional help.

LEVEL OF DIFFICULTY

This deck project requires a considerable level of carpentry skill and building know-how. Several features of this model make it a more demanding do-it-yourself project than other deck plans included in this section. One is the expense of the redwood material, which may be twice the cost of conventional deck lumber. Mistakes in measuring, layout, and cutting can cost you more, so work slowly and carefully. Another factor is the deck's height off the ground, which requires working from a step ladder and causes general inconvenience in some of the operations. A third challenging feature is the finish work required for the bench, railing, and stairway installations, all of which

demand skillful carpentry. Beginners and less skilled handymen should not attempt to complete this project on their own. They should hire a contractor to accomplish the framing and finish work and add 100% to the estimated man-hours for tasks which they intend to take on. Handymen and experts should add 50% and 20%, respectively, for the support, framing, and decking jobs and 100% and 40% for the bench, railing and stairway installations. The increase in time for these finish tasks allows for a slower work pace. This helps to minimize the waste of materials.

WHAT TO WATCH OUT FOR

If the deck is 4' or less above level grade, the installation of the supports is accomplished fairly easily; but if the deck is higher than 4' or situated over sloping terrain, the job becomes more difficult. This redwood deck, although it is moderate in size at 12' x 12', is a challenging project because of its placement at 8' above ground level. Be sure to allow for extra time because of this inconvenience. Remember that the frame is built in place or in sections, and not conveniently laid out and constructed at ground level. Other materials also have to be raised to deck level before they are placed. Plan to use a stepladder for some of the railing work, as much of the layout and fastening can be accomplished more efficiently from outside the structure. One way of saving time on both the frame and railing installations is to work with a helper. With two workers, the joists can be placed without one person having to move from end to end of the frame as each piece is installed. The railing installation can proceed more efficiently with one worker inside the perimeter and another on a stepladder outside.

SUMMARY

This redwood deck is a challenging endeavor for most do-it-yourselfers, but it is an attractive structure which will add comfort and value to your home. If you work patiently and seek advice as you go, the results of your efforts will make the undertaking worthwhile.

ELEVATED DECK, REDWOOD

Description	Quantity	Man-hours	Material
Layout, excavate post holes	6 Ea.	6.0	0.00
Concrete, field mix, 1 C.F. per bag, for posts; incl. 8" dia. forms	6 Bag	10.5	154.35
Deck material, redwood, construction grade			
Posts, 4" x 4" x 12'	72 L.F.	3.0	163.80
Headers, 2" x 8" x 12'	48 L.F.	1.5	59.25
Joists, 2" x 8" x 12'	144 L.F.	3.5	177.75
Decking, 2" x 4" x 12'	504 L.F.	14.0	268.35
Stair material, stringers 2" x 10" x 16'	32 L.F.	1.0	35.25
Treads, 2" x 4" x 3'-6", 3 per tread	144 L.F.	3.0	76.70
Landing, precast concrete, 14" wide	4 L.F.	1.0	32.90
Railing material, redwood			
Posts, 2" x 4" x 3', doubled	120 L.F.	3.5	135.05
Railings, 2" x 4" stock	72 L.F.	3.0	38.35
Balusters, 2" x 2", 6" O.C.	240 L.F.	8.0	37.15
Cap rail, 2" x 6" stock	96 L.F.	3.0	118.48
Bench material, seat & braces, 2" x 4" stock	48 L.F.	1.5	25.55
Joist hangers, 18 ga. galvanized	12 Ea.	1.0	8.00
Nails, #10d galvanized	14 LB.	0.0	11.86
Bolts, 3/8" lag bolt	18 Ea.	0.0	17.20
Totals		63.5	$1360.00

Project Size	12' x 12'	Contractor's Fee Including Materials	$4630

Key to Abbreviations
C.Y. - cubic yard   Ea. - each   L.F. - linear foot   Pr. - pair   Sq. - square (100 square feet of area)
S.F. - square foot   S.Y. - square yard   V.L.F. - vertical linear foot

ELEVATED DECK, "L"-SHAPED

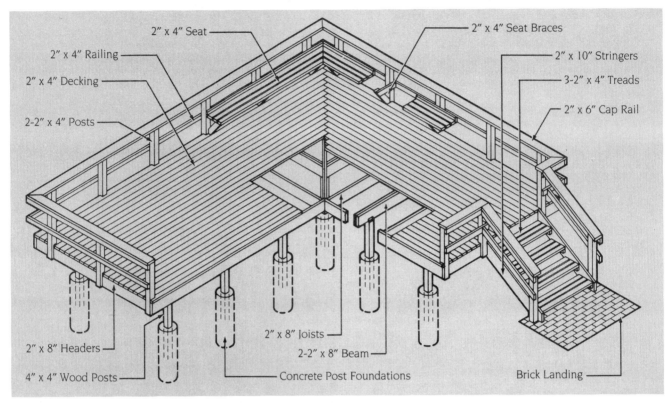

2" x 4" Seat
2" x 4" Seat Braces
2" x 4" Railing
2" x 10" Stringers
2" x 4" Decking
3-2" x 4" Treads
2-2" x 4" Posts
2" x 6" Cap Rail
2" x 8" Headers
2" x 8" Joists
4" x 4" Wood Posts
2-2" x 8" Beam
Concrete Post Foundations
Brick Landing

One of the most exciting features of deck construction is that an unlimited variety of shapes and configurations can be used to style the facility to the house and surrounding terrain. Swimming pools, sloping grades, and unusual house layouts offer opportunities to install imaginative decks, custom-planned to complement the design features of the home. This L-shaped plan demonstrates how a deck installation can be modularized to create an attractive and functional facility. Basically, it consists of two separate decks which have been tied into one L-shaped structure, bordering two sides of the house. The same modular construction method can also be used for U-shaped, angled, and multi-level deck designs. Although more careful planning and layout are necessary to build a modularized deck, the carpentry skills required are no different from those needed to build a conventional straight deck. With proper instruction before they start and guidance along the way, many do-it-yourselfers can tackle this L-shaped deck with professional results.

MATERIALS

The materials used in the L-shaped deck plan are the standard pressure-treated products employed for other deck projects. The legs of the "L" are formed from two separate, but attached, deck frames, each with its own 4" x 4" post and footing support system. More time is required to lay out the footings for this deck because there are more of them, but the process is the same as with other decks of simpler design. The most important aspect of the footing and post placement is the establishment of a square and level support system for the rest of the structure. If you are inexperienced in this procedure, get some help from a knowledgeable person and take the job in steps, building the frame for the large 8' x 16' section first before laying out the footing and post support for the 8' x 12' section. By proceeding in this way, you can adjust for small errors in alignment of the section and prevent potential materials waste due to inaccurate layout.

The frame consists of 2" x 8" joists and headers which are assembled as two separate units. As in the layout for the footings and support posts, be sure to double check all measurements and make sure that the corners of each section are properly squared. Since this L-shaped facility is built only 3' off the ground, most of the frame for the 8' x 16' section should be built in place. If the adjacent terrain allows, it may be laid out and started on the ground and then positioned on the 4" x 4"s to be finished in place. The 8' x 12' frame can be built in the same way.

The decking used in this L-shaped format consists of 2" x 4"s, but 2" x 6"s may also be installed on frames with 24" joist spacing. If thinner deck boards are to be installed, the joists will have to be placed at closer intervals and their number will be increased, so plan accordingly. Measure and cut the boards accurately, so that the shorter, cut-off pieces can be used to fill out the courses as the decking is placed. When laying the boards, place the cup side down and leave a space between courses. Also, keep a check on the gain at both ends and the middle as you proceed, to be sure that the decking is square to the frame. After all of the boards have been placed and fastened, snap a chalk line and saw the ragged ends to an even finished length.

The railing, bench, and stairway design offer the opportunity to add a distinctive and imaginative touch to the deck. This plan, for example, suggests using a corner bench design, but various other configurations are possible. The railing system, too, can be modified to suit the desired function and personal taste. In both cases, the cost of the project will be affected by alterations. A balustered railing design is an attractive addition to the deck's appearance and safety, but the added expense of the material used for the balusters, as well as their installation time, is considerable. Built-in benches also use a substantial amount of material, so plan to spend more money and allow more installation time if you are

adding to the length or the number of benches. The ship's ladder stairway design enhances the open motif of the deck, but conventional stringers and treads can also be placed. The materials cost is the same for both stairway designs, but the cutting of the stringers takes a little longer. If you are not experienced in stairway building, read up on it and seek instruction before you start. Accurate layout of tread height is a must to ensure a usable set of stairs.

LEVEL OF DIFFICULTY

As noted in the introduction to this deck plan, the carpentry skills required to complete this project are the same as for standard straight, square, or rectangular decks. A more intricate layout is involved in the alignment of the two sections; but if the project is taken in steps, the layout is simply a matter of more time, not more skill. Beginners, if they are given ample instruction and guidance, can do much of the work on this project, but they will need time to proceed slowly and must be willing to seek advice as

they go. Handymen and experts should also allow additional time for the layout and placement of the support system for this L-shaped facility. Otherwise, the project should pose no challenges greater than those encountered in other deck projects. Beginners should triple the professional time estimates for most tasks; handymen should add about 60% to the estimates; and experts should add about 20%. If the facility is to be built more than 6' off ground, more time will be required for do-it-yourselfers of all ability levels.

WHAT TO WATCH OUT FOR

Modular decks of different shapes and levels are more expensive to build because they usually demand more material and installation time. But if your budget allows for a deluxe deck facility, the resulting structure can add considerably to the appearance and value of your home. Take some time to draw up the plans and do some reading on the subject before you decide on a deck design. Multi-level decks are not that difficult to build, particularly if they are close to ground level. U-shaped, angled configurations, and even hexagonal or octagonal designs, where appropriate, can be built to professional standards by do-it-yourselfers if they are willing to learn first and then work slowly. In addition to imaginative basic designs, other amenities like built-in planters, eating and serving facilities, and sitting areas can be included to enhance the deck's appearance and function. Of course, all of these extras add to the expense of the project, but if you are doing the work on your own, some of what you save on labor costs can be applied to the cost of materials for extras and deluxe design features.

SUMMARY

This L-shaped plan demonstrates how deck construction can be modularized to create an attractive and practical exterior recreation and sitting area. Many do-it-yourselfers can complete this plan with professional results and considerable savings.

ELEVATED DECK, L-SHAPED

Description	Quantity	Man-hours	Material
Layout, excavate post holes	12 Ea.	12.0	0.00
Concrete, field mix, 1 C.F. per bag, for posts including 8" diameter forms	12 Bag	12.0	308.70
Deck material, pressure treated lumber			
Posts, 4" x 4" x 6'	84 L.F.	3.0	95.55
Headers, 2" x 8" x 16'	80 L.F.	3.0	49.35
Joists, 2" x 8" x 8'	96 L.F.	3.5	59.25
Joists, 2" x 8" x 12'	72 L.F.	2.5	44.45
Decking, 2" x 4" x 12'	720 L.F.	21.0	296.20
Stair material, stringers 2" x 10" x 6'	12 L.F.	0.5	14.25
Treads, 2" x 4" x 3'-6", 3 per tread	60 L.F.	2.0	24.70
Landing, brick on sand, no mortar	16 S.F.	2.5	42.60
Railing material, posts 4" x 4" x 3'	56 L.F.	2.0	23.05
Railings, 2" x 4" stock	136 L.F.	4.0	55.95
Cap rail, 2" x 6" stock	72 L.F.	2.5	44.45
Bench material, seats & braces, 2" x 4" stock	96 L.F.	3.0	39.50
Joist hangers, 18 ga galvanized	18 Ea.	1.0	12.00
Nails, #10d, galvanized	20 LB.	0.0	16.95
Bolts, 3/8" lag bolts, long	40 Ea.	0.0	38.25
Totals		74.5	$1165.20

Project Size	8' x 12' + 8' x 16'	Contractor's Fee Including Materials	$4310

Key to Abbreviations
C.Y. - cubic yard   Ea. - each   L.F. - linear foot   Pr. - pair   Sq. - square (100 square feet of area)
S.F. - square foot   S.Y. - square yard   V.L.F. - vertical linear foot

ROOF DECK

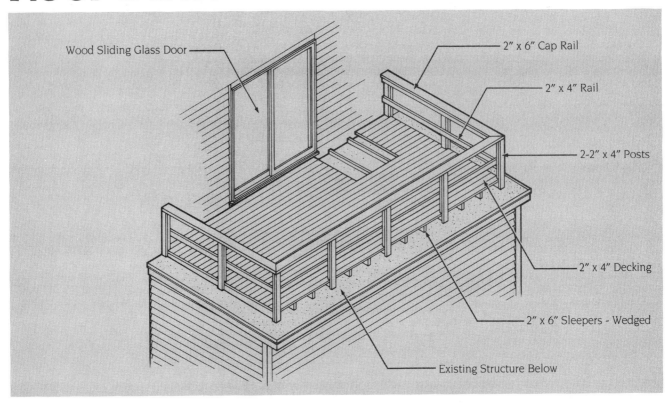

Wood Sliding Glass Door

2" x 6" Cap Rail

2" x 4" Rail

2-2" x 4" Posts

2" x 4" Decking

2" x 6" Sleepers - Wedged

Existing Structure Below

Not all houses can conveniently accommodate a roof deck, but those that can have the potential for a unique outdoor living area. This plan demonstrates how normally unused roof area can be turned into deck space. It is a challenging project for the do-it-yourselfer because of the general inconvenience involved in all roof work and because of the many carpentry skills that are required. Generally, a flat or gently sloping roof is best suited to a deck. A steeper roof can also accommodate a deck, but a different support system must be employed. The critical factor is the dormer or exterior wall, which must be able to accommodate a door for access to the proposed deck. Without this basic structural condition, the project cannot be accomplished without costly preliminary work.

MATERIALS

Conventional deck materials and design are used in this roof deck plan, with the addition of sleepers which

function as the deck frame and support system. As in the other deck plans presented in this section, pressure-treated lumber is employed for the basic components, including the sleepers, decking, and railing. If the roof is flat, the 2" x 6" sleepers can be laid on edge as in the example; but if the roof is slanted, they have to be sawn at an angle to compensate for the slope. Be sure to make the angled cut precise and consistent for all of the sleepers to ensure stability and equal load distribution. Some shimming will also be needed. Before you place the sleeper system, carefully check the condition of the roof and its rafters. If there are questionable areas, take steps to correct the situation, seeking professional advice and assistance if needed. Take care not to damage or puncture the roofing material during the deck installation process. Be sure to use proper caulking at points where the deck is attached to the roof.

After the sleeper frame has been placed, fastened, and squared, the decking and railing are installed as in any other deck. The 2" x 4" boards are laid with staggered end joints and with a space between courses to allow for drainage. The railing consists of doubled 2" x 4" posts, fitted and lagged into the sleeper frame, 2" x 4" rails, and a 2" x 6" cap. Great care should be taken in the design of the railing system for the roof deck; safety should be a primary feature. Check local building codes and regulations before construction begins to determine the minimum requirements for safety railings on off-ground decks. Adding balusters spaced at 6" or 8" along the railing on the open side of the deck, will increase the cost of the project, but the result will be a stronger, safer, and more durable railing.

The doorway to the roof deck should be installed before the deck is constructed to provide a convenient means of access to the roof site during construction. Many options are available in the choice of doors, so long as they are compatible with the structure and size of the wall. This plan includes the cost of materials for framing a 6' sliding glass door. The preparations will vary for other types and sizes of doors. Work carefully when cutting the opening to prevent excessive damage to the interior wall and exterior siding. Whenever possible, it pays to use an existing window space as part of the new door opening. You will have to enlarge and modify the rough window opening, but you will still be a step ahead in your door installation by using this approach.

LEVEL OF DIFFICULTY

Beginners should not attempt to build this deck on their own unless it is to be located on a flat roof. Even then,

they should seek professional advice before they begin the job. They should also leave the entire door installation to a professional, as the cutting of the opening and placement of the new unit involves considerable carpentry know-how. Handymen should be able to complete the deck construction in about twice the professional man-hours, but they should add more time if the roof area is not easily accessible. Plan to work slowly and seek guidance. Hole-cutting and door installation are not tasks for the handyman who is inexperienced in these areas. Experts should add about 30% to the professional time for all tasks. They should allow a bit more time for the hole-cutting and door installation, as hidden problems tend to arise in these operations, especially in older homes. If electrical wiring is located in the wall, shut off the supply before cutting the hole. Hire an electrician to rewire the affected area if you are unfamiliar with electrical work. All do-it-yourselfers should consider the risks and inconvenience of working on a

roof before they start this project, and make plans to acquire the appropriate equipment for safe and efficient roof work.

WHAT TO WATCH OUT FOR

Several important factors must be considered before installing a roof deck to prevent overloading the existing roof. Remember that the weight of the 8' x 16' deck will increase when in use. Be sure that the existing rafters and roofboards are in good condition and are sturdy enough to support more than the anticipated load. If additional support members are needed, they will have to be installed before you begin construction of the new deck. If you are in doubt as to how to reinforce the roof support, consult a contractor and hire him to do the work. The additional expense for his services will be well worth the investment to ensure proper and safe support for the new deck.

SUMMARY

If the conditions of the house are right, a roof deck addition can provide a unique dimension in exterior living space. For do-it-yourselfers who can handle some or all of the work, the project can be completed at a surprisingly reasonable cost.

ROOF DECK

Description	Quantity	Man-hours	Material
Deck material, pressure-treated lumber			
Sleepers, 2" x 6" x 8'	112 L. F.	4.0	69.15
Header, 2" x 6" x 16'	16 L.F.	0.5	9.85
Decking, 2" x 4" x 12'	408 L.F.	12.0	167.85
Railing material, posts, 2" x 4" x 3', doubled	72 L.F.	2.5	81.90
Railings, 2" x 4" stock	72 L.F.	2.5	29.65
Cap rail, 2" x 6" stock	36 L.F.	1.5	22.25
Cut opening for sliding glass door	1 Ea.	15.5	0.00
Frame for door, 2" x 4" to support header	48 L.F.	1.0	15.10
Header, 2" x 8", doubled	14 L.F.	1.0	9.65
Door, sliding glass, stock, wood frame, 6' wide	1 Ea.	4.0	508.20
Nails, #10d galvanized	10 LB.	0.0	8.45
Bolts, 3/8" lag bolts, long	24 Ea.	0.0	22.95
Totals		44.5	$945.00

Project Size	8' x 16'	Contractor's Fee Including Materials	$2980

Key to Abbreviations
C.Y. - cubic yard   Ea. - each   L.F. - linear foot   Pr. - pair   Sq. - square (100 square feet of area)
S.F. - square foot   S.Y. - square yard   V.L.F. - vertical linear foot

GABLE DORMER, 4' WIDE

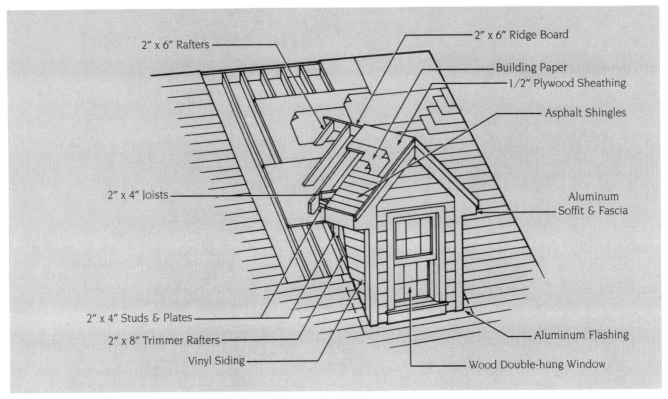

2" x 6" Rafters

2" x 4" Joists

2" x 4" Studs & Plates

2" x 8" Trimmer Rafters

Vinyl Siding

2" x 6" Ridge Board

Building Paper

1/2" Plywood Sheathing

Asphalt Shingles

Aluminum Soffit & Fascia

Aluminum Flashing

Wood Double-hung Window

The addition of a dormer or pair of dormers can add window area and living space to second or third-story rooms or an attic, while enhancing the exterior appearance of the house. Several different dormer designs have been used over the years, especially on Cape Cod style houses and other dwellings with gable roofs. The two most commonly installed dormer types are the gable dormer and the shed dormer, both of which require adequate area and ridge height. The size and design of the dormer depends greatly on the style of the house and the amount of area available for the structure. While gable dormers are smaller than shed dormers, their installation still requires significant carpentry know-how and skill. This small gable dormer plan can enlarge and brighten the upper floor of your home.

MATERIALS

Basically, dormers use the same building materials employed in the exterior wood construction of a complete house, just in smaller amounts. This dormer consists of a wood-frame support system, wall and roof materials, and other exterior construction products for the finish work. All of these materials are commonly used in home building and remodeling and are readily available from most lumber yards. Because of their abundant supply, it pays to shop for them and compare prices to get the best deal. The materials order for this project should be trucked, so make sure that delivery arrangements are made before the purchase is finalized.

Before the new dormer is constructed, extensive site preparation must be completed. The location of the dormer on the roof must first be precisely determined, and then the opening cut from outside. Be sure to make the cut adjacent to existing roof rafters and strip the roofing materials carefully in the area of the opening before you saw the roof sheathing. After the rafters in the dormer opening have been cut and the sections removed, the cut ends have to be headed off, and trimmer rafters of the same cross section added as support to the full length of the existing rafters. These doubled support rafters are important in that they maintain the structural integrity of that part of the roof and help to support the load of the new dormer. After the opening has been prepared, the dormer can be framed in basically the same order as the framing of a house. The 2" x 4" wall studs are placed, and the 2" x 4" ceiling joists and 2" x 6" rafters are installed. The placing of the framing members for this gable dormer takes time because of the number of angle cuts and the extensive amount of fitting involved in the process. Remember, too, that the cutting and placement will probably be done under less than favorable conditions, with some traveling up and down a ladder, or in and out of the opening as part of the job.

Once the frame has been completed, 1/2" plywood sheathing is applied to the walls and roof and then covered with roofing felt. The roofing material suggested in this example plan is standard asphalt shingling, but your choice of materials should match as closely as possible the existing roofing. Cedar and some other materials will be more expensive than the standard roofing listed in the plan. The same applies to the selection of the siding, soffit, fascia, and window. The vinyl siding and the aluminum soffit and fascia, for example, should be used only if they are compatible with the materials that are already in place on the house. When selecting the window, purchase a quality unit that will be energy efficient and require minimum maintenance. Before placing the siding, make sure that the seams between the old roof and the dormer walls have been correctly fastened. This process and the installation of the valley require time and roofing know-how, so seek the help of a professional if you are inexperienced in these tasks. After the dormer has been completed on the exterior, the insulation can be placed in preparation for the interior finish work. Remember that this cost estimate covers the work necessary to complete only the exterior of the dormer.

LEVEL OF DIFFICULTY

All of the dormer projects included in this section require moderate to advanced carpentry skills and a knowledge of roof structure and framing. There are, in addition, the challenges of awkwardness and height in any work done on the roof. Often, specialized equipment, such as roof jacks and staging, will need to be rented or borrowed to ensure convenience and safety for the workers. Steep roofs can be particularly difficult to work on without the right equipment. Hand-held power tools will have to be operated in awkward and inconvenient positions. For these reasons, beginners and do-it-yourselfers with limited skills are not encouraged to tackle dormer installations and should leave the entire project to a contractor. Experts and capable handymen can complete most of the operations, but they should proceed cautiously on the hole-cutting and all of the roofing and siding tasks. Even experts should consider hiring an experienced roofer to install the valley and to restore the disturbed sections of the old roofing. A poor roofing job can cause interior water damage that will exceed the roofer's fee many times over. Experts and handymen should add 50% and 100%, respectively, to the professional time for most tasks, and more for the roofing and flashing installations if they are inexperienced in these areas.

WHAT TO WATCH OUT FOR

The cutting of the roof opening for the dormer is one of the most critical operations in this project. Accurate measurement, both inside and out, is required to lay out the cuts before they are made. Because small gable dormers like this one are often installed in pairs, their symmetrical placement on the roof can further complicate the layout process. If the proposed opening is easily accessible from the inside, the job becomes much easier, especially if you have a helper. With two workers, one inside and one outside the roof, the rafters can be more easily located, the corners of the opening established, and the cutting efficiently accomplished. Remember that rapid completion of the dormer is desirable in order to restore the weathertight condition of the roof as soon as possible.

SUMMARY

Installing one or a pair of gable dormers can add space and window area to the upstairs of your house and improve its exterior appearance. With the right equipment and know-how, experts and capable handymen can complete much of the dormer construction on their own to reduce the cost. Beginners, however, should leave all of this project to a professional contractor.

GABLE DORMER, 4' WIDE

Description	Quantity	Man-hours	Material
Roof cutout & demolition	1 Ea.	12.0	0.00
Framing, rafters, 2" x 6" x 4', 16" O.C.	56 L.F.	1.5	26.45
Ridge board, 2" x 6" stock	8 L.F.	0.5	3.80
Trimmer rafters, 2" x 8" x 18' long	36 L.F.	1.5	24.85
Studs & plates, 2" x 4" stock	72 L.F.	1.5	22.65
Sub-fascia, 2" x 6" stock	12 L.F.	0.5	5.65
Headers, double, 2" x 6" stock	16 L.F.	1.0	7.55
Ceiling joists, 2" x 4", 16" O.C.	20 L.F.	0.5	6.30
Gable end studs, 2" x 4" stock	4 L.F.	0.5	1.25
Sheathing, roof & walls, 1/2" thick	4 Sheets	1.5	63.50
Building paper, 15 lb. felt	95 S.F.	0.5	3.45
Drip edge, aluminum, .016" thick, 5" girth	20 L.F.	0.5	3.65
Flashing, aluminum, .019" thick	35 S.F.	2.0	27.95
Shingles, asphalt strip, 235 lb./square	2 Bundles	1.0	24.85
Soffit & fascia, aluminum, vented	20 L.F.	3.0	33.90
Window, double hung, 3' x 3'-6", plastic clad	1 Ea.	1.0	223.85
Siding, vinyl, double 4" pattern	50 S.F.	2.0	38.15
Insulation, fiberglass, 3-1/2" thick, R-11, paper backed	60 S.F.	0.5	16.00
Totals		31.5	$ 533.80

Project Size: 4' x 6'-6"

Contractor's Fee Including Materials: **$2080**

Key to Abbreviations
C.Y. - cubic yard   Ea. - each   L.F. - linear foot   Pr. - pair   Sq. - square (100 square feet of area)
S.F. - square foot   S.Y. - square yard   V.L.F. - vertical linear foot

GABLE DORMER, 7' WIDE

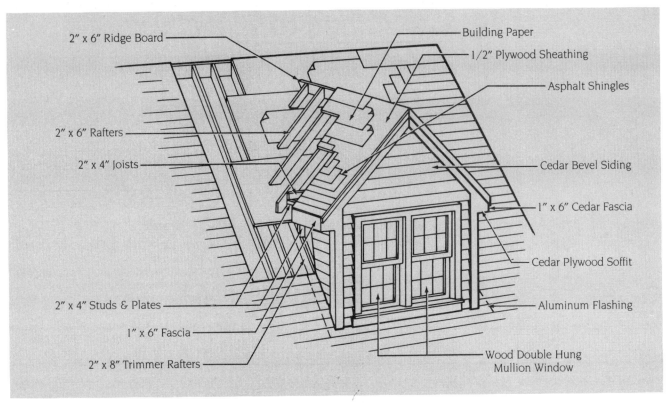

2" x 6" Ridge Board
Building Paper
1/2" Plywood Sheathing
Asphalt Shingles
2" x 6" Rafters
2" x 4" Joists
Cedar Bevel Siding
1" x 6" Cedar Fascia
Cedar Plywood Soffit
2" x 4" Studs & Plates
1" x 6" Fascia
Aluminum Flashing
2" x 8" Trimmer Rafters
Wood Double Hung Mullion Window

In houses with the roof area to accomodate them, large gable dormers can significantly increase the amount of light and living space in second- or third-floor rooms. As noted in the small gable dormer plan, style, size, and location are crucial elements in dormer design. When placed on the roof of a house, they become a prominent feature, and the homeowner should make sure that they meet both aesthetic and practical needs. This double-window gable dormer plan demonstrates how a larger-size dormer can be installed for a reasonable cost.

MATERIALS

The materials used in this gable dormer plan include standard framing lumber, sheathing, and exterior finishing products. The exterior of a dormer is in some ways like a miniature wood-framed house in that it requires a wood support system, framed walls, and a roof. Because these materials, including 2" x 4"s, 2" x 6"s, siding, roofing materials, and

window unit, are usually in good supply, the do-it-yourselfer is encouraged to do some price comparing before buying. Once again, where standard building materials are concerned, it is to the homeowner's advantage to purchase everything from the same retailer. Consolidation of the order is less complicated and provides the buyer with the leverage to get the best prices. Further, an all-in-one order is probably large enough to warrant free local delivery from the supplier.

The first major procedure in this project is the layout out and cutting of the opening in the roof to receive the new structure. Because gable dormers are often installed in pairs, and sometimes threes, the location of the structures on the roof, in relation to one another, is paramount to a successful design. Whenever possible, the longitudinal cuts for the roof opening should be made next to existing rafters. The width of the dormer, therefore, may have to be adjusted to fit the rafter spacing on a

given roof. The roofs of most houses have rafters spaced at 16" on center, but in some homes they may be spaced at 20", 24", or even larger intervals. In the latter case, plan on increasing the cost of this operation, as additional rafters and supports may have to be placed to restore the roof structure to safe standards. While the roof is open, check the condition of the other rafters and sheathing. If either of these components is questionable, have an inspection done by a professional. Any problems should be corrected before you proceed with the new installation. Placing a new dormer on a weak or deteriorated roof surface is a waste of time and money and can cause serious structural problems later on.

After the opening has been made, new support materials have to be placed, even on newer roofs. The most important of these supports are the trimmer rafters, which double the existing rafters next to the opening, and span the entire length from the ridge to the wall plate. The ends of the cut rafters must be capped with doubled headers. In both cases, the lumber should match the dimensions of the existing rafter material.

The walls, ceiling, and roof of the dormer are framed and covered after the opening has been fully prepared. Because of the number of angle cuts and the individual fitting required for many of the framing members, this procedure is time consuming and requires a patient approach by the do-it-yourselfer. If you are unfamiliar with the task, plan on making a few mistakes at first and allow some extra time for double checking the measurements and angles as you work. Remember, too, that the cutting will usually have to be done in an area remote from the dormer site, on the ground or a suitable surface inside the opening; so you will use up more time going up and down a ladder or climbing in and out of the opening as the cuts are made. Plywood sheathing is placed on the dormer walls and roof after the framing has been completed. Be sure to scribe the angled side pieces accurately, as a tight fit is desirable. Remember, too, that the roofing, siding, and trim materials should match the products already in place on your house. Also, trim and structural features, such as the width of the fascia and the proportions of the soffit, should be duplicated as closely as possible. These matching materials and design features could change the cost estimates for both labor and materials, if the products in this plan have to be replaced to meet the needs of your particular installation. The most important decision in the selection of finish materials is the choice of the window unit, the design and size of which should approximate or complement, if not match, the other windows in the house.

LEVEL OF DIFFICULTY

This gable dormer project is a difficult job which requires considerable carpentry skill and know-how to complete. Beginners and handymen whose remodeling experience is limited should not tackle it. The structure itself is a challenging undertaking, and its inconvenient roof location makes it a bit more complex. Do-it-yourselfers who undertake this project should anticipate some problems inherent to roof work. Some of these include height, limited access to the site, and the awkward position from which power and hand tools must be operated. Two steps in the project are critical to the overall success of the installation. One is the adequate restoration of the roof support with trimmer rafters and headers after the opening has been cut. The other is correct roofing and flashing installation to restore weathertight conditions to the roof. The roofing work, particularly, may require the services of an experienced tradesman, and even expert do-it-yourselfers are encouraged to consult a qualified roofer before attempting this task. Generally, experts should add 50% to the professional time for all procedures, and more for the finish roofing and flashing jobs. Handymen should add 100% to the man-hours estimates and should hire a professional for the roofing work if they are inexperienced in this area. Beginners should not attempt any of the tasks in this project for the reasons given earlier.

WHAT TO WATCH OUT FOR

Because of their inconvenient roof location, dormers are notoriously difficult to paint and maintain. As a result, you will want to select finish materials which will cut the time and difficulty of painting, window washing, and other maintenance chores. For example, window units with removable sashes may cost a little more initially, but the convenience of washing or painting from inside the house, rather than from the roof or an outside ladder, might make the extra expense worthwhile. In most cases, stained surfaces are easier to apply and maintain than painted ones. If you can match the trim color of your house with a stain, use it on the dormer instead of paint to reduce the scraping and application time of future paint jobs.

SUMMARY

This large gable dormer project is a challenging undertaking for all levels of do-it-yourselfers. Nevertheless, if you have good remodeling skills and are willing to work at a slow pace, you can complete this improvement at reasonable cost while adding to the value, living space, and appearance of your home.

GABLE DORMER, 7' WIDE

Description	Quantity	Man-hours	Material
Roof cutout & demolition	1 Ea.	16.0	0.00
Framing, rafters, 2" x 6", 16" O.C.	108 L.F.	3.0	50.95
Ridge board, 2" x 8" stock	12 L.F.	0.5	5.65
Trimmer rafters, 2" x 8" x 18' long	36 L.F.	1.5	24.85
Studs & plates, 2" x 4" stock	120 L.F.	2.5	37.75
Sub-fascia, 2" x 6" stock	16 L.F.	0.5	7.55
Headers, double 2" x 6" stock	24 L.F.	1.5	11.35
Ceiling joists, 2" x 6", 16" O.C.	36 L.F.	0.5	11.35
Gable end studs, 2" x 4" stock	10 L.F.	0.5	3.15
Sheathing, roof & walls, 1/2" thick	7 Sheets	2.5	111.15
Building paper, 15 lb. felt	210 S.F.	0.5	7.65
Drip edge, aluminum, .016" thick, 5" girth	28 L.F.	1.0	5.10
Flashing, aluminum, .019" thick	62 L.F.	3.5	49.50
Shingles, asphalt, multi-layered, 285 lb./square	6 Bundles	4.0	115.80
Fascia, 1" x 6", rough sawn cedar, stained	28 L.F.	1.0	40.00
Soffit, 3/8" rough sawn cedar plywood, stained	14 S.F.	0.5	18.15
Window, double window, double hung, 5' x 3', vinyl-clad, thermopane	1 Ea.	2.0	423.50
Siding, cedar, beveled, rough sawn, stained	120 S.F.	4.0	288.95
Insulation, fiberglass, 3-1/2" thick, R-11, paper backed	140 S.F.	1.0	87.25
Totals		46.0	$1249.65

Project Size	6'-8" x 10'-6"	Contractor's Fee Including Materials	$3540

Shed Dormer, 12' Wide

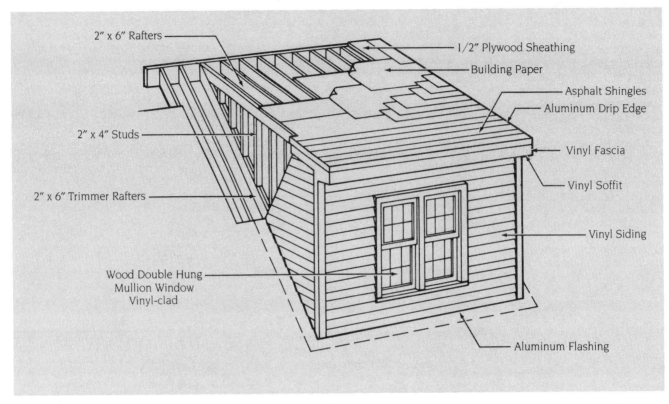

2" x 6" Rafters

1/2" Plywood Sheathing

Building Paper

Asphalt Shingles

Aluminum Drip Edge

2" x 4" Studs

Vinyl Fascia

Vinyl Soffit

2" x 6" Trimmer Rafters

Vinyl Siding

Wood Double Hung
Mullion Window
Vinyl-clad

Aluminum Flashing

Although they are not as intricate in design as gable dormers, shed dormers are an efficient means of increasing the living space and window area of second and third floor rooms. Also, although all dormer installations are challenging projects, shed dormers are generally easier to install than those with gable designs. Because of the simplicity of their roof lines, the framing and roofing operations, particularly, can be done more easily. These tasks can be accomplished by do-it-yourselfers with moderate to advanced skill levels. As long as the ridge height and area of the roof can accommodate the dormer, it can be installed. If you feel confident in your carpentry abilities, understand the structural composition of roofs, and are willing to cope with the inconveniences of roof work, you can complete this major home improvement on your own while benefitting from the experience and the savings on labor costs.

MATERIALS

The amount of construction material used for shed dormer projects is usually greater than for gable dormers because they tend to be larger structures. Yet, the same basic materials are employed in essentially the same sequence of operations. One of the reasons that they tend to be larger structures is that a shed dormer roof often extends from the ridge of the existing roof to a point near or directly over the exterior wall. Because the dormer roof is flat, not gabled or peaked, the amount of usable open space enclosed by the structure is increased, and maximum ceiling height is attained. As in most exterior house improvements, framing lumber of varying dimensions, plywood sheathing, roofing, siding, and various finish products are used in this plan. Because these materials are usually in

good supply, the do-it-yourselfer can save by comparison shopping before buying. For an order this size, the difference can mean substantial savings. If you consolidate the order with one retailer, free local delivery will usually be included.

The removal and reconditioning of the affected roof area is a critical operation in preparing the house for the new structure. The roofing, sheathing, and rafters must be torn out, the structural integrity of the old roof restored, and the rafter support for the dormer installed. In most cases, it is best to make the longitudinal cuts beside existing rafters, which are then reinforced with trimmers. These new supports must span from the ridge to the eaves. The existing rafters are usually spaced at 16" on center, but they may be located at odd intervals in some older houses.

Be sure to match or exceed the dimensions of the existing rafters with the trimmer material. Any deficiencies or weaknesses in the existing roof or its support system should be corrected before the framing of the new dormer begins.

The frame for the shed dormer consists of 2" x 4" walls and 2" x 6" rafters and ceiling joists. After the front wall of the dormer has been framed, placed, and temporarily braced, the joists and rafters are installed. As in other roof framing operations, the general rule is consistency of length, angling and notching, and spacing of the roof framing members. The framing of the side walls must be accomplished one piece at a time, with two different angles cut at each end of the studs to fit the roof lines. This process takes some time, so plan accordingly, especially if the task is new to you.

Once the framing has been completed, 1/2" plywood sheathing is applied and then covered with 15-pound felt building paper. As in other dormer plans, the finish materials which are used on the dormer should match the products already in place on the rest of the house. This plan suggests low maintenance vinyl siding and aluminum soffit and fascia coverings; but other materials, such as cedar shingles and clapboards and conventional wood trim, may be more appropriate for your house. A gutter

and downspout for the shed roof have not been included in the plan, but it might be a good idea to add them if the dormer is located above a doorway. If the face of the dormer is a continuation of the house wall, a gutter and downspout will be necessary. The roofing should match the existing roof material, except where prohibited by the pitch of the roof. If the ridge is low and the pitch of the new shed roof nearly flat, rolled roofing of matching color might have to be used, as shingles are not recommended for roofs with shallow slopes. When selecting the window unit, try to acquire thermopane sash in the same design of your present windows. The extra expense for a high-quality, energy-efficient window unit will be returned in energy savings and comfort over the years. These and other changes from the materials list in this plan will affect the cost of the finish work as well as the man-hours estimate.

LEVEL OF DIFFICULTY

This dormer project is challenging, even for experts and accomplished handymen, and is out of the reach of beginners. Whenever you open a roof and tamper with major structural components, like rafters, you have to have the building skill to accomplish the work efficiently and correctly. All

do-it-yourselfers should be prepared to cope with the inconvenience and difficulties associated with roof work. Skilled handymen and experts should be able to complete all of the tasks involved in the project. They should add 50% and 20%, respectively, to the professional time for all of the procedures. The new roofing may pose some challenges and require some extra time, especially in the flashing and the restoration of disturbed sections of the old roof. Nevertheless, once the drip edge has been placed and the job correctly laid out, the roofing material should go on smoothly. Remember to allow extra time and to get some help for hauling bundles of roofing to the work area. As with most of the exterior wood structures outlined in this book, experience in using power tools is a prerequisite for tackling this dormer project.

WHAT TO WATCH OUT FOR

All dormer installations should be completed or, at the least, closed in as rapidly as possible to protect the inside of the house from the elements. If you are doing the job on your own, arrange to have an adequate amount of time available for several successive days of work. Although sudden weather changes cannot be predicted, you can reduce the chance of getting caught off guard by scheduling the dormer project during the warm and dry time of year. Nevertheless, always have an emergency cover ready to use in the event of a sudden rainstorm, and then hold off on the resumption of construction until the roof area dries. Be aware that wet roofs can also be dangerous. These basic precautions can prevent serious water damage to your house's interior.

SUMMARY

This small shed dormer can increase bedroom area and other second- or third-floor space without the expense of putting on a full addition. Although it is a challenging undertaking, many accomplished do-it-yourselfers can complete the project on their own for the cost of the materials and the investment of several days of their time.

SHED DORMER, 12' WIDE

Description	Quantity	Man-hours	Material
Roof cutout and demolition	1 Ea.	12.0	0.00
Framing, rafters, 2" x 6" x 12', 16" O.C.	12 Ea.	4.0	67.95
Trimmer rafters, 2" x 8" x 18' long	2 Ea	1.5	24.85
Studs & plates, 2" x 4" stock	192 L.F.	3.5	60.40
Sub-fascia, 2" x 6" stock	14 L.F.	0.5	6.60
Header, double, 2"x 8", 5' long	10 L.F.	0.5	6.90
Header, double, 2" x 12", 20' long	24 L.F.	1.5	26.45
Ceiling joists, 2" x 6", 12' long	12 Ea.	2.0	67.95
Sheathing, roof & wall, 1/2" thick, 4' x 8' sheets	9 Sheets	3.5	142.90
Building paper, 15 lb. felt	150 S.F.	0.5	5.45
Drip edge, aluminum, .016" thick, 5" girth	36 L.F.	1.0	6.55
Flashing, aluminum, .019" thick	24 S.F.	1.5	19.15
Shingles, asphalt, strip, 235 lb./square	6 Bundles	3.0	74.50
Siding, vinyl, double, 4" pattern	90 S.F.	3.0	68.60
Soffit & fascia, vinyl vented	36 L.F.	5.0	58.80
Window, double window, 4' wide x 3' high, double-hung, plastic coated, premium	1 Ea.	2.0	423.50
Insulation, fiberglass, 3-1/2" thick, R-11, paper backed	192 S.F.	1.0	51.10
Totals		46.0	$1111.65

Project Size	12' x 8'	Contractor's Fee Including Materials	$3490

Key to Abbreviations
C.Y. - cubic yard   Ea. - each   L.F. - linear foot   Pr. - pair   Sq. - square (100 square feet of area)
S.F. - square foot   S.Y. - square yard   V.L.F. - vertical linear foot

SHED DORMER, 20' WIDE

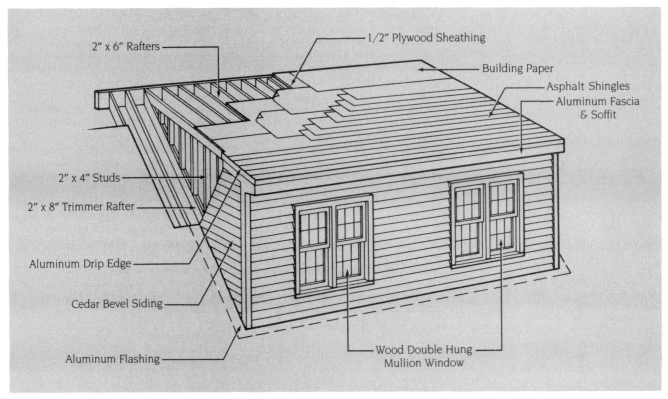

2" x 6" Rafters

1/2" Plywood Sheathing

Building Paper

Asphalt Shingles

Aluminum Fascia & Soffit

2" x 4" Studs

2" x 8" Trimmer Rafter

Aluminum Drip Edge

Cedar Bevel Siding

Aluminum Flashing

Wood Double Hung Mullion Window

Larger shed dormers provide the means to effectively utilize upper floor space. They are usually placed on the rear roofs of cape-style houses and other structures with gable roof designs large enough to accommodate them. Before you begin the planning for any shed dormer, large or small, take some time to measure your attic to see that you have enough ridge clearance to accept the dormer and enough roof and floor area to make the project worthwhile. A height of roughly 9' from the bottom of the ridge board to the floor of the room below or, in the case of an attic improvement, to the top of the ceiling joists, is a reasonable minimum measurement. Once the minimum height requirement has been met, the width and length of the dormer can be determined according to the intended use of the facility, the rafter spacing in the existing roof, and the location of interior partitions. Because there are many variables here, good judgement and careful planning are necessary to ensure that the dormer will meet your interior space needs without harming the appearance of your house or interfering with its structural design.

MATERIALS

This plan presents a basic design for the exterior shell of an 8' x 20' shed dormer with no interior materials included, except wall insulation. Although the structure is basic in its design, a substantial number of exterior materials is needed to construct it. If you are doing the building on your own, get prices from several different suppliers and compare them before you place the order. Also, make sure that delivery is included in the final price, as the materials will have to be trucked. The process of constructing the dormer requires different materials for the various components as the structure is built, including 2" x 4"s and 2" x 6"s for the support system and frame, plywood sheathing, and various exterior coverings and finish materials.

The most critical step in the project is determining the location and laying out the section of roof to be opened for the new dormer. In most cases, the new structure will be located in an area which begins on the lower part of the roof and runs to the ridge board.

This width measurement will vary with each case, depending on the size and pitch of the roof, aesthetic considerations, and the desired amount of new living space. The length of the roof area to be opened depends on such variables as the location of existing interior partitions, the design of the new living space, and wherever possible, the spacing of the existing roof rafters. The cost of this shed dormer project is based on an 8' x 20' structure placed on a roof with a steep pitch, but costs will vary somewhat if the dormer dimensions are modified. Once the location has been determined and laid out, the roof section can be opened by removing the roofing, sheathing, and rafters.

After the opening has been made, the new work begins with the installation of trimmer rafters and the heading off of the cut rafter ends and, if conditions warrant, the placing of additional support. Again, each case will vary, and additional costs and time may be required to bring the roof and dormer support system to safe standards. The frame of the new dormer should not be placed until its support system has been correctly installed and fastened. Professional consultation or subcontracting will save you money in the long run if extensive roof support reconditioning is required. The framing and closing in of the shed dormer proceeds in much the same order as that of other wood-frame structures. The face of the dormer is framed with 2" x 4"s and then braced temporarily while 2" x 6" ceiling joists and rafters are placed. The side walls are then framed and the entire enclosure sheathed with 1/2" plywood. A layer of felt building paper is applied to the walls and, optionally, to the roof. The roofing material, in this case asphalt shingles, is then applied to the shed roof before the window units are installed and the finished siding applied. The roofing, siding, and window units will also vary with each installation, as the products which are selected for the dormer should match or approximate the materials already in place on the house.

If the materials differ from those listed in the estimate, the cost may be affected. For example, the cedar roofing included in this materials list costs more than asphalt shingles, and quite a bit more than asphalt roll roofing. The windows included in this plan are quality thermopane double-hung units; but standard single-pane units can be installed for less expense. Remember, though, that the cost for storm windows, if you choose to install uninsulated windows, will have to be added. Generally, quality window units are worth the extra cost in the long run because of their return in energy savings and low maintenance. Additional cost may also be incurred and more installation time required if a gutter and downspout are needed for the dormer. If the face of the dormer is far enough back from the edge of the existing roof, you probably won't need it; but if it is positioned close enough to the edge to cause spattering or icing problems from the roof run-off, then you should spend the extra money to install one.

LEVEL OF DIFFICULTY

This project is a major home improvement that demands a considerable amount of carpentry skill and know-how. Further, the roof location of the dormer increases the difficulty and adds significantly to the time and general inconvenience of the operations. In many instances, special equipment may have to be employed for roof and upper story work - staging, roof jacks, sturdy extension ladders, and pump jacks, to name a few. Some of these devices may have to be rented, so allow for their rental cost and plan ahead to ensure their availability during the construction period. Be sure that you get some instruction in their operation before you use them if they are unfamiliar to you. Generally, beginners should not attempt this or other dormer projects, as the necessary skills and location of the work are too demanding. Experts and handymen should add 25% and 75%, respectively, to the man-hours estimates and be willing to seek professional advice when necessary.

WHAT TO WATCH OUT FOR

This dormer project plan consists of a listing of the materials and the estimated installation time for only the exterior of the structure. As the work progresses, though, take advantage of opportunities to make the subsequent interior finishing easier. Some of these odds and ends will take a little more time and money during the placement of the dormer, but they can provide substantial labor savings later on. For example, electrical or plumbing rough-in required for the interior of the new enclosure may be prepared for or relocated. Attic locations with hard-to-get-at places for insulation may be more accessible before the dormer is closed in. Plywood decking for a new attic room may be easier to stack or to place while the roof is open. Remember, however, that expediency is important for all dormer projects, so use discretion and take advantage of extra tasks that require only a minimum of time.

SUMMARY

If the ridge height and roof area are adequate, a relatively large dormer like this one will reclaim wasted floor space. Although the project is fairly costly and time consuming, it remains an economical way of adding space that will return years of service while increasing the value of your home.

SHED DORMER, 20' WIDE

Description	Quantity	Man-hours	Material
Roof cutout & demolition	1 Ea.	20.0	0.00
Framing, rafters, 2" x 6" x 12', 16" O.C.	16 Ea.	5.5	90.60
Trimmer rafters, 2" x 8" x 18'	2 Ea.	1.5	24.85
Studs & plates, 2" x 4" x 8', 16" O.C.	240 L.F.	4.5	75.50
Sub-fascia, 2" x 6"	22 L.F.	1.0	10.40
Headers, double 2" x 8" x 4' long	16 L.F.	1.0	11.05
Headers, double 2" x 12" x 20' long	40 L.F.	2.5	44.05
Ceiling joists, 2" x 6" x 12'	16 Ea.	2.5	90.60
Sheathing, roof & walls, 1/2" thick, 4' x 8' sheets	12 Sheets	4.5	190.50
Building paper, 15 lb felt	240 S.F.	0.5	8.70
Drip edge, aluminum, .016" thick, 5" girth	44 L.F.	1.0	8.00
Flashing, aluminum, .019" thick	40 S.F.	2.5	31.95
Shingles, Asphalt, Multi-layered, 285 lb./sq.	3 Sq.	2.0	57.90
Siding, cedar, beveled, rough sawn, stained	130 S.F.	4.5	313.05
Soffit & fascia, aluminum, vented	42 L.F.	6.0	71.15
Windows, double window, double hung, insulating glass, 4' x 3'	2 Ea.	3.5	653.40
Insulation, fiberglass, 3-1/2" thick, R-11, paper-backed	344 S.F.	4.0	91.55
Totals		67.0	$1773.25

Project Size	20' x 8'	Contractor's Fee Including Materials	$5280

Key to Abbreviations
C.Y. - cubic yard Ea. - each L.F. - linear foot Pr. - pair Sq. - square (100 square feet of area)
S.F. - square foot S.Y. - square yard V.L.F. - vertical linear foot

SHED DORMER, 30' WIDE

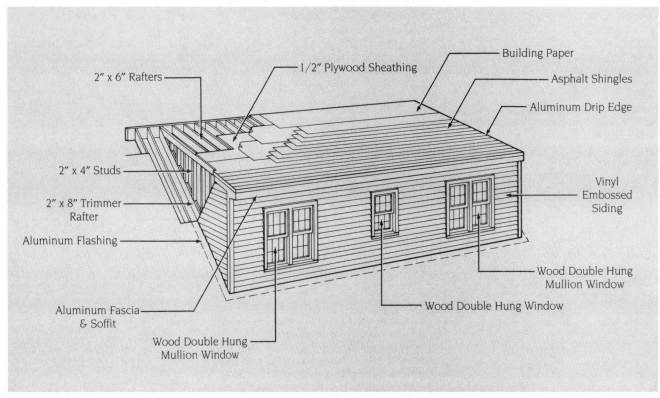

2" x 6" Rafters

1/2" Plywood Sheathing

Building Paper

Asphalt Shingles

Aluminum Drip Edge

2" x 4" Studs

2" x 8" Trimmer Rafter

Aluminum Flashing

Vinyl Embossed Siding

Wood Double Hung Mullion Window

Aluminum Fascia & Soffit

Wood Double Hung Window

Wood Double Hung Mullion Window

Like other attached exterior structures, dormers should be carefully planned to meet the needs of the homeowner without harming the exterior appearance of the dwelling. For a large structure like this 29'-4" x 8' full shed dormer, the planning and design become even more critical, to ensure the efficient use of space and the appropriate architectural impact. Although shed dormers are usually placed on the rear roofs, they can often be seen from the front and side of the house. For this reason, the pitch and location of the new shed dormer should complement the roof lines and style of the house. Like other dormer plans included in this section, this project is a major home improvement, requiring competence in carpentry and a significant amount of construction know-how.

MATERIALS

This plan calls for standard construction materials which are common to most wood-framed structures. Construction grade 2" x 4", 2" x 6", and 2" x 8" lumber is needed to frame the roof opening and dormer.

Standard sheathing covers the frame and serves as the subsurface for the roof and finished siding. Prefabricated window units and other finish and trim products are employed to complete the exterior of the structure.

The most important task involved in the project, after the layout and location of the dormer have been determined, is the cutting of the roof opening and the placement of the proper support for the structure. In a dormer project this size, time is an important factor because of the large opening that temporarily exposes the house's interior to the elements. Be sure to have plenty of help on hand, as there is a considerable amount of work to be done in a short period of time. Before opening the roof, double check to see that all supplies, tools, and equipment are readily available and in good working order. In short, all precautions should be taken to ensure expedient opening of the roof and closing in of the new dormer. Make sure that an emergency cover-up plan has been prepared.

Once the trimmer rafters and other support members have been placed, the new dormer is framed and sheathed. Because of its length, the face should be assembled and raised into position in sections with properly placed rough openings framed for the new windows. Double check all measurements for the locations and dimensions of the rough openings; correcting mistakes will be difficult and time consuming once the partition is in place. After the face wall has been installed and temporarily braced, the 2" x 6" rafters and ceiling joists are placed. Because of the large area of this dormer roof, consistent angle cuts, notching and squaring of the rafters is paramount to ensure rapid placement of the roof sheathing and finish material. Accuracy of measurement and cutting is also important for the framing of the side walls, as the studs require two different angle cuts and have to be placed individually. The 1/2" plywood sheathing which covers the frame should be applied with the seams staggered to add strength to the roof and walls.

The finish materials and coverings which are installed over the sheathing will have the greatest impact on changes in the estimated cost for this project. The roofing and siding materials and the window units, especially, must be selected to match or complement those already in place on the house. The asphalt-strip shingle material suggested for the roofing, for example, is a commmonly used product, but it may not be an appropriate choice for your roof. Remember too, that roll roofing should be used if the new shed roof has a little slope. The double-hung, vinyl-clad windows suggested in this plan may be replaced with thermopane casement units if house design features will allow. The embossed vinyl siding is low in maintenance, as are the aluminum soffit and fascia, but they may not be in keeping with the style of a house that features wood siding and trim. A contractor may have to be called in for the application of the roofing and siding, as these materials require particular skills and, often, specialized

tools and equipment. The restoration of a weathertight condition to the roof and new dormer is vital to the prevention of leaks caused by rain and icing. Particular care should be given to the flashing of the old roof where it meets the dormer walls. A gutter with downspouts may have to be included at extra cost if the location of the dormer roof poses potential drainage problems. The insulating of the dormer ceiling and walls should be accomplished as part of the exterior work.

LEVEL OF DIFFICULTY

This project is a difficult undertaking for all do-it-yourselfers because of the large size of the structure, the inconvenience of its location, and the expediency with which it must be completed. Also, many different carpentry skills must be employed during the project, including advanced framing tasks and precise fitting and angle cutting of framing, sheathing, and finish materials. The general inconvenience of the roof location often adds time and extra effort to even basic jobs, and special equipment for roof work usually has to

be employed to ensure safe and efficient working conditions. Generally, beginners should not attempt this or any other dormer installation, primarily because the project includes too many tasks requiring advanced carpentry skills within a very limited time span. Ambitious handymen and experts should seek professional advice before beginning the project and to arrange to have plenty of help on hand during the roof opening and framing operations. A dormer project of this magnitude involves a considerable effort just to open the roof, aside from the new building structure. Handymen should add 75% to the professional time for all tasks, and more for specialized jobs like the installation of the flashing, vinyl siding, and aluminum soffit and fascia. Experts should add 25% to all of the man-hours estimates throughout the project.

WHAT TO WATCH OUT FOR

The venting of any attic is an important part of its construction. This plan recommends the installation of a vented aluminum soffit to handle the attic's ventilation needs. If a wood soffit and fascia are placed, be sure to add enough vent area to ensure air movement through the attic space. Many different types of vents are available, from circular plug-in models of different sizes to larger rectangular fixtures and ventilation strips. If the vents cannot be accommodated by the soffit, they may have to be placed on the roof or engineered into the gable end of the dormer. The materials installation time required for additional vents has not been included in the plan.

SUMMARY

This 29'-4" x 8' shed dormer can add enough living area to the upper floor of your house to accommodate two moderate size bedrooms and a full bath. With the correct planning and layout, the new dormer can also enhance your home's appearance and increase its value.

SHED DORMER, 30' WIDE

Description	Quantity	Man-hours	Material
Roof cutout & demolition	1 Ea.	24.0	0.00
Framing, rafters, 2" x 6" x 12', 16" O.C.	24 Ea.	8.0	121.95
Trimmer rafters, 2" x 8" x 18'	2 Ea.	2.0	21.75
Studs & plates, 2" x 4" x 8', 16" O.C.	340 L.F.	6.5	94.65
Sub-fascia, 2" x 6"	32 L.F.	1.0	13.55
Headers, double 2" x 8" x 4' long	24 L.F.	1.5	16.55
Headers, double 2" x 12" x 20' long	60 L.F.	3.0	61.00
Ceiling joists, 2" x 6" x 12'	24 Ea.	4.0	135.90
Sheathing, roof & walls, 1/2" thick, 4' x 8' sheets	18 Sheets	6.5	285.75
Building paper, 15 lb. felt	360 S.F.	1.0	13.05
Drip edge, aluminum, .016" thick, 5" girth	54 L.F.	1.5	9.15
Flashing, aluminum, .019" thick	50 S.F.	3.0	38.15
Shingles, asphalt strip, 235 lb./square	13 Bundles	1.5	37.25
Siding, vinyl-embossed, 8" wide	180 S.F.	6.0	135.05
Soffit & fascia, aluminum, vented	52 L.F.	7.0	88.10
Window, double-hung, insulating glass plastic-clad, 2'-6" x 3'	1 Ea.	1.0	181.50
Windows, double window, double hung, insulating glass plastic-clad, 5' x 4'	2 Ea.	8.0	1113.20
Insulation, fiberglass, 3 1/2" thick, R-11, paper-backed	484 S.F.	2.5	117.15
	Totals	88.0	$2483.70

Project Size	29'-4" x 8'	Contractor's Fee Including Materials	$6980

Key to Abbreviations
C.Y. - cubic yard   Ea. - each   L.F. - linear foot   Pr. - pair   Sq. - square (100 square feet of area)
S.F. - square foot   S.Y. - square yard   V.L.F. - vertical linear foot

SINGLE GARAGE, ATTACHED

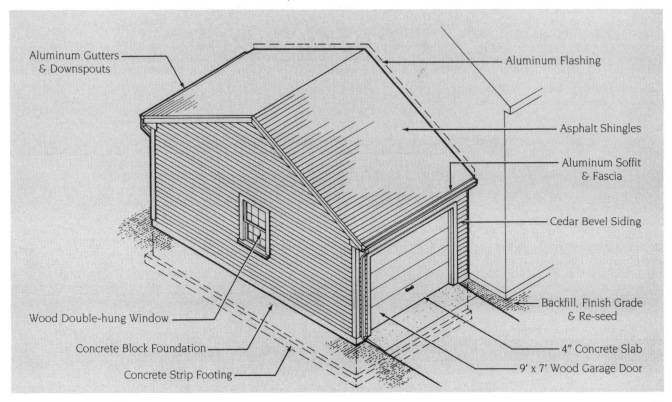

Aluminum Gutters & Downspouts

Aluminum Flashing

Asphalt Shingles

Aluminum Soffit & Fascia

Cedar Bevel Siding

Wood Double-hung Window

Concrete Block Foundation

Concrete Strip Footing

Backfill, Finish Grade & Re-seed

4" Concrete Slab

9' x 7' Wood Garage Door

A garage can boost the value of a house, as it provides protection for vehicles and sheltered work and storage space. Like carports, garages can be attached or freestanding, with single or double bays. They should be carefully planned around such factors as their intended use and the style and size of your house, as well as the available land and the characteristics of the site. This model is a basic single car garage, attached to the house and built on level ground. Many do-it-yourselfers can accomplish this project with limited assistance and subcontracting. The result is a practical home improvement completed at reasonable cost.

MATERIALS

The components of this garage plan include materials for the foundation and floor, three walls, and the roof, as well as some specialized products like the gutters and garage door unit. Because all of these items are usually in good supply, prices are competitive and it pays to shop around for them.

You probably will get a better "package" price if you buy all of the materials from the same retailer.

Before the foundation and floor are placed, the site for the new garage must be cleared and a perimeter trench excavated to a depth of about 4'. The site conditions of the garage location will have an impact on cost. For example, a severe slope in the grade may require a higher foundation or backfill to raise the grade. If needed, such operations will add to the cost of the project. Generally, if the terrain is level and free of trees and other obstructions, no extra cost will be incurred in the site preparation. The excavation of the 12' x 22' foundation trench should be dug to a level below the frost line and should be deep and wide enough to allow for an 8" x 16" footing and a 3' to 4' foundation. Where no frost line exists, it might be possible to decrease the foundation depth. The estimate for this garage provides for hand excavation and the installation of 8" concrete blocks for the foundation. It is probably best to

hire specialty contractors for the foundation work. At the very least, they can will complete the process more rapidly and with less aggravation. The concrete slab can be placed at any time after the foundation has been completed. When excavating for the slab, be sure to allow for several inches of sub-base, 4" of concrete, and at least one exposed course of block above the floor surface, except in the section that will include the door. If you are installing the floor on your own, be sure to allow a gradual slope toward the door opening for drainage.

Once the foundation has been placed and backfilled, the three walls can be framed and sheathed. Standard grade 2" x 4"s placed 16" on center, with a doubled plate on the top and a single shoe plate on the bottom, make up the walls. Be sure to fasten the shoe plate firmly to the 2" x 6" sill, which is anchored to the top of the foundation wall. The rear wall of this garage is solid, but the side and front partitions require openings for the window and door. The cost for 2" x 8" headers and 2" x 4" jack studs and their installation time have been included in the plan. Remember to allow additional time for removing some or all of the siding from the house wall before the framing begins. The other walls can then be framed, 2" x 6" joists can be placed, and the roof framing can be performed.

The framing of the roof is more difficult than that of the partitions; but this roof is still small enough to provide a good chance for do-it-yourselfers to pick up experience in placing a ridge board and rafter system. With some advice before you start and guidance as you go, your skills will improve as you progress. Consistency of rafter length and accurate angling and notching are the key to a square and level roof frame. Once the rafters have been laid out and cut from a template, the placement and fastening operations usually move quickly. After the frame is complete, the sheathing, drip edge, and roofing are installed. The

shingling can be done by most do-it-yourselfers because the roof is straight and basic in its design. Get some assistance on placing the flashing, however, if the process is unfamiliar to you. A poor or incorrect flashing job can cause water damage to the interior of the garage and to the adjacent house wall and ceiling.

There are several options for the exterior finish products to be used on this garage. An economical, standard double-hung model is a good choice for the window. This plan suggests low-maintenance aluminum fascias, soffits, and gutters, but wood products could also be employed for these components. The design and cost of these items should be considered along with your house's style and your budget limitations. Similarly, garage door units are available in expensive wood-paneled models, as well as in economical fiberglass and hardboard designs.

LEVEL OF DIFFICULTY

Foundation, framing, and roofing operations are challenging tasks, regardless of the type of structure being built. Inexperienced do-it-yourselfers should assess their level of skills and the amount of time they can give to the project before taking it on. Because this structure is relatively small, with one side already in place, handymen can improve their building skills while working on the project; but they should seek assistance when they need it. The concrete and masonry work may be out of the reach of many do-it-yourselfers. Digging trenches, constructing forms, and laying concrete blocks are physically demanding, time-consuming operations. Ambitious beginners can complete most of the project once the foundation is in, but they should get instruction at the start and guidance along the way. They should double the man-hours for the tasks they attempt. Handymen and experts should add 40% and 10%, respectively, for the carpentry work, and more for specialty operations like the foundation, floor, and garage door installations.

WHAT TO WATCH OUT FOR

An automatic garage door opener is a convenient accessory which can be installed by most handymen. These devices can be adapted to all types of door units and garage interiors and installed in just a few hours' time. The cost of an automatic opener has not been included in this plan, but some of the money saved by doing the project on your own might be applied to this convenience item.

SUMMARY

Adding a garage improves the value of your home while providing shelter for your vehicle and increasing storage and protected work space. If you do some or all of the work on your own, this attached one-car facility can be built at a surprisingly low cost.

SINGLE GARAGE, ATTACHED

Description	Quantity	Man-hours	Material
Site clearing, layout, excavate for footing	1 Lot	6.0	0.00
Footing, 8" thick x 16" wide x 44'	2 C.Y.	5.5	167.00
Foundation, 6" concrete block, 3'-4" high	200 Blocks	18.5	363.00
Edge form at doorway	10 L.F.	0.5	2.45
Floor slab, 4" thick, 300 psi, w/sub-base, reinforcing, finished	265 S.F.	9.0	506.65
Wall framing, 2" x 4" x 10' @ 16" O.C.	38 L.F.	6.5	139.80
Headers over openings, 2" x 8"	14 L.F.	1.0	9.65
Sheathing for walls, 1/2" thick, 4' x 8' sheets	12 Sheets	5.0	190.50
Ridge board, 1" x 8" x 12'	12 L.F.	0.5	4.10
Roof framing, rafters, 2" x 6" x 14', 16" O.C.	280 L.F.	4.5	132.15
Joists, 2" x 6" x 22', 16" O.C.	220 L.F.	3.0	103.85
Gable framing, 2" x 4"	45 L.F.	1.5	14.15
Sheathing for roof, 1/2" thick, 4' x 8' sheets	11 Sheets	4.0	174.65
Sub-fascia, 2" x 8" x 12'	24 L.F.	2.0	16.55
Felt paper, 15 lb.	340 S.F.	0.5	12.35
Shingles, asphalt, standard strip	4 Sq.	6.5	149.05
Drip edge, aluminum, 5"	52 L.F.	1.0	9.45
Flashing, aluminum	21 S.F.	1.5	16.75
Fascia, aluminum	21 S.F.	1.5	52.85
Soffit, aluminum	38 S.F.	1.5	33.55
Gutters & downspouts, aluminum	44 L.F.	3.0	44.20
Window, wood, standard, 34" x 22"	1 Ea.	1.0	157.30
Garage door, wood, incl. hardware, 9' x 7'	1 Ea.	2.0	453.75
Siding, cedar, rough sawn, stained	400 S.F.	13.5	963.15
Painting, door & window trim, primer & 2 coats	85 S.F.	2.0	7.20
Totals		101.5	$3724.10

Project Size	12' x 22'	Contractor's Fee Including Materials	$9110

Key to Abbreviations
C.Y. - cubic yard   Ea. - each   L.F. - linear foot   Pr. - pair   Sq. - square (100 square feet of area)
S.F. - square foot   S.Y. - square yard   V.L.F. - vertical linear foot

DOUBLE GARAGE, FREESTANDING

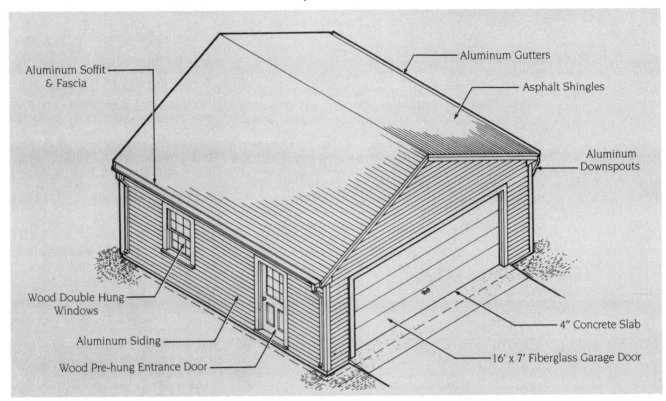

Aluminum Soffit & Fascia

Aluminum Gutters

Asphalt Shingles

Aluminum Downspouts

Wood Double Hung Windows

Aluminum Siding

Wood Pre-hung Entrance Door

4" Concrete Slab

16' x 7' Fiberglass Garage Door

If your house lot is large enough to accommodate the addition of a free-standing garage, you might consider using this model for a two-car facility. This plan is basic in both design and materials; but it is still a major project, and one that will challenge do-it-yourselfers of all ability levels. With patient and careful work, however, handymen can save on labor costs by completing some or all of the project on their own.

MATERIALS

The basic components of this two-car garage are commonly available building materials used in wood frame structures. A 4" reinforced concrete slab with a thickened perimeter comprises the foundation and finished floor of the structure. Standard 2" x 4" framing materials, plywood, and asphalt shingles are employed for the roof. Several specialty products are also included to finish the structure, including aluminum gutters, soffits, and fascias, and a double-width fiberglass garage door. Bear in mind

that all of these materials are competitively priced at building supply outlets. With this size order, you have some leverage in getting the best possible price. Arrange for local delivery in the final purchase agreement, as most of these materials require trucking. Cost, quality, and convenience are factors to consider before making your materials purchase.

If the site for the new garage is level and dry, the suggested 4" reinforced concrete slab with a thickened perimeter is generally all that is required for a foundation. Such factors as poor soil conditions, frost, and the possibility of future attachment to an existing structure may require the placement of a footing and foundation wall at extra cost. The site clearing and excavation will take some time because of the large surface area, so plan accordingly, particularly if you intend to clear and dig by hand. If you are unfamiliar with concrete installations, seek some advice from a knowledgeable person or subcontract

the job to a professional. Incorrect slab placement can be the cause of wasted time and materials later on in the construction.

Installing the wall materials for this four-sided structure requires a command of basic carpentry skills. If you have not framed a four-sided structure before, you will need some assistance in the layout, erecting, squaring, and securing of the partitions. After the wall framing is in place, 1/2" exterior plywood sheathing should be installed for support and as a base for the finished siding.

The roof framing is the most difficult task in the entire project, as the 2" x 6" rafters and 1" x 8" ridge board have to be positioned with accuracy. Poor workmanship can cause wasted time and material, and result in variations in the finished roofing. Like the straight roof in the free-standing carport project, this shingling job can be handled by most do-it-yourselfers.

Roofing felt is an extra weather-proofing material which is applied under the asphalt shingles in this project. It is not an essential item, however, if you are looking for a way to cut costs.

Once the roof has been completed, the structure is ready to receive the windows, entrance door, siding, garage door, and other finish products. A wide variety of standard pre-hung window and door units can be used, depending on the style of your home, the garage's visibility, and your budget. The extra expense for insulating glass or deluxe airtight units is unnecessary unless you plan to insulate and heat the facility. This plan features low-maintenance aluminum siding, soffits, and gutters, but standard wood products can be used in their place at varying costs. If you choose the suggested aluminum material, a specialty contractor should be consulted or called in, as these products require particular tools and expertise for fast and efficient installation. Many different types of garage doors are available in a wide range of prices, in both wood and man-made materials. The large fiberglass door suggested in this plan is recommended for its light weight, durability, and maintenance-free properties. A specialty door contractor should also be consulted or hired before the installation.

LEVEL OF DIFFICULTY

If you are familiar with framing operations and reasonably skilled in exterior home improvements, you should be able to complete this garage project. As noted earlier, it is a major undertaking and will take considerable time to complete, but if you are willing to work slowly and carefully, the results will be worthwhile. Two critical procedures, the slab installation and roof framing, can be costly if they are not done correctly. Seek professional assistance for these tasks if you feel that they are beyond your abilities. Beginners should not attempt the concrete, framing, and specialty installations; and they should add 100% to the professional time for other jobs like the sheathing and roofing. They should get professional help or guidance for all tasks that are new to them. Handymen and experts should add 40% and 10%, respectively, to the man-hours estimates for the jobs they attempt. They should add more for the slab placement and roof framing if they are inexperienced in these operations. Handymen and experts should also consider hiring professionals for the specialty work, like the aluminum siding and garage door installation.

WHAT TO WATCH OUT FOR

This two-car garage project provides an excellent opportunity for the homeowner to create storage and workshop space in addition to shelter for vehicles. If the peak of the structure is high enough, over 300 square feet of usable storage space exists in the attic above the ceiling joists. Although it will add to the cost and time of the project, decking can be laid over the joists, and an access door can be framed into the gable above the garage door opening. Remember that the ceiling joists suggested in this plan are only 2" x 6"s; 2" x 8"s should be used for the joists if heavy materials are to be stored in this area. Electrical service can also be added to the plan for safety or convenience lighting, or for workshop use.

DOUBLE GARAGE, FREESTANDING

Description	Quantity	Man-hours	Material
Grading, by hand, for slab area	576 S.F.	8.5	0.00
Edge forms for floor slab	88 L.F.	5.0	21.30
Concrete floor slab, 4" thick, 3000 psi, complete	484 S.F.	4.0	925.30
Anchor bolts, embedded in slab	20 Ea.	1.0	8.25
Wall framing, 2" x 4" x 8', 24" O.C., studs & plates	80 L.F.	10.5	224.60
Headers over openings, 2" x 12"	28 L.F.	1.5	30.85
Sheathing for walls, 1/2" thick, plywood, 4' x 8' sheets	23 Sheets	10.5	365.15
Ridge board, 1" x 8" x 12'	24 L.F.	1.0	8.15
Roof framing, rafters, 2" x 6" x 14', 24" O.C.	336 L.F.	5.5	158.55
Joists, 2" x 6" x 22', 24" O.C.	264 L.F.	3.5	124.60
Gable framing, 2" x 4"	75 L.F.	2.5	23.60
Sheathing for roof, 1/2" thick, plywood, 4' x 8' sheets	21 Sheets	7.5	375.05
Sub-fascia, 2" x 8" x 12'	48 L.F.	3.5	33.10
Felt paper, 15 lb.	625 S.F.	1.0	22.70
Shingles, asphalt, standard strip	7 Sq.	10.5	260.90
Drip edge, aluminum, 5"	100 L.F.	2.0	18.15
Fascia, aluminum	50 S.F.	3.0	125.85
Soffit, aluminum	70 S.F.	3.0	61.85
Gutters & downspouts, aluminum	64 L.F.	4.5	64.30
Windows, wood, standard, 2' x 3'	2 Ea.	2.0	314.60
Garage door, incl. hardware, hardboard, 16' x 7', standard	1 Ea.	3.0	677.60
Entrance door, wood, pre-hung, 2'-8" x 6'-8"	1 Ea.	1.0	199.65
Siding, aluminum, double 4" pattern, 8" wide	680 S.F.	21.5	798.15
Painting, entrance door & window trim, primer & 2 coats	50 S.F.	1.0	4.25
Totals		117.0	$4846.50

Project Size 22' x 22'

Contractor's Fee Including Materials **$12,230**

SUMMARY

If your lot and dwelling can accommodate a large free-standing garage, this economical and practical design might be the right choice. Although it is a major project, handymen who have the time can complete much of the work on their own, with a substantial savings in the cost of construction.

Key to Abbreviations
C.Y. - cubic yard   Ea. - each   L.F. - linear foot   Pr. - pair   Sq. - square (100 square feet of area)
S.F. - square foot   S.Y. - square yard   V.L.F. - vertical linear foot

OCTAGONAL GAZEBO, 4' SIDES

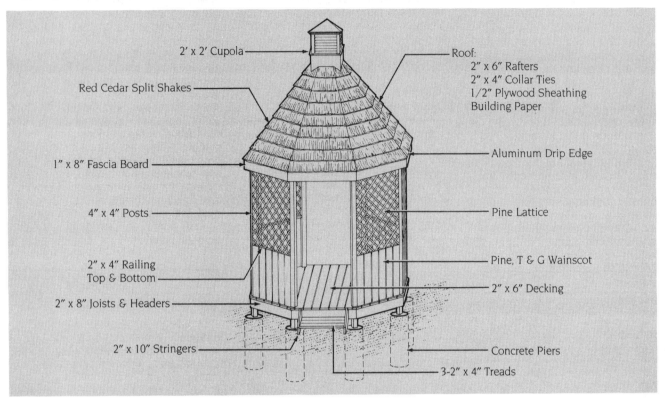

2' x 2' Cupola

Red Cedar Split Shakes

Roof:
2" x 6" Rafters
2" x 4" Collar Ties
1/2" Plywood Sheathing
Building Paper

1" x 8" Fascia Board

Aluminum Drip Edge

4" x 4" Posts

Pine Lattice

2" x 4" Railing
Top & Bottom

Pine, T & G Wainscot

2" x 8" Joists & Headers

2" x 6" Decking

2" x 10" Stringers

Concrete Piers

3-2" x 4" Treads

Building a gazebo can be a fun project for do-it-yourselfers, although a considerable amount of carpentry skill is required. The convenience of the backyard location, working on level ground, and not being pressed to finish quickly are all factors which help make the project managcable. This small octagonal gazebo may appear complex, but with a patient, step-by-step approach, it can be completed with professional results.

MATERIALS

In many ways, a gazebo is like the shell of a small house, as it consists of a foundation or support system, framed and covered walls, and a roof. Standard construction lumber and finish materials can be used throughout, or you might prefer pressure-treated wood, which is used in this model. As in other home improvement projects which require a substantial order of readily available materials, it pays to shop around before buying.

The foundation system for this octagonal gazebo consists of concrete pedestals set 3' deep at each of the eight points of the structure. Before the concrete is placed, the post holes must be carefully laid out and dug by hand. Be sure to dig the holes precisely where they are staked, as inaccurate pedestal placement will cause problems later on in the project. You might consider the extra expense of ''tube'' forms for the pedestals, as they are easy to level and provide a neat, cylindrical shape for any exposed concrete.

After the pedestals are finished and allowed to set up, the support posts, platform, and sides are installed. Again, there are several methods that can be used, all of which work well and require about the same amount of material, though they may vary in installation time. One method is to assemble the 4" x 4" support posts and the frame for the platform in the same operation. This approach guarantees integral support between

the platform, posts, and later, the roof, and it makes for a neat carpentry job. Be sure to maintain plumb and level during this operation and the subsequent installations of the decking, railings, and wainscoting.

Various options in both materials and methods are open to the do-it-yourselfer throughout the construction of the platform and sides. Decorative floorboard patterns and angled wainscoting are among the possibilities, and an ornate cap with trim could replace a standard 2" x 4" railing. These are just a few of the possible variations from this plan. Generally, extra cost and installation time should be added for all decorative work, as more material and intricate angle-cutting are usually involved. The lattice included in this plan adds a delicate design feature typical to many gazebos, but other options are also possible, including the fabrication of heavier lattice with a larger grid, or leaving the space above the wainscoting open. If you intend to use lattice, hold off on placing it until the roof has been completed.

The most challenging procedure in the construction of the gazebo is the roof. Because it features a design with triangular sections, skillful carpentry and application of geometry are required. Remember that it is a very visible component of the structure, both inside and out, so take your time and work carefully. The use of precisely made templates throughout the roof construction will ensure a consistent size in the framing members and sheathing pieces and will help the job go smoothly. Like the sides of the gazebo, the design and style of the roof can also be chosen from many possible variations. This plan suggests red cedar shakes with an 8-1/2" exposure and a prefabricated cupola. Another option is squared-end white cedar shingles, which create a more delicate appearance.

The finishing touches, including the stairs, lattice, built-in benches, and the painting, allow for much creative leeway. The stairs can be of standard wood design, as suggested in this plan, or they can be made of brick over a poured concrete base. The lattice, as noted earlier, can be altered in pattern, size, and material. Prefabricated lattice made from pressure-treated wood is recommended here because of its longevity and low maintenance. Although they are convenient, built-in benches do take up platform space that could be used by more comfortable patio furniture. As in other exterior projects, the style and type of materials chosen for the finish work on this gazebo will have a considerable impact on the overall cost.

LEVEL OF DIFFICULTY

This small gazebo is difficult to build because of the moderate to advanced carpentry skills and the number of odd angles, saw cuts, and fastening techniques that are required. Nevertheless, it can still be a fun and educational project which can serve as a training ground for improving your carpentry abilities. With a patient approach, some preliminary reading on the subject, and help and guidance along the way, many do-it-yourselfers can successfully complete this gazebo. Be prepared to make some mistakes and, possibly, waste some materials if you are a beginner. The most challenging tasks in the project are the initial layout and the roof construction. Beginners might want to consider hiring a contractor for these aspects of the project. Handymen should plan on extra time for both of these operations, as precise measuring, angling, and saw cutting are key to correct installation. Experts should add 20% or more to the professional time throughout the project. Beginners and handymen should add 100% and 50% for all tasks, except the layout and the roof placement. If they choose to take on these jobs, beginners should add 150% to the time estimate, and handymen, 100%.

OCTAGONAL GAZEBO, 4' SIDES

Description	Quantity	Man-hours	Material
Excavate post holes, incl. layout	8 Ea.	8.0	0.00
Concrete, field mix, 1 C.F. per bag, for posts, incl. 8" diam. form	8 Bags	8.0	145.20
Framing materials, pressure-treated lumber			
Posts 4" x 4" x 12'	96 L.F.	3.5	109.20
Headers, 2" x 8" x 12'	36 L.F.	1.5	31.80
Joists, 2" x 8" x 10'	70 L.F.	1.5	61.85
Flooring, 2" x 6" x 10'	200 L.F.	6.0	123.45
Railing, top & bottom, 2" x 4" stock	60 L.F.	2.0	24.65
Wainscot, white pine, rough-sawn, 1" x 8", natural, T & G	72 S.F.	2.5	53.15
Lattice, stock pine, 1/4" x 1-1/8" stock	216 L.F.	6.5	47.05
Roofing material, headers, 2" x 6" stock	36 L.F.	1.5	22.25
Rafters, 2" x 6" x 8'	128 L.F.	3.5	60.40
Collar ties, 2" x 4" stock	16 L.F.	0.5	5.05
Fascia board, 1" x 8" stock	36 L.F.	1.0	32.65
Sheathing, 1/2" plywood, 4' x 8' sheets	8 Sheets	3.0	127.00
Building paper, 15 lb. felt paper	140 S.F.	0.5	5.05
Drip edge, aluminum, 5" girth	32 L.F.	1.0	5.80
Shakes, hand split red cedar, 18" long, 8-1/2" exposure	2 Sq.	8.0	193.60
Stair material, stringers, 2" x 10" stock	16 L.F.	1.0	39.50
Treads, 2" x 4" x 3'-6", 3 per tread	24 L.F.	1.0	31.05
Cupola, stock unit, 2' x 2' x 2'	1 Ea.	2.0	223.85
Painting, primer & 2 coats	700 S.F.	6.0	220.25
	Totals	68.5	$1562.80

Project Size	10'-6" x 10'-6"	Contractor's Fee Including Materials	$3940

Key to Abbreviations
C.Y. - cubic yard   Ea. - each   L.F. - linear foot   Pr. - pair   Sq. - square (100 square feet of area)
S.F. - square foot   S.Y. - square yard   V.L.F. - vertical linear foot

WHAT TO WATCH OUT FOR

A good set of carpentry tools will help facilitate work on most home improvements and the gazebo project is no exception. Having the right hand and power tools makes many of the challenging carpentry operations less difficult. It's a good idea to have some extra, sharpened blades handy, as pressure-treated wood dulls them faster than standard lumber. Several different nailsets of various sizes will also help in the toenailing of angled pieces and in the finish nailing of the floor, wainscoting, lattice, fascia, and other trim pieces. An accurate 2' or 3' level, calipers, and an adjustable square will all help to make the layouts and angle cutting much easier and more precise.

SUMMARY

If you have the time and are willing to learn some carpentry as you go, constructing this gazebo can be an enjoyable and educational undertaking. Once finished, it will provide many years of practical and pleasurable use.

OCTAGONAL GAZEBO, 6' SIDES

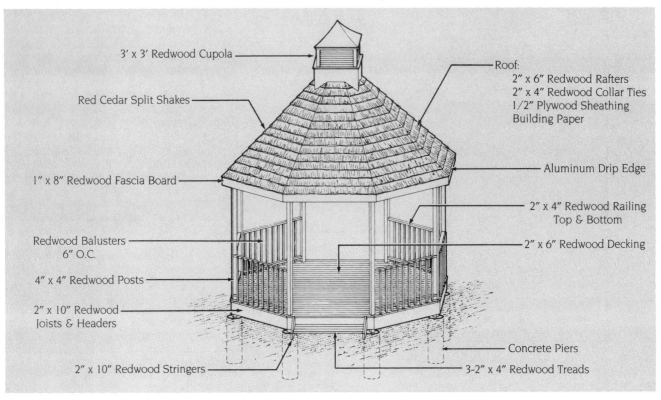

3' x 3' Redwood Cupola

Red Cedar Split Shakes

1" x 8" Redwood Fascia Board

Redwood Balusters
6" O.C.

4" x 4" Redwood Posts

2" x 10" Redwood
Joists & Headers

2" x 10" Redwood Stringers

Roof:
2" x 6" Redwood Rafters
2" x 4" Redwood Collar Ties
1/2" Plywood Sheathing
Building Paper

Aluminum Drip Edge

2" x 4" Redwood Railing
Top & Bottom

2" x 6" Redwood Decking

Concrete Piers

3-2" x 4" Redwood Treads

Gazebos can range from plain and rustic to very decorative and can be constructed from a wide variety of materials, from basic to deluxe. This model has 6' sides, a floor area of nearly 170 square feet, and a balustered railing. It is built of attractive, long-lasting redwood material. Because of its size and the skillful carpentry required in its construction, it is a challenging project. The extra expense of redwood underscores the importance of good workmanship. Beginners and inexperienced handymen are advised to hire a carpenter to complete some portions of the work. Despite the challenges and the expense of this project, the rewards are an attractive outside structure and years of pleasurable use for your friends and family.

MATERIALS

The materials used in this plan consist of basic products found in all exterior structures. The difference is that redwood is used instead of standard construction lumber for many of the components. Because redwood is not readily available in some areas of the country, you may have to special order it. In this case, the price may exceed the one given in the model's estimate. The plywood sheathing and the cedar for the roof are standard products generally available at building supply outlets, regardless of geographical location. When purchasing the materials, be sure to arrange delivery, as it is a large enough order to require trucking.

The most important procedure in the early stages of the project involves establishing the layout for the gazebo and accurately placing 3' concrete pedestals, which serve as its basic support. Because of the octagonal shape and the number of pedestals required, the operation is tricky; and careful planning and workmanship are crucial if the rest of the project is to go smoothly. Be sure to double check all measurements before placing the concrete. The use of "tube" forms will add to the cost of this procedure, but they will make it easier to place and level the pedestals accurately.

The next phase of the project involves the placement of the platform and 4" x 4" support posts. One method is to build the 2" x 10" frame in place and then mortise it into the posts so that short legs of about 6" extend below the frame onto the tops of the pedestals. Another way is to place the frame directly on the pedestals and set the posts beside the perimeter of the frame at each point. Still another is to plant the 4" x 4" legs in the concrete at rough height, level them by sawing after the concrete has cured, and then build the frame of the platform around them. Later, the 4" x 4" roof supports should transmit the load of the roof directly to the pedestals. The costs vary only slightly between these three methods.

After the 4 x 4's are positioned, they should be temporarily braced while the 2" x 6" headers for the roof perimeter are installed. The 2" x 6" roof rafters are difficult to place, as they must be precisely angled on both ends if they are to fit correctly. Ceiling joists are not called for in this plan, but they can be used in place of the collar ties if the new gazebo is to have a finished ceiling. Sheathing and finished roofing are applied after the roof frame is completed. Red cedar shingles are suggested in this plan, but any other type of finished roofing can be used, including tile, slate, and various grades of asphalt and cedar. Although the roof is relatively small, its installation can be challenging because of the hips and the triangular shape of the roof sections. Seek some assistance if you are an inexperienced roofer, and plan on allowing extra time for cutting and scribing the roofing material. Also be aware that considerable waste is expected on roofs of this design. The cupola can be placed at any time after the roof has been completed. Hiring a carpenter for this job might be a good idea, as extensive cutting of the base is required to install this expensive fixture.

The railing and steps of the gazebo also require skillful carpentry if you choose to follow the design of this plan. Here, a top and bottom rail are constructed with 2" x 2" balusters set at 8" intervals. There are many other options, however, for the railing design. Fancy balusters, lattice, and wainscoting are some of the possibilities. Lattice and various trim styles can also be used for the opening above the rail and the fascia. Ornate trim designs tend to be more expensive than simpler styles, so compromises might be made to stay within a budget. Many stairway designs are also possible, from basic wood steps, like the ones included in this plan, to decorative styles made of concrete, brick, and stone.

LEVEL OF DIFFICULTY

The size, expense, and advanced carpentry skills required to construct this gazebo make it a challenging project, even for expert do-it-yourselfers. Beginners and handymen, therefore, should consider hiring a carpenter to complete the roof and some other aspects of the job.

Mistakes can always be costly and time-consuming, but when redwood is involved, the price can be twice as high. The most challenging task in the project is the roof frame. The rental of staging may be an extra cost for this phase of the project. The detailed work of the finished roof and cupola may also be troublesome for many do-it-yourselfers. Generally, handymen and beginners should not attempt any of the roof work. They should add 50% and 100%, respectively, to the estimated time for all other tasks, and slightly more for fancy trim work which involves expensive materials. Experts should add 20% to the professional time for all jobs, and more for all aspects of the roof work. All do-it-yourselfers are reminded of the high cost of redwood and should consider the potential liability of working with it.

WHAT TO WATCH OUT FOR

Both of the gazebos outlined in this section are octagonal in shape, but six- and five-sided configurations are also authentic Victorian gazebo designs. The eight-sided structures presented in the book provide more platform space, but they also require more materials and time to construct. The hexagonal and pentagonal types are slightly easier to build, because fewer pedestals are required; but the same kinds of complications still exist in angling the roof frame and applying its covering. However they may differ in size and shape, gazebos can be decoratively trimmed and authentically styled from the same kinds of materials.

SUMMARY

This large, octagonal redwood gazebo is a home improvement that will enhance the atmosphere of your backyard landscape and expand your outdoor living space. While some aspects of the project may be out of reach for inexperienced do-it-yourselfers, it can still be your own personal creation, taking shape from the decorative features you choose to incorporate.

OCTAGONAL REDWOOD GAZEBO, 6' SIDES,

Description	Quantity	Man-hours	Material
Excavate, post holes, including layout	8 Ea.	8.0	0.00
Concrete, field mix, 1 C.F. per bag, for posts, incl. 8" diam. forms	8 Bags	4.0	98.35
Framing materials, redwood			
Posts, 4" x 4" x 12'	96 L.F.	3.5	218.40
Headers, 2" x 10" x 12'	48 L.F.	1.5	113.85
Joists, 2" x 10" x 16'	192 L.F.	6.0	455.35
Flooring, 2" x 6" x 16'	448 L.F.	12.0	552.95
Railing, top & bottom, 2" x 4"	72 L.F.	2.0	59.25
Balusters, 2" x 2" x 3'	180 L.F.	7.0	69.70
Roof framing materials, redwood			
Headers, 2" x 6" stock	48 L.F.	1.0	59.25
Rafters, 2" x 6" x 10'	240 L.F.	7.0	296.20
Collar ties, 2" x 4" stock	24 L.F.	1.0	19.75
Fascia board, 1" x 8" stock	48 L.F.	1.5	87.15
Sheathing, 1/2" plywood, 4' x 8' sheets	12 Sheets	4.0	190.50
Building paper, 15 lb. felt paper	250 S.F.	0.5	9.10
Drip edge, aluminum, 5" girth	48 L.F.	1.0	8.70
Shakes, hand split red cedar, 18" long, 8-1/2" exposure	3 Sq.	12.0	290.40
Stair materials, redwood, stringers, 2" x 10" stock	16 L.F.	0.5	37.95
Treads, 2" x 4" x 4", 3 per tread	24 L.F.	0.5	19.75
Cupola, stock unit, 1" redwood, 3' x 3' base, 3' high, copper roof	1 Ea.	2.5	363.00
Sealer, 2 coats, brushwork	1100 S.F.	10.0	119.80
Totals		85.5	$3069.40

Project Size	16' x 16'	Contractor's Fee Including Materials	$7330

Key to Abbreviations
C.Y. - cubic yard   Ea. - each   L.F. - linear foot   Pr. - pair   Sq. - square (100 square feet of area)
S.F. - square foot   S.Y. - square yard   V.L.F. - vertical linear foot

Lean-to Greenhouse, Small

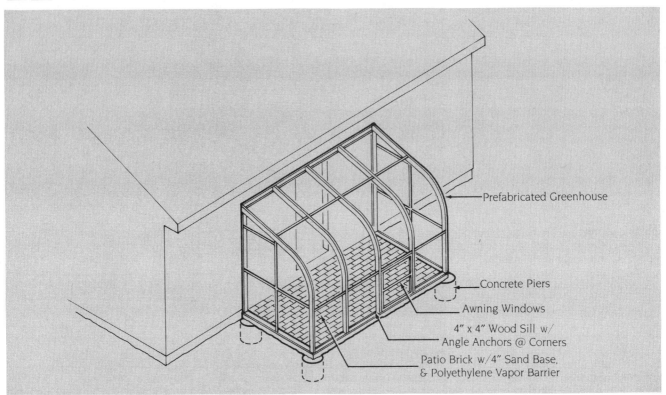

Prefabricated Greenhouse

Concrete Piers

Awning Windows

4" x 4" Wood Sill w/
Angle Anchors @ Corners

Patio Brick w/4" Sand Base,
& Polyethylene Vapor Barrier

Like decks, patios, and gazebos, greenhouses can enhance the atmosphere of your home while adding to its comfort. Of the aforementioned improvements, greenhouse projects may be the most time-consuming, but also reward you with some unique benefits that the other facilities do not provide. Their primary function is as a practical and aesthetically pleasing enclosed garden area, but they can also increase interior living space, provide solar heat, and improve the lighting and ventilation of adjacent rooms. This plan presents a small greenhouse project that most do-it-yourselfers can complete with a modest investment of time and expense.

MATERIALS

Like other attached exterior structures, greenhouses require a foundation or some other means of support, a basic framing system, flooring, and inside and outside finish work. If you plan to use a factory-prepared greenhouse kit, as this plan recommends, much of the framing and covering material for the structure has been taken care of by the manufacturer. The foundation, flooring, and finish materials are standard construction products which can be purchased at most building supply outlets. Additional materials and installation time may be needed if the new greenhouse requires an entryway into the house.

Before the greenhouse kit is assembled and placed, a considerable amount of preliminary work must be completed. Aluminum-framed greenhouses with fiberglass or tempered glass panels require a sturdy and deep foundation or ground support system. In colder climates, especially, ground frost can cause heaving, settling, and possibly, warping of the frame or cracking of the greenhouse panels if the foundation is inadequate. This plan calls for four concrete pedestals set 3' deep, and a 4" x 4" frame secured with galvanized angle anchors. Be sure to lay out the post holes precisely and dig them to a proper depth. The extra investment in

"tube" forms might be worthwhile because they are easy to work with. They also provide a neat finished appearance for the tops of the pedestals. Because the frame is placed in direct contact with the ground, it should be constructed from pressure-treated lumber. After the pedestals and frame have been installed, the flooring can be put into place. There are several possibilities for floor material, but dry-set bricks, patio blocks, and crushed stone all provide surfaces which drain well. Before a brick floor is installed, the area should be excavated to a depth of about 7" to allow for 4" of sand base and 3" for the thickness of the bricks. The brick-in-sand patio plan outlined in this book provides detailed information on the cost and placement procedures of surfaces of this type.

The greenhouse itself is the most important and expensive component included in the project. The unit suggested in this plan features aluminum framing, tinted tempered glass panels, an exterior door, and two awning windows. However, many other designs and options are available, so do some research and thoroughly investigate all of the possibilities before you buy. Because of the craftsmanship involved and specialized materials required for their manufacture, greenhouse kits are expensive products. Further, their cost and quality vary widely, depending on the type of materials used in their frame and panels, and the engineering of their structural and tie-in systems. As with other specialized factory-made home building products, the selection of a quality item with a proven reputation for durability and low maintenance is usually worth the extra cost. Some additional expense will, be incurred if you choose to include thermal shades, screens, vents, fans, and other options. Further costs will be incurred if any electrical, plumbing, or heating components are to be included in the project.

When erecting the new facility, be sure to fasten it correctly to the base frame and tie it into the house with acceptable flashing methods. This plan does not include the cost of

adding or redesigning an entryway from the house. If there is not already a doorway, you might consider installing one. In colder climates, especially, arranging direct access from the house makes sense because of convenience and the potential benefits of passive solar heating. Like other attached structures, the new greenhouse should blend with the rest of the house, so some compromises may have to be made in determining its location. Factors to consider include the extent to which the greenhouse is to be used, the design of the house, and its orientation to the sun.

LEVEL OF DIFFICULTY

This project presents an opportunity for do-it-yourselfers of all ability levels to take part in its construction. It is a small structure which involves only a limited amount of foundation and other preliminary work. Once the support pedestals and frame are correctly located, leveled, and squared, the rest of the work is very straightforward. There may be some challenges in the fabrication of the greenhouse itself; but if you follow the manufacturer's directions and guidelines included in the kit, that operation should also go smoothly.

Slow, patient work and the willingness to get help if problems arise are important aspects of any home improvement project, and this one is no different. While beginners may find the pedestal and frame work out of reach, they should add 100% to the man-hours for the brick floor installation and for any other finish work. Handymen should figure on an additional 40% time allowance; and experts, about 10%. Because the greenhouse kit is expensive and intricate in its materials and design, all do-it-yourselfers should allow extra time for its assembly and installation.

WHAT TO WATCH OUT FOR

Even a small, basic greenhouse like this one can collect a considerable amount of passive solar heat in the course of a winter day. The brick floor, house wall, and the plants themselves absorb heat from the sunlight, store it, and then provide a source of radiant warmth after the sun has gone down. With a little ingenuity and a modest investment, this energy can be put to use to heat the greenhouse at night, and can even help to heat the house. One way of collecting more solar heat is to paint the house wall and other surfaces, like plant racks and floor borders, a dark color. Another easy way to collect more heat is to place portable dark-colored containers filled with water against the house wall. To transfer the heat from the greenhouse to the main house during the day and, sometimes, even at night, you might install a small exhaust fan in the house wall near the ceiling of the greenhouse. For a modest extra investment, you can purchase a thermostatic fan control which will turn it on and off to ensure a stable temperature. All of these means of collecting and controlling passive solar heat energy are economical to install and their benefits can be surprisingly great.

LEAN-TO GREENHOUSE, SMALL

Description	Quantity	Man-hours	Material
Excavate, post holes, including layout	4 Ea.	4.0	0.00
Concrete, field mix, 1 C.F. per bag, for posts, incl. 8″ diam. forms	4 Bags	2.0	49.20
Angle anchors for 4″ x 4″ wood frame	4 Ea.	0.5	1.60
Wood frame for base, 4″ x 4″ treated lumber	36 L.F.	1.5	40.95
Polyethylene vapor barrier,. 008″ thick	72 S.F.	0.5	2.60
Washed sand for 4″ base	1 C.Y.	0.0	3.80
Grade & level sand base	60 S.F.	2.0	0.00
Patio brick, 4″ x 8″ x 1-1/2″ thick, laid flat	60 S.F.	9.0	159.75
Greenhouse, prefab., 5′-6″ x 10′-6″ x 7′ high, w/2 awning windows	1 Ea.	16.0	4961.00
Flashing, aluminum, .016″ thick	24 S.F.	1.5	19.15
Totals		36.5	$5238.05

Project Size	5′-6″ x 10′-6″	Contractor's Fee Including Materials	$9020

Key to Abbreviations
C.Y. - cubic yard Ea. - each L.F. - linear foot Pr. - pair Sq. - square (100 square feet of area)
S.F. - square foot S.Y. - square yard V.L.F. - vertical linear foot

SUMMARY

This greenhouse project offers rewards for gardeners and homeowners who want to enhance the atmosphere of their homes. For a small additional investment, you can also reap the benefits of passive solar heat.

LEAN-TO GREENHOUSE, LARGE

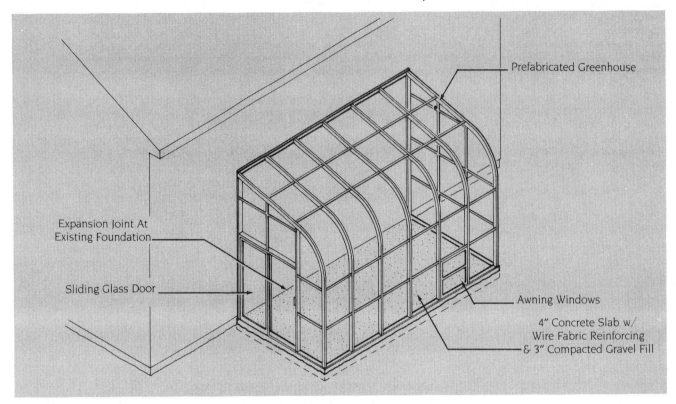

Prefabricated Greenhouse

Expansion Joint At
Existing Foundation

Sliding Glass Door

Awning Windows

4" Concrete Slab w/
Wire Fabric Reinforcing
& 3" Compacted Gravel Fill

One of the options for attached greenhouses is an exterior structure with its access limited to the outside. As long as some type of heating and ventilation system is employed to stabilize the air temperature inside, such a facility can serve as an attractive, yet practical, interior garden independent of the household. In some cases, a doorway to the interior might be planned as another part of the project, to be completed at a later date. In this way, the homeowner can adjust to the energy demands of the greenhouse without interfering with the normal operation of the house's heating or air conditioning system. In other cases, a doorway between the inside living area and the greenhouse simply may not be desired. This plan demonstrates how a medium-sized greenhouse can be erected with exterior access only. Should an inside doorway be needed for a similar sized greenhouse, simply add to this estimate the extra cost of the door installation from one of the other greenhouse plans. Many experienced do-it-yourselfers can complete this project on their own, but beginners should consider hiring a contractor for some of the procedures.

MATERIALS

The construction supplies for this project consist of the concrete and other materials needed to form the slab, as well as the factory-prepared greenhouse kit, and the items required to attach it to the slab and house wall. Before purchasing the greenhouse kit, do some research and shopping to find out about brand names, designs, levels of quality, and prices of the various units. Some offer more operational accessories and better craftsmanship and engineering than others. As with the purchase of any home building product, it pays in the long run to buy a quality item.

The support system for this greenhouse installation is comprised of a 4" concrete slab which has been placed over a 3" bed of compacted gravel fill. Before the slab is put into place, the area must be dug out by hand to a depth of 7". Accurate measuring, squaring, and leveling of the form is a critical procedure in the operation, as the base of the greenhouse has fixed dimensions and the unit as a whole must fit snugly against the house wall. If the foundation is not true in its placement, the greenhouse will not sit properly on the slab or against the house wall; and, consequently, the enclosure may develop leaks. In climates where deep frost occurs, the slab recommended in this plan may not be adequate, and a deeper foundation may be required. Any movement or heaving of the surface can cause the seams along the house and foundation to open, the mullions and weatherstripping in the greenhouse to separate, and, possibly, the glass panels to crack. Other floor and foundation systems could also be used; for example, redwood and pressure-treated pine are options for the base. These can be set in or on one of the following: concrete pedestals, concrete block foundations set on footings, or established supports like decks and patios. The cost for the greenhouse support system will vary from this model's estimate according to your requirements and preferences.

Once the slab or foundation and floor have been placed, the house wall is prepared to receive the greenhouse, and the kit is assembled. Even if you plan to keep the house siding as is, you may have to make a channel in it for the greenhouse frame, and apply flashing and caulking where needed along the seams between the new structure and the house. If your house is painted a light color, you might consider applying two coats of dark, flat paint to the siding in the area to be enclosed by the greenhouse. Painting before the greenhouse is placed will save some time. You might also consider applying dark paint to the concrete floor. Both of these surfaces will absorb sunlight and provide radiant heat.

The greenhouse kit included in this plan features a sliding glass door, an awning window, and double-layered tempered glass in an aluminum frame. All of the hardware needed to interconnect the greenhouse's components and base fittings is included in the kit. Other accessories, such as screens, shades, additional awning windows, fans and heaters are available at extra cost. If the greenhouse is to be used exclusively as an exterior facility, some of these optional accessories, especially a fan and heater, may become necessities and, therefore, will add to the basic cost.

LEVEL OF DIFFICULTY

Many experienced do-it-yourselfers can complete this project on their own, but beginners and less-skilled handymen may find some aspects of the undertaking out of reach. Basically, the installation involves two challenging operations, the placement of the slab and the erection of the greenhouse itself. Both of these procedures require skilled and precise workmanship. Further, because the greenhouse kit is expensive and the structure intricate, mistakes can be costly and difficult to correct. In short, beginners should leave the slab and greenhouse installations to a

professional and limit their efforts to such tasks as excavation and finish work. They should allow some added time for these tasks. Skilled handymen and experts who have masonry experience should add 50% and 20%, respectively, to the man-hours for the placement of the slab. They should add even more time for the greenhouse fabrication and erection to allow for patient and careful workmanship.

WHAT TO WATCH OUT FOR

Although all of the greenhouse projects in this section involve attached structures with shed roofs, other roof designs and building configurations are also possible. A gable roof, for example, might be a better choice if the greenhouse will look or perform better with its length running at right angles to the house. If the greenhouse is placed on a wall with an east or west exposure, such an alignment may utilize available sunlight more effectively. In hot weather, the larger area of a vented gable roof will increase the ventilation and rate of exhaust in the greenhouse. In addition to attached greenhouses, factory-prepared freestanding models offer other options for greenhouse projects.

SUMMARY

For the active year-round or seasonal gardener, this improvement can provide many years of enjoyable and practical service. Although this model is essentially an exterior facility, it can be easily incorporated into the house's interior with the addition of an entryway.

LEAN-TO GREENHOUSE, LARGE

Description	Quantity	Man-hours	Material
Clearing & excavation for slab, by hand	1 Ea.	12.0	0.00
Gravel fill, 3" deep, compacted	140 S.F.	1.0	18.65
Edge forms, 4" high	32 L.F.	2.0	7.75
Expansion joint at existing foundation, premolded bituminous fiber	16 L.F.	0.5	9.30
Reinforcing, welded wire fabric, 6 x 6-10/10	140 S.F.	1.0	13.55
Concrete, ready mix, 3000 psi	2 C.Y.		135.05
Placing concrete	2 C.Y.	1.0	0.00
Finishing, broom finish	128 S.F.	1.5	0.00
Greenhouse, prefab., 8' x 16' x 11'-6" high, w/awning window & sliding glass door	1 Ea.	24.0	10,376.95
Flashing, aluminum, .016" thick	32 S.F.	2.0	25.25
Finish, grade & re-seed	1 Ea.	2.0	2.60
	Totals	47.0	$10,589.10

Project Size	8' x 16'	Contractor's Fee Including Materials	$16,900

Key to Abbreviations
C.Y. - cubic yard   Ea. - each   L.F. - linear foot   Pr. - pair   Sq. - square (100 square feet of area)
S.F. - square foot   S.Y. - square yard   V.L.F. - vertical linear foot

SUNROOM-GREENHOUSE, SMALL

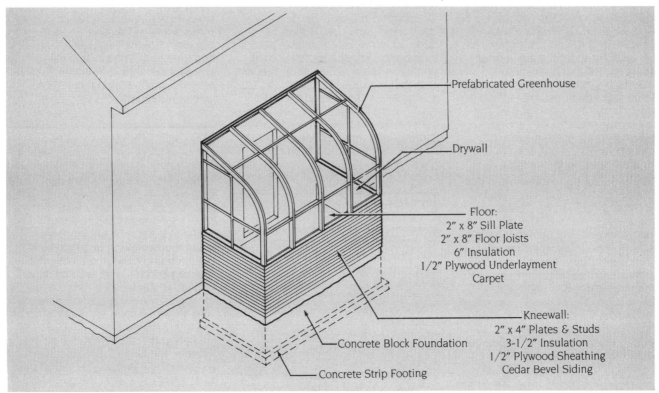

Prefabricated Greenhouse

Drywall

Floor:
2" x 8" Sill Plate
2" x 8" Floor Joists
6" Insulation
1/2" Plywood Underlayment
Carpet

Kneewall:
2" x 4" Plates & Studs
3-1/2" Insulation
1/2" Plywood Sheathing
Cedar Bevel Siding

Concrete Block Foundation

Concrete Strip Footing

One of the best features of an attached greenhouse is its potential as a sitting and recreation area as well as an interior garden. If the location and access are appropriate, the greenhouse can become an integral part of your home's floor plan and provide an attractive improvement. A sunroom can be costly to install, but the benefits to your lifestyle, energy savings, and increased property value can make it worthwhile. Although this model is relatively small in scale, it is a challenging project; and inexperienced do-it-yourselfers might consider hiring a professional contractor to perform some of the work.

MATERIALS

The materials used in this project include standard construction components for the foundation, floor, and knee wall in the new structure, and for the entryway into the house. The biggest item is the factory-prepared greenhouse-sunroom kit, which consists of an insulated aluminum frame and double-layered tempered glass. The basic structural and finish materials are readily available from building supply retailers, but the greenhouse kit is usually a special-order product. Before you purchase the materials for this project, do some research and shop around, especially for the greenhouse unit. Because there are many brand names and variations in quality and cost, you can take advantage of competitive pricing while selecting the greenhouse unit that meets your practical needs and aesthetic standards.

Other than the fabrication and placement of the greenhouse itself, the most important operation in the project is the construction of the foundation and floor systems. The foundation for this plan is built to a height of 2' 8", but a higher or deeper foundation may be required if the grade is several feet below or slopes sharply away from the house. Once the

foundation has been completed, a doubled 2" x 8" sill plate is fastened to it, and the floor framed with 2" x 8"s and sheathed with 3/4" exterior plywood. Insulating the foundation, floor and, later, the knee wall, is strongly advised, as temperature variations and drafts are detrimental to the operation and comfort of the greenhouse. Like the foundation and floor, the knee wall must be precisely placed to receive the greenhouse kit. In most cases, the finished siding and any trim features on the knee wall should blend with the design and style of the rest of the house. The cost for these materials may vary from that provided in the plan.

Before selecting the type and design of the greenhouse kit, consider its thermal and aesthetic impact on the house. Because the greenhouse kit is being used to create a year-round sunroom, the extra investment for insulating glass and frames is recommended. Be sure to investigate the many operational and design features offered by the various manufacturers. Some of the kits come complete with screens, shades, and vent windows, while others offer these items as options at additional cost. When assembling the greenhouse, work carefully to maintain precise alignment. The base fasteners for the greenhouse are usually included in the kit, but flashing for the base, roof, and walls is extra.

Before the finish work can begin on the interior of the greenhouse-sunroom, the doorway from the house must be installed or reconditioned. This plan allows for the cost of removing a window, enlarging and framing the 3' opening, and installing the necessary trim. The old exterior siding must also be removed and a layer of drywall and paneling applied to the house wall and knee wall. Standard interior or indoor-outdoor carpeting provides comfort and additional warmth to the floor. The interior design and the selection of finish materials offer a wide range of choice and the opportunity to use your imagination in blending the new facility with your home's decor.

LEVEL OF DIFFICULTY

Compared to a basic attached greenhouse, this combined greenhouse and sunroom facility requires more time, skill, and expense to install. The building of the foundation and knee wall are operations which demand, at the least, a moderate level of masonry and carpentry skills. Further, because the foundation and knee wall must be precisely set at level and squared to match the fixed dimensions of an expensive greenhouse, greater liability is involved, and mistakes can be very costly. Beginners and inexperienced handymen should, therefore, consider hiring a contractor to perform these operations, and then finish the project on their own. Because of the out-of-the-way location of most greenhouse sites, the light finish work can be completed at a comfortable pace and under convenient conditions. Beginners should add 100% to the man-hours estimate for all of the basic finish work, and more for the wall opening, if they tackle it. They should seek professional advice, as needed, throughout the project. Handymen and experts should add 40% and 10%, respectively, to the professional time for all tasks. All do-it-yourselfers should plan to add extra time to assemble and install the greenhouse kit, as the cost of the product and the intricacy of its design demand careful workmanship.

WHAT TO WATCH OUT FOR

Before finalizing the master plan for your greenhouse project, be sure to make provisions for electrical and plumbing fixtures. Although these items are not listed in this plan, you might consider installing at least one electrical outlet and, perhaps, a light fixture for the interior wall. The knee wall provides a convenient support for a recessed outlet and a cavity for the supply wires, doing away with the need for a surface-mounted box and exposed conduit. For an extra cost, a small sink or other fixture can also be included in the plan. If these electrical and plumbing conveniences are roughed in during the construction process, the procedure will cost less and look better.

SUMMARY

With imagination, creative design, and some extra expense, a basic attached greenhouse can become a delightful sunroom as well as an interior garden. If you want to add a few of the special options, it can become the showpiece of your home while providing the practical benefits of passive solar heating and increased interior living space.

SUNROOM GREENHOUSE, SMALL

Description	Quantity	Man-hours	Material
Site clearing, layout & excavation for foundation wall	1 Lot	4.0	0.00
Footing, 6" thick x 16" wide x 32'	2 C.Y.	5.5	167.00
Foundation, 8" concrete block, 2'-8" high	105 Blocks	10.0	190.60
Perimeter, insulation, molded bead board, 1" thick, R-4	100 S.F.	1.5	24.20
Sill plate, 2" x 8" x 12'	36 L.F.	1.5	31.80
Floor joists, 2" x 8", 16" O.C.	132 L.F.	2.0	91.05
Floor insulation, fiberglass blankets, foil-backed, 6" thick, R-19	60 S.F.	1.0	28.30
Underlayment, plywood, 1/2" thick, 4' x 8' sheets	3 Sheets	1.5	47.65
Framing for knee wall, 2" x 4" plates & studs, 3' high, 16" O.C.	108 L.F.	2.5	34.00
Knee wall insulation, fiberglass blankets, foil backed, 3-1/2" thick, R-11	70 S.F.	1.0	22.85
Sheathing, plywood on knee walls, 1/2" thick	3 Sheets	1.5	47.65
Greenhouse, sun room, prefab., 5'-6" x 10'-6" x 6'-6" high, insul. double temp. glass	1 Ea.	12.5	3968.80
Flashing, aluminum, .019" thick	25 S.F.	1.5	19.95
Remove window & siding for opening in existing building	1 Job	1.0	0.00
Frame opening, 2" x 8" stock	24 L.F.	1.0	16.55
Jamb & casing for opening, 9/16" x 3-1/2", interior & exterior	48 L.F.	1.5	40.65
Drywall for interior knee wall & sides of opening, 1/2" thick	4 Sheets	2.0	38.75
Paneling, plywood, prefinished, 1/4" thick	4 Sheets	4.0	85.20
Flooring, carpet, 26 oz. nylon, w/pad	60 S.F.	1.5	143.05
Siding for exterior knee wall, cedar beveled, rough-sawn, stained	80 S.F.	3.0	192.65
Totals		60.0	$5190.70

Project Size	5'-6" x 10'-6"	Contractor's Fee Including Materials	$9900

Key to Abbreviations
C.Y. - cubic yard   Ea. - each   L.F. - linear foot   Pr. - pair   Sq. - square (100 square feet of area)
S.F. - square foot   S.Y. - square yard   V.L.F. - vertical linear foot

SUNROOM-GREENHOUSE, LARGE

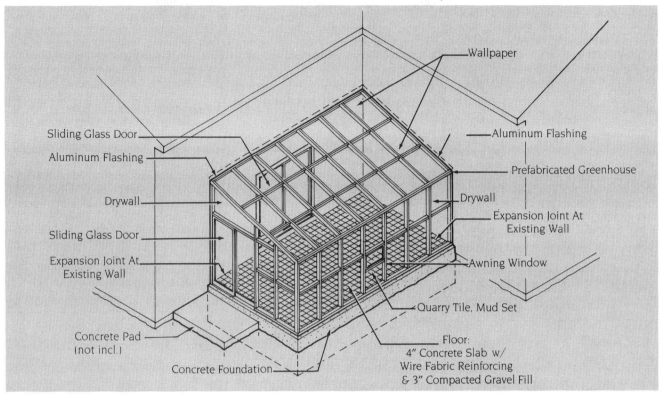

Sliding Glass Door

Aluminum Flashing

Drywall

Sliding Glass Door

Expansion Joint At Existing Wall

Concrete Pad (not incl.)

Concrete Foundation

Wallpaper

Aluminum Flashing

Prefabricated Greenhouse

Drywall

Expansion Joint At Existing Wall

Awning Window

Quarry Tile, Mud Set

Floor:
4" Concrete Slab w/
Wire Fabric Reinforcing
& 3" Compacted Gravel Fill

Combination greenhouse-sunrooms have become popular home improvements, because they combine the beauty of plants and open natural lighting with the practical benefits of passive solar heating and increased year-round interior living area. This plan demonstrates how a large greenhouse-sunroom addition can be nestled into the corner between wings of a house. Because of its size and the deluxe products used in its construction, it is an expensive improvement, but one which will return more than the homeowner's investment in increased property value. It is a challenging project for all levels of do-it-yourselfers, and beginners and inexperienced handymen should consider hiring a contractor for much of the work.

MATERIALS

The materials required to construct this deluxe greenhouse-sunroom consist of ready-mixed concrete for the foundation and floor, the

factory-prepared greenhouse, and the basic building materials included in the finishing of the interior walls and entryway. Except for the greenhouse kit, all of the materials used in the project are readily available, so shopping for the best prices is usually worth the effort. Even ready-mixed concrete can be competitively priced, although a minimum charge is to be expected for a small order like this one. Remember that two separate deliveries, a few days apart, will be required to place the foundation, and, later, the slab.

Before the foundation work begins, however, a substantial amount of excavation must be completed. A perimeter trench must be dug to receive the form for the concrete. This task may have to be done by hand if the location of the site prohibits machine excavation. After the concrete has been allowed to set up for several days, a gravel subsurface, reinforcing, and expansion joints are installed, and the slab poured. The surface of the slab is troweled and

then broom-finished to provide an acceptable base surface for the floor covering. These are difficult tasks for most do-it-yourselfers. Not only are they physically demanding, but they also require specialized masonry skills and equipment. In most cases, a contractor should be hired to complete these operations. Mistakes in concrete work can be difficult and expensive to correct, and a precisely set foundation is a must for the fixed dimensions of the greenhouse.

After the foundation and slab have been installed, the greenhouse itself is assembled on-site and secured to the foundation and house walls. As in the other greenhouse projects in this section, this plan includes a quality factory-prepared unit with an insulated aluminum framing system and tempered glass panels. Be sure to do some research before buying this expensive component. There are many brand names and designs available in a wide range of quality and price. The extra cost of a fully insulated, well-made product will be justified by years of energy-efficient, durable service. Most do-it-yourselfers will need some professional assistance with this installation. In any case, be sure that the final placement of the greenhouse is secure and weathertight before proceeding with the interior work.

Within the enclosure, the two walls of the house must be prepared to receive the finish materials, and the floor should be covered with its finish surface. In most cases, the exterior siding must be removed and, in this plan, a window opening enlarged and framed to receive a 6' sliding glass door unit. If the new sunroom is to be incorporated into the house's interior for year-round use, the opening can be enlarged even more and then trimmed with a jamb and facings. In this way you can deduct the expense of the slider unit, but you may have to add slightly to the cost of preparing the rough opening. A second doorway, through the other common wall, is another option you might want to consider. If you are tackling this task for the first time, be sure to seek some advice before you start. If the opening is greater than 6' in width, larger headers and, possibly, a beam or

girder may be required to bear the load. The ceiling adjacent to the opening may also require temporary bracing during the procedure. After the opening has been made and sliders or a doorway frame installed, the walls are covered with 1/2" sheetrock or other suitable veneer and finished. This plan suggests 1/2" thick quarry tile for the finished floor. Its durability, low maintenance, and rustic appearance make it an ideal covering for plant and sunroom floors, but brick, flagstone, and other tile materials are viable options. If you plan to use the sunroom as a source of passive solar heat, install finish materials that are dark in color and dull in surface texture to increase their rate of heat absorption. The cost of the finish products will vary according to their design and quality.

LEVEL OF DIFFICULTY

This greenhouse-sunroom project is a challenging undertaking which most do-it-yourselfers should leave, at least in part, to a professional contractor. The extensive concrete work and the erection of the greenhouse are jobs which require special skills and

equipment and involve considerable liability if mistakes are made. Most do-it-yourselfers can handle the interior wall finish work, but some might consider hiring a mason or tilesetter to install the finished floor. As a general rule, beginners should limit their involvement to the finishing of the walls and should double the professional time for that operation. They should get instruction before attempting any new tasks. Handymen, too, should probably stick to the interior finishing at a rate of 50% over the estimated man-hours. If they attempt to lay the tile or brick floor, they should add 100% to the professional time to allow for slow and careful work. Experts should leave the foundation and slab installations to a specialist and consider hiring a contractor to erect the greenhouse. For the basic tasks, they should add 20% to the estimated man-hours, and for the finished floor, about 40%.

WHAT TO WATCH OUT FOR

In order for greenhouses and sunrooms to utilize the full benefits of solar energy, they must be properly located. For most installations, a south or west exposure is ideal because of the longer duration of available sunlight at all times of the year. East exposure is acceptable in some open locations, such as that of a waterfront home, but north exposures are generally unacceptable sites in this hemisphere. Another important consideration for locating the greenhouse-sunroom is protection from the wind. Wherever possible, an alcove, or in this case, the corner of an "ell", should be utilized. Even though both the glass and the frame of this greenhouse are insulated, heat loss can be rapid when the sun goes down. Windy conditions might further accelerate the heat loss, but this protected corner location helps to head off such problems.

SUMMARY

This deluxe greenhouse-sunroom will add beauty, increased living area, and comfort to homes which are spacious enough to accommodate it. Although the expertise of a contractor may be required for the construction of the exterior, do-it-yourselfers can save on installation costs by finishing the inside themselves.

SUNROOM-GREENHOUSE, LARGE

Description	Quantity	Man-hours	Material
Site clearing, layout & excavation for foundation	1 Lot	7.0	0.00
Concrete wall, 8" thick, 3000 psi, incl. form, reinforcing & sill plates, 42" high	100 S.F.	14.5	603.00
Gravel fill, 3" deep, compacted	200 S.F.	1.0	26.65
Expansion joints, premolded bituminous fiber	57 L.F.	1.5	33.15
Reinforcing, welded wire fabric, 6' x 6-10/10	200 S.F.	1.0	19.35
Concrete, ready mix, 3000 psi	3 C.Y.	0.0	202.55
Placing concrete	3 C.Y.	1.5	0.00
Finishing, broom finish	190 S.F.	2.5	0.00
Greenhouse, sunroom, prefab, 10'-6" x 18' x 10' high, double temp. glass, incl. sliding door & 1 awning window	1 Ea.	32.0	11,491.35
Flashing, aluminum, .019" thick	46 S.F.	2.5	36.75
Remove window & siding for sliding glass door opening & end wall	1 Job	6.5	0.00
Frame opening, 2" x 8"	20 L.F.	1.0	13.80
Door, sliding glass, aluminum, 6' wide	1 Ea.	4.0	435.60
Drywall, 1/2" thick, for sides of opening	6 Sheets	3.5	58.10
Trim, jamb for door, 1" x 6" pine Crown molding stock pine, 9/16" x 3-5/8"	40 L.F. 30 L.F.	1.5 1.0	33.90 39.95
Painting, trim, incl. puttying, primer & 1 coat	70 L.F.	1.5	4.25
Painting, walls, primer and 1 coat	200 S.F.	2.0	21.80
Flooring, quarry tile, mud set, 6" x 6", 1/2" thick	190 S.F.	22.0	643.75
	Totals	106.5	$13,663.95

Project Size	10'-6" x 18'	Contractor's Fee Including Materials	$23,060

Key to Abbreviations
C.Y. - cubic yard   Ea. - each   L.F. - linear foot   Pr. - pair   Sq. - square (100 square feet of area)
S.F. - square foot   S.Y. - square yard   V.L.F. - vertical linear foot

BRICK PATIO, IN SAND

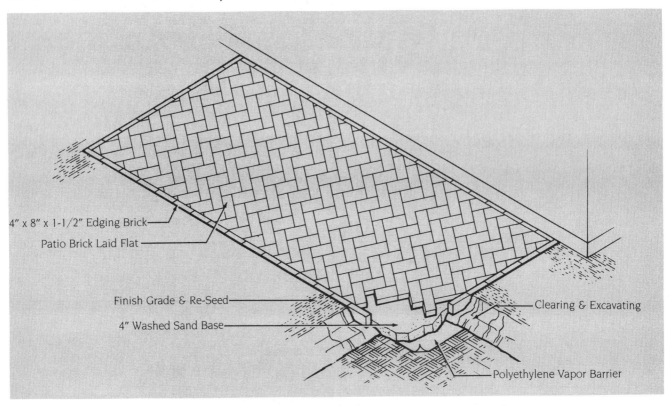

4" x 8" x 1-1/2" Edging Brick

Patio Brick Laid Flat

Finish Grade & Re-Seed

4" Washed Sand Base

Clearing & Excavating

Polyethylene Vapor Barrier

There are many advantages to working with brick, concrete, and stone as building materials. They are durable, strong, and attractive; and they can be used in a wide variety of installations, from interior fireplace facings to exterior walkway and patio surfaces. Once you have learned some of the basic skills, acquired the fundamental hand tools, and gained some experience, working with these materials can be enjoyable and rewarding. If you are inexperienced with masonry tasks, it is best to start with a project that is small in size and not too demanding. This 6' x 12' brick patio plan presents such an opportunity. Also, because the bricks are set in sand, mistakes can be easily corrected, with little or no waste of materials. The results of the project will be an attractive outdoor sitting area or entryway apron, built for just the cost of the materials and a few incidental items.

MATERIALS

Patio projects utilize the same basic materials, though they may vary in form, size, and method of placement. The first step is arranging some type of a form system to set the limits and the perimeter design of the patio. Then, a subsurface of sand, gravel, or concrete is put into place to establish a level base and support for the installation. Lastly, the surface material of brick, stone, or concrete is applied and then grouted or finished. All of these materials are readily available from building and masonry supply outlets, so it pays to shop for the best prices. In most cases, they have to be trucked, so be sure to arrange delivery as a part of the purchase agreement. The retailer may or may not charge you for curb delivery, depending on the size of the order and the distance to the site. In addition to the masonry supplies, some basic hand tools are needed for all brick or stone patio installations. These include a stonemason's hammer, flat stone chisel, 3' or 4' level, square, and long tape measure.

Before the bricks can be set for this 6' x 12' patio, the area must be laid out, excavated, and prepared with a sand base. Minimal materials cost is involved in this stage of the installation process, but a significant amount of time is required to dig out the site to the required depth and to place the sand. If the area is level, the procedure is basic, but more time and expense may be involved if you have to contend with a slope. Be sure to dig out completely all vegetation, especially grass and other perennial plants that are hardy enough to re-establish themselves later on between the bricks. This plan suggests that a polyethylene barrier be placed below the layout of base sand to prohibit the growth of deep-rooting vegetation, but some hardy plants with shallow root systems may still establish themselves above the barrier if they are left unattended. The cost of the barrier is minimal and its benefits are many, so be sure to include it. Once the base sand has been leveled and tamped, and a course of perimeter bricks placed, the surface can be laid.

The bricks themselves are the most important and costly component of the project, so be sure to make the right selection. There are many different types, sizes, and grades of brick available, but not all of them can be used for paving purposes. In most cases, bricks that can be used for paving are referred to as "all purpose bricks," "hard brick," or "pavers," and are rated as "SW" (severe weathering). Bricks with a rating less than "SW" may crack and even disintegrate in time when exposed to water, icing, and constant freeze-thaw weather conditions. Be sure to verify the rating of the brick with your retailer before you buy it, as a softer, less durable product will necessitate premature replacement of the patio materials. Paving brick is more expensive than the softer "MW," or "NW" brick, but it will last longer if properly installed.

The method and pattern for laying the brick on the sand base should be carefully planned. One of the advantages of setting the bricks in sand is that trial and error will usually only cost you more time. As a general rule, patterns which require little or no brick cutting are desirable because

they install faster and create minimal waste. Simple jack-on-jack and basket-weave patterns in various configurations require little or no cutting. There is some cutting involved, however, in the intricate running bond and herringbone patterns, like the one illustrated. In short, the more imaginative the design, the more cutting is required, and the more waste of material is incurred. Once you have gotten the knack of "striking" brick and cutting it accurately, the waste will be minimal. However, some mistakes will occur as you learn this art, so allow for extra material if you are a beginner. A masonry saw can make the job easier. You might also seek professional advice or ask an experienced friend for help before you start.

After the brick has been set and leveled in the desired pattern, the seams are grouted with screened sand or stone dust and packed solid. Doing this process correctly takes time, but it is a vital operation in the project. If the sand grout is not packed tightly, the bricks will wobble and eventually become misaligned. Several treatments are usually required to solidify the surface. A light watering with a hose should follow each packing session. Be sure to kneel outside of the patio, whenever possible, when you work at grouting. If you have to walk or kneel on the newly placed bricks, use a piece of plywood to distribute your weight. Keep the new patio wetted down for a couple of weeks after it is finished, and regrout it from time to time.

LEVEL OF DIFFICULTY

This project presents an excellent opportunity for all levels of do-it-yourselfers to acquire some basic masonry skills without the worry of wasting materials. As long as you take time to lay out the site, prepare it properly, and select a design that is commensurate with your ability, little can go wrong; and the result will be of professional quality. Beginners should allow an additional 75% to the professional time for simple patterns and 100% for more intricate designs. Handymen and experts should add 40% and 10%, respectively, to the man-hours for all tasks included in the project. All do-it-yourselfers should allow for additional time and materials if they choose patterns which require brick cutting, and are unfamiliar with the procedure.

WHAT TO WATCH OUT FOR

The cost for the brick paving material in this 6' x 12' patio allows for a perimeter course of brick laid lengthwise on edge, and for surface courses laid flat. More material will be required if the pattern includes bricks laid in soldier or sailor style or in other vertical or angled arrangements. Sawtooth or sailor edging, for example, requires more perimeter bricks than standard edging. Extra material and installation time are also required for special patterns or angled surface courses. This herringbone design uses about 20% more brick than a basketweave or jack-on-jack pattern because some waste occurs when the bricks are cut.

SUMMARY

This brick-in-sand patio project can enhance an entranceway or create a small outdoor sitting area at a modest cost. Because it is basic in design, small in size, and easy to install, you can benefit from the satisfaction and reduced cost of completing it entirely on your own.

BRICK PATIO, IN SAND

Description	Quantity	Man-hours	Material
Layout, clearing & excavation for patio, by hand	1 Job	4.5	0.00
Polyethylene vapor barrier, .008" thick	80 S.F.	0.5	2.90
Washed sand for 4" base	1 C.Y.	0.0	15.65
Grade & level sand base	72 S.F.	2.0	0.00
Edging brick 4" x 8" x 1-1/2", laid on edge	36 L.F.	1.5	31.35
Patio brick, 4" x 8" x 1-1/2" thick, laid flat, herringbone pattern	72 S.F.	11.0	197.75
Finish grade & re-seed	1 Job	1.5	5.85
Totals		21.0	$253.50

Project Size	6' x 12'	Contractor's Fee Including Materials	$1020

Key to Abbreviations
C.Y. - cubic yard   Ea. - each   L.F. - linear foot   Pr. - pair   Sq. - square (100 square feet of area)
S.F. - square foot   S.Y. - square yard   V.L.F. - vertical linear foot

BRICK PATIO, IN MORTAR

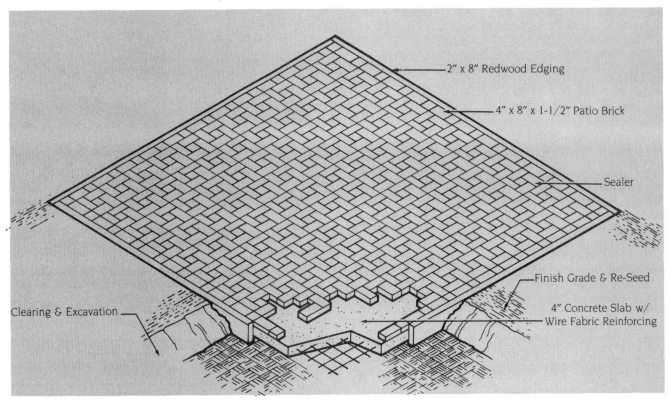

2" x 8" Redwood Edging

4" x 8" x 1-1/2" Patio Brick

Sealer

Finish Grade & Re-Seed

4" Concrete Slab w/ Wire Fabric Reinforcing

Clearing & Excavation

The process of placing bricks in mortar on a concrete slab is more difficult than setting them in sand, but it is well within the reach of many do-it-yourselfers. If the slab is already in place and the laying of the brick is all that has to be done, the job is fairly easy. However, if you begin from scratch and place the concrete slab first, the project becomes more difficult, costly, and time-consuming. This home improvement plan presents a cost estimate and outline for the installation of a 12' x 12' brick-in-mortar patio, which includes the placement of a reinforced concrete slab. Because of the specialized know-how required for all masonry installations, inexperienced do-it-yourselfers should seek some assistance before they start and might also want to do some reading on the subject. Mistakes are not easily corrected when they involve mortar, bricks, and concrete, so work slowly and get help and guidance when needed as the project progresses. One of the advantages of a patio project is that its convenient location allows the do-it-yourselfer to do the work in

stages at a comfortable pace. Once the patio is completed, it will provide years of enjoyment for you and your family.

MATERIALS

The materials included in this project consist of the concrete and metal reinforcement for the slab, a 2" x 8" redwood border, the brick, and mortar mixed in various portions with sand. These are all common construction materials and, except for the ready-mixed concrete, can be purchased from most building and masonry supply retailers. It pays to shop for the best deal, especially on the brick, which is the most costly product included in this project. As for the ready-mixed concrete, some price comparing may help here as well; but because the amount of material required for this patio is relatively small, you may have to pay a minimum delivery charge to cover the supplier's trucking expenses. If you don't want to complete the project all at once, the slab can be placed and

the brick surface applied at a later date, with full use of the facility between steps of the project.

Before the slab is placed, a substantial amount of excavating has to be done. The patio area should be carefully located, measured, squared, and then dug out by hand to a size slightly larger than that of the finished surface. Remember to leave room for the slab form and for the redwood edging. Some additional cost may be incurred for a layer of gravel if the slab is being placed on poor subsoil. This precautionary measure will help to reduce cracking and heaving of the slab during freezes. The form for the slab may be made from the 2" x 8" redwood border or from conventional lumber. The use of the redwood will save you time later on because once it has been placed, it is there for good as the trim for the finished patio. Be aware, however, that the edges may take some abuse during the slab placement. If you are fussy about its appearance, you might consider placing the border after the concrete has set up. Doing it this way will take more time, and extra expense will be incurred for the purchase of temporary form lumber. Be sure to square the form to its precise dimensions and then brace the corners and stake the sides to hold it firmly in place while the slab is poured. A slight pitch off level in one direction away from adjacent structures will help to drain the surface. Remember, too, that the pattern of bricks to be used on the finished surface has to be considered before the concrete is placed. An error of an inch or two can add time and expense later because of the extra brick cutting required to adjust for the error in measurement or square.

Once the form has been placed and the reinforcing wire positioned, the slab is poured and finished. This process can be challenging if you are inexperienced because you have to work quickly and efficiently. Be sure to get some advice beforehand and to have plenty of help available on the day that the ready-mix truck arrives. Getting prepared for the truck's arrival requires much organization and a set plan to minimize the time of the delivery. If the truck is tied up for too long, you will be charged extra. If the site is inaccessible to the truck, wheelbarrows will have to be used in the delivery. In some cases, ramps or wood tracks may have to be used as access routes to protect the landscaping from the weight and traffic of the wheelbarrows. After the delivery has been completed, the concrete is leveled and rough finished in preparation for the placement of the bricks.

The process of laying the bricks on the finished slab also requires basic masonry knowledge. The entire brick surface does not have to be completed in one session, so work very slowly at first with the anticipation of faster placement as you get better at it. Never mix more mortar than you will use in an hour of brick laying. If any brick cutting is required, do it before mixing the mortar or starting the brick placement for that session. As in all construction projects, keep an eye on level and square as you proceed. Investment in a stringline, long mason's level, and a good trowel will add to your efficiency and to the appearance of the finished patio. The time and money invested in an application of masonry sealer will be returned many times over in protection for the finished patio.

LEVEL OF DIFFICULTY

This project is challenging for most do-it-yourselfers, but manageable if it is taken in small steps. With patient work, even inexperienced handymen can complete the patio with professional results. Seek advice and guidance as you proceed, and complete one phase before going on to the next. Impatience will only cause frustration, poor workmanship, and wasted time and materials. The most demanding part of the project is the placing of the slab, because a great deal of work has be be compressed into a four-hour period. Novices may consider hiring a contractor to form

and pour the slab and could then follow up with the brick work. Experts and most handymen should be able to complete the entire project on their own. They should add 10% and 40%, respectively, to the man-hours estimate for the project. Beginners should add 75% to the professional time for all tasks. All do-it-yourselfers who are inexperienced in laying pavement bricks can expect a very slow work pace at first, with a gradual increase in productivity as the surface is laid.

WHAT TO WATCH OUT FOR

The border trim requires careful planning because it has both a practical and an aesthetic role in the overall design of the patio. Although special border features and materials usually cost more and take longer to install, they can bring the design of the patio to life and add lasting protection to the edge of the surface. This plan calls for 2" x 8" redwood edging, but there are other options for rot-resistant wood edges, such as cedar, locust, or pressure-treated pine. Patios which are recessed or terraced can be made even more attractive with appropriate wood edging. Bricks set in soldier, sailor, or sawtooth arrangements can also enhance the surface design while adding durability to the patio's edge. Be sure to point all joints in the edging, including those that are hidden by the backfill, to protect them from water penetration and to maintain the strength of the border. Bricks with rounded, angled, and beveled edges are also available on special order for patio borders. Whatever the type or arrangement of the edging, be sure that it extends far enough below the level of the surface bricks to ensure a solid, protective border.

SUMMARY

The 12' x 12' brick-in-mortar patio presented in this plan will make an attractive and practical addition to the exterior of any home. Although its installation requires a moderate level of masonry know-how, the project can be completed in small steps and at a comfortable pace for do-it-yourselfers who are willing to learn as they go.

BRICK PATIO, In Mortar

Description	Quantity	Man-hours	Material
Layout, clearing & excavation for patio, by hand	1 Ea.	7.0	0.00
Edging, redwood, 2" x 8"	48 L.F.	2.0	41.85
Base, 4" thick concrete slab Reinforcing, welded wire fabric 6' x 6' - 10/10	160 S.F.	1.0	15.50
Concrete, ready mix, 2000 psi, 4" thick	2 C.Y.	0.0	135.05
Place concrete	2 C.Y.	5.0	0.00
Patio brick, 4" x 8" x 1-1/2" thick, grouted, 3/8" joint	144 S.F.	25.0	327.55
Finish grade, & re-seed	1 Job	2.0	11.70
Sealer, silicone or stearate, 1 coat	144 S.F.	0.5	31.35
Totals		42.5	$563.00

Project Size	12' x 12'	Contractor's Fee Including Materials	$2050

Key to Abbreviations
C.Y. - cubic yard   Ea. - each   L.F. - linear foot   Pr. - pair   Sq. - square (100 square feet of area)
S.F. - square foot   S.Y. - square yard   V.L.F. - vertical linear foot

CONCRETE PATIO, 6' x 12'

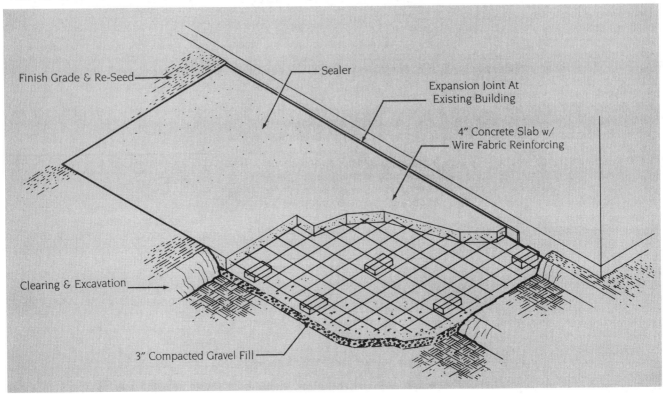

Finish Grade & Re-Seed

Sealer

Expansion Joint At Existing Building

4" Concrete Slab w/ Wire Fabric Reinforcing

Clearing & Excavation

3" Compacted Gravel Fill

One of the most economical patio materials is concrete. It can be formed to complement just about any area and custom shaped and textured in a variety of surface finishes. As long as it is placed correctly, with provisions made for drainage, expansion, and reinforcement, it will provide many years of low maintenance and durable service. This 6' x 12' patio plan demonstrates how a small area, perhaps outside of a sliding door, next to a deck, or between garage and house, can be economically converted to a patio. Because it is a relatively small project which includes basic carpentry and masonry tasks, it is an ideal home improvement for do-it-yourselfers to undertake. If you learn some of the fundamental procedures and guidelines for concrete work before you start, you can complete this patio yourself. Although the project may add only modestly to the value of your home, it will provide years of practical service and perhaps give you the confidence to tackle other, more challenging masonry improvements.

MATERIALS

The materials list for the 6' x 12' patio is small compared to other exterior projects, but the process is still challenging. As in other patio installations, the site for the new facility has to be laid out first, then excavated, and prepared to receive the concrete. Next, the form for the slab has to be constructed, positioned, and braced. After reinforcement has been installed, the concrete is put into place, leveled, and finished to the desired texture. All materials, except for the ready-mixed concrete, are available at most building and masonry supply outlets.

Even though the 6' x 12' area of this patio looks small, a significant amount of excavation has to be completed before the form is built. Be sure to dig to a depth of 7" to allow for 3" of gravel under the 4" slab. The amount of subsurface material will vary with

the consistency of the soil, and the cost may increase or decrease proportionately. For example, if the soil is hard-packed and drains poorly, more gravel will be called for; if it is sandy and porous, less will be required. When in doubt, consult a professional who has installed concrete surfaces in your area and get advice on how much subsurface to use. The form for the slab should be constructed from 2 x 4's or 2 x 6's positioned in the excavated area. When the slab is to be bordered on one side by the house or garage foundation, or by a concrete walk, only three sides have to be formed. The form is then squared, set at a slight pitch off level in one direction, away from surrounding structures, then braced and staked in position. Be sure to install an asphalt-impregnated expansion joint at the seam between the foundation and patio before the concrete is placed. Even though these preliminary tasks are fairly easy, doing the job right takes some time. Be sure to double check the form for pitch and square before the concrete placement begins.

After the form is completed, welded wire fabric is installed to reinforce the slab. This material is sold in rolls and sheets in various widths, and it may have to be cut so that it fits several inches inside the slab's perimeter. To be effective, it should be located at the center of the slab's thickness, so you might consider propping it up on bricks or small stones to allow the concrete to flow through it and bond in equal thicknesses above and below the fabric. Steel rods and fabrics of varying gages and sizes can also be used - at extra cost - for the reinforcing.

If you plan to use ready-mixed concrete, considerable preparation is required to ensure trouble-free delivery and installation. In most cases, the charge for concrete delivery will depend on the amount of material and the time required to deliver it. However, a minimum charge may be levied for small orders like this one. For a job of this size no more than an hour and perhaps as little as 45 minutes will be allowed before extra charges are made for truck tie-up. If you are not well organized and prepared to receive the delivery in the allotted time, the extra costs can be

substantial. Arrange to have some help, procure some extra rakes and shovels, and if necessary, wheelbarrows for the delivery period. If the truck can get to the site without damaging your lawn, landscaping, or septic system, the delivery can be made directly from the truck's chute. If access is a problem, however, the concrete will have to be transported from the street or driveway by wheelbarrow. Ramps and tracks may have to be arranged beforehand to make the wheeling easier.

After the delivery has been made and the concrete roughly spread in the form, the surface should be screeded or leveled, allowed to set for a short period, and then troweled and finished to the desired surface texture. Care should be taken when finishing the surface, as concrete can be troweled to a slick, even dangerous, smoothness. This plan calls for a broom finish which provides a safe, non-skid textured surface. Other finishes are also possible, but they may require more time to complete. Imitation flagstone designs can be tooled into the surface, for example, or coarse ripples and swirls can be made by moistening the surface and reworking it with a sponge, float or trowel. Generally, a broom finish is the most popular texture and the easiest to accomplish for inexperienced do-it-yourselfers.

Level of Difficulty

This small patio project provides an excellent opportunity for inexperienced do-it-yourselfers to acquire some knowledge and skill in concrete work while saving on labor costs. It is still a challenging project, however, as mistakes cannot be easily remedied unless they are caught in time. Knowing how to use a level, square, and common hand tools is important, but this know-how is easily acquired if you seek assistance from an experienced person. The delivery of the concrete and its subsequent finishing operations are critical parts of the installation process. If you are unfamiliar with these procedures, get some advice beforehand. You might also have a knowledgeable friend help you during these phases. Beginners should add 75% to the estimated time for the form and reinforcement installation and plan to have an experienced helper available for the concrete placement. Handymen and experts should add 40% and 10%, respectively, to the professional time for all tasks.

What to Watch Out For

Even a small patio of this size should have one or two joints placed in the surface to control the cracking that is part of all concrete installations. As a general rule, control joints should be placed at 4' to 6' intervals to a depth of about 3/4". When the surface has been finished and allowed to set up enough so that it will support your weight when distributed on a piece of plywood or lumber, use a jointing or edging tool to place the joint in a straight line across the slab. The three exterior edges of the slab should then be rounded or beveled with an edging tool before the finishing job is completed.

Summary

This 6' x 12' patio can provide a small, but important contribution to the exterior of your home. For most do-it-yourselfers, it is a manageable undertaking that can also serve as a starter masonry project. It can be installed with a modest investment of time and money.

Concrete Patio, 6' x 12'

Description	Quantity	Man-hours	Material
Layout, clearing & excavation for patio, by hand	1 Job	4.0	0.00
Gravel fill, 3" deep, compacted	80 S.F.	1.0	4.45
Edge forms, 4" high	24 L.F.	1.5	5.80
Expansion joint at existing foundation, premolded bituminous fiber	12 L.F.	1.0	7.00
Reinforcing, welded wire fabric, 6 x 6 - 10/10	80 S.F.	1.0	7.75
Concrete, ready mix, 3000 psi	1 C.Y.	0.0	67.55
Place concrete	1 C.Y.	3.0	0.00
Finishing, broom finish	72 S.F.	1.5	0.00
Finish, grade & re-seed	1 Job	2.0	5.85
Sealer for concrete	72 S.F.	1.0	15.70
Totals		16.0	$114.10

Project Size	6' x 12'	Contractor's Fee Including Materials	$520

Key to Abbreviations
C.Y. - cubic yard   Ea. - each   L.F. - linear foot   Pr. - pair   Sq. - square (100 square feet of area)
S.F. - square foot   S.Y. - square yard   V.L.F. - vertical linear foot

CONCRETE PATIO, 12' x 16'

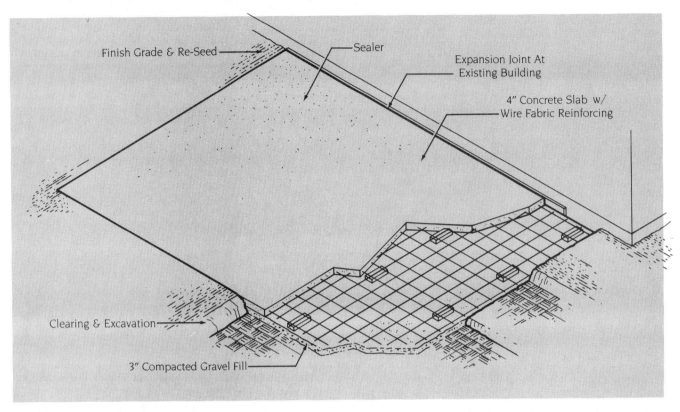

Finish Grade & Re-Seed

Sealer

Expansion Joint At
Existing Building

4" Concrete Slab w/
Wire Fabric Reinforcing

Clearing & Excavation

3" Compacted Gravel Fill

The primary advantages of concrete as a patio, walkway, or floor material are its strength and durability, but as an added benefit, it can also be shaped and molded into a variety of configurations and forms. It can take on many surface textures and can be colored before it is placed, or painted after it is installed. With imaginative planning and design, a standard concrete patio can be enlivened with the addition of colored stones, terracing, or redwood bordering or sectioning. If you want to leave the surface in its natural state, be sure to locate it appropriately and build in the proper drainage, expansion, and reinforcement controls required in all concrete and slab work. This 12' x 16' patio is a moderately challenging project for do-it-yourselfers. If the work is done in stages, experts, handymen, and many beginners can complete the project on their own.

MATERIALS

This patio is double the size of the previous project, but the materials and methods of installation are the same.

The site has to be laid out and excavated, the forms built, the subsurface and reinforcement placed, and the concrete poured and finished. As long as the grade on which the patio is to be built is level or gently sloped, and the subsoil easy to dig into, the project can be completed as estimated with no extra costs. All masonry work which involves mortar and concrete requires efficient organization and detailed preparation. Before you begin work, you will need some basic masonry hand tools: shovels, stiff rakes, a sturdy wheelbarrow, trowels, a float, and an edging or jointing tool. A stringline, square, 3' or 4' level, 16' tape measure, and hammer are required for the construction of the forms. Extra cost will be incurred if you have to buy some of these tools, but all of them are necessary to complete this project. The specialized concrete finishing tools, reinforcement materials, and premolded expansion joint can be purchased from a masonry supplier.

The excavation work required for this patio is substantial, as the 12' x 16' area has to be dug out by hand to a

depth of at least 7" to allow for 3" of gravel fill for a subbase under the 4" slab. Be sure to dig out the edges of the cavity throughly to permit easy placement of the form and to allow some leeway for squaring and leveling. The form should be pitched slightly away from any adjacent structures, squared, and braced firmly with stakes and corner ties to its final position. The subsurface material, reinforcement wire, and expansion joint should then be placed in preparation for the concrete delivery.

The concrete for a relatively small job like this one may cost more per cubic yard than it would for a complete foundation or cellar floor, because of the dealer's overhead for trucking costs. A minimum charge, therefore, is not unlikely. Be sure to work out all of the conditions of delivery with the retailer before the order is placed. The amount of time allowed for the delivery and the cost of additional truck tie-up time are important details that you should be aware of. Good organization and advance preparation will keep the costs down. If the site is accessible to the truck and the concrete poured directly from the chute, the job will go quickly, efficiently, and most economically. If it has to be transported from the street or driveway, then more time, manpower, and possibly, expense will be involved. Wheelbarrowing concrete is a physically demanding task which involves concentrated, rigorous work during the delivery period.

After the concrete has been put into place, several hours can elapse before the material hardens to an unworkable state. Always keep some fresh concrete handy during the screeding to add to low spots and to offset settling as the surface is finished. On warm days, you may have to work a little faster in the finishing process, but there still will be enough time to create the desired texture. If the surface sets up too quickly, it can be enlivened with mist from a hose. Do not give it the full spray of a hose at this time, however, as this may expose the aggregate and damage the finish. Also, do not overwork the surface during finishing, as too much troweling can cause the aggregate to settle and separate from the rest of the slab. Be sure to tamp the edges only enough to fill voids and to create

a solid side surface. Control joints and rounded edges should be added after the finishing process.

LEVEL OF DIFFICULTY

Although this 12' x 16' patio plan involves more installation time and a greater quantity of material than the 6' x 12' project, it can be accomplished by most do-it-yourselfers. The most difficult procedures are the actual placement of the concrete and its subsequent finishing, both of which can be troublesome for inexperienced workers. Remember that several hours of intense, physically demanding work are involved in accomplishing this phase of the project. Beginners, therefore, should make arrangements to have at least one experienced person on the job during the pour and for some time after to oversee the operation. Novices should add 75% to the professional time for all of the preliminary tasks, like the setting of the form and placement of the reinforcing. Handymen with experience in concrete work and experts should add 40% and 10%, respectively, to the man-hours estimate for the entire project.

WHAT TO WATCH OUT FOR

Many alternatives to the conventional square, single-level patio are possible if the surrounding terrain is suitable and if you are willing to exercise your imagination and ingenuity. Terracing the patio is one example which is not so complex as it may seem. The same basic techniques used for single-level slabs are employed in multi-level installations, only in modular arrangements. Where the land slopes away from the house, two- and three-tier patio designs are an option, with interconnecting pressure-treated pine or redwood steps. Railroad ties and other rot-resistant border materials can be used to shore cutouts in the embankment. Single-level concrete patios can also be sectioned off in interesting configurations and grids with redwood or cedar dividers. Rounded corners and oval shapes are among the alternatives to conventional square and rectangular patio shapes. Masonite or 1/4" plywood can be used to form the curved edges. Custom-colored surface materials are also available on special order from concrete dealers and masonry suppliers if you want to mix them on your own. All of these variations from the standard patio design will add expense to the project, but they can enhance the facility's appearance, and, in some cases, contribute to its practical functions.

SUMMARY

Most do-it-yourselfers can complete this 12' x 16' patio plan if they are willing to put in several sessions of hard work. If you are unfamiliar with concrete construction, be sure to seek advice and arrange to have a knowledgeable person available to assist you during the slab placement and finishing. Your efforts will produce substantial savings and a home improvement that will give you and your family years of enjoyment.

CONCRETE PATIO, 12' x 16'

Description	Quantity	Man-hours	Material
Layout, clearing & excavation for patio, by hand	1 Job	12.0	0.00
Gravel fill, 3" deep, compacted	210 S.F.	1.5	13.35
Edge forms, 4" high	40 L.F.	2.5	9.70
Expansion joint at existing foundation, premolded bituminous fiber	16 L.F.	1.5	9.30
Reinforcing, welded wire fabric, 6 x 6 - 10/10	210 S.F.	1.5	20.35
Concrete, ready mix, 3000 psi	3 C.Y.	0.0	202.55
Place concrete	3 C.Y.	4.0	0.00
Finishing, broom finish	192 S.F.	3.0	0.00
Finish grade & re-seed	1 Job	4.0	11.70
Sealer for concrete	72 S.F.	1.5	15.70
Totals		31.5	$282.65

Project Size	12' x 16'	Contractor's Fee Including Materials	$1270

Key to Abbreviations
C.Y. - cubic yard   Ea. - each   L.F. - linear foot   Pr. - pair   Sq. - square (100 square feet of area)
S.F. - square foot   S.Y. - square yard   V.L.F. - vertical linear foot

FLAGSTONE PATIO, IN SAND

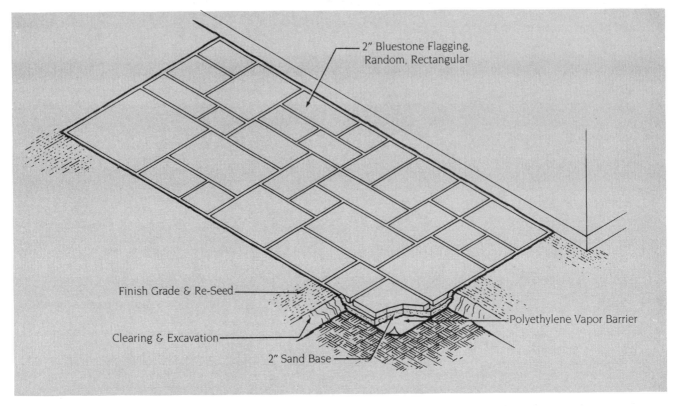

2" Bluestone Flagging, Random, Rectangular

Finish Grade & Re-Seed

Clearing & Excavation

2" Sand Base

Polyethylene Vapor Barrier

In addition to brick and concrete, many natural stone materials can be used to create attractive and functional patios. In geographical areas where the material is quarried or close to an abundant supply, the cost for both rough and cut stone can be surprisingly affordable. Like brick and concrete, stone is durable and can maintain its appearance with little upkeep throughout years of wear. This plan features a 6' x 12' patio constructed from bluestone flags of random-sized squares and rectangles, set in a sand bed. Like the brick-in-sand patio outlined earlier in this section, this project can be completed by most do-it-yourselfers for just the cost of the materials.

MATERIALS

The basic materials used for patio projects of this type tend to be readily available from masonry suppliers, though the choice of stone may be limited. Flagstone, slate, and bluestone are the most common, but you may have to compromise on the

size of the rectangular cut pieces if you plan to buy from the retailer's stock. Planning far enough in advance of the project will allow you to special order the type of stone and its size, but you may have to pay more for the custom cutting.

No special type of sand is required for the base, as long as it is not too fine to restrict drainage, nor too coarse to prohibit easy placement of the stones. Sand that has been screened and washed, like mason's sand, works the best and is usually the most economical. Only a small amount is needed to cover this 6' x 12' area to a depth of 2" and to provide the grouting between the pieces of stone. If you live in an area where clean sand (not sandy soil) is naturally available, it can be used for the base. Be sure that you screen it first through 1/4" wire screen to remove pebbles and organic matter. Money saved by acquiring or transporting the sand yourself should be weighed against the time and trouble required in its preparation.

Before the sand base is installed, the area for the new patio should be measured, squared, and staked out. Check the diagonal measurements of the rectangular area to be sure that they are equal. The site must then be excavated to a depth of about 4" to allow for a minimum of 2" of sand base and approximately 2" of stone depth. A polyethylene barrier is placed under the sand to restrict grass and other hardy plants from growing between the stone. No permanent border strip is included in this plan, but a temporary form made from 2" x 4"s may be used to keep the sand base intact and to ensure straight edges for the laying of the perimeter stones. After the sand has been placed, it is leveled with a straight piece of wood cut to the 6' width of the surface. It should then be tamped and watered, allowed to set for a day or two, and then tamped and watered again. A third treatment may be required before the base is firm enough to receive the surface stones.

The stones are then placed on the sand bed in the desired configuration or pattern. If you are installing rectangular flags of random size, as suggested in this plan, you might consider roughly laying out the entire patio, or a good portion of it, to get an idea of the trial-and-error fitting procedure. This preliminary layout will also give you a sense of how to place the material with maximum coverage and as little cutting as possible. By minimizing the cutting, you save time and avoid damaging or wasting the material. The permanent placement of the surface stones is easier and faster if they are uniform in their shape and thickness. Like bricks, stones of a generally consistent proportion can be placed on the leveled base with little fuss or readjustment. If there is much variation in thickness, the process takes longer, as each stone has to be leveled separately by adding or taking away sand. In most cases, rectangular bluestone flags maintain a consistent 2" thickness, but common flagstone and other paving materials are apt to be irregular. The trouble-free placement of regular stones might be worth their extra cost as you save on installation time. If you have not cut stones before, be sure to get some advice or have an experienced person show you the technique. You may have to invest in a stone chisel or brickset because a conventional cold chisel or other substitute will not do the job as well. The damage to the flags resulting from incorrect cutting methods may cause considerable waste and, therefore, expense. Even with the right tools and technique, a 20% waste allowance should be expected for irregular flagstone.

The joints between the stone can be grouted as each section is laid, but it is better to wait until the entire surface is completed. The same material used for the base sand can also be employed for the grouting, though there are other alternatives. Preprocessed grouting, stone dust, and fine sand will cost more, but they can provide more effective packing for the stones and enhance the design of the patio. The grouting material should be dampened after it has been swept into the joints with a stiff broom. Use a jointing tool, brickset, or similar device to pack the material, and then wet it again. Repeat this process several times until the grout is level with the surface of the stones and tightly packed. Whenever possible, kneel on the ground outside of the patio when installing the grout. If you have to walk or kneel on the newly set, ungrouted stones, distribute your weight with a piece of plywood or a wide board.

LEVEL OF DIFFICULTY

This project can be completed by homeowners who have the time to devote to it. Working with regular stone flags is not a difficult undertaking, and the results can be very rewarding. The advantage of installing a sand-set patio is that you can work at a comfortable pace and rectify mistakes easily. The most difficult task in the project is the cutting of the stones; but with careful planning, even this job is within the reach of the do-it-yourselfer. Those who are inexperienced in stone cutting should get instruction in the technique before they begin the project. Beginners should add 75% to the professional time for the project; handymen 40%; and experts, 10%. Extra time should be allowed for the installation of stones with irregular shapes and/or thicknesses and for those which require extensive cutting.

WHAT TO WATCH OUT FOR

Patios which are constructed from brick or stone and set in sand are not as easy to maintain as those set in mortar. Some of the stones may have to be reset periodically, and the grout replenished because of frost heaving or loosening from foot traffic. Even though the plastic barrier will prevent deep-rooted plants from becoming established, smaller surface plants will grow between the stones during warmer times of the year. If you use an inert grouting material like stone dust or professionally prepared exterior grout, the problem will still exist, but the amount of growth will be reduced. Careful application of a mild herbicide will reduce the amount of plant growth. If you use a hose to clean the patio, keep the spray light, as the grout is easily dislodged.

FLAGSTONE PATIO, IN SAND

Description	Quantity	Man-hours	Material
Layout, clearing & excavation for patio, by hand	1 Job	4.0	0.00
Polyethylene vapor barrier, .008" thick	80 S.F.	0.5	2.90
Washed sand for base, 2" thick	1 C.Y	0.0	15.65
Grade & level sand base	72 S.F.	2.0	0.00
Flagging, bluestone, snapped random rectangular, 2" thick	86 S.F.	17.0	324.65
Finish grade & re-seed	1 Job	2.0	5.85
Totals		25.5	$349.05

Project Size	6' x 12'	Contractor's Fee Including Materials	$1360

Key to Abbreviations
C.Y. - cubic yard   Ea. - each   L.F. - linear foot   Pr. - pair   Sq. - square (100 square feet of area)
S.F. - square foot   S.Y. - square yard   V.L.F. - vertical linear foot

SUMMARY

This small flagstone-in-sand patio project provides an ideal opportunity for do-it-yourselfers to learn the basics of dry-set masonry. With time, patient work, and a modest investment for materials, the exterior of your home can be enhanced with this comfortable and attractive sitting area or entryway apron.

FLAGSTONE PATIO, IN MORTAR

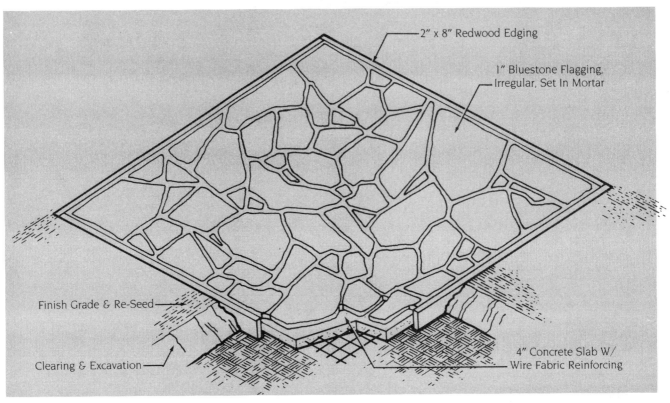

2" x 8" Redwood Edging

1" Bluestone Flagging, Irregular, Set In Mortar

Finish Grade & Re-Seed

Clearing & Excavation

4" Concrete Slab W/ Wire Fabric Reinforcing

Flagstone, bluestone, slate and other paving stones can be set in mortar to create attractive patio surfaces. Like brick, these materials offer the advantages of durability, low maintenance, and rugged beauty. They differ from brick in that they can be more expensive and often take longer to install because of their irregular sizes and shapes. This plan provides a cost estimate for the installation of a 12' x 12' irregular flagstone patio, including excavation, placement of the slab, and application of the finished surface. Because of the relatively large size of the patio and the number of masonry tasks required to complete it, beginners may consider hiring a contractor to do some of the work. However, many do-it-yourselfers, including some advanced beginners, can complete the entire project if they pace their work, proceed slowly, and seek advice and instruction before they tackle unfamiliar jobs. With careful and correct installation, this patio will be an attractive addition to the exterior of any home.

MATERIALS

This plan calls for the basic masonry materials used in most mortar-set patios. The project is really two installations in one. The first involves excavating and preparing the site and then placing the slab; the second includes the placement of the flagstone in the mortar bed and the finish work. For both phases of the project, several basic masonry tools are needed. Some of these tools may have to be purchased or rented, and this extra cost may have to be figured in. As for the materials themselves, no additional costs should arise if the patio as planned is installed under normal conditions on level ground. Be sure to compare prices before you buy the materials to get the best deal.

Before construction begins, you will need to carefully determine the location of the patio and lay it out. Generally, level, well-drained areas near the house are best suited to patio installations. Conveniently located spots that are protected from the wind and exposed to moderate sun are ideal. Although only 6" of

earth has to be removed, the excavation of a 12' x 12' area requires a considerable effort. Be sure to dig out several inches more than the patio dimensions so that you will be able to move the form freely while setting it. If the subsoil condition is poor, you may have to allow for extra time and expense to place a layer of gravel or crushed stone under the slab. Set and brace the form precisely at square and pitch it slightly away from the foundation before you stake it into final position. Standard welded wire reinforcing or steel rods will add strength and reduce cracking in the slab. If the new concrete abuts the foundation or a concrete walk, an asphalt-impregnated expansion joint should be placed along the seam.

The slab can be put into place at any time after the form has been completed, but you may be rushing things if you try to build and set the form and place the concrete all in the same work session. The general rule to follow for the concrete delivery is "Be Prepared." Have all of the necessary tools, plenty of manpower, and a detailed plan of operation ready when the truck arrives. Disorganization and poor preparation can add time and, therefore, expense to the procedure, as you may tie up the truck for longer than the allotted delivery time. Once the concrete has been placed, you have about four hours to finish the slab, so work patiently, but methodically. The finish does not have to be troweled extensively because a rough surface is best for bonding the mortar to be placed later.

Allow the slab time to set up and cure before proceeding with the second stage of the project, the placement of the mortar bed and flagstone. As in the brick-in-mortar patio project, the important aspect of this operation is to complete small, manageable sections at first, with increased production as the project progresses. Flagstone, however, does require more know-how, skill, and installation time than brick because its irregular shape necessitates cutting and fitting some pieces. Be sure to select flags of uniform thickness, as adjustments cannot be easily made for variations of thickness. Before laying a section of stones, place the pieces on the slab and position them by trial and error until you arrive at a combination that provides maximum coverage and joints that average about 3/4" in width. Some cutting of the stone may be required, but only as a last resort. Then, remove the pieces in order and reconstruct the pattern in a nearby area. Moisten the slab in the area to be covered, spread the mortar to a thickness of about 1", reposition the stones, and tap them into place with a

mallet or a hammer and block of wood. Precisely maintain level as you lay the stones so that the finished surface will look neat and drain properly. After the entire surface has been set and the mortar has cured, grout is packed into the joints, pointed, and allowed to set up for a week before a sealer is applied. This plan suggests a redwood border for the patio; but if no border material is installed, use extra care in grouting the edges of the surface.

LEVEL OF DIFFICULTY

Because of the various masonry tasks required to complete this project, all do-it-yourselfers will find it a challenging undertaking. If you are inexperienced in placing concrete slabs, mixing mortar to the right consistency, and cutting and fitting stone, get some assistance and instruction before you start the project. Beginners might consider hiring a contractor to install the slab, then finishing the surface on their own. As long as you place the flagstone in sections small enough to complete in one hour at your work pace, you can't go wrong. Working in this fashion, the job may take a little longer to finish, but the results should be lasting and attractive. The most difficult operation in the project is the placing of the slab because it involves considerable work in a limited time frame. Beginners should tackle the slab placement only if an experienced person is on hand to assist. If the slab

is installed incorrectly and the surface and edges are uneven, the flagstone placement will become a much more difficult and time-consuming operation. Beginners should add 75% to the man-hours for most of the tasks, and more for the flagstone placement. Handymen and experts should add 40% and 10%, respectively, to the professional time for all tasks, and more for the flagstone placement if they are inexperienced in stone cutting and fitting. All do-it-yourselfers can anticipate a gradual increase in productivity as they progress in the flagstone placement.

WHAT TO WATCH OUT FOR

The grouting for the flagstone can bring the surface of the patio to life, but it must be done neatly to achieve the desired effect. There are several methods which can be employed to quicken the pace of this time-consuming task and still produce neat results. One is to work with a trowel in one hand and a jointing tool in the other. A small portion of grout is placed on the trowel and scooped off as needed with the jointing tool. After the joints in a small section have been filled, the grout is packed. If voids occur, extra mortar is added where needed and packed. A second method employs a small piece of sheet metal which is shaped into a "V" and carries a small amount of grout. The point of the "V" is placed on the joint and guided into the opening with a jointing tool or the point of the trowel. The packing and pointing of the grout is the same as for the first method. Either way, an enriched mortar is used, mixed at dry consistency. Part of a neat job is minimizing the amount of mortar that gets on the stones. Clean up any drops or smears with a damp cloth or sponge before they dry as you proceed with the grouting. A final cleaning can be done with muriatic acid after the grout has cured.

FLAGSTONE PATIO, IN MORTAR

Description	Quantity	Man-hours	Material
Layout, clearing and excavation for patio, by hand	1 Job	4.0	0.00
Edging, redwood, 2" x 8"	48 L.F.	2.0	79.00
Base, concrete slab, 4" thick Reinforcing, welded wire fabric 6 x 6 - 10/10	160 S.F.	2.0	15.50
Concrete, ready mix, 2000 psi 4" thick	2 C.Y.	0.0	135.05
Place concrete	2 C.Y.	5.5	0.00
Flagging, bluestone, irregular shapes, 1" thick	170 S.F.	30.0	384.65
Finish grade & re-seed	1 Job	4.0	11.70
Totals		47.5	$625.90

Project Size	12' x 12'	Contractor's Fee Including Materials	$2680

Key to Abbreviations
C.Y. - cubic yard   Ea. - each   L.F. - linear foot   Pr. - pair   Sq. - square (100 square feet of area)
S.F. - square foot   S.Y. - square yard   V.L.F. - vertical linear foot

SUMMARY

This patio project involves a considerable number of masonry tasks, all of which can be completed by most do-it-yourselfers. With patient fitting and mortaring of the flagstones, the resulting patio will be an attractive, functional, and lasting addition to the exterior of your home.

PORCH, ENCLOSED WITH WINDOWS

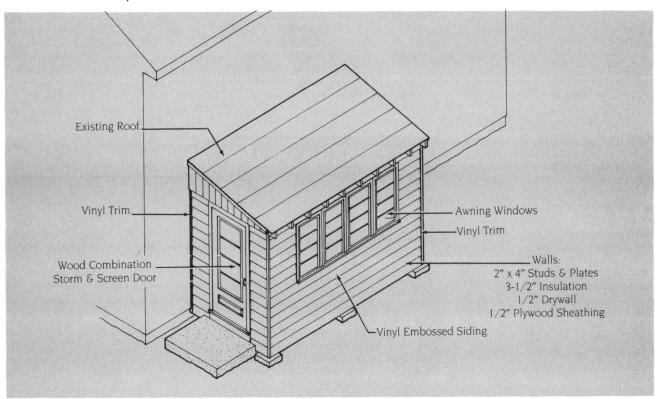

Existing Roof

Vinyl Trim

Wood Combination
Storm & Screen Door

Awning Windows

Vinyl Trim

Walls:
2" x 4" Studs & Plates
3-1/2" Insulation
1/2" Drywall
1/2" Plywood Sheathing

Vinyl Embossed Siding

Like breezeways, porches and roofed-over entryways can also be converted into comfortable interior space. If the porch structure already has a good roof and a sturdy floor and support system, the project is that much easier. This plan demonstrates how a 6' x 12' porch can become a small, but practical interior room. With the roof, floor, and support system already in place, the conversion can be accomplished quickly and economically by most do-it-yourselfers.

MATERIALS

The materials used in this plan are standard construction products commonly employed in home remodeling. The amount of required material will depend on the dimensions of the existing structure, the style and design of the house, and the extent to which the porch must be prepared and reconditioned. If the porch is large enough to warrant conversion, the materials order will

probably be large enough to require trucking. Be sure to work out the conditions of delivery before you finalize the purchase agreement.

Two critical areas of the existing porch should be examined before you begin the construction of the new room. These are the roof and the support system. Especially in older structures, these two vital components may need reconditioning and even replacing if they are to protect the new interior and carry the load of the new materials. Examine the flashing and general condition of the roof covering and rafters for signs of leakage and deterioration. If you can crawl under the structure, make a thorough inspection of the floor joists and decking, as well as the foundation. Rot, insect infestations, moisture, and weakness of the frame and flooring are problems which must be corrected before the project continues. If you cannot get under the porch, the condition of the floor and its frame can be checked by removing some of

the floor boards in several places and performing the inspection from above. These preliminary measures take time and may involve extra expense if reconditioning work is called for. If a problem looks serious, hire a specialist to investigate further and correct the situation. In short, be sure that the existing porch roof, floor, and foundation are in top condition before you install any new material.

After the porch has been reconditioned, the 2" x 4" walls are framed and the exterior of the structure is sheathed, equipped with new windows and a door, and then sided. In most cases, the framing will fill areas between the existing roof support posts, so allow extra time, and possibly cost, for extra cutting and measuring. If any of the posts have to be replaced or relocated, be sure to provide temporary roof support posts during the framing operaton. The 1/2" plywood sheathing and new window and door units are put into place once the framing is complete. This plan includes medium-sized thermopane casement window units, but double-hung or jalousie models may be more appropriate for your home. Embossed vinyl siding is suggested in this model, but cedar, aluminum, or a different style and grade of vinyl may better suit the exterior of your home. Your total cost will vary somewhat with these substitutions. Refurbishing or changing the exterior trim or adding a gutter and downspout, if required, will also add time and expense to the project.

Within the enclosure, the old exterior wall must be prepared for new materials. Ceiling joists and insulation must be installed, and finish coverings applied to the ceiling, walls, and floor. The wall preparation involves stripping the old siding and reconditioning the existing entryway for the new interior door. The exterior ends of the new ceiling joists must be tapered to fit the existing roof line and the interior ends plated and lagged into the side of the house. The ceiling and new exterior walls should be insulated to the recommended R-value ratings for your geographical area. Before drywall or paneling is applied, all rough electrical

work should be completed. You can place the underlayment for the carpeting or vinyl flooring directly on the old porch floorboards, but be sure to use threaded flooring nails and then level the surface before the finish is applied. A layer of building paper between the old floor and underlayment will reduce the chance of moisture penetration while helping to eliminate squeaks.

LEVEL OF DIFFICULTY

This porch conversion can be performed by all levels of do-it-yourselfers. Because the site is conveniently located and much of the heavy exterior work has already been done, the project is considerably less difficult and expensive than a complete room addition of the same size. Assuming that only minimal reconditioning is needed, the most challenging operations in the project are the wall framing and ceiling joist placement. If you are unfamiliar with framing, the procedures can be learned from an experienced carpenter. As in other conversion projects, like the breezeway, attic, and garage plans, the work can usually be

completed at a comfortable pace without disturbing the routine of the house. Beginners should double the professional time estimates throughout the project and get help before they begin tasks that are new to them. Handymen should add 50% to the estimated man-hours, and experts 20%, for all procedures. All do-it-yourselfers should consider hiring an electrician and a carpet installer for these aspects of the job.

WHAT TO WATCH OUT FOR

Particularly in colder climates, the floor of the converted room should be insulated for comfort and energy savings. This task can be challenging, however, even if the floor is accessible from underneath the structure. You may have to place the insulation from a prone position and under cramped conditions. Space problems may require that batts, rather than rolled material be used. Once the insulation is in place, some means of permanent support should be installed. Strapping can be nailed across the joists at 16" intervals, or chicken wire or inexpensive screening can be stapled to the supports to cover the newly insulated area. If the floor is inaccessible from below, styrofoam sheets can be placed between sleepers made from strapping or 2" x 4"s on the old floor surface. With this method, however, new decking as well as underlayment must be installed before the finished floor is laid. In this case, you may also have to make adjustments for the new floor height at both entryways. Although the materials and extra work required to insulate the floor will add cost and time to the project, the benefits of a warm floor and reduced heating costs may make the investment worthwhile.

SUMMARY

Winterizing an existing porch like this one can increase the interior space of your home without the large expense of a complete room addition. Because the roof and support system are already in place, many do-it-yourselfers can handle the finishing tasks at their convenience, without having to deal with the challenges of a completely new structure.

PORCH, ENCLOSED WITH WINDOWS

Description	Quantity	Man-hours	Material
Remove siding & door inside porch	1 Ea.	4.0	0.00
Wall framing, studs & plates, 2" x 4" x 8', 16" O.C.,	24 L.F.	4.0	74.35
Headers over openings, 2" x 6" stock	24 L.F.	1.5	11.35
Sheathing, plywood, 1/2" thick, 4' x 8' sheets	6 Sheets	3.0	95.25
Ceiling joists, 2" x 6" x 12', 16" O.C.	60 L.F.	1.0	28.30
Insulation, ceiling, 6" thick, R19, paper-backed	72 S.F.	0.5	34.00
Walls, 3-1/2" thick, R-11, paper-backed	160 S.F.	1.0	52.30
Sheetrock, walls & ceilings, 1/2" thick, 4' x 8' sheets, taped & finished	12 Sheets	6.5	116.15
Door, wood entrance, birch solid core, 2'-8" x 6'-8"	1 Ea.	1.0	145.20
Lockset, exterior	1 Ea.	1.0	116.20
Door, prehung exterior, combination storm & screen, 6'-9" x 2'-8"	1 Ea.	1.5	99.20
Windows, awning, average quality, 2' x 3' insulating glass	4 Ea.	3.5	706.65
Trim, colonial casing, windows, door & base	88 L.F.	3.0	38.35
Siding, vinyl embossed, 8" wide, w/trim	40 S.F.	1.5	30.50
Flooring, vinyl sheet, .25" thick	72 S.F.	2.5	196.00
Paint walls, ceiling & trim, primer & 2 coats	288 S.F.	5.0	24.40
	Totals	40.5	$1768.20

Project Size	6' x 12'	Contractor's Fee Including Materials	$3960

Key to Abbreviations
C.Y. - cubic yard   Ea. - each   L.F. - linear foot   Pr. - pair   Sq. - square (100 square feet of area)
S.F. - square foot   S.Y. - square yard   V.L.F. - vertical linear foot

PORCH, ENCLOSED WITH SCREENS

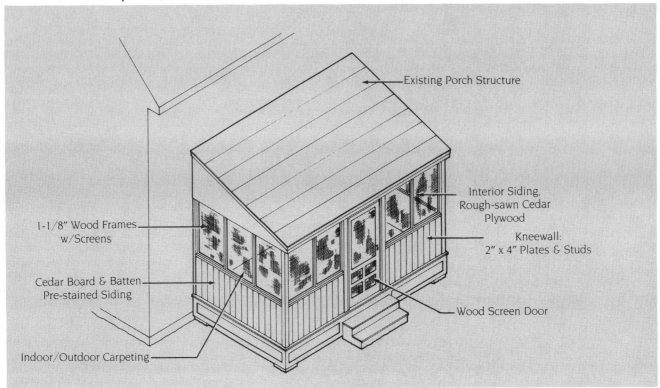

Existing Porch Structure

Interior Siding, Rough-sawn Cedar Plywood

Kneewall: 2" x 4" Plates & Studs

1-1/8" Wood Frames w/Screens

Cedar Board & Batten Pre-stained Siding

Wood Screen Door

Indoor/Outdoor Carpeting

This plan demonstrates how a roofed-over exterior space, such as a porch, can be screened in for a modest investment of time and money by the homeowner. It is an ideal project for do-it-yourselfers of all ability levels, as only a limited amount of specialized work is required.

MATERIALS

As in other porch and breezeway conversions, the amount and type of materials are determined by the fixed dimensions of the structure and the style of the house to which it is attached. If the dimensions of your project differ from this model, the total cost will have to be adjusted. All of the products are conventional construction materials which can be purchased at competitive prices from most building supply outlets.

Before the new materials are installed, the existing porch should be thoroughly inspected and its condition evaluated. If the roof or floor is in need of repair, it should be restored to dry and safe conditions. Some

additional costs may be incurred during this stage of the project if repairs or restorations are needed. Any extra exterior work, like installing a gutter and downspout, finishing the fascia and soffit, or building a new set of stairs, should also be completed at this stage.

The frame for the knee wall of the porch is constructed from standard 2" x 4"s between the existing roof support posts. Unless there is good reason to move them, all support posts should be kept in position to maintain the structural integrity of the roof support system. In situations where a post has to be relocated or replaced, temporary bracing must be provided. Extra cost and man-hours will also have to be added. Inexperienced do-it-yourselfers should consult a contractor if extensive post relocation or replacement is required. Once the framing has been completed, the exterior walls are covered with a single layer of sheet siding, or sheathed and then covered with appropriate cedar, vinyl, or aluminum

exterior finish. A decorative cap with trim for the knee wall is an option which can be applied at extra cost. With some ingenuity, the trim for the cap can be designed to serve as the bottom stop for the screen panels.

Inside the enclosure, 2" x 6" ceiling joists are put into place, and the finish coverings for the ceiling, walls, and floor are applied. Many options are available for the type and quality of materials used in the interior, depending on the degree of finish work desired. If you want the effect of a rustic finish, the ceiling can be left open to the rafters, the inside of the exterior walls left uncovered, and the existing floor repainted or left as is. The cost of the project will be reduced significantly in this case, and the finishing touches could be added at a later date. The moderate finish work suggested in this plan provides covering for the ceiling, knee wall, and floor, but not the interior wall. Sheet goods, like the rough-sawn cedar plywood included in this materials list, install quickly and provide an attractive, low maintenance surface. Barnboard, tongue-and-groove, and plank coverings are also available, but they are usually more expensive and require more time to install. Electrical work is not included in this plan, but you might consider installing outdoor-approved outlets and an overhead or wall lighting fixture. If you plan to include these electrical amenities, be sure that the rough-in is completed before the wall and ceiling coverings are put into place.

The screen panels for the new porch are the most important components in the structure. They deserve special consideration before you decide on their design and the best installation method. In most cases, removable wood-framed panels are the most effective system to use. They may cost more and take longer to fabricate than permanent models, but they have many advantages. They last longer because they can be removed and stored during the months when the porch is not in use. They can also be cleaned and painted more easily on the ground and then put in place. Furthermore, repair work, restretching, and replacement can be performed more conveniently because of the

modular design of these panels. Beginners might consider hiring a carpenter to manufacture the panels and, later, to install the screen door. Both of these operations require some know-how, and precision carpentry skills are a prerequisite. Handymen and experts who intend to make the screen panels should weigh the benefits of the potential savings in labor costs against the expediency and professional workmanship of an experienced carpenter. Screen panels are also available in standard factory-prepared models with both wood and aluminum frames, but they may require special ordering. If you intend to make the panels on your own, be sure to read up on the techniques involved in their manufacture and consult a knowledgeable person for tips. Priming and painting the stock for the frames will save time in the finishing stages of the project.

LEVEL OF DIFFICULTY

The carpentry skills required to complete this medium-sized porch enclosure are within the realm of most do-it-yourselfers. As noted earlier, the heavy exterior work is already done,

and the filling in of the shell is all that is required. Professional help may be needed if extensive reconditioning is necessary for the roof, floor, or support system, but minor problems can be corrected by the do-it-yourselfer. Beginners should consider hiring a contractor or retailer who specializes in screen fabrication to manufacture the screen panels. For all other tasks, beginners should add 100% to the man-hours estimates. Handymen and experts who tackle the screen panel manufacture should add extra time to their normal work rate to allow for the precise nature of the operation. For all other procedures, they should add 50% and 20%, respectively.

WHAT TO WATCH OUT FOR

Before you make a decision on the screen panel design and installation method, investigate all of the possibilities. Conventional wood-framed panels meet durability standards, but they require maintenance and are prone to bowing and warping if they are poorly made or installed. Aluminum-framed panels may not be as attractive as wood-framed units, but they will last longer, and periodic cleaning is the only required maintenance. The options for the screen material include aluminum, which is long-lasting and capable of withstanding abuse, but it discolors with corrosion after a few years. Fiberglass screening is another possibility. It tends to stretch and bow more easily than aluminum, but it retains its original luster and attractive appearance longer. Copper screening is a material which performs and looks better than both aluminum and fiberglass, but it is very expensive. The type of screening should be carefully considered before the final design has been determined.

PORCH, ENCLOSED WITH SCREENS

Description	Quantity	Man-hours	Material
Framing for knee wall, 2" x 4" plates	96 L.F.	2.0	30.20
Studs, 2" x 4" x 3', 16" O.C.	84 L.F.	2.0	26.45
Framing, for doorway, 2" x 4" x 8'	32 L.F.	1.0	10.10
Celing joists, 2" x 6" x 8', 16" O.C.	88 L.F.	1.5	41.55
Ceiling & knee walls, rough-sawn cedar plywood, 3/8" thick, stained	7 Sheets	5.5	290.00
Siding, exterior, for knee wall, cedar board & batten, pre-stained	90 S.F.	3.0	128.50
Wood screens, 1-1/8" frames, pre-fabricated	140 S.F.	6.0	423.50
Screen door, wood, 2'-8" x 6'-9"	1 Ea.	2.0	190.00
Indoor/outdoor carpet, 3/8" thick	112 S.F.	3.0	383.55
Paint, door, screens & trim, primer & 2 coats	100 L.F.	3.0	9.70
Totals		29.0	$1533.55

Project Size	8' x 14'	Contractor's Fee Including Materials	$3180

Key to Abbreviations
C.Y. - cubic yard   Ea. - each   L.F. - linear foot   Pr. - pair   Sq. - square (100 square feet of area)
S.F. - square foot   S.Y. - square yard   V.L.F. - vertical linear foot

SUMMARY

A screened-in porch like this one can provide years of enjoyment for you and your family. If the basic roof and support structure are already in place, the facility can be completed at a reasonable cost, as the work can be done by most do-it-yourselfers.

PORCH, ENCLOSED WITH SLIDING GLASS DOORS

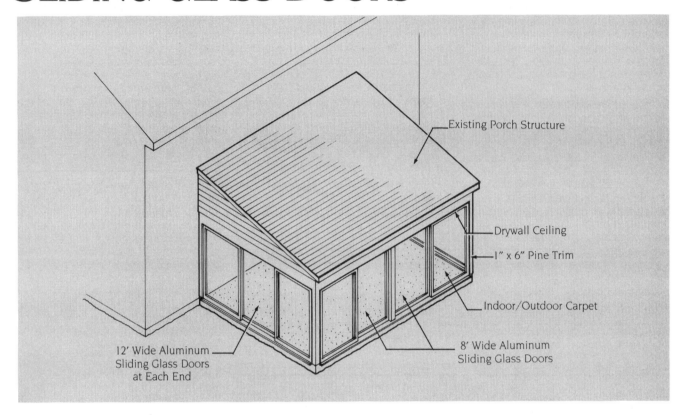

Existing Porch Structure

Drywall Ceiling

1" x 6" Pine Trim

Indoor/Outdoor Carpet

8' Wide Aluminum Sliding Glass Doors

12' Wide Aluminum Sliding Glass Doors at Each End

Open, attached porch areas can be remodeled with a very standard approach, or converted to a more deluxe kind of interior space. This plan presents the latter type of improvement, and features insulated sliding glass doors to provide the benefits of natural light and fresh air. If you want to increase the light and ventilation still further, you might invest a bit more by adding skylights. Generally, this is a moderate to difficult project because of the size of the porch area and the specialized skills required to accomplish several of the tasks. Once the enclosure has been finished, it will provide years of enjoyable and practical service for you and your family, while increasing the value of your home.

MATERIALS

As in other porch plans included in this section, it is assumed that a weathertight, sturdy roof and a solid foundation and support system are already in place before the work begins. The materials list, therefore, includes only those products which are required to fill in the walls, finish the interior, and otherwise enhance the porch's function and appearance. Because many variables exist, the particulars of an individual project will modify this estimate. The size, roof style, and the amount of reconditioning required for the existing structure will affect the overall cost, as will the type and extent of finish work that goes into the new room. The basic structural materials are readily available from building supply retailers, but some sliding glass door models may require special ordering.

Before any new materials are installed, the existing structure should be thoroughly inspected and evaluated. The roof should be dry and its sheathing solid and free from rot or deterioration. Carefully check the flashing along the seam between the roof and the wall of the house, and examine the underside of the roof's subsurface and rafters. If the roof is held up by a post-and-beam support system, check the condition and alignment of the supporting members. This plan depicts a concrete slab as the floor and foundation for the porch, but a concrete block or poured-in-place foundation with a wood floor may better describe your porch's arrangement. Regardless of the type, check and evaluate its condition before continuing. If deficiencies or weaknesses are found in the existing porch's components, correct them before proceeding with the project. Extensive reconditioning may require the services of a roofing or foundation specialist.

The sliding glass doors are the primary components of the conversion, so give careful consideration to their selection and installation. Generally, the extra expense for top quality units is worthwhile, as they will provide years of reliable, weathertight service. If you should choose to incorporate skylights into this project, consult the skylight plans in the "Exteriors" section. Various models are described there, along with details on price, selection, and installation.

The most important aspect of the sliding glass door installation is the correct sizing and precise leveling, plumbing, and squaring of the rough openings. The units are available in various standard sizes, like the 6' and 8' models suggested in this plan. Odd sizes require special ordering and cost more because they must be custom made. The estimate given in this plan is for a high quality slider unit which, because of its expense, should be handled carefully, with plenty of time allowed for its installation.

The doorway from the porch area to the house may require some attention after the sliders and interior finish are put into place. If the porch area is to become a new room in the house, you may want to enlarge the existing doorway, build a rough frame with appropriate jack studs and headers,

and then trim the opening. A slider unit or French door can also be installed in this location. If the porch is to be winterized but will still be considered more as an exterior area, the old doorway can be left as is with no additional work required. The exterior siding and any existing windows can be left in place or removed, depending on the extent of finish desired in the new porch. Your choice of treatment for this area will have a substantial impact on the cost of the project. Plan carefully if the access is to be redesigned.

LEVEL OF DIFFICULTY

Because of the specialty work involved in the sliding glass door installations, beginners and handymen with limited remodeling experience should consider hiring professionals to complete this task. Even experts and experienced handymen should seek some assistance. The components are expensive, and precise workmanship is required to ensure that the results of the installation are commensurate

with the investment in materials. The rest of the project, with the exception of any extensive reconditioning work, should be within the reach of most do-it-yourselfers. Beginners should double the professional time for all work and seek advice when needed. Handymen and experts should add 50% and 20%, respectively, to the man-hours estimates for basic procedures, and 60% and 30% for the sliding door installations. All do-it-yourselfers will have to add both time and expense for extra interior finish work if the porch is to be integrated into the first floor room plan of the house.

WHAT TO WATCH OUT FOR

If the new glassed-in porch is to be used essentially as an interior facility, local building codes may require a minimum number of electrical outlets. Extra lighting fixtures and wall switches may also be desired by the homeowner. These necessities and amenities should be provided for before the ceiling and walls are framed and covered, to save time and money and to simplify the procedure. Remember that space may be required between the rough framing members of the slider units if wiring and switch or outlet boxes are to be installed in this location. Also, supply wires for the wall switches, outlets, and overhead lighting fixtures must be run above the finished ceiling and then fed to the electrical service panel. A qualified electrician should tie in the new circuit to the electrical supply and perform any parts of the installation which are too difficult for the do-it-yourselfer. Beginners should hire a professional for all of the electrical work.

SUMMARY

This glassed-in porch enclosure will add an attractive and comfortable new living space to your home. If the conditions of the existing roofed-over structure are right, this deluxe conversion can be performed for a reasonable cost.

PORCH, ENCLOSED WITH SLIDING GLASS DOORS

Description	Quantity	Man-hours	Material
Remove existing door & enlarge opening	1 Ea.	4.0	0.00
Frame opening into house, 2" x 4" studs	32 L.F.	1.5	8.90
Header over opening, 2" x 10" stock	20 L.F.	1.0	9.45
Trim at opening, 1" x 6" jamb, stock pine	24 L.F.	1.0	9.60
Casing, stock pine, 11/16" x 2-1/2"	24 L.F.	1.0	21.20
Sliding glass doors, aluminum, 5/8" insul. glass, 8' wide, premium	2 Ea.	11.0	1113.20
Sliding glass doors, aluminum, 5/8" insul. glass, 12' wide, premium	2 Ea.	13.0	1318.90
Miscellaneous wood blocking for ceiling, 2" x 4" stock	48 L.F.	1.5	15.10
Insulation, fiberglass, kraft-faced batts, 6" thick, R-19	192 S.F.	1.5	90.60
Sheetrock at ceiling, 1/2" thick, 4' x 8' sheets, taped & finished	6 Sheets	4.5	58.10
Trim, cove molding, 9/16" x 1-3/4"	60 L.F.	2.0	163.35
Indoor/outdoor carpet, 3/8" thick	21 S.Y.	4.5	171.20
Paint trim, primer & 2 coats	50 L.F.	1.5	4.25
Paint ceiling, primer & 1 coat	192 S.F.	1.5	20.90
	Totals	49.5	$3004.75

Project Size	12' x 16'	Contractor's Fee Including Materials	$6660

Key to Abbreviations
C.Y. - cubic yard   Ea. - each   L.F. - linear foot   Pr. - pair   Sq. - square (100 square feet of area)
S.F. - square foot   S.Y. - square yard   V.L.F. - vertical linear foot

ROOM ADDITION, 8' x 8'

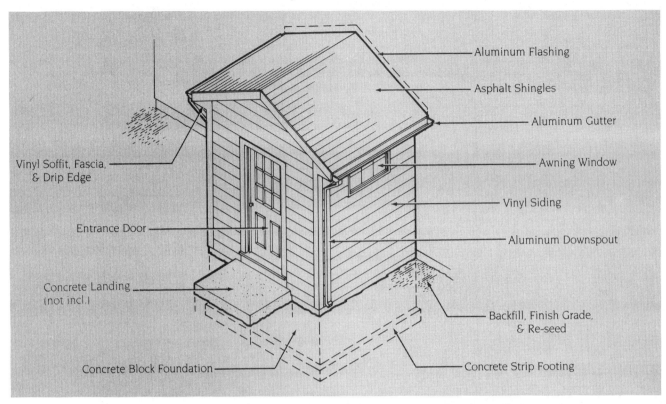

Aluminum Flashing

Asphalt Shingles

Aluminum Gutter

Awning Window

Vinyl Siding

Aluminum Downspout

Backfill, Finish Grade, & Re-seed

Concrete Strip Footing

Concrete Block Foundation

Concrete Landing (not incl.)

Entrance Door

Vinyl Soffit, Fascia, & Drip Edge

Room additions, like other projects involving attached structures, should complement the style and design of the house while meeting the need for new living area. Because of budget limitations, major remodeling projects like this one often require modifications in the structure's design and materials. This give-and-take process may lengthen the planning stages, but it helps ensure the livability, appearance, and value of the addition. This plan demonstrates how an 8' x 8' structure can be built for modest cost. Because the project is small scale and at first-floor level, do-it-yourselfers can take a hand in its construction and enjoy the benefits of lower costs.

MATERIALS

It is possible to dig the foundation for this addition by hand to its required 4' below-grade depth, however, machine excavation is a practical alternative, the cost of which is included in this estimate. The excavation should be wide enough to accommodate the

footing and foundation walls and deep enough to rest on firm, frost-free subsoil. Once the footing has been carefully laid out and put into place, the concrete block wall can be built to the desired height. A formed and poured concrete wall is a slightly more expensive option. Generally, do-it-yourselfers should leave the excavation and masonry tasks to a professional contractor, as specialized skills and equipment and considerable physical exertion are involved in foundation work.

The exterior of the structure is comprised of framing, sheathing, and finish materials common to wood-framed houses. The support for the floor of the room consists of 2" x 8" joists placed 16" on center and covered with 5/8" plywood sheathing. Before the floor frame is placed, a 2" x 8" sill should be lagged or bolted into the top of the foundation wall. A little extra expense for pressure-treated lumber for the sill plate will provide protection against rot and deterioration. If pressure-treated lumber is not used, you might consider treating the sill lumber with

wood preservative before the floor frame is placed. A vent should also be included in the foundation as protection against dampness and deterioration.

When planning the roof frame, be sure to match or complement the pitch of the house roof and the design of its soffit and fascia. This part of the project requires substantial carpentry skills and a basic knowledge of framing procedures. Seek advice and help if these tasks are new to you. The sheathing and exterior finish materials can be applied once the framing is completed. This plan includes economical asphalt strip shingles, vinyl siding, and aluminum soffits and fascias. If other finish products are more appropriate to the style of your house, these substitutions will alter both the cost of materials and the estimated time for installation. Most do-it-yourselfers can accomplish this roof work if they are given instruction on laying it out and flashing it correctly at the house wall. But do allow plenty of time to work slowly if you are not an experienced roofer.

Inside, many different surface coverings and trim materials can be used, according to your home's decor and practical requirements. For example, if this addition is to be used as a mud room and entryway, the low-maintenance vinyl flooring suggested in this plan might be a better choice than carpet. The possible wall and ceiling coverings include taped and finished 1/2" drywall, wood paneling, or other sheet products. Be sure to take care of all the preliminary work, like the electrical rough-in, insulating, and the placing of underlayment, before you apply the finish surfaces.

LEVEL OF DIFFICULTY

Because of its small size and first floor location, much of this 8' x 8' addition project can be completed by do-it-yourselfers. As noted earlier, the foundation work should be left to a contractor; but the framing and finish work can be performed by homeowners with a moderate level of remodeling skill. Beginners should get help before starting new procedures and seek guidance as they progress. Homeowners should weigh the savings on labor costs against the investment of their time in jobs which require specialized skills and know-how. Siding, roofing, electrical work, and flooring can be done much faster and with better results by a specialty contractor than by the handyman who is unfamiliar with the tools, materials, and the ins and outs of these jobs. Generally, beginners should add 100% to the man-hours estimates for the basic tasks and hire a professional for the time-consuming, technically-demanding specialty operations. Handymen should add 50% to the time for basic tasks and carpentry procedures and 70% for any specialty work that is new to them.

Experts should add about 20% to the professional time for all tasks in this project. Almost all do-it-yourselfers should hire a contractor to do the electrical rough-in, and even experts should leave the circuit tie-in to a qualified tradesman.

WHAT TO WATCH OUT FOR

The type and placement of windows and doors are among the most important design features of any room addition. Although they are also some of the more expensive items in any home improvement project, it does not pay to compromise on the quality or design of these components. Whenever possible, purchase well-made thermopane window units. Not only do they provide on-going energy savings, but they usually include screens, and do not require the extra expense of storm windows. The door used in this plan is a new fixture; however, the old exterior door could be relocated to the entryway of the new room. Existing window units can be relocated in the same way to reduce the materials cost. If you choose to reuse the old door and windows, be sure that they are in good enough condition to make their relocation worthwhile. While cosmetic deficiencies are usually fairly simple to correct, structural defects involve a considerable amount of repair time.

SUMMARY

This 8' x 8' addition can add to the comfort and convenience of your home. It is an approachable project for the do-it-yourselfer because it is relatively small in size and is conveniently located.

ROOM ADDITION, 8' x 8'

Description	Quantity	Man-hours	Material
Excavate, with machine, 4' deep	1 Job	6.0	0.00
Footing, 8" thick x 16" wide x 20'	1 C.Y.	4.0	106.00
Foundation, 8" concrete block, 4' high	96 Blocks	16.0	428.65
Frame, floor, 2" x 8" joists, 16" O.C., 8' long	80 L.F.	1.5	55.15
Floor sheathing, 5/8" plywood, 4' x 8' sheets	2 Sheets	1.0	34.05
Frame, walls, 2" x 4" studs & plates, 8' high	20 L.F.	3.5	71.40
Header over window, 2" x 8" stock	8 L.F.	0.5	5.25
Wall sheathing, 1/2" x 4' x 8' plywood	6 Sheets	3.0	95.25
Frame, roof, 2" x 6" rafters, 16" O.C.	80 L.F.	1.5	37.75
Ridge board & sub-fascia, 2" x 8" x 8' long	24 L.F.	1.5	16.55
Ceiling, 2" x 6" joists, 16" O.C.	48 L.F.	1.0	22.65
Roof sheathing, 1/2" x 4' x 8' plywood	3 Sheets	1.5	47.65
Siding, vinyl embossed, 8" wide, with trim	180 S.F.	6.0	135.05
Soffit, 12" wide vented, fascia & drip edge	35 L.F.	5.0	59.30
Roofing, standard strip shingles & felt paper	1 Sq.	2.0	57.90
Flashing, aluminum stop flashing	20 S.F.	1.5	15.95
Gutters, 5" aluminum, .027" thick	16 L.F.	1.5	16.10
Downspouts, 2" x 3", embossed aluminum	20 L.F.	1.0	12.60
Wall insulation, fiberglass, 3-1/2" thick, R-11	180 S.F.	1.0	58.80
Ceiling, insulation, fiberglass, 6" thick, R-19	50 S.F.	0.5	23.60
Window, clad awning type, 40" x 22", thermopane	1 Ea.	1.0	225.05
Exterior door, wood, 2'8" x 6'8", prehung with lockset	1 Ea.	2.0	372.70
Drywall, 1/2" x 4' x 8', standard, finished	10 Sheets	6.0	96.80
Underlayment, 3/8" particleboard	2 Sheets	1.0	31.75
Flooring, vinyl sheet, .125" thick	50 S.F.	2.0	196.65
Trim, ranch base & casing	50 L.F.	2.0	42.35
Paint walls, ceiling & trim, primer & 2 coats	320 S.F.	5.0	69.70
Electrical wiring, 4 outlets, 1 switch	1 Lot	7.0	74.95
Backfill, finish grade & re-seed	1 Job	13.0	12.10
Totals		98.5	$2421.90

Project Size	8' x 8'	Contractor's Fee Including Materials	$6680

Key to Abbreviations
C.Y. - cubic yard   Ea. - each   L.F. - linear foot   Pr. - pair   Sq. - square (100 square feet of area)
S.F. - square foot   S.Y. - square yard   V.L.F. - vertical linear foot

ROOM ADDITION, 8' x 12'

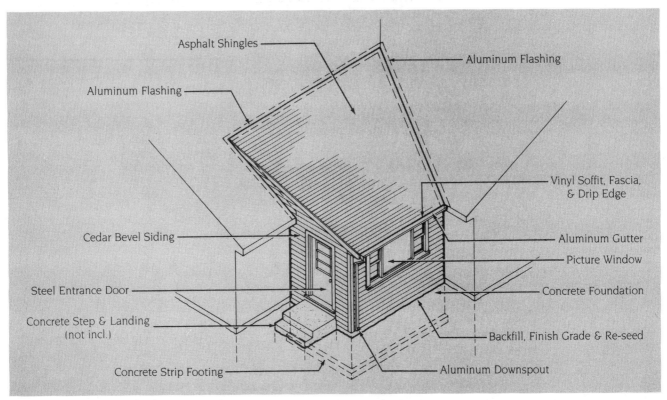

Asphalt Shingles

Aluminum Flashing

Aluminum Flashing

Vinyl Soffit, Fascia, & Drip Edge

Cedar Bevel Siding

Aluminum Gutter

Picture Window

Steel Entrance Door

Concrete Foundation

Concrete Step & Landing (not incl.)

Backfill, Finish Grade & Re-seed

Concrete Strip Footing

Aluminum Downspout

The proximity of property boundaries, design of the existing house, and other factors often prevent the conventional construction of a room addition. In these circumstances, unusual designs may be called for, such as this 8' x 12' addition between the wings of the house. Although the structure is moderate in size, it is a challenging project for most do-it-yourselfers, as it calls for quite a few carpentry and building skills.

MATERIALS

One of the benefits of placing the addition in a corner location is that two of the walls are already in place. Thus, you can save on the materials and labor which are normally required to frame and cover these walls. For the new construction, a 4' foundation is required on the remaining two sides. The other materials are standard framing lumber and interior and exterior coverings and finish products appropriate to the style of the house.

Before placing the order, do some comparative pricing at several building supply outlets. Also, because of the size of the order and the number and weight of materials, trucking is required, so make arrangements for delivery before you close the deal.

The foundation suggested in this plan is constructed from poured concrete, but concrete blocks can also be used and will function as well. The extra time and expense required to install foundation vents are well invested, as they will help to increase air circulation and prevent moisture from accumulating underneath the structure. In most cases, excavations and foundation installations of this size are best left to the contractor. Accurate location and leveling of the forms, and skillful concrete placement are vital to the successful completion of the project.

The shell of this addition is comprised of standard materials commonly used in exterior framing and finishing. After the sill, floor joists, and floor sheathing have been placed, the two exterior walls are framed on the deck and raised into position. The roof framing of corner structures can be tricky, so plan ahead and get some help if you think you will need it. After the roof structure has been completed, the gable end must be framed with 2" x 4"s, placed individually. The sheathing for the walls in this plan is 3/4" rigid styrofoam, but standard 1/2" plywood can also be used. The roof also requires plywood sheathing before it is covered with a layer of building paper and asphalt shingles. Because of the amount of flashing required, most do-it-yourselfers should consider hiring a professional to do the roofing work.

Before the interior finish materials are applied, the exterior walls and the ceiling should be insulated at the recommended R-values for your area of the country. In colder climates, the floor should also be insulated before the sheathing is placed. Additional materials cost will have to be added to the project; but your floors will be warmer during the cold months, and your heating bill lower. After the electrical work has been roughed in, the interior finish materials can be installed. Cost will vary here according to your choice of products, the amount of trim, and decorative considerations. Standard 1/2" drywall requires know-how and skill to install and finish, but most handymen can do the job if they are given some assistance at the outset. Underlayment should be installed beneath the carpet and laid at right angles to the floor sheathing, with no coincidental seams. All trim materials should match or complement the decor in the rest of your home.

LEVEL OF DIFFICULTY

As in other complete room additions, this project requires a moderate to advanced level of skill in many construction procedures, including framing, roofing, siding, and exterior finish work. However, once the structure is closed in, the interior tasks can be completed one at a time over an extended period. This situation works to the benefit of all do-it-yourselfers who proceed patiently and learn as they go. Beginners can approach the interior work at a relaxed pace on weekends and evenings, but they should leave most of the exterior work on this project to contractors.

The foundation, framing, roofing, siding, and other specialized tasks require skill and experience, but for the more basic tasks, like painting, sheathing, and landscaping, beginners should add 100% to the professional time. Handymen should add 50% for all but the roof framing and finishing, electrical, and carpet installations. They should allow more time for these specialty tasks, and, depending on their ability, should hire professionals to do the work. Experts should add 20% to allow for a slow and patient installation process. All do-it-yourselfers should hire a contractor for the excavation and foundation work.

WHAT TO WATCH OUT FOR

The unusual roof lines of structures like this corner room addition provide a good situation for a skylight. Adding this amenity to the project will increase the cost, but the installation will be much easier and faster if it is done while the roof is being built, rather than later. Skylights are available in many sizes, models, and levels of quality. The good ones are expensive; but as with other window units, the extra cost for a quality product will be returned in energy efficiency and durability over the years.

SUMMARY

Corner room additions such as this 8' x 12' design require imaginative planning and skillful installation, but offer a great potential for reward. When appropriately tailored to the roof lines and setting of your house, they can add an attractive exterior feature while increasing the living area and value of your home.

ROOM ADDITION, 8' x 12'

Description	Quantity	Man-hours	Material
Excavate, with machine, 4' deep	1 Job	6.0	0.00
Footing, 8" thick x 16" wide x 20' long	1 C.Y.	3.0	88.30
Foundation walls, 8" thick, c.i.p. concrete	2 C.Y.	12.0	296.20
Frame, floor, 2" x 8" joists, 16" O.C., 8' long	120 L.F.	2.5	82.75
Floor, sheathing, 5/8" plywood 4' x 8' sheets	3 Sheets	1.5	51.10
Frame, walls, 2" x 4" studs and plates, 8' long	20 L.F.	4.0	194.80
Header over window & door, 2" x 8" stock	18 L.F.	1.0	38.30
Wall sheathing, 3/4" x 4' x 8' rigid styrofoam	5 Sheets	2.0	79.40
Frame, roof, 2" x 6" rafters, 16" O.C.	169 L.F.	3.0	84.95
Sub-fascia, 2" x 6" stock	14 L.F.	0.5	6.60
Ceiling, 2" x 6" joists, 16" O.C.	90 L.F.	1.5	47.20
Support beam, double 2" x 10"	28 L.F.	1.5	52.85
Roof sheathing, 5/8" x 4' x 8' plywood	7 Sheets	3.0	114.10
Siding, cedar bevel, 1/2" x 8", A grade	160 S.F.	6.0	452.55
Soffit, 12" wide vented, fascia & drip edge	22 L.F.	3.5	37.25
Roofing, standard strip shingles & felt paper	2 Sq.	4.0	115.80
Flashing, at valley	20 S.F.	2.5	33.55
Gutters, 5" aluminum, .027" thick	12 L.F.	1.0	12.05
Downspouts, 2" x 3", embossed aluminum	10 L.F.	0.5	6.30
Wall insulation, fiberglass, 3-1/2" thick, R-11	160 S.F.	1.0	52.25
Ceiling insulation, fiberglass, 6" thick, R-19	100 S.F.	1.0	47.20
Door, steel 24 ga., 3' x 6'-8", half glass, complete	1 Ea.	1.0	232.30
Picture window, 60" x 48", thermopane	1 Ea.	1.5	268.60
Drywall, 1/2" x 4' x 8', standard, finished	10 Sheets	6.0	96.80
Underlayment, 3/8" particleboard	3 Sheets	1.5	27.90
Carpet, 22 oz. nylon, with pad	12 S.Y.	3.0	237.85
Trim, ranch base & casing	70 L.F.	2.5	59.30
Paint walls, ceiling & trim, primer & 2 coats	320 S.F.	5.0	69.70
Electrical wiring, 4 outlets, 1 switch	1 Lot	7.5	74.95
Backfill, finish grade & re-seed	1 Job	13.5	12.10
Totals		**91.5**	**$2973.00**

Project Size	8' x 12'	Contractor's Fee Including Materials	**$7470**

Key to Abbreviations
C.Y. - cubic yard   Ea. - each   L.F. - linear foot   Pr. - pair   Sq. - square (100 square feet of area)
S.F. - square foot   S.Y. - square yard   V.L.F. - vertical linear foot

ROOM ADDITION, 12' X 16'

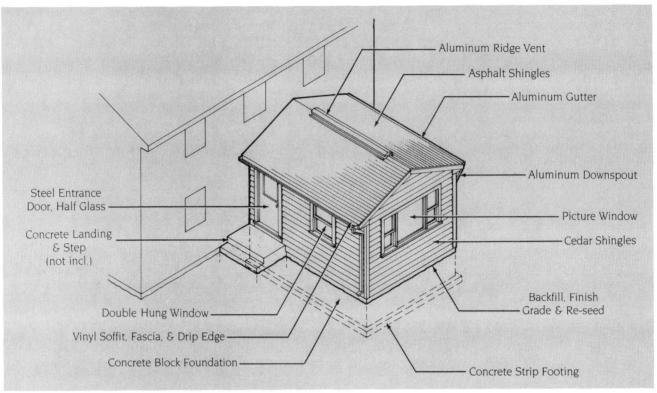

Aluminum Ridge Vent
Asphalt Shingles
Aluminum Gutter
Aluminum Downspout
Picture Window
Cedar Shingles
Backfill, Finish Grade & Re-seed
Concrete Strip Footing
Concrete Block Foundation
Vinyl Soffit, Fascia, & Drip Edge
Double Hung Window
Concrete Landing & Step (not incl.)
Steel Entrance Door, Half Glass

If you have sufficient yard area and adequate distance to property lines, an "ell" configuration is usually the most convenient and appropriate design to use for a room addition. The new structure, though attached, is essentially a miniature house with its own foundation, frame, and interior and exterior finish. Care should be taken in determining its location, roof lines, and exterior trim to ensure that it will become an integral part of the existing house. Just as important are local zoning regulations, which should be checked before you begin any work. Like other room addition projects in this section, it's a major home improvement which requires considerable carpentry and building skills. Because it is also relatively large in size, beginners and handymen with limited remodeling experience should plan to hire a contractor to do much of the work, especially on the exterior of the structure.

MATERIALS

The covering and finish materials for room additions and attached structures tend to vary with each project, as they should match or complement the style features of the existing house. However, the support and subsurface materials have little variation from structure to structure. The materials in this plan, especially the basic subsurface components, are readily available at building supply outlets, and you can shop around for the best deal. For an order of this size, the savings can be considerable, with free local delivery a part of the purchase agreement.

Most do-it-yourselfers should have the excavation and foundation work for this addition done by a contractor. A substantial amount of earth has to be removed to allow for the 4' foundation depth. Additional expense should be

figured in if some of the excavated material has to be trucked from the site. This plan suggests a concrete block foundation; but a formed and poured foundation can also be used. If you plan to install the foundation yourself, but don't have any experience with masonry, get some professional advice before you start. A poorly constructed or misaligned foundation can cause major problems.

After the foundation has been placed, the framing, sheathing, and exterior finishing tasks can be accomplished. A 2" x 8" sill plate is secured to the top of the foundation wall, and the 2" x 10" floor joists installed. Be sure to use at least 5/8" plywood for the decking and to stagger the termination seams for additional floor strengthening. Standard 2" x 4" partitions with appropriate headers and jack studs are erected for the door and window opening and are then covered with 1/2" sheathing. If you are not experienced in framing, be sure to get some help for this part of the wall and roof work. The gable roof is basic in its framing design, but it requires skill and know-how to construct. The most critical aspect of the roof framing procedure is the layout of the rafter template, which must duplicate or complement the roof pitch and overhang features of the existing house. This plan also includes a 10' ridge vent strip, which should be installed as part of the finish roofing procedure. The final steps in the exterior work include finishing the soffit and trim, placing the door and window units, and applying the siding.

Within the new room, preliminary work on the floor, ceiling, and walls has to be completed before the finish products are placed. The subfloor has to be covered with appropriate underlayment if carpeting or resilient flooring is to be installed. The ceiling and walls should be insulated and roughed in for the desired electrical fixtures. Once the rough wiring is in place, the fixtures can be purchased and tied in later. When installing the drywall, always hang the ceiling pieces first and then the wall sheets. This plan calls for wainscoting constructed from 1/4" paneling on the lower part of the walls. Before the paneling is put into place, 3/8" plywood backing is applied to the studs as a support, furring, and fastening subsurface.

LEVEL OF DIFFICULTY

Most of the exterior work on this addition demands considerable skill and know-how. Beginners, therefore, should plan to restrict their efforts primarily to the interior finishing. The exterior painting, landscaping, and other basic operations are tasks which beginners can tackle, but advanced procedures such as framing and roofing should be left to a contractor. Beginners should add at least 100% to the man-hours estimates for all of the tasks which they undertake. Handymen should attempt only those exterior operations which they feel comfortable in taking on. The roof framing and finish work are especially challenging undertakings which may require professional assistance. Handymen should be able to handle all of the interior operations, except the carpeting and electrical installations, with 50% added to the professional time. Experts should add 20% for all interior and exterior jobs. As noted earlier, do-it-yourselfers should hire a contractor for the excavation, and in most cases, for the foundation installation as well.

WHAT TO WATCH OUT FOR

The existing house wall which is included in the addition requires considerable preparation before it can be finished to blend in with the new room. The exterior siding has to be removed and any structural alterations made before the drywall or other finish material is applied. If an acceptable entryway from the house to the new room already exists, no structural work is required and the rough opening can simply be trimmed with the appropriate materials. If there is no access or an existing entryway has to be widened, the wall will have to be opened and new structural members added. This procedure will add significantly to the cost and time of the wall preparation.

SUMMARY

This good-sized room addition will boost the value of your home by adding to its living space and enhancing its exterior appearance. With careful planning and professional assistance where needed, it is a manageable job for many do-it-yourselfers.

ROOM ADDITION, 12' x 16'

Description	Quantity	Man-hours	Material
Excavate, with machine, 4' deep	1 Job	6.0	0.00
Footing, 8" thick x 16" wide x 20' long	2 C.Y.	7.0	194.30
Foundation walls, 8" concrete block, 4' high	176 S.F.	31.0	805.00
Frame, floor, 2" x 10" joists, 16" O.C., 12' long	192 L.F.	3.5	132.40
Sill plates, 2" x 8" stock	48 L.F.	1.5	33.10
Floor, sheathing, 3/4" plywood 4' x 8' sheets	6 Sheets	2.5	102.20
Frame, walls, 2" x 4" plates, 12' long	144 L.F.	3.0	45.30
2" x 4" studs, 8' long	320 L.F.	5.0	100.65
Header over window & door, 2" x 8" stock	36 L.F.	2.0	24.85
Wall sheathing, 1/2" x 4' x 8' plywood	12 Sheets	5.5	190.50
Frame, roof, 2" x 6" rafters, 16" O.C., 8' long	208 L.F.	3.5	98.15
Ceiling, 2" x 6" joists, 16" O.C.	156 L.F.	2.0	73.60
Ridge board & sub-fascia, 2" x 8" stock	50 L.F.	2.5	34.50
Roof sheathing, 5/8" x 4' x 8' plywood	9 Sheets	3.5	153.40
Felt paper, 15 lb., on roof & walls	700 S.F.	1.0	25.40
Roofing, asphalt shingles, 285 lb. premium	3 Sq.	7.0	282.40
Flashing at wall .016" thick	16 S.F.	1.0	6.40
Ridge vent strip, aluminum	10 L.F.	0.5	26.25
Siding, no. 1 red cedar shingles, 7 1/2" exp.	370 S.F.	14.5	358.20
Soffit, 12" wide vented, fascia & drip edge	48 L.F.	7.0	81.30
Gutters, 5" aluminum, .027" thick	34 L.F.	2.5	34.15
Downspouts, 2" x 3", embossed aluminum	20 L.F.	1.0	12.60
Wall insulation, fiberglass, 3-1/2" thick, R-11	400 S.F.	2.0	130.70
Ceiling, insulation, fiberglass, 6" thick, R-19	200 S.F.	1.5	94.40
Door, steel 24 ga., 3' x 6'-8", half glass, complete	1 Ea.	1.0	232.35
Picture window, 60" x 48", thermopane	1 Ea.	1.5	268.60
Double-hung window, 36" x 48", thermopane	2 Ea.	2.0	423.50
Drywall, 1/2" x 4' x 8', standard finished	12 Sheets	8.0	116.20
Paneling, 1/4" thick for wainscot	5 Sheets	6.5	164.55
Plywood, 3/8" thick, backing for paneling	5 Sheets	3.0	77.45
Carpet, 24 oz. nylon, with pad	23 S.Y.	5.0	455.85
Trim, ranch base, casing & wainscoting	155 L.F.	6.0	168.80
Paint walls, ceiling & trim, primer & 2 coats	420 S.F.	4.0	91.50
Electrical wiring, 4 outlets, 1 switch	1 Lot	7.0	74.95
Backfill, finish grade & re-seed	1 Job	13.0	12.10
Totals		**173.5**	**$5125.60**

Project Size	12' x 16'	Contractor's Fee Including Materials	**$13,140**

Key to Abbreviations
C.Y. - cubic yard   Ea. - each   L.F. - linear foot   Pr. - pair   Sq. - square (100 square feet of area)
S.F. - square foot   S.Y. - square yard   V.L.F. - vertical linear foot

ROOM ADDITION, 20' x 24'

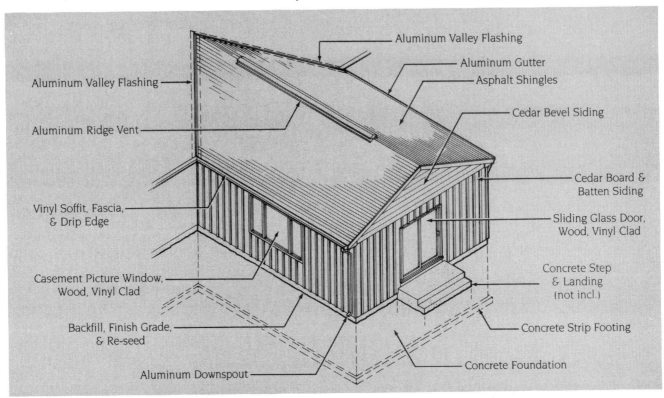

Aluminum Valley Flashing

Aluminum Valley Flashing

Aluminum Gutter

Asphalt Shingles

Aluminum Ridge Vent

Cedar Bevel Siding

Cedar Board & Batten Siding

Vinyl Soffit, Fascia, & Drip Edge

Sliding Glass Door, Wood, Vinyl Clad

Casement Picture Window, Wood, Vinyl Clad

Concrete Step & Landing (not incl.)

Backfill, Finish Grade, & Re-seed

Concrete Strip Footing

Aluminum Downspout

Concrete Foundation

The need for greater living space often leads to substantial room additions, approaching the dimensions of small houses. This plan demonstrates how a large room can be attached at first floor level to the eave end of a house. It has over 400 square feet of floor area, a full 20' x 24' basement, and a roof structure that is neatly tied into the existing house. As with all room additions, its design must be carefully planned to suit the architectural style and layout of the original house. Good organization is needed for the purchase of materials, hiring of subcontractors, and the sequence of construction operations.

MATERIALS

One of the primary considerations in buying the components for this addition is the size of the order and the logistics involved in storing the materials. Unless you have a good-sized garage or sheltered enclosure, you should wait to have interior materials delivered until after the shell

has been erected and made weathertight. Even the exterior items require a large outside area adjacent to the site for stockpiling. Your retailer may be willing to stagger the delivery of these goods to help you out if storage is a problem.

All of the foundation work for this large addition should be completed by a professional contractor. The 9' excavation has to be performed by machine and the excess material hauled away. The cost for the excavation will vary depending on the topographical features of the site. If the adjacent grade falls off to or below basement walk-out level, the amount of excavation may be reduced. The basement floor slab can be placed at any time after the foundation has been completed, providing there is proper access.

The materials in the exterior shell of the addition are conventional products employed in most wood-frame structures. Because of the 20' width of this room, a tripled 2" x 10"

center support beam must be installed to bear the load of the floor and its frame. This primary structural component must be properly supported with lally columns or other suitable posts placed at regular intervals and set into a preformed notch in the foundation wall. After the sill has been placed and the 2" x 10" floor joists installed, 5/8" plywood sheathing will cover the frame. The 2" x 4" walls are then laid out, built on the deck, positioned, fastened, and covered with 1/2" sheathing. The 2" x 6" ceiling joists and roof rafters are then placed and sheathed, and the gable end studded and sheathed to complete the framing operation. After the layout and placement of the new roof frame has been completed, the finished roofing, soffit and trim, window and door units, and siding are installed to close in the new structure.

All of these exterior finish materials should be carefully selected to match the existing finish on the house. The costs and installation time for these products will affect the estimate.

Like the exterior products, the interior finish materials should be selected to complement the style of your house. The shell should first be thoroughly insulated on the ceiling, walls, and, in colder areas, the floor. The electrical rough-in should also be installed before the finish coverings are placed. The standard 1/2" sheetrock for the walls and ceiling can be taped and finished or, at extra cost, skim-coated with plaster. The nylon carpet included in this plan will provide years of durable, low maintenance service. Wood floors, though they are more expensive to install and require more maintenance, may be a more appropriate choice for some homes.

All of these interior finish products demand careful and patient installation, and specialty contractors may have to be hired for this job.

LEVEL OF DIFFICULTY

Because of the size of this room addition, most do-it-yourselfers should plan to hire a general contractor or various subcontractors to do the heavy exterior work and the specialty installations. Once the exterior has been finished, the inside work can be done at a slower pace and, therefore, by the homeowner at his convenience. The insulating, drywalling, trim work, and painting are jobs which can be performed during weekends or evenings over an extended period. Generally, beginners should limit their work to the interior

tasks mentioned above and to basic exterior work like painting and landscaping. They should add 100% to the professional time for these jobs and seek professional advice as they go. Most handymen should not tackle the framing on this project, and they should consider hiring a roofer unless they have substantial experience in this area. They should tack on 50% to the man-hours for the other non-specialty tasks. Experts should add 20% to all procedures except the roof framing and finish. Slightly more time should be allowed for these advanced exterior operations and for specialty interior work. All do-it-yourselfers should leave the foundation work and the basement floor installation to a professional contractor.

WHAT TO WATCH OUT FOR

The full basement included in this room addition plan adds interior space that can be used for storage, a workshop, or living area. Access is an important consideration, and it should be carefully planned to suit the function of the new room installation and the existing structure. The stairway from the new room does take away valuable floor space and may require extra cost for a partition and a door to enclose the stairwell. Exterior cellar access is an option, but provisions for it will have to be included in the foundation design at extra cost. If the existing house already has a basement, it may be possible to gain access from it. Be aware, however, that considerable expense may be incurred in hiring a concrete specialist to cut an opening in the foundation for the doorway. The important thing to remember is to make some provision for cellar access before the project begins.

SUMMARY

This 20' x 24' room addition is a comprehensive project which requires a total commitment by the homeowner - both in the preliminary planning and in the carrying out of required construction standards. Most do-it-yourselfers will need professional help for the exterior work, but can still handle many interior finishing tasks. In this way, you can reduce your costs and still be assured of a weathertight exterior shell, appropriately tied into the existing house.

ROOM ADDITION, 20' x 24'

Description	Quantity	Man-hours	Material
Excavate basement & haul away excess	1 Job	32.5	0.00
Footing, 8" thick x 16" wide x 20'	3 C.Y.	11.5	300.30
Foundation walls, 8" thick c.i.p. concrete	535 S.F.	81.0	2014.20
Basement floor slab, 4" thick concrete	480 S.F.	15.5	592.45
Frame floor, 2" x 10" joists, 16" O.C., 12' long	540 L.F.	10.0	509.65
Center support beam, triple 2" x 10" stock	24 L.F.	1.0	45.30
Sheathing, 3/4" plywood 4' x 8' sheets	15 Sheets	6.5	302.00
Frame & trim basement stairs, complete including railing around stair opening	1 Ea.	5.5	868.80
Frame, walls, 2" x 4" plates & studs	216 L.F.	13.5	242.75
Header over window & door, 2" x 8" stock	60 L.F.	3.0	41.40
Wall sheathing, 25/32" x 4' x 8' wood fiberboard	17 Sheets	7.5	269.90
Corner bracing, 16 ga. steel straps. 10' long	8 Ea.	1.0	50.35
Frame, roof, 2" x 6" joists & rafters, 16" O.C.	1008 L.F.	8.5	251.05
Ridge board & sub-fascia, 2" x 8" stock	88 L.F.	3.5	60.70
Roof sheathing, 1/2" x 4' x 8' plywood	25 Sheets	11.5	396.90
Roofing, asphalt shingles, 285 lb. premium	8 Sq.	21.5	718.25
Felt paper, 15 lb., on roof	800 S.F.	1.5	29.05
Ridge vent strip, aluminum	20 L.F.	1.0	52.50
Siding, cedar board & batten, pre-stained	540 S.F.	17.5	771.00
Cedar bevel, 1/2" x 8", pre-stained	50 S.F.	1.5	113.15
Soffit, 12" wide vented, fascia & drip edge	48 L.F.	6.5	92.95
Flashing, at valley	80 S.F.	4.5	63.90
Gutters & downspouts, aluminum	68 L.F.	5.5	78.40
Wall insul., fiberglass, 3-1/2" thick, R-11	550 S.F.	3.0	179.70
Ceiling, insulation, fiberglass, 6" thick, R-19	480 S.F.	2.5	226.50
Door, sliding glass 6' x 6'-8", clad, insul. glass	1 Ea.	4.0	794.95
Casement window, 8' x 5', clad, thermopane	1 Ea.	1.5	1258.40
Casement window, 24" x 52", clad, thermopane	2 Ea.	2.0	469.50
Drywall, 1/2" x 4' x 8', standard, finished	37 Sheets	20.0	358.20
Carpet, 26 oz. nylon, with pad	54 S.Y.	11.5	1070.25
Trim, ranch base & casing	168 L.F.	5.5	142.30
Paint walls, ceiling & trim, primer & 2 coats	1200 S.F.	19.0	261.35
Electrical wiring, 8 outlets, 2 switches	1 Lot	15.0	149.90
Backfill, finish grade & re-seed	1 Job	13.5	12.10
Totals		369.0	$12,788.10

Project Size	20' x 24'	Contractor's Fee Including Materials	$32,130

Key to Abbreviations
C.Y. - cubic yard   Ea. - each   L.F. - linear foot   . Pr. - pair   Sq. - square (100 square feet of area)
S.F. - square foot   S.Y. - square yard   V.L.F. - vertical linear foot

SECOND-STORY ADDITION, 8' x 12'

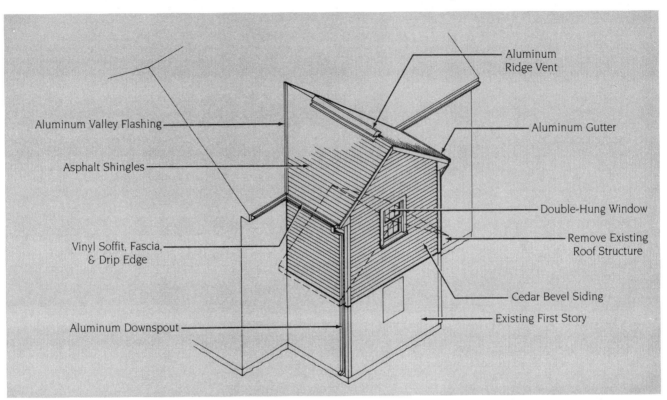

Aluminum Valley Flashing

Asphalt Shingles

Vinyl Soffit, Fascia, & Drip Edge

Aluminum Downspout

Aluminum Ridge Vent

Aluminum Gutter

Double-Hung Window

Remove Existing Roof Structure

Cedar Bevel Siding

Existing First Story

Second floor living space can be increased by means of attic conversions or the placement of dormers, but still more interior area can be created with a complete room addition. If the conditions are right and there is an existing attached structure on which to build, adding a second story may be the answer. Because of the difficulties in removing the old roof, the potential for hidden problems, and the need to work rapidly, most do-it-yourselfers should hire a contractor to perform the exterior work.

MATERIALS

The materials used in this project are the same as those employed in first floor room additions. Conventional framing, sheathing, and finish products are placed on top of the supporting first-floor. What makes the installation of the new components difficult is the general inconvenience of the second-story location and the extra time required to complete any off-ground construction.

Before the new materials are placed, an extensive amount of preliminary planning has to be done, as well as preparation of the old structure to receive the new one. The first step is to evaluate the condition of the existing wood structure and its foundation. Even expert do-it-yourselfers should hire a qualified inspector if there is any question about its strength or ability to support the load of the new materials. Foundation work and added lumber may have to be included in the estimate to reinforce the original structure before the new work begins. The next step is the removal of the old roof covering, sheathing, and rafters. As in dormer installations, this procedure can be time consuming, yet expediency is important because part of the interior of the house will be opened to the elements. If you plan to do this part of the project without the services of a contractor, be sure to have plenty of help on hand to move the job quickly. Whenever possible, try to salvage the old lumber and sheathing. If they are in good condition, they may come in handy later in the project.

After the roof has been removed, the existing ceiling joists become the floor joists for the new room. If they are 2" x 8"s or larger, they are probably strong enough as they are; but if they are 2" x 6"s, they will need some reinforcing. Check with a professional to determine the size of required reinforcement materials and the methods of installing them. The deck is then sheathed with 5/8" plywood before the wall partitions are framed. Be sure to prepare the area of the existing house wall to receive the new framing. The roof is then framed with 2" x 6" rafters and a 2" x 8" ridge board tapered into the existing roof. The sheathing and finished roofing, selected to match the existing finish roof material, are then applied. After the window unit and siding are installed, the structure is ready for the interior work.

All of the operations involved in the exterior construction require a thorough knowledge of carpentry, skilled handling of tools, and safe equipment for work above ground level. Since complications tend to arise in this type of work, it is best to build in some extra time and, possibly, cost. The given estimate will also vary depending on the size and shape of the room. Use this plan's price guide to get an accurate idea of what a similar structure would cost; then figure the expense of your own particular improvement by making any necessary modifications.

Before work can begin on the addition's interior, the type of access must be determined. This plan assumes that access to the new room will come through a finished second-story room or hallway. Whenever possible, existing window openings should be utilized as part of the future rough opening for a door. If you cannot use an existing window opening, then the wall will have to be opened at a convenient place and

headers and jack studs placed to rough in the entryway. If you want to open the entire wall or a large portion of it, more support will be required. Additional cost and time may have to be included in the estimate for the entryway installation, according to its type, size, and conditions of placement. As for the rest of the room, many different interior products can be installed to meet the practical and aesthetic standards of its intended use. When the rough electrical work and insulating have been completed, the walls and ceiling can be drywalled and finished. Carpeting or other appropriate flooring material is put into place after the trim work and painting are done.

LEVEL OF DIFFICULTY

This project is one of the most challenging home improvements included in this book. The exterior operations require not only advanced carpentry and tool handling skills, but

also fast and efficient work at roof level. As in the dormer project described later in the "Exteriors" section, expediency is a critical factor in any operation which involves opening a section of the roof. Here, the entire roof must be removed; the ceiling joists must be blocked off and, possibly, reinforced; and a new structure built and tied into the wall and roof of the existing house, all in a relatively short period of time. All levels of do-it-yourselfers, therefore, are encouraged to hire a specialty contractor for the exterior work. Even experts should consider professional help for the roof removal, and plan to have several experienced helpers on hand to assist with the framing and roofing tasks. Beginners and handymen should restrict their efforts to the interior work only and tack on an additional 100% and 50%, respectively, to the professional man-hours. Experts should add 30% to the time estimates for all exterior tasks which they feel they can handle, and 20% to the interior operations.

SECOND-STORY ADDITION, 8' x 12'

Description	Quantity	Man-hours	Material
Remove existing roof structure & siding, etc.	1 Ea.	40.0	0.00
Frame, boxing at existing joists, 2" x 6" stock	32 L.F.	0.5	15.10
Floor, sheathing, 5/8" plywood, 4' x 8' sheets	3 Sheets	1.5	51.10
Frame, walls, 2" x 4" studs & plates, 8' long	32 L.F.	6.0	114.20
Headers over windows, 2" x 8" stock	12 L.F.	1.0	8.30
Gable end studs, 2" x 4" stock	12 L.F.	0.5	3.80
Wall sheathing, 1/2" x 4' x 8' plywood	9 Sheets	4.0	142.90
Frame, roof, 2" x 6" rafters, 16" O.C.	192 L.F.	3.5	90.60
Sub-fascia, 2" x 6" stock	24 L.F.	0.5	11.35
Ceiling, 2" x 6" joists, 16" O.C.	90 L.F.	1.5	42.45
Roof sheathing, 1/2" x 4' x 8' plywood	7 Sheets	2.5	119.25
Siding, cedar bevel, 1/2" x 8", A grade	270 S.F.	8.0	610.95
Soffit, 12" wide vented, fascia & drip edge	40 L.F.	5.0	77.40
Roofing, standard strip shingles & felt paper	3 Sq.	5.5	190.60
Ridge vent strip, aluminum	8 L.F.	0.5	21.00
Flashing, at valley	40 S.F.	2.0	31.95
Gutters, 5" aluminum, .027" thick	24 L.F.	1.5	24.10
Downspouts, 2" x 3", embossed aluminum	36 L.F.	1.5	22.65
Wall insul., fiberglass, 3-1/2" thick, R-11	260 S.F.	1.5	84.50
Ceiling, insul., fiberglass, 6" thick, R-19	100 S.F.	1.0	47.20
Window, double-hung, 3' x 3'-6", thermopane, plastic clad	1 Ea.	1.0	211.75
Drywall, 1/2" x 4' x 8', standard, finished	13 Sheets	7.0	125.85
Underlayment, 3/8" particleboard	3 Sheets	1.5	47.65
Carpet, 22 oz. nylon, with pad	12 S.Y.	2.5	237.85
Trim, ranch base & casing	70 L.F.	2.0	59.30
Paint walls, ceiling & trim, primer & 2 coats	420 S.F.	6.5	91.50
Electrical wiring, 4 outlets, 1 switch	1 Lot	7.0	74.95
Totals		115.5	$2558.25

Project Size	8' x 12'	Contractor's Fee Including Materials	$7730

Key to Abbreviations
C.Y. - cubic yard   Ea. - each   L.F. - linear foot   Pr. - pair   Sq. - square (100 square feet of area)
S.F. - square foot   S.Y. - square yard   V.L.F. - vertical linear foot

WHAT TO WATCH OUT FOR

If there is one guiding principle for room addition plans, it is that the new attached structure should blend with the house and complement its style, and not look "tacked on." Roofing and siding lines are particularly important in this blending process. This plan, for example, requires that the roof line of the new room align with that of the existing house, and that the courses of asphalt roofing meet precisely at the valley. The new siding should follow the same spacing of the structure below, and its course lines should align at the seam between the house and the addition. The soffit and trim features, roof pitch, and door and window design should all be considered in the proper blending of old and new. The overall size and architectural proportion of the new room are equally important to the design.

SUMMARY

If the conditions are right, this second-story room addition can add space to the upstairs of your house. Although it requires a considerable effort to construct, it provides an alternative plan to attic conversion or dormer installation.

SECOND-STORY ADDITION, 20' x 24'

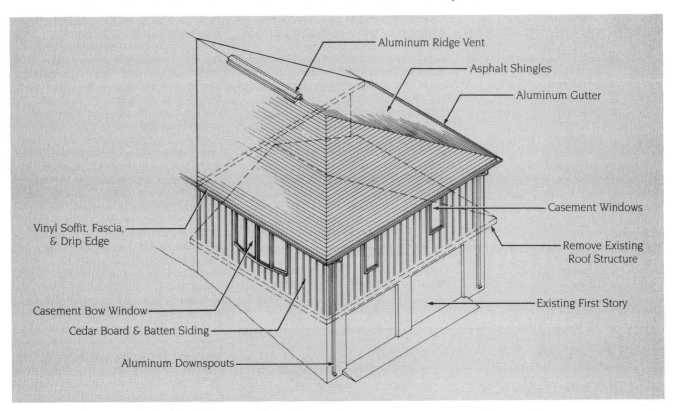

Aluminum Ridge Vent

Asphalt Shingles

Aluminum Gutter

Casement Windows

Remove Existing Roof Structure

Existing First Story

Vinyl Soffit, Fascia, & Drip Edge

Casement Bow Window

Cedar Board & Batten Siding

Aluminum Downspouts

If more interior space is needed, but restricted building area prohibits the construction of a ground-level addition, a large second-story structure may be the answer. This room addition plan demonstrates how nearly 500 square feet of new interior space can be created above a two-car, attached garage. Such a project is an expensive, time consuming undertaking which requires a major commitment on the part of the homeowner. The time schedule for the procedure has to be carefully planned to ensure expedient completion of the exterior enclosure. An architect can help you to determine the style, design, and structural aspects of the project. Because this addition demands professional expertise and assistance, do-it-yourselfers should consider hiring a contractor to complete the exterior work. Once the structure has been enclosed, handymen can reduce the cost of the project by completing some of the interior tasks.

MATERIALS

This project involves the cost of roof removal and, in most cases, the strengthening of the support system for the new room. This expense is offset by the fact that a foundation already exists, and thus, you avoid the costs of its excavation and construction. Once the support system has been reconditioned to acceptable standards, the same materials used in other wood frame structures are employed in constructing this new room. All materials used in this project are readily available at building supply outlets, so shop around for the best prices, in working out the delivery conditions, you might arrange to receive the exterior and interior products in two separate loads.

Before the new decking can be applied to this 20' x 24' room, the existing garage roof has to be removed and the ceiling joists reinforced to safe

standards. If the existing joists are 2" x 8"s or larger and are supported by a center beam, the amount of reinforcement will be minimal. If they are 2" x 6"s, then a substantial amount of reinforcement will be required. The cost for this procedure will vary with each situation. After the 5/8" plywood decking has been installed, the walls and roof are framed with standard 2" x 4" and 2" x 6" lumber and sheathed with 1/2" plywood or comparable material. Care should be taken to blend the new structure to the old so that the roof line, the style of the overhang, and other design features complement one another.

The new exterior finish products should also be selected to harmonize with the style of the house. For example, premium asphalt shingles are suggested in this plan, but standard asphalt or cedar shingles can also be used. Tile and slate are two more possibilities. Some of the options for exterior walls are cedar shingles, clapboards, aluminum siding, stucco, or the cedar board and batten siding suggested in this plan. All of these materials vary in price, and the selection of one product over another will have a considerable impact on the estimated cost.

After the exterior has been completed and the structure made weathertight, a doorway or opening into the new room must be created. If you are completing the interior work on your own and are unfamiliar with cutting and framing a wall opening, get some advice before you start. The placement of a standard-sized 30" or 32" door requires 2" x 8" headers and jack studs for the rough opening frame, but a 6' or 8' wall opening necessitates more support and, possibly, temporary ceiling bracing during the installation procedure. Remember to allow time for stripping the siding on the wall where the entry is placed.

One of the advantages of this and most other room addition projects is that the interior work can be completed by the do-it-yourselfer, one task at a time, when convenient. The insulating, rough electrical work, and any partitioning are completed first, and then the ceiling and walls are covered and finished. Partitioning for closets or room dividers will add to the total cost and the installation time. A wide range of wall and ceiling coverings and finishes is available, and once again, their selection will depend on the style of your house. Wall-to-wall nylon carpeting blends well with many interior styles, but hardwood and other flooring materials are other alternatives if they better suit the decor, location, and use of the room. The costs for these interior coverings and their trim work will vary according to the style and quality of the products.

LEVEL OF DIFFICULTY

This large second-story addition is one of the most challenging home improvement projects presented in this book. The removal of the roof and subsequent framing and roofing are difficult operations that must be completed as expediently as possible to protect the interior from the elements. All do-it-yourselfers, therefore, are encouraged to leave the exterior work to a professional and concentrate their efforts on the inside tasks. As noted earlier, the convenient location of the addition permits the homeowner to work at his own pace. Do-it-yourselfers should be able to handle most of the interior operations, though they should leave the electrical and carpet installations to professionals. Beginners should add 100% to the man-hours estimate for all of the tasks they undertake. Handymen and experts should add 50% and 20%, respectively, to the estimate for the interior jobs, and more for the specialty work.

WHAT TO WATCH OUT FOR

Painting is one exterior job that all do-it-yourselfers can accomplish to keep the costs down. If you install the aluminum soffit, fascia, and gutter products and the vinyl-clad windows suggested in this plan, the only thing you will have to paint is the siding. That, too, can be purchased pre-stained, but the chances of matching it to the color of the existing house are slim. Apply a minimum of two coats, one primer and one finish, to all new exterior materials which require painting. Skimping on the paint job is unwise, as it will not only detract from the appearance of the structure, but could also necessitate premature repainting and replacement of materials.

SECOND-STORY ADDITION, 20' x 24'

Description	Quantity	Man-hours	Material
Remove existing roof structure & siding, cut opening	1 Job	80.0	0.00
Frame, floor, 2" x 8" joists, 16" O.C., 12' long	540 L.F.	8.5	372.45
Floor sheathing, 3/4" plywood, 4' x 8' sheets	15 Sheets	6.5	302.00
Frame, walls, 2" x 4" plates, 12' long	264 L.F.	13.0	228.45
2" x 4" studs, 8' long			
Headers over windows, 2" x 8" stock	24 L.F.	1.5	16.55
Wall sheathing, 25/32" x 4' x 8' wood fiber board	22 Sheets	9.5	255.55
Corner bracing, 16 ga. steel straps, 10' long	8 Ea.	1.0	50.35
Frame, roof, 2" x 6" rafters, 16" O.C., 14' long	238 L.F.	4.0	112.30
Ridge board, 2" x 8" stock	22 L.F.	1.0	15.20
Hip rafters, 2" x 8" x 18'	36 L.F.	1.0	24.85
Hip jack rafters, 2" x 6" stock, 16" O.C.	336 L.F.	9.5	158.55
Sub-fascia, 2" x 6" stock	84 L.F.	2.0	39.65
Ceiling, 2" x 6" joists, 16" O.C.	416 L.F.	5.5	196.30
Roof sheathing, 5/8" x 4' x 8' plywood	30 Sheets	11.5	511.10
Roofing, asphalt shingles, 285 lb. premium	10 Sq.	23.0	941.40
Felt paper, 15 lb., on roof	1000 S.F.	2.0	36.30
Ridge vent strip, aluminum	14 L.F.	1.0	36.75
Siding, cedar board & batten, pre-stained	525 S.F.	16.5	749.60
Soffit, 12" wide vented, fascia & drip edge	90 L.F.	12.0	174.25
Gutters, 5" aluminum, .027" thick	68 L.F.	5.0	68.30
Downspouts, 2" x 3", embossed aluminum	36 L.F.	1.5	22.65
Wall insulation, fiberglass, 3-1/2" thick, R-11	525 S.F.	3.0	171.50
Ceiling, insulation, fiberglass, 6" thick, R-19	480 S.F.	2.5	226.50
Casement window. 8' x 5', clad thermopane	1 Ea.	2.0	1292.30
Casement window, 24" x 52", clad thermopane	4 Ea.	4.0	948.65
Drywall, 1/2" x 4' x 8', standard, finished	37 Sheets	20.0	358.15
Carpet, 26 oz. nylon, with pad	54 S.Y.	12.0	1070.25
Trim, ranch base & casing	186 L.F.	6.0	157.55
Jamb, 1" x 6" clear pine, at opening to house	1 Ea.	1.0	12.65
Paint walls, ceiling & trim, primer & 2 coats	1200 S.F.	19.0	261.35
Electrical wiring, 8 outlets, 2 switches	1 Lot	14.5	149.90
Totals		299.5	$8961.35

Project Size	20' x 24'	Contractor's Fee Including Materials	$23,160

Key to Abbreviations
C.Y. - cubic yard   Ea. - each   L.F. - linear foot   Pr. - pair   Sq. - square (100 square feet of area)
S.F. - square foot   S.Y. - square yard   V.L.F. - vertical linear foot

SUMMARY

This 20' x 24' second-story addition is a major home improvement which requires the services of a professional contractor for much of the structural and exterior work. However, most do-it-yourselfers can substantially reduce the cost of the project by completing the interior work themselves. The combined efforts of contractor and homeowner can result in a lot of new living space at a reasonable cost.

BUBBLE SKYLIGHT, FIXED

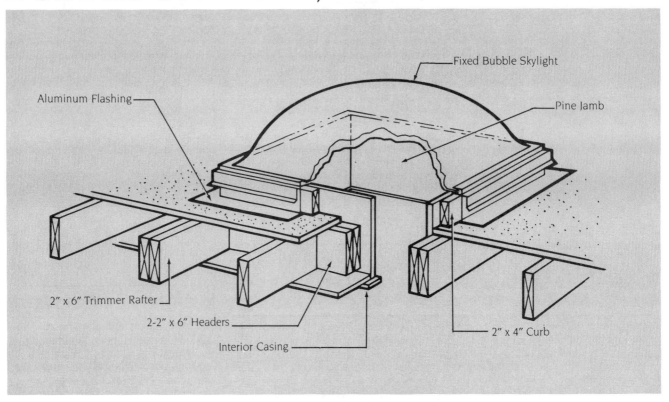

Aluminum Flashing

Fixed Bubble Skylight

Pine Jamb

2" x 6" Trimmer Rafter

2-2" x 6" Headers

Interior Casing

2" x 4" Curb

As in other exterior home improvements, the overall planning, layout, and design of a skylight installation must be determined with care. This plan features a small fixed bubble skylight which can provide an economical solution to lighting problems in an interior room or porch. Although this project involves the general inconveniences of roof work and the complications of roof hole-cutting, many do-it-yourselfers can complete the installation in a surprisingly short time.

MATERIALS

Other than the skylight itself, the materials required to complete this project consist of the standard construction products needed to support the unit. These basic materials include lumber for adding strength to the rafters, flashing, incidental items for making the roof weathertight, and various interior trim products to finish the shaft and to refurbish the ceiling area affected by

the installation. Because each project will present a different set of conditions, the type and amount of these materials may vary from the estimate. Slight increases or decreases in cost, therefore, are to be expected in installations of this type.

Before the prefabricated skylight unit can be placed, an extensive amount of preliminary work must be completed. The roof and ceiling areas to be opened must be carefully laid out, the holes cut, and support restored to the rafters and, if necessary, the ceiling joists. Determining the location of the skylight is a critical procedure for both practical and aesthetic reasons. Generally, a central location in the ceiling between existing rafters is ideal, as the hole-cutting is easier and trimmer rafters do not have to be placed. However, these conditions apply only when the unit you are installing is small enough to fit within your rafter spacing (usually 16"). In most cases, at least one rafter must be cut, and trimmers and headers installed to restore roof support. This

operation can often be difficult and time consuming, as the trimmers may have to span a major portion of the length from the ridge to the top of the outside wall. The cutting of the holes in the roof and ceiling, the placing of the trimmer and header rafters and joists, and the installing of extra support can be difficult jobs which require know-how and moderate to advanced carpentry skills. Inexperienced do-it-yourselfers are advised to seek help if they are unfamiliar with these operations. Additional costs may be incurred during the preliminary phase of the project if extensive roof reconditioning is required. All do-it-yourselfers should have a professional contractor evaluate and, if necessary, correct any deficiencies in the structure of the roof before proceeding with the project.

The design and the size of the skylight unit should also be carefully selected so that it meets practical and aesthetic needs. This plan calls for a small fixed bubble, but a larger fixed unit or a ventilating model may be more appropriate for a given situation. In addition to the amount of light and ventilating capacity of the skylight, factors like the roof pitch, exposure, and exterior design of the fixture should also be considered. Generally, fixed dome skylights like this one are a good choice for well ventilated rooms, high ceilings above stairwells and hallways, and screened-in porches. As with other prefabricated building materials that will be exposed to the weather for many years, the quality of the skylight unit should be taken into consideration. Double-layered plastic bubbles like this one, for example, must be hermetically sealed to prevent condensation between the layers of plastic and to ensure efficient energy control. Most models include a base flange or provision for a curb and self-flashing. Be sure to follow precisely the manufacturer's guidelines when installing the skylight unit.

The time and material required to finish the interior of the skylight shaft will vary, as each installation will present a different set of conditions. This plan assumes that the skylight shaft extends only the thickness of the roof frame, as in attic rooms or basic porch locations where the ceiling follows the line of the roof. A longer shaft will be required, however, if the roof and ceiling are separated by attic space. In these cases, more materials and installation time will be necessary to build, insulate, and finish the shaft. The installation can also be more difficult when flared or angled shaft designs are needed or desired. Where long shafts are required, the extra cost and time will be considerable.

LEVEL OF DIFFICULTY

With good conditions such as 16" rafter spacing and no extra shaft requirements, most do-it-yourselfers can handle this skylight installation. Small, fixed plastic bubbles of this type tend to be relatively inexpensive, so there isn't the worry of working with very costly or complicated components. The units are often installed in porches and attics, on flat or gently sloping roofs, and while the hole-cutting is never easy, it is less difficult in these locations. As long as conditions are favorable, beginners can complete this installation with the addition of 150% to the professional time; but they should proceed cautiously and seek instruction beforehand from a knowledgeable person. For skylight placement on a steep roof or where long shafts and extensive preliminary work are necessary, beginners should consider hiring a professional installer. Handymen and experts should add 75% and 25%, respectively, to the man-hours estimate for all tasks. All do-it-yourselfers should build in extra time for the general inconvenience of roof work.

WHAT TO WATCH OUT FOR

Although they do not allow for increased ventilation, fixed skylights like this one provide many other advantages which make them the right choice for certain installations. One is that they are ideal for flat roofs and for roofs that tend to drain slowly, ice up, or collect snow. Once the sealed unit has been correctly placed and made weathertight, the chances of its leaking are minimal. A second advantage is the bubbled shape of the exterior, which exposes more domed surface area to natural light. This feature makes them a good choice for roofs with northern exposures. A third advantage is that they are economically priced. For locations like porches and breezeways, they function as well as more expensive operable windows.

SUMMARY

This basic fixed bubble skylight will dramatically increase the amount of light and sense of spaciousness in a bedroom, attic area, porch, or breezeway. If the conditions are right, it can be installed by most do-it-yourselfers for just the cost of the unit and a few basic construction materials.

BUBBLE SKYLIGHT, FIXED

Description	Quantity	Man-hours	Material
Roof cutout & demolition including layout	1 Ea.	2.5	0.00
Trimmer rafters, 2" x 6" x 14'	28 L.F.	0.5	26.45
Headers, double 2" x 6" stock	8 L.F.	0.5	3.80
Curb, 2" x 4" stock	10 L.F.	0.5	3.15
Skylight, fixed bubble, 24" x 24"	1 Ea.	2.0	260.15
Flashing, aluminum, .013" thick	9 S.F.	0.5	3.05
Trim interior, casing, 9/16" x 3-1/2"	10 L.F.	0.5	8.45
Jamb, 1" x 8" clear pine	10 L.F.	0.5	9.10
Painting trim, incl. puttying, primer & 1 coat	20 L.F.	0.5	1.20
Totals		8.0	$315.35

Project Size	24" x 24"	Contractor's Fee Including Materials	$780

Key to Abbreviations
C.Y. - cubic yard   Ea. - each   L.F. - linear foot   Pr. - pair   Sq. - square (100 square feet of area)
S.F. - square foot   S.Y. - square yard   V.L.F. - vertical linear foot

BUBBLE SKYLIGHT, VENTILATING

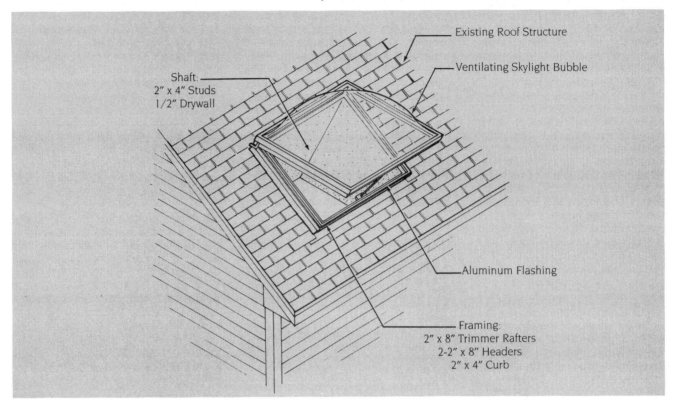

Existing Roof Structure

Ventilating Skylight Bubble

Shaft:
2" x 4" Studs
1/2" Drywall

Aluminum Flashing

Framing:
2" x 8" Trimmer Rafters
2-2" x 8" Headers
2" x 4" Curb

Ventilating skylights have some unique advantages; and when they are installed under the right conditions, they can greatly improve the appearance and air quality of an interior space. The large 52" x 52" ventilating bubble featured in this plan can considerably increase air circulation while providing nearly 18 square feet of window area. When the skylight is closed, the benefits of natural light continue, while the unit's double-layered insulating dome helps to keep the interior warm in winter and cool in the summer. Because of the large size of the skylight unit and the considerable preparation required to install it, this project is challenging. Beginners and handymen with limited remodeling experience should consider hiring a professional, at least for the more difficult exterior phase of the project.

MATERIALS

The primary component in this remodeling project is the skylight unit, but several basic construction materials are also included in the plan. These are needed to restore the roof structure, to make the installation weathertight, and to finish the interior around the new skylight. There are many styles and brand names of skylights available to the consumer in a wide range of quality and price. Therefore, it pays to do some research before you decide on the unit that meets your needs and budget requirements.

The most challenging task faced in this skylight project is that of locating the fixture on the roof and ceiling, and the subsequent hole-cutting. Although only a few new materials are included in this preliminary work, the procedure is time consuming and demands considerable know-how to accomplish correctly and safely. To install a skylight of this size under normal conditions, about 20 square feet of

roofing must be stripped, an equal area of sheathing removed, and two or, possibly, three rafters cut. If a finished ceiling is involved, a comparable area of interior covering will have to be removed and an equal number of joists cut. Temporary bracing may be required for the severed rafters and joists until the trimmers and doubled headers are placed. This plan suggests 2" x 8" trimmer rafters and headers, but 2" x 6"s and even 2" x 10"s may be needed if the existing rafters match these dimensions. Extra time and cost may be required for the preliminary work if extensive reconditioning and strengthening of roof framing members are needed.

Once the hole cutting and rafter trimming have been completed, the skylight unit can be placed in the opening and fastened into position. A unit of this size is heavy and awkward enough to cause problems in getting it to the site. You should have several workers available to help in getting it onto the roof and to position it from inside and outside of the opening. Remember that these expensive units are preframed, often prefinished, and fragile. Dropping or banging one can cause cosmetic damage at the very least, and worse, misalignment or breakage. After the skylight has been placed, the surrounding roof and perimeter seams are made weathertight with flashing, caulking, and reroofing. Reusing some of the old roofing can be a bit of a challenge, but it can also help to blend the new installation into the roof. Follow the manufacturer's guidelines and instructions throughout the placement operation, including the recommendations for proper flashing and weatherstripping.

The amount of interior finish material and installation time will vary according to the location and arrangement of the ceiling. If the finished covering is applied directly to the rafters, as in some attic and cathedral ceiling designs, the amount of finish material and the man-hours to install it will be fairly limited. In such cases, the hole is closed in with finished wood and then faced with

trim. If, as in this plan, the finished ceiling lies below several feet of attic space and joists, the job becomes more difficult, costly, and time consuming. A light shaft must be built to span the attic space and joists to the level of the finished ceiling. A frame of 2 x 4's is normally used for the walls of the shaft. Finish material like sheetrock, pine boards, or paneling can then be applied to the inside of the shaft and appropriate casing used to trim the opening. Insulation of the recommended R-value for your area should be placed on the outside of the shaft walls. Further expense will be incurred for the shaft construction if special effects like flaring and angling are desired. Remember that triming and heading off the ceiling joist are a necessary preliminary tasks for the installation of a light shaft.

LEVEL OF DIFFICULTY

This large skylight installation is a major project for do-it-yourselfers of all ability levels. If the project is complicated by the need to build a light shaft, the undertaking becomes even more challenging. Remember, too, that because the skylight unit is

an expensive product, the risks of damaging it have to be weighed against the savings in labor costs when you install it on your own. Experts and skilled handymen can handle all procedures in the project, but they should add 25% and 75%, respectively, to the professional time estimate. They should allow even more time for placing the skylight itself, as careful handling and workmanship are important considerations. Any do-it-yourselfers who are inexperienced in roofing should get some advice on the task of replacing the disturbed roofing and applying the flashing. Beginners and less skilled handymen should leave all of the exterior work to a professional installer; but they may be able to handle the interior finish if the required ceiling work is minimal. They should double the man-hours estimate for all basic tasks, including painting.

WHAT TO WATCH OUT FOR

Determining the size, shape, and type of the skylight or sky window deserves ample consideration before the master plan for the project is finalized. For example, a large unit like this one can overwhelm a small room, and, conversely, skylights that are too small can look out of place on an expansive ceiling. Often, several medium sized units will look better and provide more flexibility for your ventilation, lighting, and aesthetic needs. Of course, more expense is incurred for more units; but if they are small enough to be placed between the roof framing members, installation costs for each one will be reduced. Remember that the exterior appearance of the skylight, especially on front roofs, is also important. The choice between fixed and ventilating models should be given careful consideration as well, since each type has qualities which make it more or less suitable to a particular location and set of conditions.

BUBBLE SKYLIGHT, VENTILATING

Description	Quantity	Man-hours	Material
Layout, roof & ceiling cutout & demolition	1 Ea.	4.0	0.00
Trimmer rafters, 2" x 8" x 14'	28 L.F.	0.5	38.65
Headers, double 2" x 8"	18 L.F.	1.0	12.40
Curb, 2" x 4" stock	18 L.F. stock	0.5	5.65
Skylight, ventilating bubble, 52" x 52"	1 Ea.	3.0	580.80
Flashing, aluminum, .019" thick	21 S.F.	1.5	7.10
Shaft construction, 2" x 6" x 12' trimmer joists	24 L.F.	0.5	22.65
Headers for joists, 2" x 6" stock	20 L.F.	1.0	9.45
Framing, 2" x 4" stock	64 L.F.	2.0	20.10
Drywall, 1/2" x 4' x 8' sheets, taped & finished	2 Sheets	1.5	19.35
Painting, shaft walls, primer & 1 coat	64 S.F.	5.5	6.95
Insulation, foil-faced batts, 3-1/2" thick, R-11	64 S.F.	0.5	20.90
Trim, interior casing, 9/16" x 4-1/2"	18 L.F.	1.0	19.60
Painting, trim, primer & 1 coat	18 L.F.	0.5	1.10
Totals		23.0	$764.70

Project Size	52" x 52"	Contractor's Fee Including Materials	$1710

Key to Abbreviations
C.Y. - cubic yard   Ea. - each   L.F. - linear foot   Pr. - pair   Sq. - square (100 square feet of area)
S.F. - square foot   S.Y. - square yard   V.L.F. - vertical linear foot

SUMMARY

This large bubble skylight can improve the livability of your home by bringing in new light and ventilation. If the right design and roof location are chosen, this improvement can also enhance the exterior appearance of your home.

SKY WINDOW, FIXED

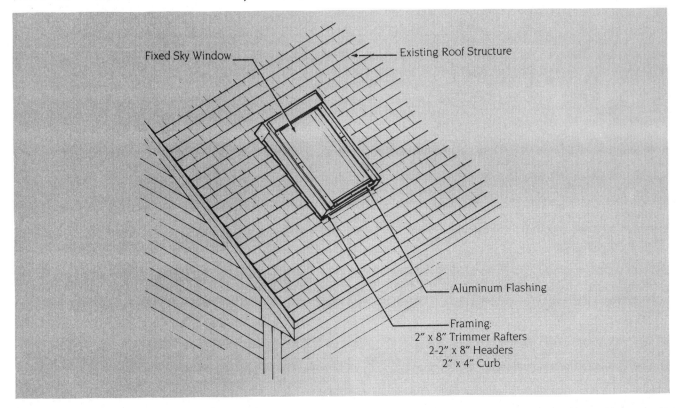

Fixed Sky Window — Existing Roof Structure

Aluminum Flashing

Framing:
2" x 8" Trimmer Rafters
2-2" x 8" Headers
2" x 4" Curb

Sky windows, like bubble skylights, are available in square and rectangular shapes and various sizes, levels of quality, and price. The homeowner should research the possibilities and then purchase the unit that best serves his needs. This model features a medium-sized rectangular sky window with awning hinges and tinted insulated glass. Like other large, operating skylight installations, this project can be a challenge for do-it-yourselfers. Beginners and less-skilled handymen are encouraged to hire a professional for the exterior work and, in some cases, for the interior part of the installation as well.

MATERIALS

Except for the skylight unit itself, the materials needed to complete this project under normal conditions are relatively inexpensive. Trimmer rafters, constructed from 2" x 6"s or framing lumber that matches the existing roof rafters, and a 2" x 4" curb are needed for the opening. The other basic construction materials for this project are flashing and milled trim for the interior casing. All of these items can

be purchased at most lumber yards and building supply outlets. The sky window is a factory-prepared unit which includes a flashing kit, basic fasteners, and complete installation instructions, in addition to the preassembled window. These units are available under many brand names from building supply outlets, door and window retailers, and specialty solar equipment stores.

Aside from the actual placement of the skylight, the most important operation in the project is the preparation of the roof and ceiling to receive the unit. In some situations, this preliminary procedure is basic, but in others it can be quite difficult and costly. This plan allows for the materials and installation time under basic conditions, as in an attic, loft, or winterized porch, where the finished ceiling follows the roof line and is attached to the rafters. In this case, the roof area affected by the skylight is first laid out, carefully squared, and stripped of its finish covering. The sheathing is then cut out with a reciprocating or circular saw and a section of the intermediate rafter is removed. The opening is trimmed with 2" x 6"s and 2" x 8"s, as required.

Although they will add slightly to the cost, joist hangers and angle brackets may facilitate the header installation and add strength to the reconditioned support system. If the rafters are spaced at 24", as in some older homes, rafter cutting may not be required. However, additional cost may be incurred in this case to bolster the support of the old roof. If extensive roof reconditioning is required, the increase in cost may be substantial, and a professional contractor may have to be consulted.

If the conditions are not this accommodating, the interior operation can be considerably more difficult and expensive. This is because the ceiling must be opened and the joists trimmed in a procedure similar to that done on the roof. Also, a light shaft between the openings must be framed, sheathed, insulated, and finished. Because the dimensions and design features of the shaft will be different from project to project, the cost and time to install it will vary greatly. Remember that a longer shaft is required for a skylight located near the ridge than for one placed near the eaves.

LEVEL OF DIFFICULTY

As advised earlier, beginners and less skilled handymen will find much of this project beyond their experience. The exterior installation can be particularly challenging, especially on steep roofs and those which require extra reconditioning. Joist work and the building of a shaft, if needed, might also make the interior operations too difficult for inexperienced do-it-yourselfers. Beginners, therefore, should consider hiring a qualified carpenter to complete the exterior part of the installation, and possibly, the interior. For any basic tasks which they feel they can handle, beginners should double the estimated man-hours. Experts and experienced handymen should add at least 25% and 75%, respectively, to all tasks, with slightly more time allowed for the careful handling and placing of the expensive sky window unit. All do-it-yourselfers should take into consideration the general inconvenience and hazards of roof work before they tackle the project. Extra expense may be incurred if staging or other specialized equipment is required for high ceilings and steep roofs.

WHAT TO WATCH OUT FOR

Sky windows provide their unique lighting function during the daytime, but at night they may offer little more than large dark areas on the ceiling. Also, during the warm months, they may contribute unwanted extra heat to the house if they are located on sunny roofs. Accessories are available to alleviate both of these shortcomings. To cut down on an excess of summer sunlight, you might invest in one of the many shade and sun-screen options available from the skylight manufacturer. A shade may also be used in the nighttime to insulate this area of the ceiling. This accessory will add to the cost of the project, but the benefit derived will make the added expense worthwhile.

SUMMARY

Even a medium-sized sky window like the one in this plan can make a considerable impact on interior ventilation and lighting. It is a challenging project, but one which can tremendously improve the comfort and appearance of a room.

SKY WINDOW, FIXED

Description	Quantity	Man-hours	Material
Layout, roof cutout & demolition	1 Ea.	3.5	0.00
Trimmer rafters, 2" x 8" x 14'	28 L.F.	0.5	38.60
Headers, double 2" x 8" stock	16 L.F.	1.0	11.05
Curb, 2" x 4" stock	12 L.F.	0.5	3.80
Sky window, fixed thermopane glass, metal-clad wood, 24" x 48"	1 Ea.	2.5	499.75
Flashing, aluminum, .013" thick	13.5 S.F.	1.0	4.75
Trim, interior casing, 9/16" x 4-1/2"	12 L.F.	0.5	10.20
Jamb, 1" x 8" clear pine	12 L.F.	0.5	10.90
Painting, trim, primer and 1 coat	24 L.F.	0.5	1.45
Totals		10.5	$580.50

Project Size	24" x 48"	Contractor's Fee Including Materials	$1160

Key to Abbreviations
C.Y. - cubic yard   Ea. - each   L.F. - linear foot   Pr. - pair   Sq. - square (100 square feet of area)
S.F. - square foot   S.Y. - square yard   V.L.F. - vertical linear foot

SKY WINDOW, OPERABLE

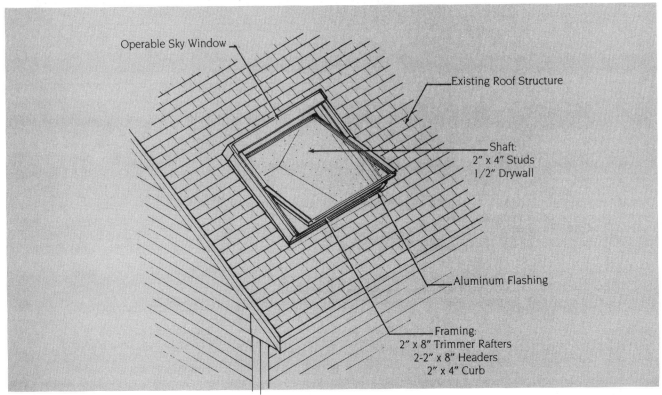

Operable Sky Window

Existing Roof Structure

Shaft:
2" x 4" Studs
1/2" Drywall

Aluminum Flashing

Framing:
2" x 8" Trimmer Rafters
2-2" x 8" Headers
2" x 4" Curb

This project features a 48" x 52" top-of-the-line sky window with an operable sash. Units like this are equipped with insulated tinted glass and factory-prepared curbing. A wide selection of accessories is also available to suit the particular needs of each installation. This window addition can dramatically improve the lighting and ventilation in an interior space.

MATERIALS

Only a small number of materials is required for this project, as the prefabricated skylight unit is designed for convenient installation. A considerable amount of preliminary roof work is necessary, however, and interior and exterior finish work will be required after the unit has been installed. The materials needed to complete these operations include inexpensive home building products, like framing lumber, flashing, and interior wood trim. These items represent only a small percentage of

the total cost of the project, but they are necessary components. The trimmer joist/rafters, especially, are vital structural elements which will be used to restore ceiling and roof support after the opening has been cut.

Before you begin the task of opening the ceiling and the roof, take time to lay out the location of the window unit. Most of the popular brands of skylights are manufactured for easy placement between standard-sized rafter spacings. The frame of this 52" skylight unit can be located in the space opened when two 16" rafters are cut and partially removed. Whenever possible, locate the skylight between existing rafters, as you will save time and disturb the roof structure only slightly. Be sure to square the layout and double check all measurements before the hole is cut. After trimmers and headers are installed, a curb may have to be fastened to the perimeter of the opening, depending on the manufacturer's recommendations. The

instructions will also provide specific information for proper fastening and flashing of the window frame. Use accepted roofing methods for replacing the disturbed area with finished materials. Reusing salvaged pieces of the old roofing will neatly blend the new work with the existing roof.

In many instances, sky windows are placed in attic rooms, family rooms with vaulted ceilings, and other rooms with slanted ceilings. The installation process is easier in these cases because the roof rafters and ceiling joists are often one and the same. After the skylight unit has been secured in its opening and made weathertight on the outside, the interior finishing is a relatively easy undertaking. The inside of the opening is trimmed with appropriate material, usually wood, and matching trim is applied for the casing.

In some instances, the interior finishing may be more difficult and costly. If, as in this plan, the roof and ceiling are separated by unused attic space and separate holes are required for the exterior and interior openings, you will have to build a light shaft between the two. The cost of this procedure and its degree of difficulty will vary with each situation, depending on the shaft's dimensions, finish, and design features. Usually, a 2" x 4" frame, sheathing, and insulation are required for the basic structure. Trim work and an appropriate covering are then applied to the shaft's interior to complete the procedure. If the bottom of the shaft is located on a horizontal ceiling, the opening could be flared to gain the maximum benefits of light and ventilation. Remember to figure in some extra time and cost for cutting and trimming the ceiling opening and joists as part of the shaft installation.

LEVEL OF DIFFICULTY

If the basic conditions are right, the installation of this sky window can be a manageable project for do-it-yourselfers experienced in the use of tools and routine roof work. Beginners and less-skilled handymen, however, should not rush into the undertaking without considering the risks involved in roof hole-cutting and related procedures. Steep roofs and inaccessible attic locations can provide dangerous and troublesome conditions for inexperienced workers. Remember that you must also use power tools in awkward positions such as from a roof ladder. Because nearly 20 square feet of roof will be opened, rapid and effective work is required to cut the hole, trim it, place and flash the unit, and restore the finish roofing to weathertight condition within a few hours time. Experts and skilled handymen should be able to complete these tasks with 25% and 75%, respectively, added to the professional time. Inexperienced do-it-yourselfers should not attempt the exterior work and should double the estimated man-hours for finishing the interior. All do-it-yourselfers are reminded to allow extra time for handling this expensive and fragile skylight unit and for the general inconvenience of roof work.

WHAT TO WATCH OUT FOR

If a long light shaft is required for the installation of your sky window, you might want to put some extra effort into planning its design features. Although the length and width of the shaft's top opening are fixed, the sides, bottom, and length of its run can be creatively arranged to provide maximum practical operation and aesthetic appeal. One of the best ways to increase ventilation and light penetration is to flare the shaft by increasing the length and width of the opening at the ceiling end. This design requires more time and expertise to install because the rafters, joists, 2" x 4"s for the frame, and sheathing must be cut at precise angles; but any additional cost for materials is small. Although this modification to the conventional shaft design will add some time and expense to the project, it can significantly improve its appearance and function.

SUMMARY

Installing a large sky window like the one featured in this plan can transform a gloomy interior area into attractive and pleasant living space. With the addition of a clever shaft design and the appropriate accessories, the installation can produce spectacular results.

SKY WINDOW, OPERABLE

Description	Quantity	Man-hours	Material
Layout, roof & ceiling cutout, demolition	1 Ea.	4.0	0.00
Trimmer rafters, 2" x 8" x 14'	28 L.F.	0.5	38.65
Headers, double 2" x 8"	16 L.F.	1.0	11.05
Curb, 2" x 4" stock	14 L.F.	0.5	4.40
Sky window, operating, thermopane glass, 48" x 52"	1 Ea.	5.5	682.45
Flashing, aluminum, .019" thick	14 S.F.	1.0	4.75
Shaft construction, 2" x 6" x 12' trimmer joists	24 L.F.	0.5	22.65
Headers for joists, 2" x 6" stock	20 L.F.	1.0	9.45
Framing, 2" x 4" stock	64 L.F.	2.0	20.15
Drywall, 1/2" x 4' x 8' sheets, taped and finished	2 Sheets	1.0	19.35
Painting, shaft walls, primer & 1 coat	64 S.F.	5.5	9.95
Insulation, foil-faced batts, 3-1/2" thick, R-11	64 S.F.	0.5	20.90
Trim, interior casing, 9/16" x 4-1/2"	18 L.F.	0.5	19.60
Painting, trim, primer & 1 coat	18 L.F.	0.5	1.10
Totals		24.0	$864.45

Project Size	52" x 55"	Contractor's Fee Including Materials	$1850

Key to Abbreviations
C.Y. - cubic yard   Ea. - each   L.F. - linear foot   Pr. - pair   Sq. - square (100 square feet of area)
S.F. - square foot   S.Y. - square yard   V.L.F. - vertical linear foot

SAUNA ROOM

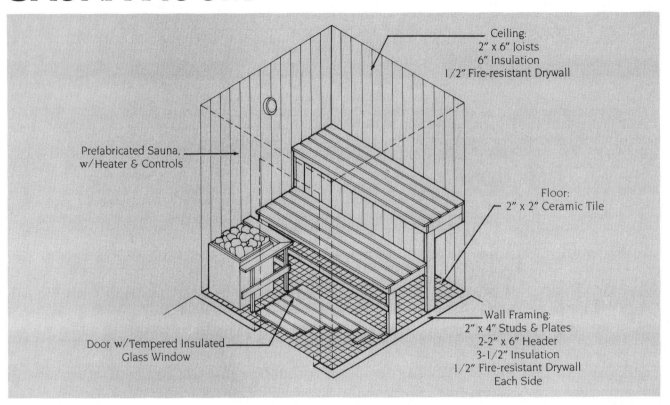

Ceiling:
2" x 6" Joists
6" Insulation
1/2" Fire-resistant Drywall

Prefabricated Sauna,
w/Heater & Controls

Floor:
2" x 2" Ceramic Tile

Door w/Tempered Insulated
Glass Window

Wall Framing:
2" x 4" Studs & Plates
2-2" x 6" Header
3-1/2" Insulation
1/2" Fire-resistant Drywall
Each Side

Saunas are a popular home improvement, not only as a health and luxury item, but also because they require little space and are only moderately difficult to install. Other than some basic electrical hook-ups, there is no specialized trade work involved. Unlike a steam bath, no plumbing or floor drain installation is required, and ceramic tile or concrete are the desirable floor coverings. This plan outlines a sauna project that can be completed by most experienced handymen. The installation features a 6' x 6' factory-prepared sauna room which is delivered complete with ready-to-assemble walls, ceiling, benches, heater, and basic accessories.

MATERIALS

In addition to the prefabricated sauna room, standard framing, surface covering, and insulating materials are needed for the exterior shell of the facility. These basic construction products can be purchased from most building supply retailers at competitive prices. The sauna room itself is a specialty item. Many brand names are presently on the market, and as with other prefabricated building products, the costs vary widely. The design features, types of materials, and levels of quality also have a wide range.

The first phase of this project involves determining the location and layout of the sauna room and then constructing its exterior shell. Because the prefabricated units are not that heavy and can be ordered in a wide range of sizes and configurations, they can be located almost anywhere in the house. If you have the space off a bedroom and near a shower area, a second-floor location is ideal. However, first-floor, basement, and even exterior areas can also be utilized. This plan allows for enough material to construct the shell of a sauna room in a corner of a basement where two walls are already in place. The two new walls must be framed with 2" x 4"s and then covered with 1/2" fire-resistant drywall on both sides. A ceiling must also be framed with 2" x 6"s and similarly covered on the interior side.

Insulation is required on the new walls and ceiling to ensure energy savings. Some additional expense may be incurred if the existing walls must also be insulated or covered with fireproof material. During the framing of the shell, follow the manufacturer's recommended rough measurement guidelines and maintain precise level, plumb, and square. Inaccurate framing will cause misalignment of the prefabricated components, and, consequently, heat-losing cracks and spaces at the corners and between panels.

The second phase of the project involves assembling the sauna room and its accessories. Various designs and materials are employed in sauna units, but most of them feature soft-wood walls and ceilings. Economical units may employ pine, spruce, and hemlock, for example; and the more expensive ones, cedar and redwood. The benches, safety heater railing, and optional duckboards and back rests are usually manufactured from wood which matches the ceiling and walls.

At the heart of the installation is the heater, which has been carefully engineered to provide the correct output for its particular size of sauna room. A light fixture, switch, and controls for the heater are also normally included in the basic sauna package. Most manufacturers feature prewiring for these electrical devices within the wall panels of their products. No special electrical service is required for the heater; and under normal conditions, a certified electrician can routinely tie the lead wires from the sauna into your house's electrical supply. Throughout the assembly of the sauna unit, follow the manufacturer's instructions and guidelines. Work patiently and follow accepted carpentry practices, as the naturally finished softwood is particularly susceptible to marks and dents caused by careless hammering or handling.

Once the sauna unit has been assembled and fastened, the finished floor can be laid and the special prehung sauna door installed. This plan includes attractive low maintenance ceramic floor tile. If you intend to install ceramic flooring,

be sure to use appropriate grout and to seal it thoroughly, as frequent floor cleaning is recommended by most manufacturers. Duckboards are available as an accessory flooring material at extra cost from most sauna manufacturers. Depending on the brand of sauna, several styles of prehung doors are available. All of them are insulated and have wood interior handles, and some include small or full-size insulated glass windows and exterior decoration. The door is usually included in the sauna unit price, but is sometimes an extra, which is chosen from several styles. Many optional accessories are available, usually at extra cost. These include recessed light fixtures, sophisticated thermostat and time controls, hygrometers, and convenience items, such as back rests, towel bars, and robe racks.

LEVEL OF DIFFICULTY

This project calls for moderate to advanced carpentry skills and know-how. Although the sauna facility

measures only 6' x 6', it requires an accurate layout and a precise fit of both the exterior shell and interior wall and ceiling assembly. Careless workmanship can be problematic if the exterior shell is misaligned or inaccurately plumbed or squared. Beginners, therefore, should seek assistance in the framing phase of the installation. They may also consider hiring a professional for the sauna assembly after weighing the cost of the unit and the chance of damaging it against the potential savings in labor. Beginners should add 100% to the professional time for insulating, finishing the drywall, and painting. If they tackle the ceramic floor installation, they should add slightly more time to allow for careful work. Handymen and experts should add 50% and 20%, respectively, to the estimated time for all basic carpentry procedures, and more for the sauna assembly, door installation, and ceramic floor.

WHAT TO WATCH OUT FOR

Although this plan is for an economical sauna inside your house, there are several other options, both interior and exterior. Some manufacturers of prefabricated sauna units provide completely finished rooms which can be erected without the need of a shell. These units come with insulated walls, interior and exterior finish, and the full range of electrical and convenience accessories. In some areas of the country, they also provide the services of expert installers at extra cost. Exterior sauna locations are a possibility if interior space is limited or if you prefer an outdoor setting. As long the enclosure for the facility is well insulated and weathertight, interior sauna kits can be safely and effectively adapted to an exterior setting. The complete room kit, and especially the outdoor kit, will increase the cost of the project.

SUMMARY

For a reasonable investment of time and money, the unique pleasure of a sauna room can become part of your home life. Skilled do-it-yourselfers can substantially reduce the cost of this amenity by building it on their own.

SAUNA ROOM

Description	Quantity	Man-hours	Material
Wall framing, plates, 2" x 4", top & bottom	36 L.F.	1.0	11.30
Studs, 2" x 4" x 8", 16" O.C.	112 L.F.	2.0	35.25
Blocking, misc. 2" x 4"	20 L.F.	1.0	7.50
Header over door opening, 2" x 6", doubled	8 L.F.	0.5	3.80
Ceiling joists, 2" x 6", 16" O.C.	60 L.F.	1.0	28.30
Insulation, walls, 3-1/2" thick, R-11, 15" wide	170 S.F.	1.0	55.55
Ceiling, 6" thick, R-19, 15" wide	36 S.F.	0.5	17.00
Drywall, gypsum plasterboard, 1/2" thick on ceiling & both sides of walls, fire-resistant, taped & finished	11 Sheets	6.0	123.52
Sauna, 6' x 6' prefabricated kit, including heater & controls	1 Ea.	16.0	3872.00
Door, pre-hung w/tempered insulated glass window, including jambs & hardware	1 Ea.	1.5	229.90
Flooring, ceramic tile, 1 color, 2" x 2"	36 S.F.	3.5	145.95
Painting, exterior walls, primer & 1 coat	85 S.F.	1.0	9.25
Totals		35.0	$4539.32

Project Size	6' x 6'	Contractor's Fee Including Materials	$8250

Key to Abbreviations
C.Y. - cubic yard   Ea. - each   L.F. - linear foot   Pr. - pair   Sq. - square (100 square feet of area)
S.F. - square foot   S.Y. - square yard   V.L.F. - vertical linear foot

HOT TUB, REDWOOD

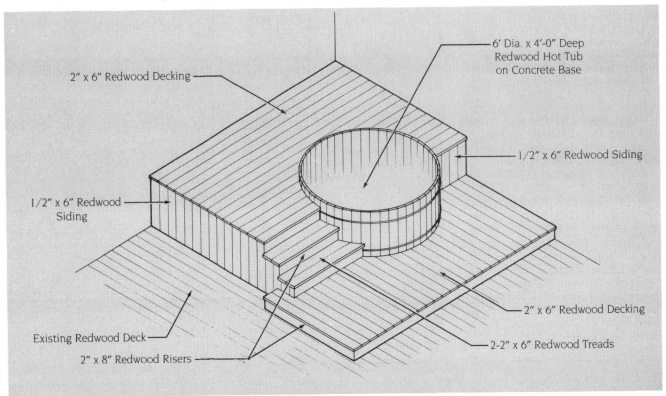

2" x 6" Redwood Decking

6' Dia. x 4'-0" Deep Redwood Hot Tub on Concrete Base

1/2" x 6" Redwood Siding

1/2" x 6" Redwood Siding

Existing Redwood Deck

2" x 8" Redwood Risers

2" x 6" Redwood Decking

2-2" x 6" Redwood Treads

Hot tubs can be installed in interior or exterior settings and often complement another facility, such as a deluxe bath, exercise room, sauna, sun deck, or swimming pool. This plan demonstrates how a 6' factory-prepared redwood hot tub can be placed on an existing redwood deck. Although many locations and designs are possible, this project covers the basic materials, procedures, and considerations for a medium-sized exterior installation.

MATERIALS

The materials list starts with redwood support members and decking. These are required to alter and prepare the existing deck to receive the hot tub. The remaining components are the precut and prefinished 6' hot tub kit and incidental finish products. The framing and decking lumber are available from most lumber yards, as are some of the finish materials. Redwood may have to be special ordered, however, in some areas of the

country. The redwood tub kit can be purchased from a specialty retailer, but some general building suppliers may also carry hot tubs and spas on a special-order basis. Because the redwood deck materials and hot tub are expensive products, do-it-yourselfers should thoroughly research their options before finalizing the design of the facility and the materials order.

The 6' hot tub suggested in this plan weighs well over three tons when filled and in use. Consequently, a considerable amount of support must be added to the existing deck if it is to bear the load. Each installation will present a different set of conditions, and the requirements for reinforcing your deck's support system may vary from what is recommended in this plan. Consult local building codes, follow the manufacturer's guidelines, and get a professional opinion before you determine the arrangement and size of the deck joists and supports. In some cases, extra joists and bridging

may be enough; in others, additional footings, posts, and supports may be required. Most manufacturers of hot tubs recommend an independent ground support system for the unit, separate from the deck. Whenever possible, this method of installation should be employed, even though it may involve considerable extra work and expense. When placing the knee wall and partial perimeter deck structure around the hot tub, be careful not to drive the fasteners into the side of the unit. Also, leave a small space for expansion and drainage between the tub and the deck frame. Use quality hot-dipped galvanized nails and lag screws for the decking and supports to prevent corrosion and rusting.

Many different sizes, shapes, and material options are open to you when selecting the hot tub kit. The unit in this plan features standard-grade bottom pieces and redwood staves collared with adjustable stainless steel hoops. The kit is precision cut and fitted at the factory, and delivered unassembled to the consumer. Also included in the price of the kit are the basic plumbing and electrical support packages for the operation of the facility. Many specialty retailers will provide, at extra charge, an on-site assembly service for the tub itself. Handymen and beginners might consider this service, as the hot tub is fairly complicated and must be accurately fitted together so that it will be sturdy and watertight. The cost of this service covers only the basic tub and its attached components, however, and does not include plumbing and electrical work. As noted earlier, careful planning and research will help you determine the size and design features that meet your practical and aesthetic requirements. In addition to redwood, hot tubs are available in teak, cedar, mahogany, and cyprus. Coated fiberglass, stainless steel, and other materials are also used. Whatever they are made of, hot tubs come in different sizes and are designed as free-standing, exposed units or as inserts for redwoood or other raised perimeter decks. Still others can be recessed into the raised section of an interior floor. The cost of these alternative sizes, designs, and settings, will, of course, significantly affect the cost of the project.

After the support system, perimeter decking, and hot tub are in place, the installation can be left as is or finished with stain or sealer. If left untreated, the redwood will eventually weather to a tanned leather color, but it will not rot or deteriorate. However, because of the dampness, a sealer with a mildewcide additive is recommended for the exposed exterior surfaces of the tub and the surrounding deck. If the deck and tub are made from different materials, one or both may be stained to blend the new and old installations. In most cases, a qualified plumber and electrician should be hired to tie in the support packages to the house utilities. Because the water pump, heater, filters, and other tub support facilities are often remotely located, extra expense may be incurred for additional piping and underground placement. Increased cost is to be expected for convenience options such as air switches, therapy jets, chemical feeders, timers, lighting, and solar heat packages. Shelves, steps, and ladders are some other options that can be obtained at additional cost.

LEVEL OF DIFFICULTY

This project calls for some expensive materials — both the redwood decking and the tub kit. This factor, together with precise installation requirements, makes it a challenge for all do-it-yourselfers. Beginners and most handymen might want to stick to the more basic tasks, like the preliminary site preparation and the surface finishing. Experts who opt to assemble the kit themselves should follow the manufacturer's instructions precisely and consult a professional before tackling the operation. Experts should add 25% to the man-hours for all carpentry work. Beginners and handymen should add 100% and 50%, respectively, to the time estimate for the basic tasks which they attempt. All do-it-yourselfers should hire qualified tradesmen to accomplish the electrical and plumbing work.

WHAT TO WATCH OUT FOR

Provisions should be made in the planning stages of this project for features such as proper drainage piping and protection against the effects of freezing temperatures. The installation should allow for complete drainage during the period when the facility is not in use. In cold climates, where the tub is to be used year-round, an optional freeze protection package can be purchased at additional cost. Floating or attached covers made of wood and plastic are other extras which will reduce heat loss and protect the tub. If the tub is to be used during cooler weather, you might consider installing a wind screen adjacent to the facility for greater comfort and reduced heat loss. All of these components will increase the cost of the project, but they will also extend the length of the season during which the facility can be used.

SUMMARY

Although the installation of a hot tub is a relatively expensive undertaking, the comfort and potential benefits can add a unique luxury to your home life. When carefully designed to complement an existing deck, exercise area, or swimming pool, it can also enhance your home's exterior appearance.

HOT TUB, REDWOOD

Description	Quantity	Man-hours	Material
Remove portion of existing deck	1 Job	4.0	0.00
Reinforce existing deck, 2" x 8" redwood stock	24 L.F.	1.0	42.40
Base support slab, hand grading	50 S.F.	1.0	0.00
Edge forms for slab	24 L.F.	1.5	5.80
Concrete, ready mix, 3000 psi	1 C.Y.	0.0	67.55
Place & screed concrete	1 C.Y.	1.0	0.00
Platform framing, redwood, construction grade			
Posts, doubled 2" x 4" stock	48 L.F.	2.0	109.20
Joists, 2" x 6" stock	130 L.F.	4.5	160.45
Decking, 2" x 6" x 12'	252 L.F.	8.0	311.00
Stair stringers, 2" x 8" stock	12 L.F.	1.0	21.20
Stair treads, 2" x 6" stock	18 L.F.	0.5	22.20
Stair risers 2" x 8" stock	14 L.F.	1.0	24.75
Vertical siding, 1/2" x 6"	48 L.F.	1.5	77.85
Redwood hot tub kit, 6' diam. x 4' deep with circulating pump & drain system	1 Ea.	20.0	1609.30
Plumbing rough-in & supply	1 Ea.	9.5	85.40
Electrical rough-in, hook-up	1 Ea.	3.0	68.95
	Totals	59.5	$2606.00

Project Size	12' x 14'	Contractor's Fee Including Materials	$5800

Key to Abbreviations
C.Y. - cubic yard   Ea. - each   L.F. - linear foot   Pr. - pair   Sq. - square (100 square feet of area)
S.F. - square foot   S.Y. - square yard   V.L.F. - vertical linear foot

SECTION THREE
DETAILS

This "Section" is designed to supplement the previous parts of the book. It deals with the cost of unit items rather than that of whole, predetermined projects (as presented in the "Interiors" and "Exteriors" sections). You can use this section to add or substitute components in one of the "Interiors" or "Exteriors" plans, or to put together your own model, which will suit your specific space requirements, the style of your house, your budget, or your personal taste. The information given will also help you to arrive at the total cost of a smaller project, such as the installation of a single door, the replacement of a window, or the addition of a new kitchen appliance.

"Section Three" lists a variety of available materials and their comparative costs, as well as the man-hours involved in their installation and the corresponding contractors' fees. Everything from kitchen cabinets to insulation is listed in this section of the book, with a range of quality and price in each category. By knowing the prices of the available options, as well as their installation time and the contractors' charges, you can make informed choices about the fixtures and materials you need for a given home improvement project. You can also determine how much of the work you are willing to take on yourself and how much should be done by a contractor. In each part of

Section Three, an illustration is also provided with its various components identified. This feature makes planning and purchasing that much easier and helps you to visualize the renovation in progress.

While this section is presented in a straightforward and clear manner, using it can be a bit more challenging than the "Interiors" or "Exteriors" sections. For example, different standards of measure (such as square foot, linear foot, and set) are used according to the type of material; and the quantity of building components must be calculated with the measurements you make yourself. A "How-to-Use" page follows this introduction and explains the format in more detail. Some organization is required when you use Section Three to draw up plans, and a bit of imagination is helpful, too, when it comes to putting the separate elements together. The benefits of this independent approach are the ability to create your own remodeling system, to expand or reduce the size of a given system, and to change certain aspects within that system for reasons of economy, practicality, or personal preference. As a result, you can be the designer of your own room or facility and can make plans in advance according to the commitment of time, effort, and money that is right for you.

HOW TO USE SECTION THREE

Section Three is provided as a quick, efficient reference for estimating the cost of home improvements. It enables you to closely match dollars and cents to your ideas before you commit yourself to a project.

Basic building elements are grouped together to create a complete "system". These "systems" can then be used to make up a proposed project. For example, the "Gable End Roofing System" page lists all of the basic elements required to shingle a house. The result is the total cost per square foot of area to be shingled.

The "systems" can also be combined to create an estimate for a more complex project. For example, if you need to replace the roof structure before shingling, you can consult the "Gable End Roof Framing System" page to calculate the cost per square foot for framing a new roof, and then add in the cost for shingling. In this manner, an entire project, matched to your specifications for size and proposed design, can be cost-estimated.

There are two types of pages found here. The most common format is composed of a graphic illustration of the construction process and a list of the building elements that make it up. In many cases, several different options are presented. For example, the "Gable End Roof Framing System" page shows the cost per square foot for asphalt as well as wood shingles.

The second type of page contains the same kind of information in a slightly different format. These pages list the cost for items that do not require a grouping of basic building elements. For example, the "Insulation" page lists the cost per square foot for various types of building insulation.

The illustration below defines terms that appear and will help you use information presented. The illustration on the facing page shows how Section Three is organized.

Key to Abbreviations

C.Y. - cubic yard
Ea. - each
L.F. - linear foot
Pr. - pair
Sq. - square (100 square feet of area)
S.F. - square foot
S.Y. - square yard
V.L.F. - vertical linear foot

System Descriptions uniquely define the system being costed. Descriptions range from item-by-item component lists to single entries differentiating systems by size or other relevant characteristics.

Quantity of each building element or system.

Unit of measure for each item. A key to abbreviations appears on this page.

Material cost for each component of the system. In systems comprised of a group of components, the total material cost for 1 unit of the system appears in a box at the bottom of the column.

SYSTEM DESCRIPTION	QUAN.	UNIT	MAN-HOURS	MAT. COST	COST PER SQUARE FOOT
ASPHALT, ROOF SHINGLES, CLASS A					
Shingles, asphalt standard, inorganic class A, 210-235 lb./sq.	1.160	S.F.	.017	.44	
Drip edge, metal, 5" girth	.150	L.F.	.003	.04	
Building paper, #15 felt	1.300	S.F.	.001	.04	
Ridge shingles, asphalt	.042	L.F.	.001	.03	
Soffit & fascia, white painted aluminum, 1' overhang	.083	L.F.	.012	.14	
Rake trim, painted, 1" x 6"	.040	L.F.	.002	.03	
Gutter, seamless, aluminum, painted	.083	L.F.	.005	.09	
Downspouts, aluminum, painted	.035	L.F.	.001	.02	Contractor's Fee
TOTAL			.042	.83	**2.81**
WOOD, CEDAR SHINGLES, NO. 1 PERFECTIONS					
Shingles, wood, cedar, No. 1 perfections, 5" exposure, 4/12 pitch					
Drip edge, metal, 5" girth					
Building paper, #15 felt					
Ridge shingles, cedar					
Soffit & fascia, white painted aluminum, 1' overhang					
Rake trim, painted, 1" x 6"					

Man-hours required to install the system. In systems made-up of components, the total man-hours for 1 unit of the system appears in a box at the bottom of the column.

Total cost per unit for each system. This figure includes the price of materials (without sales tax), labor costs, and the contractor's overhead expenses and profit.

Note: Refer to "Location Multipliers" to adjust costs to your area.

SECTION THREE
TABLE OF CONTENTS

Information in this section is organized into the nine divisions listed here. The schematic diagram pictured below shows how the parts of a typical house fit into these divisions.

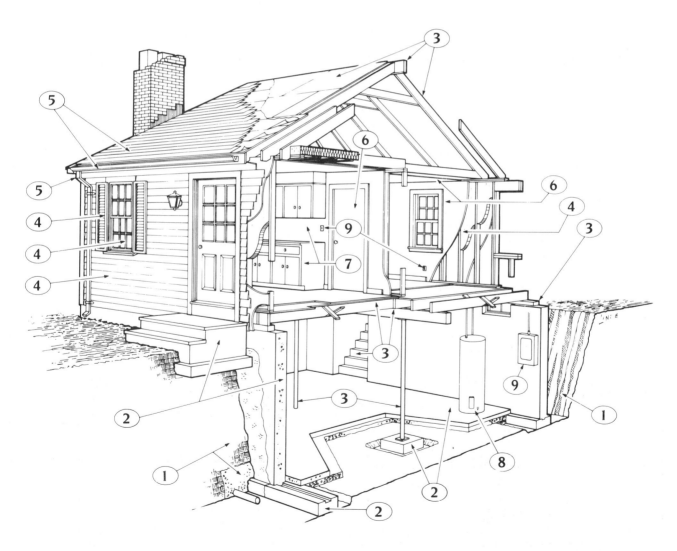

DIVISION 1
SITE WORK

Footing Excavation System

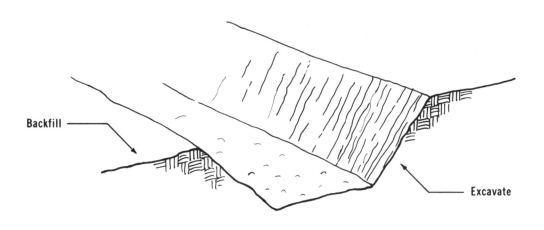

SYSTEM DESCRIPTION	QUAN.	UNIT	MAN-HOURS	MAT. COST	COST PER JOB
BUILDING, 24' X 38', 4' DEEP					
Clear and strip, dozer, light trees, 30' from building	.190	Acre	11.400		
Excavate, backhoe	174.000	C.Y.	7.656		
Backfill, dozer, no compaction	87.000	C.Y.	.870		Contractor's Fee
Rough grade, dozer, 30' from building	87.000	C.Y.	.870		
TOTAL			20.796		**1550.00**

Foundation Excavation System

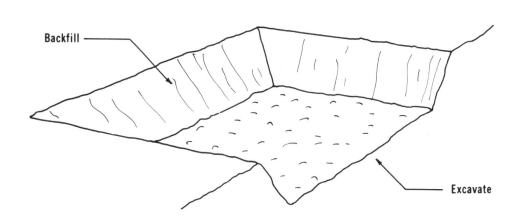

SYSTEM DESCRIPTION	QUAN.	UNIT	MAN-HOURS	MAT. COST	COST PER JOB
BUILDING, 24' X 38', 8' DEEP					
Clear and grub, dozer, medium brush, 30' from building	.190	Acre	2.027		
Excavate, track loader, 1-1/2 C.Y. bucket	550.000	C.Y.	11.550		
Backfill, dozer, no compaction	180.000	C.Y.	1.800		Contractor's Fee
Rough grade, dozer, 30' from building	280.000	C.Y.	2.800		
TOTAL			18.177		**1700.00**

Be sure to read pages 155–157 for proper use of this section.

Utility Trenching System

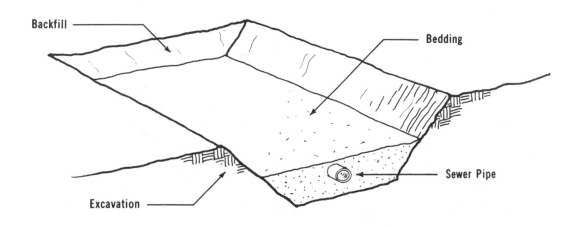

SYSTEM DESCRIPTION	QUAN.	UNIT	MAN-HOURS	MAT. COST	COST PER LINEAR FOOT
2' DEEP					
Excavation, backhoe	.296	C.Y	.032		
Bedding, sand	.111	C.Y.	.044	1.20	
Utility, sewer, 6" cast iron	1.000	L.F.	.282	6.80	
Backfill, incl. compaction	.185	C.Y.	.043		Contractor's Fee
TOTAL			.401	8.00	**26.00**

Sidewalk System

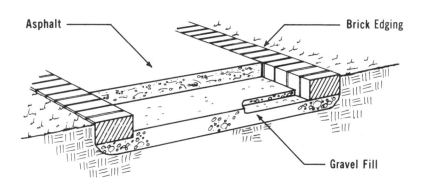

SYSTEM DESCRIPTION	QUAN.	UNIT	MAN-HOURS	MAT. COST	COST PER SQUARE FOOT
ASPHALT SIDEWALK SYSTEM, 3' WIDE WALK					
Gravel fill, 4" deep	1.000	S.F.	.001	.13	
Compact fill	.012	C.Y.	.001		
Handgrade	1.000	S.F.	.001		
Walking surface, bituminous paving, 2" thick	1.000	S.F.	.007	.42	
Edging, brick, laid on edge	.670	L.F.	.079	1.14	Contractor's Fee
TOTAL			.089	1.69	**5.25**

Be sure to read pages 155-157 for proper use of this section.

161

Driveway System

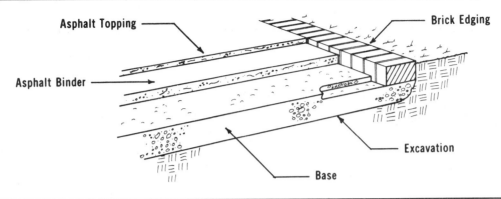

SYSTEM DESCRIPTION	QUAN.	UNIT	MAN-HOURS	MAT. COST	COST PER SQUARE FOOT
ASPHALT DRIVEWAY TO 10' WIDE					
Excavation, driveway to 10' wide, 6" deep	.019	C.Y.			
Base, 6" crushed stone	1.000	S.F.	001	.53	
Handgrade base	1.000	S.F.	.001		
Surface, asphalt, 2" thick base, 1" topping	1.000	S.F.	.007	.63	Contractor's Fee
Edging, brick pavers	.200	L.F.	.023	.34	
TOTAL			.032	1.50	**3.20**

Septic System

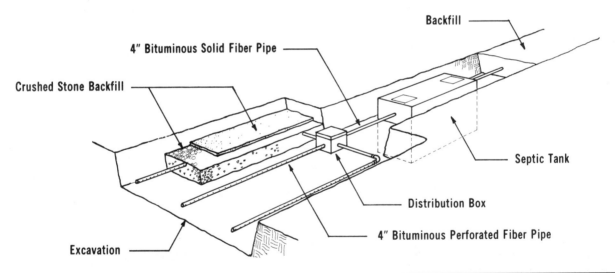

SYSTEM DESCRIPTION	QUAN.	UNIT	MAN-HOURS	MAT. COST	COST EACH
SEPTIC SYSTEM WITH 1000 S.F. LEACHING FIELD, 1000 GALLON TANK					
Tank, 1000 gallon, concrete	1.000	Ea.	3.500	510.00	
Distribution box, concrete	1.000	Ea.	1.000	60.00	
4" bituminous fiber pipe	25.000	L.F.	1.050	43.00	
Tank and field excavation	119.000	C.Y.	13.090		
Crushed stone backfill	76.000	C.Y.	12.160	1500.00	
Backfill with excavated material	36.000	C.Y.	.360		
Building paper	125.000	S.Y.	2.250	37.00	
4" bituminous fiber perforated pipe	145.000	L.F.	4.640	255.00	
4" pipe fittings	2.000	Ea.	2.280	17.55	Contractor's Fee
TOTAL			40.330	2422.55	**5595.00**

Be sure to read pages 155–157 for proper use of this section.

Chain Link Fence Pricesheet

SYSTEM DESCRIPTION	QUAN.	UNIT	MAN-HOURS	COST PER UNIT MAT.	COST PER UNIT TOTAL
Chain link fence					
Galv.9ga. wire, 1-5/8"post 10'O.C., 1-3/8"top rail, 2" corner post, 3'high	1.000	L.F.	.130	3.45	8.75
4' high	1.000	L.F.	.141	4.15	10.10
6' high	1.000	L.F.	.209	5.20	13.65
Add for gate 3' wide 1-3/8" frame 3' high	1.000	Ea.	2.000	35.00	110.00
4' high	1.000	Ea.	2.400	45.00	135.00
6' high	1.000	Ea.	2.400	69.00	170.00
Add for gate 4' wide 1-3/8" frame 3' high	1.000	Ea.	2.670	45.00	140.00
4' high	1.000	Ea.	2.670	60.00	165.00
6' high	1.000	Ea.	3.00	90.00	220.00
Alum.9ga. wire, 1-5/8"post, 10'O.C., 1-3/8"top rail, 2"corner post,3' high	1.000	L.F.	.130	4.15	9.80
4' high '	1.000	L.F.	.141	4.88	11.25
6' high	1.000	L.F.	.209	6.30	15.20
Add for gate 3' wide 1-3/8" frame 3' high	1.000	Ea.	2.000	41.00	120.00
4' high	1.000	Ea.	2.400	56.00	150.00
6' high	1.000	Ea.	2.400	82.00	190.00
Add for gate 4' wide 1-3/8" frame 3' high	1.000	Ea.	2.400	56.00	150.00
4' high	1.000	Ea.	2.670	74.00	190.00
6' high	1.000	Ea.	3.000	110.00	250.00
Vinyl 9ga. wire, 1-5/8" post 10'O.C., 1-3/8" top rail, 2" corner post,3' high	1.000	L.F.	.130	3.84	9.30
4' high	1.000	L.F.	.141	4.62	10.85
6' high	1.000	L.F.	.209	5.80	14.45
Add for gate 3' wide 1-3/8" frame 3' high	1.000	Ea.	2.000	45.00	125.00
4' high	1.000	Ea.	2.400	59.00	155.00
6' high	1.000	Ea.	2.400	90.00	205.00
Add for gate 4' wide 1-3/8" frame 3' high	1.000	Ea.	2.400	60.00	155.00
4' high	1.000	Ea.	2.670	80.00	195.00
6' high	1.000	Ea.	3.000	120.00	260.00
Tennis court chain link fence, 10' high					
Galv.11ga.wire,2" post 10'O.C., 1-3/8" top rail, 2-1/2" corner post	1.000	L.F.	.253	9.55	21.25
Add for gate 3' wide 1-3/8" frame	1.000	Ea.	2.400	120.00	245.00
Alum.11ga.wire,2" post 10'O.C., 1-3/8" top rail, 2-1/2" corner post	1.000	L.F.	.253	11.60	24.35
Add for gate 3' wide 1-3/8" frame	1.000	Ea.	2.400	150.00	295.00
Vinyl 11ga.wire,2"post 10' O.C.,1-3/8"top rail,2-1/2" corner post	1.000	L.F.	.253	10.60	23.00
Add for gate 3' wide 1-3/8" frame	1.000	Ea.	2.400	165.00	310.00

Be sure to read pages 155–157 for proper use of this section.

Wood Fence Price Sheet

SYSTEM DESCRIPTION	QUAN.	UNIT	MAN-HOURS	COST PER UNIT	
				MAT.	INST.
Basketweave, 3/8"x4" boards, 2"x4" stringers on spreaders, 4"x4" posts					
No. 1 cedar, 6' high	1.000	L.F.	.150	16.80	29.00
Treated pine, 6' high	1.000	L.F.	.160	8.60	17.20
Board fence, 1"x4" boards, 2"x4" rails, 4"x4" posts					
Preservative treated, 2 rail, 3' high	1.000	L.F.	.166	5.15	12.30
4' high	1.000	L.F.	.178	6.00	13.90
3 rail, 5' high	1.000	L.F.	.185	7.40	16.15
6' high	1.000	L.F.	.192	8.05	17.35
Western cedar, No. 1, 2 rail, 3' high	1.000	L.F.	.166	5.75	13.20
3 rail, 4' high	1.000	L.F.	.178	11.10	21.00
5' high	1.000	L.F.	.185	14.20	26.00
6' high	1.000	L.F.	.192	17.20	31.00
No. 1 cedar, 2 rail, 3' high	1.000	L.F.	.166	13.25	25.00
4' high	1.000	L.F.	.178	16.00	30.00
3 rail, 5' high	1.000	L.F.	.185	17.55	31.00
6' high	1.000	L.F.	.192	19.20	34.00
Shadow box, 1"x6" boards, 2"x4" rails, 4"x4" posts					
Fir, pine or spruce, treated, 3 rail, 6' high	1.000	L.F.	.150	7.95	16.00
No. 1 cedar, 3 rail, 4' high	1.000	L.F.	.178	15.10	27.00
6' high	1.000	L.F.	.185	16.80	30.00
Open rail, split rails, No. 1 cedar, 2 rail, 3' high	1.000	L.F.	.150	3.75	9.85
3 rail, 4' high	1.000	L.F.	.160	4.95	11.85
No. 2 cedar, 2 rail, 3' high	1.000	L.F.	.150	1.98	7.15
3 rail, 4' high	1.000	L.F.	.160	2.31	7.95
Open rail, rustic rails, No. 1 cedar, 2 rail, 3' high	1.000	L.F.	.150	3.30	9.10
3 rail, 4' high	1.000	L.F.	.160	4.09	10.60
No. 2 cedar, 2 rail, 3' high	1.000	L.F.	.150	2.10	7.35
3 rail, 4' high	1.000	L.F.	.160	2.77	8.65
Rustic picket, molded pine pickets, 2 rail, 3' high	1.000	L.F.	.171	3.10	9.45
3 rail, 4' high	1.000	L.F.	.196	3.56	10.85
No. 1 cedar, 2 rail, 3' high	1.000	L.F.	.171	6.36	14.25
3 rail,	1.000	L.F.	.196	7.32	16.40
Picket fence, fir, pine or spruce, preserved, treated					
2 rail, 3' high	1.000	L.F.	.171	3.63	10.20
3 rail, 4' high	1.000	L.F.	.185	4.24	11.55
Western cedar, 2 rail, 3' high	1.000	L.F.	.171	4.24	11.10
3 rail, 4' high	1.000	L.F.	.185	4.66	12.10
No. 1 cedar, 2 rail, 3' high	1.000	L.F.	.171	9.65	19.05
3 rail, 4' high	1.000	L.F.	.185	10.95	21.00
Stockade, No. 1 cedar, 3-1/4" rails, 6' high	1.000	L.F.	.150	12.90	23.00
8' high	1.000	L.F.	.155	20.00	34.00
No. 2 cedar, treated rails, 6' high	1.000	L.F.	.150	5.25	12.05
Treated pine, treated rails, 6' high	1.000	L.F.	.150	8.30	16.50
Gates, No. 2 cedar, picket, 3'-6" wide 4' high	1.000	Ea.	2.670	45.00	145.00
No. 2 cedar, rustic round, 3' wide, 3' high	1.000	Ea.	2.670	57.00	165.00
No. 2 cedar, stockade screen, 3'-6" wide, 6' high	1.000	Ea.	3.000	44.00	150.00
General, wood, 3'-6" wide, 4' high	1.000	Ea.	2.400	43.00	130.00
6' high	1.000	Ea.	3.000	53.00	160.00

Be sure to read pages 155–157 for proper use of this section.

Division 2
Foundations

Footing System

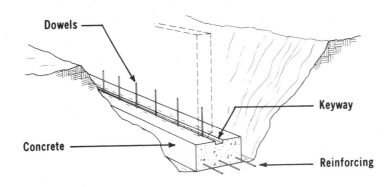

SYSTEM DESCRIPTION	QUAN.	UNIT	MAN-HOURS	MAT. COST	COST PER LINEAR FOOT
8" THICK BY 18" WIDE FOOTING					
Concrete, 3000 psi	.040	C.Y		2.68	
Place concrete, direct chute	.040	C.Y.	.016		
Forms, footing, 4 uses	1.330	SFCA	.102	.60	
Reinforcing, 1/2" diameter bars, 2 each	1.380	Lb.	.011	.45	
Keyway, 2" x 4", beveled, 4 uses	1.000	L.F.	.015	.09	
Dowels, 1/2" diameter bars, 2' long, 6' O.C.	.166	Ea.	.021	.18	Contractor's Fee
TOTAL			.165	4.00	**11.60**

Block Wall System

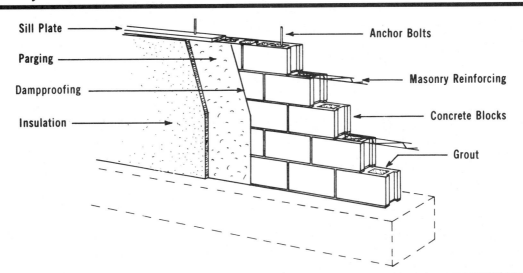

SYSTEM DESCRIPTION	QUAN.	UNIT	MAN-HOURS	MAT. COST	COST PER SQUARE FOOT
8" WALL, GROUTED, FULL HEIGHT					
Concrete block, 8" x 16" x 8"	1.000	S.F.	.093	1.82	
Masonry reinforcing, every second course	.750	L.F.	.002	.17	
Parging, plastering with portland cement plaster, 1 coat	1.000	S.F.	.012	.45	
Dampproofing, bituminous coating, 1 coat	1.000	S.F.	.012	.10	
Insulation, 1" rigid polystyrene	1.000	S.F.	.010	.50	
Grout, solid, pumped	1.000	S.F.	.038	.98	
Anchor bolts, 1/2" diameter, 8" long, 4' O.C.	.060	Ea.	.002	.02	
Sill plate, 2" x 4", treated	.250	L.F.	.007	.10	Contractor's Fee
TOTAL			.176	4.14	**12.00**

Be sure to read pages 155–157 for proper use of this section.

Concrete Wall System

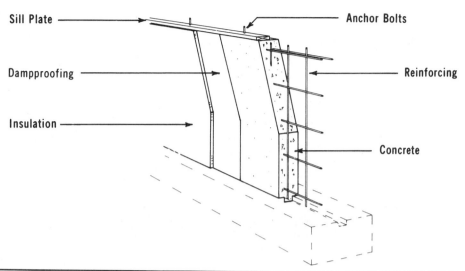

SYSTEM DESCRIPTION	QUAN.	UNIT	MAN-HOURS	MAT. COST	COST PER SQUARE FOOT
8" THICK, POURED CONCRETE WALL					
Concrete, 8" thick, 3000 psi	.025	C.Y		1.68	
Forms, prefabricated plywood, 4 uses per month	2.000	SFCA	.098	.64	
Reinforcing, light	.670	Lb.	.003	.23	
Placing concrete, direct chute	.025	C.Y.	.013		
Dampproofing, brushed on, 2 coats	1.000	S.F.	.016	.19	
Rigid insulation, 1" polystyrene	1.000	S.F.	.010	.50	
Anchor bolts, 1/2" diameter, 12" long, 4' O.C.	.060	Ea.	.002	.03	
Sill plates, 2" x 4", treated	.250	L.F.	.007	.10	Contractor's Fee
TOTAL			.149	3.37	**10.15**

Wood Wall Foundation System

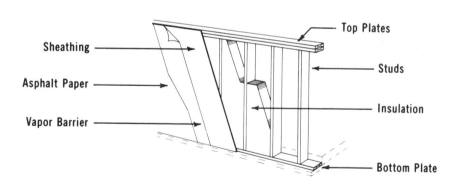

SYSTEM DESCRIPTION	QUAN.	UNIT	MAN-HOURS	MAT. COST	COST PER SQUARE FOOT
2" x 4" STUDS, 16" O.C., WALL					
Studs, 2" x 4", 16" O.C., treated	1.000	L.F.	.015	.41	
Plates, double top plate, single bottom plate, treated, 2" x 4"	.750	L.F.	.011	.31	
Sheathing, 1/2", exterior grade, CDX, treated	1.000	S.F.	.014	.68	
Asphalt paper, 15# roll	1.100	S.F.	.002	.03	
Vapor barrier, 4 mil polyethylene	1.000	S.F.	.002	.03	
Insulation, batts, fiberglass, 3-1/2" thick, R 11	1.000	S.F.	.005	.26	Contractor's Fee
TOTAL			.049	1.72	**4.31**

Be sure to read pages 155–157 for proper use of this section.

Floor Slab System

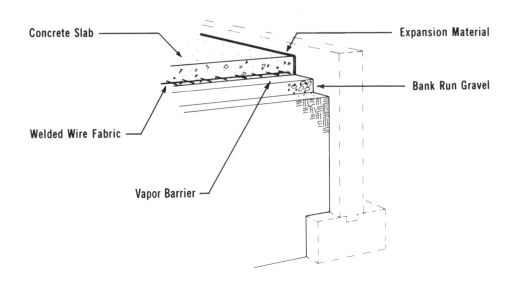

SYSTEM DESCRIPTION	QUAN.	UNIT	MAN-HOURS	MAT. COST	COST PER SQUARE FOOT
4" THICK SLAB					
Concrete, 4" thick, 3000 psi concrete	.012	C.Y		.80	
Place concrete, direct chute	.012	C.Y.	.005		
Bank run gravel, 4" deep	1.000	S.F.		.15	
Polyethylene vapor barrier, .006" thick	1.000	S.F.	.002	.03	
Edge forms, expansion material	.100	L.F.	.005	.02	
Welded wire fabric, 6 x 6, 10/10 (W1.4/W1.4)	1.100	S.F.	.005	.11	
Steel trowel finish	1.000	S.F.	.015		Contractor's Fee
TOTAL			.032	1.11	**2.84**

Be sure to read pages 155–157 for proper use of this section.

DIVISION 3 FRAMING

Floor Framing System

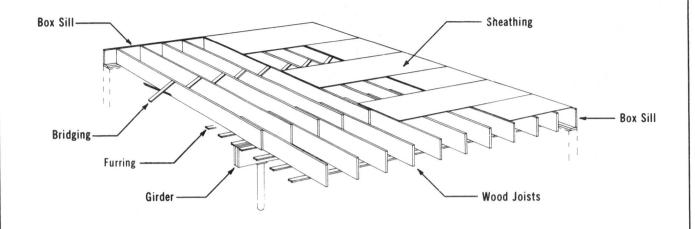

SYSTEM DESCRIPTION	QUAN.	UNIT	MAN-HOURS	MAT. COST	COST PER SQUARE FOOT
2″ X 8″, 16″ O.C.					
Wood joists, 2″ x 8″, 16″ O.C.	1.000	L.F.	.017	.69	
Bridging, 1″ x 3″, 6′ O.C.	.080	Pr.	.004	.02	
Box sills, 2″ x 8″	.150	L.F.	.002	.10	
Girder, including lally columns, 3-2″ x 8″	.125	L.F.	.015	.33	
Sheathing, plywood, subfloor, 5/8″ CDX	1.000	S.F.	.012	.53	Contractor's Fee
Furring, 1″ x 3″, 16″ O.C.	1.000	L.F.	.023	.12	**5.30**
TOTAL			.073	1.79	

Exterior Wall Framing System

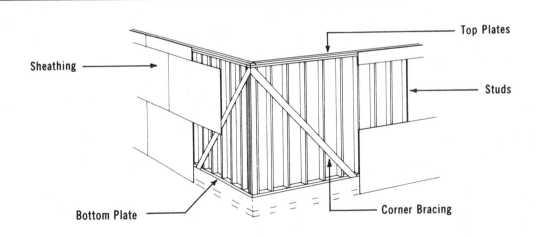

SYSTEM DESCRIPTION	QUAN.	UNIT	MAN-HOURS	MAT. COST	COST PER SQUARE FOOT
2″ x 4″, 16″ O.C.					
2″ x 4″ studs, 16″ O.C.	1.000	L.F.	.015	.32	
Plates, 2″ x 4″, double top, single bottom	.375	L.F.	.005	.12	
Corner bracing, let-in, 1″ x 6″	.063	L.F.	.003	.01	Contractor's Fee
Sheathing, 1/2″ plywood, CDX	1.000	S.F.	.013	.63	**2.92**
TOTAL			.036	1.08	

Be sure to read pages 155–157 for proper use of this section.

Gable End Roof Framing System

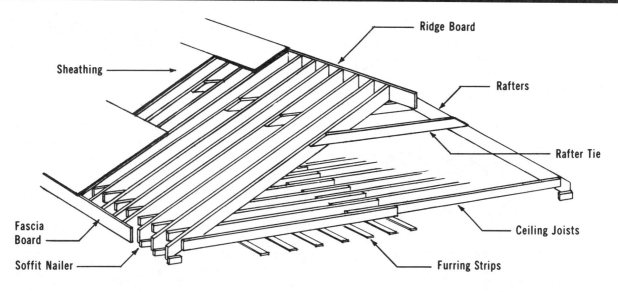

SYSTEM DESCRIPTION	QUAN.	UNIT	MAN-HOURS	MAT. COST	COST PER SQUARE FOOT
2" X 8" RAFTERS, 16" O.C., 4/12 PITCH					
Rafters, 2" x 8", 16" O.C., 4/12 pitch	1.170	L.F.	.019	.82	
Ceiling joists, 2" x 6", 16" O.C.	1.000	L.F.	.013	.47	
Ridge board, 2" x 8"	.050	L.F.	.001	.03	
Fascia board, 2" x 8"	.100	L.F.	.002	.10	
Rafter tie, 1" x 4", 4' O.C.	.060	L.F.	.001	.01	
Soffit nailer (outrigger), 2" x 4", 24" O.C.	.170	L.F.	.004	.06	
Sheathing, exterior, plywood, CDX, 1/2" thick	1.170	S.F.	.012	.58	
Furring strips, 1" x 3", 16" O.C.	1.000	L.F.	.023	.12	Contractor's Fee
TOTAL			.075	2.19	**6.10**

Truss Roof Framing System

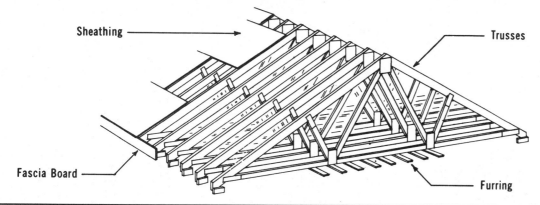

SYSTEM DESCRIPTION	QUAN.	UNIT	MAN-HOURS	MAT. COST	COST PER SQUARE FOOT
TRUSS, 16" O.C., 4/12 PITCH, INCLUDING 1' OVERHANG 26' SPAN					
Truss, 40# loading, 16" O.C., 4/12 pitch, 26' span	.030	Ea.	.021	1.78	
Fascia board, 2" x 6"	.100	L.F.	.005	.06	
Sheathing, exterior, plywood, CDX, 1/2" thick	1.170	S.F.	.012	.58	
Furring, 1" x 3", 16" O.C.	1.000	L.F.	.023	.12	Contractor's Fee
TOTAL			.061	2.54	**6.10**

Be sure to read pages 155–157 for proper use of this section.

Hip Roof Framing System

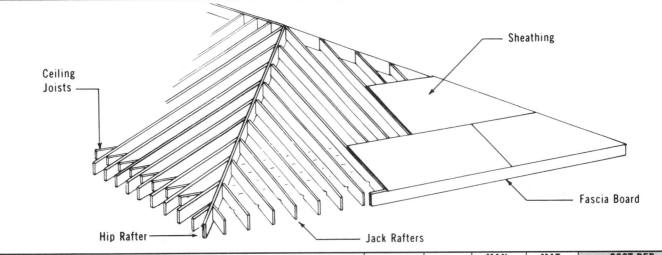

SYSTEM DESCRIPTION	QUAN.	UNIT	MAN-HOURS	MAT. COST	COST PER SQUARE FOOT
2" X 8", 16" O.C., 4/12 PITCH					
Hip rafters, 2" x 8", 4/12 pitch	.160	L.F.	.003	.11	
Jack rafters, 2" x 8", 16" O.C., 4/12 pitch	1.430	L.F.	.047	.99	
Ceiling joists, 2" x 6", 16" O.C.	1.000	L.F.	.013	.47	
Fascia board, 2" x 8"	.220	L.F.	.015	.15	
Soffit nailer (outrigger), 2" x 4", 24" O.C.	.220	L.F.	.005	.07	
Sheathing, 1/2" exterior plywood, CDX	1.570	S.F.	.017	.78	
Furring strips, 1" x 3", 16" O.C.	1.000	L.F.	.023	.12	**Contractor's Fee 8.40**
TOTAL			.123	2.69	

Gambrel Roof Framing System

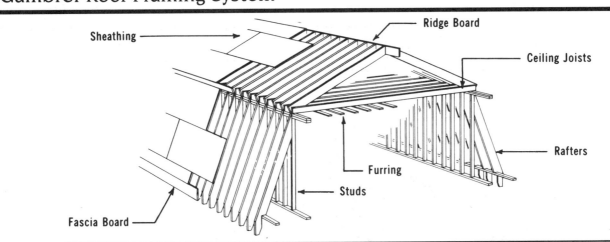

SYSTEM DESCRIPTION	QUAN.	UNIT	MAN-HOURS	MAT. COST	COST PER SQUARE FOOT
2" x 6" RAFTERS, 16" O.C.					
Roof rafters, 2" x 6", 16" O.C.	1.430	L.F.	.028	.67	
Ceiling joists, 2" x 6", 16" O.C.	.710	L.F.	.009	.34	
Stud wall, 2" x 4", 16" O.C., including plates	.790	L.F.	.012	.25	
Furring strips, 1" x 3", 16" O.C.	.710	L.F.	.016	.09	
Ridge board, 2" x 8"	.050	L.F.	.001	.03	
Fascia board, 2" x 6"	.100	L.F.	.005	.06	
Sheathing, exterior grade plywood, 1/2" thick	1.450	S.F.	.015	.72	**Contractor's Fee 6.40**
TOTAL			.086	2.16	

Be sure to read pages 155–157 for proper use of this section.

Mansard Roof Framing System

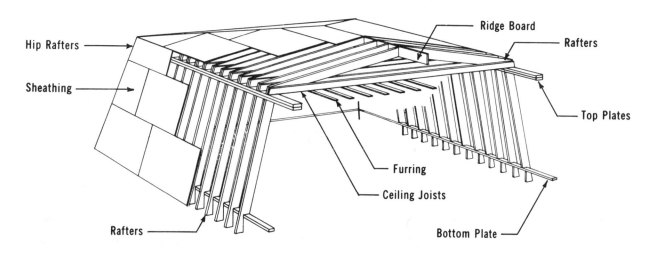

SYSTEM DESCRIPTION	QUAN.	UNIT	MAN-HOURS	MAT. COST	COST PER SQUARE FOOT
2" X 6" RAFTERS, 16" O.C.					
Roof rafters, 2" x 6", 16" O.C.	1.210	L.F.	.032	.57	
Rafter plates, 2" x 6", double top, single bottom	.364	L.F.	.009	.18	
Ceiling joists, 2" x 4", 16" O.C.	.920	L.F.	.011	.30	
Hip rafter, 2" x 6"	.070	L.F.	.002	.03	
Jack rafter, 2" x 6", 16" O.C.	1.000	L.F.	.039	.47	
Ridge board, 2" x 6"	.018	L.F.		.01	
Sheathing, exterior grade plywood, 1/2" thick	2.210	S.F.	.024	1.09	
Furring strips, 1" x 3", 16" O.C.	.920	L.F.	.021	.11	Contractor's Fee
TOTAL			.138	2.76	**9.05**

Shed/Flat Roof Framing System

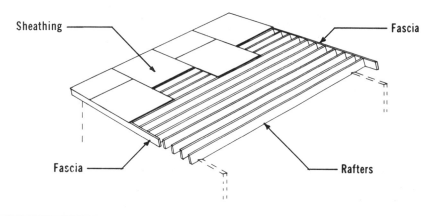

SYSTEM DESCRIPTION	QUAN.	UNIT	MAN-HOURS	MAT. COST	COST PER SQUARE FOOT
2" x 6", 16" O.C., 4/12 PITCH					
Rafters, 2" x 6", 16" O.C., 4/12 pitch	1.170	L.F.	.018	.55	
Fascia, 2" x 6"	.100	L.F.	.005	.06	
Bridging, 1" x 3", 6' O.C.	.080	Pr.	.004	.02	
Sheathing, exterior grade plywood, 1/2" thick	1.230	S.F.	.013	.61	Contractor's Fee
TOTAL			.040	1.24	**6.40**

Be sure to read pages 155–157 for proper use of this section.

Gable Dormer Framing System

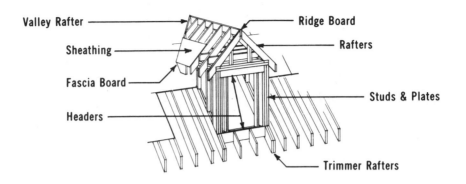

SYSTEM DESCRIPTION	QUAN.	UNIT	MAN-HOURS	MAT. COST	COST PER SQUARE FOOT
2" X 6", 16" O.C.					
Dormer rafter, 2" x 6", 16" O.C.	1.330	L.F.	.035	.63	
Ridge board, 2" x 6"	.280	L.F.	.008	.13	
Trimmer rafters, 2" x 6"	.880	L.F.	.014	.42	
Wall studs & plates, 2" x 4", 16" O.C.	3.160	L.F.	.056	1.01	
Fascia, 2" x 6"	.220	L.F.	.012	.12	
Valley rafter, 2" x 6", 16" O.C.	.280	L.F.	.008	.13	
Cripple rafter, 2" x 6", 16" O.C.	.560	L.F.	.021	.26	
Headers, 2" x 6", doubled	.670	L.F.	.020	.32	
Ceiling joist, 2" x 4", 16" O.C.	1.000	L.F.	.013	.32	
Sheathing, exterior grade plywood, 1/2" thick	.610	S.F.	.046	2.27	Contractor's Fee
TOTAL			.233	5.61	**16.75**

Shed Dormer Framing System

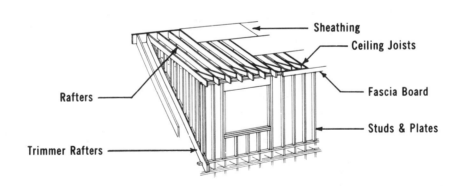

SYSTEM DESCRIPTION	QUAN.	UNIT	MAN-HOURS	MAT. COST	COST PER SQUARE FOOT
2" x 6" RAFTERS, 16" O.C.					
Dormer rafter, 2" x 6", 16" O.C.	1.080	L.F.	.029	.51	
Trimmer rafter, 2" x 6"	.400	L.F.	.006	.19	
Studs & plates, 2" x 4", 16" O.C.	2.750	L.F.	.049	.88	
Fascia, 2" x 6"	.250	L.F.	.013	.13	
Ceiling joist, 2" x 4", 16" O.C.	1.000	L.F.	.013	.32	
Sheathing, exterior grade plywood, CDX, 1/2" thick	2.940	S.F.	.038	1.85	Contractor's Fee
TOTAL			.148	3.88	**11.05**

Be sure to read pages 155–157 for proper use of this section.

Partition Framing System

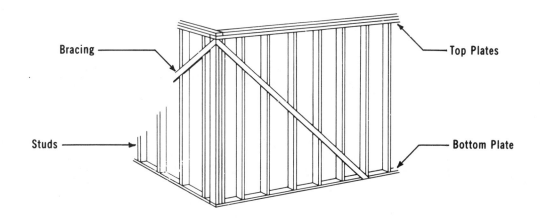

Bracing

Top Plates

Studs

Bottom Plate

SYSTEM DESCRIPTION	QUAN.	UNIT	MAN-HOURS	MAT. COST	COST PER SQUARE FOOT
2" X 4", 16" O.C.					
2" x 4" studs, #2 or better, 16" O.C.	1.000	L.F.	.015	.32	
Plates, double top, single bottom	.375	L.F.	.005	.12	
Cross bracing, let-in, 1" x 6"	.080	L.F.	.004	.02	Contractor's Fee
					1.41
TOTAL			.024	.46	
2" x 4", 24" O.C.					
2" x 4" studs, #2 or better, 24" O.C.	.800	L.F.	.012	.25	
Plates, double top, single bottom	.375	L.F.	.005	.12	
Cross bracing, let-in, 1" x 6"	.080	L.F.	.002	.02	Contractor's Fee
					1.29
TOTAL			.019	.39	
2" x 6", 16" O.C.					
2" x 6" studs, #2 or better, 16" O.C.	1.000	L.F.	.016	.47	
Plates, double top, single bottom	.375	L.F.	.006	.18	
Cross bracing, let-in, 1" x 6"	.080	L.F.	.004	.02	Contractor's Fee
					1.91
TOTAL			.026	.67	
2" x 6", 24" O.C.					
2" x 6" studs, #2 or better, 24" O.C.	.800	L.F.	.012	.37	
Plates, double top, single bottom	.375	L.F.	.006	.18	
Cross bracing, let-in, 1" x 6"	.080	L.F.	.002	.02	Contractor's Fee
					1.60
TOTAL			.020	.57	

Be sure to read pages 155–157 for proper use of this section.

DIVISION 4
EXTERIOR WALLS

Block Masonry System

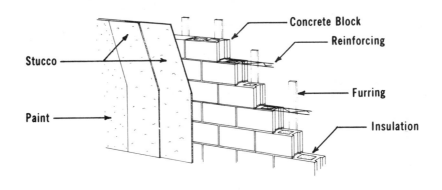

SYSTEM DESCRIPTION	QUAN.	UNIT	MAN-HOURS	MAT. COST	COST PER SQUARE FOOT
8" THICK CONCRETE BLOCK WALL					
8" thick concrete block, 8" x 8" x 16"	1.000	S.F.	.107	1.45	
Masonry reinforcing, truss strips every other course	.625	L.F.	.001	.14	
Furring, 1" x 3", 16" O.C.	1.000	L.F.	.016	.13	
Masonry insulation, poured vermiculite	1.000	S.F.	.017	.96	
Stucco, 2 coats	1.000	S.F.	.068	.21	
Masonry paint, 2 coats	1.000	S.F.	.022	.20	Contractor's Fee
TOTAL			.231	3.09	**12.00**

Brick Veneer System

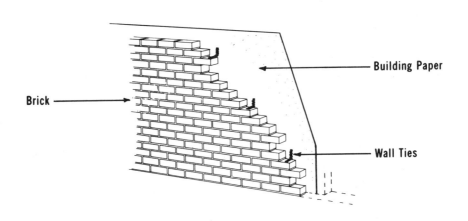

SYSTEM DESCRIPTION	QUAN.	UNIT	MAN-HOURS	MAT. COST	COST PER SQUARE FOOT
COMMON BRICK					
Brick, common, running bond	1.000	S.F.	.174	2.26	
Wall ties, 7/8" x 7", 24 gauge	1.000	Ea.	.008	.04	
Building paper, #15 asphalt	1.100	S.F.	.002	.03	
Trim, pine, painted	.125	L.F.	.004	.06	Contractor's Fee
TOTAL			.188	2.39	**9.50**

Be sure to read pages 155–157 for proper use of this section.

Wood Siding System

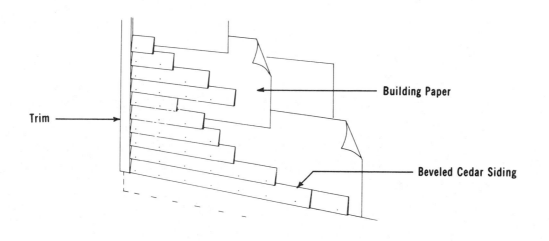

Trim

Building Paper

Beveled Cedar Siding

SYSTEM DESCRIPTION	QUAN.	UNIT	MAN-HOURS	MAT. COST	COST PER SQUARE FOOT
1/2" X 6" BEVELED CEDAR SIDING, "A" GRADE					
1/2" x 6" beveled cedar siding	1.000	S.F.	.032	1.97	
#15 asphalt felt paper	1.100	S.F.	.002	.03	
Trim, cedar	.125	L.F.	.005	.12	
Paint, primer & 2 coats	1.000	S.F.	.017	.21	Contractor's Fee
TOTAL			.056	2.33	**5.30**
1/2" x 8" BEVELED CEDAR SIDING, "A" GRADE					
1/2" x 8" beveled cedar siding	1.000	S.F.	.029	2.27	
#15 asphalt felt paper	1.100	S.F.	.002	.03	
Trim, cedar	.125	L.F.	.005	.12	
Paint, primer & 2 coats	1.000	S.F.	.017	.21	Contractor's Fee
TOTAL			.053	2.63	**5.65**
1" x 4" TONGUE & GROOVE, VERTICAL, REDWOOD, VERTICAL GRAIN					
1" x 4" tongue & groove, vertical, redwood	1.000	S.F.	.033	2.83	
#15 asphalt felt paper	1.100	S.F.	.002	.03	
Trim, redwood	.125	L.F.	.005	.12	
Sealer, 1 coat, stain, 1 coat	1.000	S.F.	.012	.14	Contractor's Fee
TOTAL			.052	3.12	**6.40**
1" x 6" TONGUE & GROOVE, VERTICAL, REDWOOD, VERTICAL GRAIN					
1" x 6" tongue & groove, vertical, redwood	1.000	S.F.	.024	2.63	
#15 asphalt felt paper	1.100	S.F.	.002	.03	
Trim, redwood	.125	L.F.	.005	.12	
Sealer, 1 coat, stain, 1 coat	1.000	S.F.	.012	.14	Contractor's Fee
TOTAL			.043	2.92	**5.75**

Be sure to read pages 155–157 for proper use of this section.

Shingle Siding System

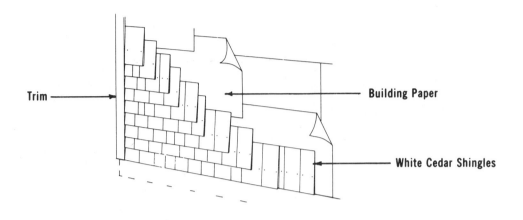

Trim

Building Paper

White Cedar Shingles

SYSTEM DESCRIPTION	QUAN.	UNIT	MAN-HOURS	MAT. COST	COST PER SQUARE FOOT
WHITE CEDAR SHINGLES, 5" EXPOSURE					
White cedar shingles, 16" long, grade "A", 5" exposure	1.000	S.F.	.033	1.33	
#15 asphalt felt paper	1.100	S.F.	.002	.03	
Trim, cedar	.125	L.F.	.005	.12	Contractor's Fee
Paint, primer & 1 coat	1.000	S.F.	.013	.13	
TOTAL			.053	1.61	**4.13**
NO. 1 PERFECTIONS, 5-1/2" EXPOSURE					
No. 1 perfections, red cedar, 5-1/2" exposure	1.000	S.F.	.029	1.40	
#15 asphalt felt paper	1.100	S.F.	.002	.03	
Trim, cedar	.125	L.F.	.005	.12	Contractor's Fee
Stain, sealer & 1 coat	1.000	S.F.	.013	.13	
TOTAL			.049	1.68	**4.14**
RESQUARED & REBUTTED PERFECTIONS, 5-1/2" EXPOSURE					
Resquared & rebutted perfections, 5-1/2" exposure	1.000	S.F.	.026	1.11	
#15 asphalt felt paper	1.100	S.F.	.002	.03	
Trim, cedar	.125	L.F.	.005	.12	Contractor's Fee
Stain, sealer & 1 coat	1.000	S.F.	.013	.13	
TOTAL			.046	1.39	**3.58**
HAND-SPLIT SHAKES, 8-1/2" EXPOSURE					
Hand-split red cedar shakes, 18" long, 8-1/2" exposure	1.000	S.F.	.040	.97	
#15 asphalt felt paper	1.100	S.F.	.002	.03	
Trim, cedar	.125	L.F.	.005	.12	Contractor's Fee
Stain, sealer & 1 coat	1.000	S.F.	.013	.13	
TOTAL			.060	1.25	**3.86**

Be sure to read pages 155–157 for proper use of this section.

Metal & Plastic Siding

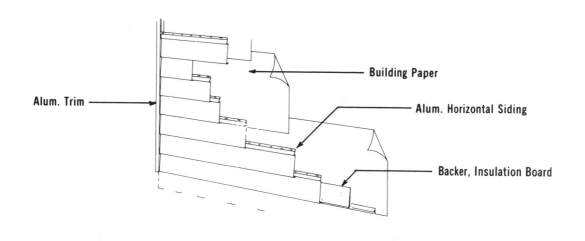

Building Paper

Alum. Trim

Alum. Horizontal Siding

Backer, Insulation Board

SYSTEM DESCRIPTION	QUAN.	UNIT	MAN-HOURS	MAT. COST	COST PER SQUARE FOOT
ALUMINUM CLAPBOARD SIDING, 8" WIDE, WHITE					
Aluminum horizontal siding, 8" clapboard	1.000	S.F.	.031	1.13	
Backer, insulation board	1.000	S.F.	.008	.47	
Trim, aluminum	.600	L.F.	.015	.55	Contractor's Fee
Paper, #15 asphalt felt	1.100	S.F.	.002	.03	
TOTAL			.056	2.18	**5.25**
ALUMINUM VERTICAL BOARD & BATTEN, WHITE					
Aluminum vertical board & batten	1.000	S.F.	.027	1.21	
Backer, insulation board	1.000	S.F.	.008	.47	
Trim, aluminum	.600	L.F.	.015	.55	Contractor's Fee
Paper, #15 asphalt felt	1.100	S.F.	.002	.03	
TOTAL			.052	2.26	**5.25**
VINYL CLAPBOARD SIDING, 8" WIDE, WHITE					
PVC vinyl horizontal siding, 8" clapboard	1.000	S.F.	.032	.70	
Backer, insulation board	1.000	S.F.	.008	.47	
Trim, vinyl	.600	L.F.	.013	.35	Contractor's Fee
Paper, #15 asphalt felt	1.100	S.F.	.002	.03	
TOTAL			.055	1.55	**4.28**
VINYL VERTICAL BOARD & BATTEN, WHITE					
PVC vinyl vertical board & batten	1.000	S.F.	.029	.70	
Backer, insulation board	1.000	S.F.	.008	.47	
Trim, vinyl	.600	L.F.	.013	.35	Contractor's Fee
Paper, #15 asphalt felt	1.100	S.F.	.002	.03	
TOTAL			.052	1.55	**4.17**

Be sure to read pages 155–157 for proper use of this section.

Double Hung Window System

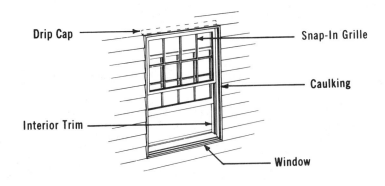

SYSTEM DESCRIPTION	QUAN.	UNIT	MAN-HOURS	MAT. COST	COST PER SQUARE FOOT
BUILDER'S QUALITY WOOD WINDOW, 2' X 3', DOUBLE HUNG					
Window, wood primed, builder's quality, 2' x 3', insulating glass	1.000	Ea.	.800	140.00	
Trim, interior casing	11.000	L.F.	.363	7.50	
Paint, interior & exterior, primer & 2 coats	2.000	Face	.888	2.71	
Caulking	10.000	L.F.	.310	.88	
Snap-in grille	1.000	Set	.333	9.10	
Drip cap, metal	2.000	L.F.	.040	.37	Contractor's Fee
TOTAL			2.734	160.56	**325.00**
PLASTIC CLAD WOOD WINDOW, 3' X 4', DOUBLE HUNG					
Window, wood, plastic clad, premium, 3' x 4', insulating glass	1.000	Ea.	.889	210.00	
Trim, interior casing	15.000	L.F.	.495	10.25	
Paint, interior, primer & 2 coats	1.000	Face	.800	4.21	
Caulking	14.000	L.F.	.434	1.23	Contractor's Fee
Snap-in grille	1.000	Set	.333	9.10	
TOTAL			2.951	234.79	**450.00**
METAL CLAD WOOD WINDOW, 3' X 5', DOUBLE HUNG					
Window, wood, metal clad, deluxe, 3' x 5', insulating glass	1.000	Ea.	1.000	310.00	
Trim, interior casing	17.000	L.F.	.561	11.60	
Paint, interior, primer & 2 coats	1.000	Face	.800	4.21	
Caulking	16.000	L.F.	.496	1.41	
Snap-in grille	1.000	Set	.235	16.00	
Drip cap, metal	3.000	L.F.	.060	.56	Contractor's Fee
TOTAL			3.152	343.78	**615.00**

Be sure to read pages 155–157 for proper use of this section.

Casement Window System

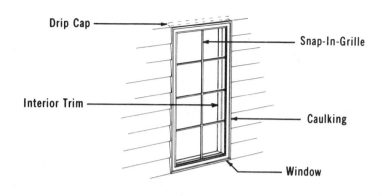

Drip Cap · Snap-In-Grille · Interior Trim · Caulking · Window

SYSTEM DESCRIPTION	QUAN.	UNIT	MAN-HOURS	MAT. COST	COST EACH
BUILDER'S QUALITY WOOD WINDOW, 2' X 3', CASEMENT					
Window, wood primed, builder's quality, 2' x 3', insulating glass	1.000	Ea.	.800	180.00	
Trim, interior casing	11.000	L.F.	.363	7.50	
Paint, interior & exterior, primer & 2 coats	2.000	Face	.888	2.71	
Caulking	10.000	L.F.	.310	.88	
Snap-in grille	1.000	Ea.	.267	10.00	
Drip cap, metal	2.000	L.F.	.040	.37	Contractor's Fee
TOTAL			2.668	201.46	**385.00**
PLASTIC CLAD WOOD WINDOW, 2' X 4', CASEMENT					
Window, wood, plastic clad, premium, 2' x 4', insulating glass	1.000	Ea.	.889	200.00	
Trim, interior casing	13.000	L.F.	.429	8.85	
Paint, interior, primer & 2 coats	1.000	Ea.	.444	1.35	
Caulking	12.000	L.F.	.372	1.06	
Snap-in grille	1.000	Ea.	.267	10.00	Contractor's Fee
TOTAL			2.401	221.26	**405.00**
METAL CLAD WOOD WINDOW, 2' X 5', CASEMENT					
Window, wood, metal clad, deluxe, 2' x 5', insulating glass	1.000	Ea.	1.000	295.00	
Trim, interior casing	15.000	L.F.	.495	10.25	
Paint, interior, primer & 2 coats	1.000	Ea.	.800	4.21	
Caulking	14.000	L.F.	.434	1.23	
Snap-in grille	1.000	Ea.	.250	13.00	
Drip cap, metal	12.000	L.F.	.040	.37	Contractor's Fee
TOTAL			3.019	324.06	**580.00**

Be sure to read pages 155–157 for proper use of this section.

Awning Window System

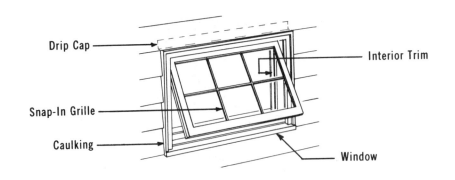

Drip Cap

Interior Trim

Snap-In Grille

Caulking

Window

SYSTEM DESCRIPTION	QUAN.	UNIT	MAN-HOURS	MAT. COST	COST EACH
BUILDER'S QUALITY WOOD WINDOW, 34" X 22", AWNING					
Window, wood primed, builder's quality, 34" x 22", insulating glass	1.000	Ea.	.800	175.00	
Trim, interior casing	10.500	L.F.	.346	7.15	
Paint, interior & exterior, primer & 2 coats	2.000	Face	.888	2.71	
Caulking	9.500	L.F.	.294	.83	
Snap-in grille	1.000	Ea.	.267	23.00	Contractor's Fee
Drip cap, metal	3.000	L.F.	.060	.56	
TOTAL			2.655	209.25	**400.00**
PLASTIC CLAD WOOD WINDOW, 40" X 28", AWNING					
Window, wood, plastic clad, premium, 40" x 28", insulating glass	1.000	Ea.	.889	230.00	
Trim, interior casing	13.500	L.F.	.445	9.20	
Paint, interior, primer & 2 coats	1.000	Face	.444	1.35	
Caulking	12.500	L.F.	.387	1.10	Contractor's Fee
Snap-in grille	1.000	Ea.	.267	23.00	
TOTAL			2.432	264.65	**475.00**
METAL CLAD WOOD WINDOW, 60" X 36", AWNING					
Window, wood, metal clad, deluxe, 60" x 36" insulating glass	1.000	Ea.	1.000	290.00	
Trim, interior casing	15.000	L.F.	.495	10.25	
Paint, interior, primer & 2 coats	1.000	Face	.800	4.21	
Caulking	14.000	L.F.	.434	1.23	
Snap-in grille	1.000	Ea.	.250	30.25	Contractor's Fee
Drip cap, metal	4.000	L.F.	.080	.74	
TOTAL			3.059	336.68	**600.00**

Be sure to read pages 155–157 for proper use of this section.

Sliding Window System

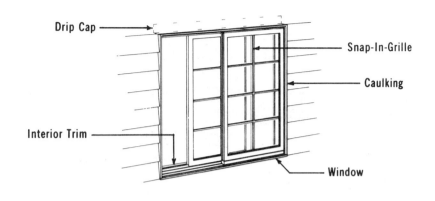

SYSTEM DESCRIPTION	QUAN.	UNIT	MAN-HOURS	MAT. COST	COST EACH
BUILDER'S QUALITY WOOD WINDOW, 3' X 3' SLIDING					
Window, wood primed, builder's quality, 3' x 3', insulating glass	1.000	Ea.	.800	150.00	
Trim, interior casing	11.000	L.F.	.363	7.50	
Paint, interior & exterior, primer & 2 coats	2.000	Face	.888	2.70	
Caulking	10.000	L.F.	.310	.88	
Snap-in grille	1.000	Set	.333	19.35	
Drip cap, metal	3.000	L.F.	.060	.56	Contractor's Fee
TOTAL			2.754	180.99	**360.00**
PLASTIC CLAD WOOD WINDOW, 4' X 3'-6", SLIDING					
Window, wood, plastic clad, premium, 4' x 3'-6", insulating glass	1.000	Ea.	.889	325.00	
Trim, interior casing	16.000	L.F.	.528	10.90	
Paint, interior, primer & 2 coats	1.000	Face	.800	4.21	
Caulking	17.000	L.F.	.527	1.50	
Snap-in grille	1.000	Set	.333	19.35	Contractor's Fee
TOTAL			3.077	360.96	**635.00**
METAL CLAD WOOD WINDOW, 6' X 5', SLIDING					
Window, wood, metal clad, deluxe, 6' x 5', insulating glass	1.000	Ea.	1.000	570.00	
Trim, interior casing	23.000	L.F.	.759	15.70	
Paint, interior, primer & 2 coats	1.000	Face	1.000	4.31	
Caulking	22.000	L.F.	.682	1.94	
Snap-in grille	1.000	Set	.364	71.00	
Drip cap, metal	6.000	L.F.	.120	1.12	Contractor's Fee
TOTAL			3.925	664.07	**1125.00**

Be sure to read pages 155–157 for proper use of this section.

Bow/Bay Window System

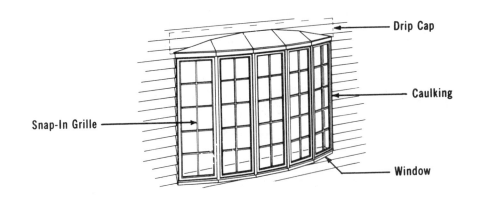

Drip Cap

Caulking

Snap-In Grille

Window

SYSTEM DESCRIPTION	QUAN.	UNIT	MAN-HOURS	MAT. COST	COST EACH
AWNING TYPE BOW WINDOW, BUILDER'S QUALITY, 8' X 5'					
Window, wood primed, builder's quality, 8' x 5', insulating glass	1.000	Ea.	1.600	840.00	
Trim, interior casing	27.000	L.F.	.891	18.40	
Paint, interior & exterior, primer & 1 coat	2.000	Face	2.000	8.60	
Drip cap, vinyl	1.000	Ea.	.533	67.00	
Caulking	26.000	L.F.	.806	2.29	Contractor's Fee
Snap-in grille	1.000	Set	1.068	40.00	
TOTAL			6.898	976.29	**1675.00**
CASEMENT TYPE BOW WINDOW, PLASTIC CLAD, 10' X 6'					
Window, wood, plastic clad, premium, 10' x 6', insulating glass	1.000	Ea.	2.290	1936.00	
Trim, interior casing	33.000	L.F.	1.089	22.50	
Paint, interior, primer & 1 coat	1.000	Face	1.600	8.45	
Drip cap, vinyl	1.000	Ea.	.615	73.00	
Caulking	32.000	L.F.	.992	2.82	Contractor's Fee
Snap-in grille	1.000	Set	1.335	50.00	
TOTAL			7.921	2092.77	**3345.00**
DOUBLE HUNG TYPE, METAL CLAD, 9' X 5'					
Window, wood, metal clad, deluxe, 9' x 5', insulating glass	1.000	Ea.	2.670	1585.00	
Trim, interior casing	29.000	L.F.	.957	19.75	
Paint, interior, primer & 1 coat	1.000	Face	1.600	8.45	
Drip cap, vinyl	1.000	Ea.	.615	73.00	
Caulking	28.000	L.F.	.868	2.46	Contractor's Fee
Snap-in grille	1.000	Set	1.068	40.00	
TOTAL			7.778	1728.66	**2815.00**

Be sure to read pages 155–157 for proper use of this section.

Picture Window System

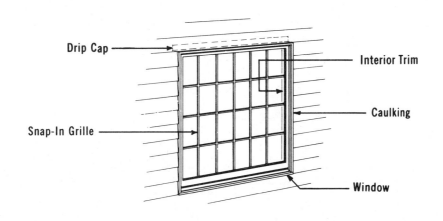

SYSTEM DESCRIPTION	QUAN.	UNIT	MAN-HOURS	MAT. COST	COST EACH
BUILDER'S QUALITY PICTURE WINDOW, 3'-6" X 4'					
Window, wood, primed, builder's quality, 3'-6" x 4', insulating glass	1.000	Ea.	1.330	230.00	
Trim, interior casing	17.000	L.F.	.561	11.60	
Paint, interior & exterior, primer & 2 coats	2.000	Face	1.600	8.45	
Caulking	16.000	L.F.	.496	1.41	
Snap-in grille	1.000	Ea.	.267	67.00	Contractor's Fee
Drip cap, metal	4.000	L.F.	.080	.75	
TOTAL			4.334	319.21	**620.00**
PLASTIC CLAD WOOD WINDOW, 4' X 6'					
Window, wood, plastic clad, premium, 4' x 6', insulating glass	1.000	Ea.	1.450	355.00	
Trim, interior casing	23.000	L.F.	.759	15.70	
Paint, interior, primer & 2 coats	1.000	Face	.800	4.21	
Caulking	22.000	L.F.	.682	1.94	
Snap-in grille	1.000	Ea.	.267	67.00	Contractor's Fee
TOTAL			3.958	443.85	**795.00**
METAL CLAD WOOD WINDOW, 6' X 6'					
Window, wood, metal clad, deluxe, 6' x 6', insulating glass	1.000	Ea.	1.600	765.00	
Trim, interior casing	27.000	L.F.	.891	18.40	
Paint, interior, primer & 2 coats	1.000	Face	1.000	4.31	
Caulking	26.000	L.F.	.806	2.29	
Snap-in grille	1.000	Ea.	.267	67.00	
Drip cap, metal	6.500	L.F.	.130	1.22	Contractor's Fee
TOTAL			4.694	858.22	**1425.00**

Be sure to read pages 155–157 for proper use of this section.

Entrance Door System

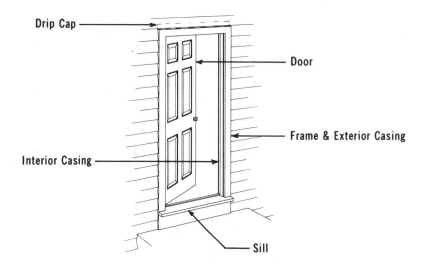

Drip Cap

Door

Frame & Exterior Casing

Interior Casing

Sill

SYSTEM DESCRIPTION	QUAN.	UNIT	MAN-HOURS	MAT. COST	COST EACH
COLONIAL, 6 PANEL, 3' X 6'-8", WOOD					
Door, 3' x 6'-8" x 1-3/4" thick, pine, 6 panel colonial	1.000	Ea.	1.070	188.00	
Frame, pine, 5-13/16" deep, including exterior casing & drip cap	17.000	L.F.	.731	62.00	
Interior casing, 2-1/2" wide	18.000	L.F.	.594	12.30	
Sill, 8/4 x 8" deep	3.000	L.F.	.480	31.00	
Butt hinges, brass, 4-1/2" x 4-1/2"	1.500	Pr.		19.05	
Lockset	1.000	Ea.	.571	21.00	
Weatherstripping, metal, spring type, bronze	1.000	Set	1.050	7.25	Contractor's Fee
Paint, interior & exterior, primer & 2 coats	2.000	Face	4.580	19.50	
TOTAL			9.076	360.10	**830.00**
SOLID CORE BIRCH, FLUSH 3' X 6'-8"					
Door, 3' x 6'-8", 1-3/4" thick, birch, flush solid core	1.000	Ea.	1.070	85.00	
Frame, pine, 5-13/16" deep, including exterior casing & drip cap	17.000	L.F.	.731	62.00	
Interior casing, 2-1/2" wide	18.000	L.F.	.594	12.30	
Sill, 8/4 x 8" deep	3.000	L.F.	.480	31.00	
Butt hinges, brass, 4-1/2" x 4-1/2"	1.500	Pr.		19.05	
Lockset	1.000	Ea.	.571	21.00	
Weatherstripping, metal, spring type, bronze	1.000	Set	1.050	7.25	Contractor's Fee
Paint, interior & exterior, primer & 2 coats	2.000	Face	4.260	9.90	
TOTAL			8.756	247.50	**655.00**

Be sure to read pages 155–157 for proper use of this section.

Sliding Door System

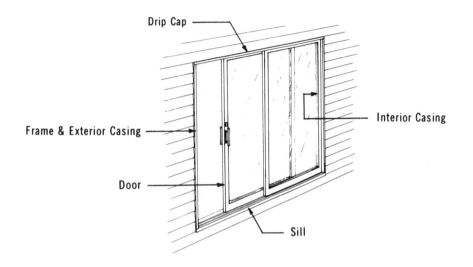

Drip Cap

Interior Casing

Frame & Exterior Casing

Door

Sill

SYSTEM DESCRIPTION	QUAN.	UNIT	MAN-HOURS	MAT. COST	COST EACH
WOOD SLIDING DOOR, 8' WIDE, PREMIUM					
Wood 5/8" thick, tempered insul. glass, 8' wide, premium	1.000	Ea.	5.330	1000.00	
Interior casing	22.000	L.F.	.726	15.00	
Exterior casing	22.000	L.F.	.726	15.00	
Sill, oak, 8/4 x 8" deep	8.000	L.F.	1.280	82.00	
Drip cap	8.000	L.F.	.160	1.50	
Paint, interior & exterior, primer & 2 coats	2.000	Face	2.992	10.65	Contractor's Fee
TOTAL			11.214	1124.15	**2075.00**
ALUMINUM SLIDING DOOR, 8' WIDE, PREMIUM					
Aluminum 5/8" thick, tempered insul. glass, 8' wide, premium	1.000	Ea.	5.330	555.00	
Interior casing	22.000	L.F.	.726	15.00	
Exterior casing	22.000	L.F.	.726	15.00	
Sill, oak, 8/4 x 8" deep	8.000	L.F.	1.280	82.00	
Drip cap	8.000	L.F.	.160	1.50	
Paint, interior & exterior, primer & 2 coats	2.000	Face	1.496	5.32	Contractor's Fee
TOTAL			9.718	673.80	**1330.00**

Be sure to read pages 155–157 for proper use of this section.

Garage Door System

Exterior Trim

Drip Cap

Door

Jamb

Weatherstripping

SYSTEM DESCRIPTION	QUAN.	UNIT	MAN-HOURS	MAT. COST	COST EACH
OVERHEAD, SECTIONAL GARAGE DOOR, 9' X 7'					
Wood, overhead sectional door, standard, including hardware, 9' x 7'	1.000	Ea.	2.000	455.00	
Jamb & header blocking, 2" x 6"	25.000	L.F.	.900	11.85	
Exterior trim	25.000	L.F.	.825	17.05	
Paint, interior & exterior, primer & 2 coats	2.000	Face	9.160	39.00	
Weatherstripping, molding type	1.000	Set	.759	15.70	
Drip cap	9.000	L.F.	.180	1.68	Contractor's Fee **1250.00**
TOTAL			13.824	540.28	
OVERHEAD, SECTIONAL GARAGE DOOR, 16' x 7'					
Wood, overhead sectional door, standard, including hardware, 16' x 7'	1.000	Ea.	2.670	845.00	
Jamb & header blocking, 2" x 6"	30.000	L.F.	1.080	14.20	
Exterior trim	30.000	L.F.	.990	20.00	
Paint, interior & exterior, primer & 2 coats	2.000	Face	13.740	58.00	
Weatherstripping, molding type	1.000	Set	.990	20.00	
Drip cap	16.000	L.F.	.320	2.99	Contractor's Fee **2050.00**
TOTAL			19.790	960.19	
OVERHEAD, SWING-UP TYPE, GARAGE DOOR, 16' X 7'					
Wood, overhead, swing-up type, standard, including hardware, 16' x 7'	1.000	Ea.	2.670	470.00	
Jamb & header blocking, 2" x 6"	30.000	L.F.	1.080	14.20	
Exterior trim	30.000	L.F.	.990	20.00	
Paint, interior & exterior, primer & 2 coats	2.000	Face	13.740	59.00	
Weatherstripping, molding type	1.000	Set	.990	20.00	
Drip cap	16.000	L.F.	.320	2.99	Contractor's Fee **1500.00**
TOTAL			19.790	586.19	

Be sure to read pages 155–157 for proper use of this section.

Aluminum Window System

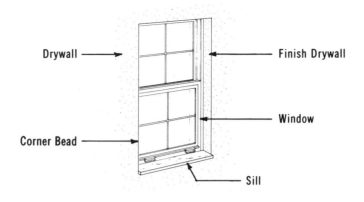

Drywall → ← Finish Drywall

← Window

Corner Bead → ← Sill

SYSTEM DESCRIPTION	QUAN.	UNIT	MAN-HOURS	MAT. COST	COST EACH
SINGLE HUNG, 2' X 3' OPENING					
Window, single hung, 2' x 3' opening, enameled, insulating glass	1.000	Ea.	1.600	175.00	
Blocking, 1" x 3" furring strip, nailers	10.000	L.F.	.150	1.21	
Drywall, 1/2" thick, standard	5.000	S.F.	.040	1.21	
Corner bead, 1" x 1", galvanized steel	8.000	L.F.	.224	.79	
Finish drywall, tape and finish corners, inside and outside	16.000	L.F.	.240	1.23	Contractor's Fee
Sill, slate	2.000	L.F.	.400	13.30	
TOTAL			2.654	192.74	**390.00**
SLIDING, 3' X 2' OPENING					
Window, sliding, 3' x 2' opening, enameled, insulating glass	1.000	Ea.	1.600	120.00	
Blocking, 1" x 3" furring strip, nailers	10.000	L.F.	.150	1.21	
Drywall, 1/2" thick, standard	5.000	S.F.	.040	1.21	
Corner bead, 1" x 1", galvanized steel	7.000	L.F.	.196	.69	
Finish drywall, tape and finish corners, inside and outside	14.000	L.F.	.210	1.08	Contractor's Fee
Sill, slate	3.000	L.F.	.600	20.00	
TOTAL			2.796	144.19	**320.00**
AWNING, 3'-1" X 3'-2"					
Window awning, 3'-1" opening, enameled, insulating glass	1.000	Ea.	1.600	160.00	
Blocking, 1" x 3" furring strip, nailers	12.500	L.F.	.187	1.52	
Drywall, 1/2" thick, standard	4.500	S.F.	.036	1.10	
Corner bead, 1" x 1", galvanized steel	9.250	L.F.	.259	.91	
Finish drywall, tape and finish corners, inside and outside	18.500	L.F.	.277	1.43	Contractor's Fee
Sill, slate	3.250	L.F.	.650	21.00	
TOTAL			3.009	185.96	**390.00**

Be sure to read pages 155–157 for proper use of this section.

Storm Door & Window System

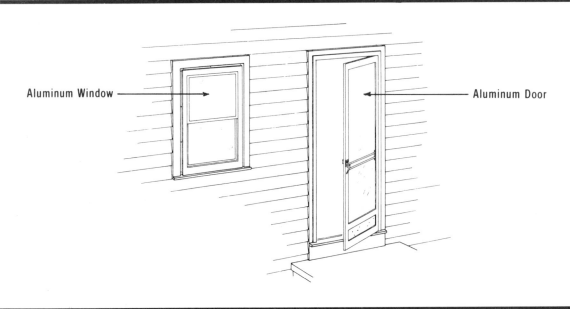

Aluminum Window

Aluminum Door

SYSTEM DESCRIPTION	QUAN.	UNIT	MAN-HOURS	COST EACH	
				MAT.	TOTAL
Storm door, aluminum, combination, storm & screen, anodized, 2'-6" x 6'-8"	1.000	Ea.	1.070	175.00	300.00
2'-8" x 6'-8"	1.000	Ea.	1.140	180.00	305.00
3'-0" x 6'-8"	1.000	Ea.	1.140	195.00	330.00
Mill finish, 2'-6" x 6'-8"	1.000	Ea.	1.070	165.00	280.00
2'-8" x 6'-8"	1.000	Ea.	1.140	165.00	280.00
3'-0" x 6'-8"	1.000	Ea.	1.140	170.00	290.00
Painted, 2'-6" x 6'-8"	1.000	Ea.	1.070	180.00	305.00
2'-8" x 6'-8"	1.000	Ea.	1.140	185.00	315.00
3'-0" x 6'-8"	1.000	Ea.	1.140	185.00	315.00
Wood, combination, storm & screen, crossbuck, 2'-6" x 6'-9"	1.000	Ea.	1.450	180.00	320.00
2'-8" x 6'-9"	1.000	Ea.	1.600	180.00	330.00
3'-0" x 6'-9"	1.000	Ea.	1.780	230.00	345.00
Full lite, 2'-6" x 6'-9"	1.000	Ea.	1.450	145.00	265.00
2'-8" x 6'-9"	1.000	Ea.	1.600	150.00	280.00
3'-0" x 6'-9"	1.000	Ea.	1.780	155.00	295.00
Windows, aluminum, combination, storm & screen, basement, 1'-10" x 1'-0"	1.000	Ea.	.533	30.00	65.00
2'-9" x 1'-6"	1.000	Ea.	.533	31.00	65.00
3'-4" x 2'-0"	1.000	Ea.	.533	28.00	60.00
Double hung, anodized, 2'-0" x 3'-5"	1.000	Ea.	.533	57.00	100.00
2'-6" x 5'-0"	1.000	Ea.	.571	63.00	115.00
4'-0" x 6'-0"	1.000	Ea.	.640	115.00	140.00
Painted, 2'-0" x 3'-5"	1.000	Ea.	.533	56.00	100.00
2'-6" x 5'-0"	1.000	Ea.	.571	57.00	105.00
4'-0" x 6'-0"	1.000	Ea.	.640	75.00	135.00
Fixed window, anodized, 4'-6" x 4'-6"	1.000	Ea.	.640	105.00	175.00
5'-8" x 4'-6"	1.000	Ea.	.800	120.00	210.00
Painted, 4'-6" x 4'-6"	1.000	Ea.	.640	96.00	160.00
5'-8" x 4'-6"	1.000	Ea.	.800	110.00	190.00

Be sure to read pages 155–157 for proper use of this section.

Shutter/Blinds System

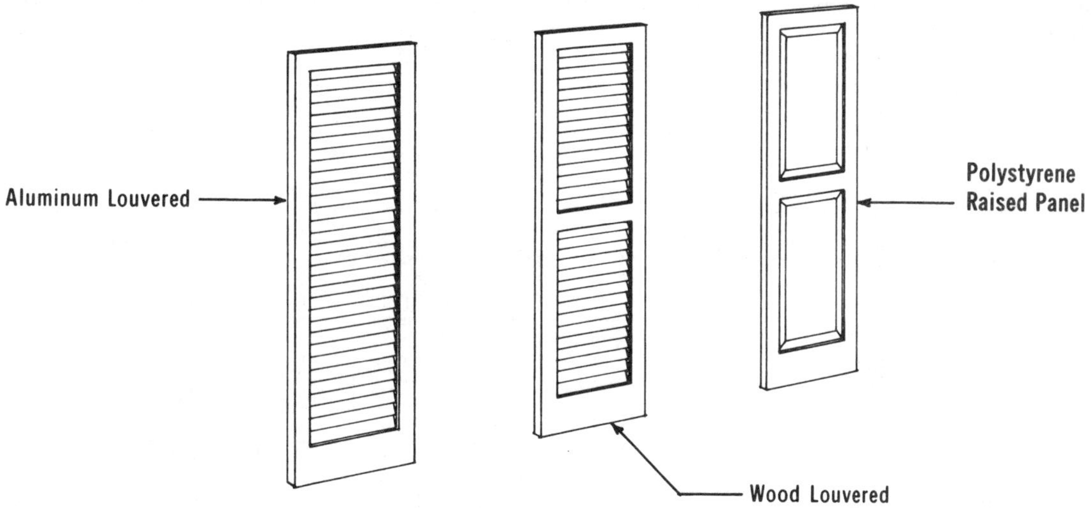

Aluminum Louvered

Polystyrene Raised Panel

Wood Louvered

SYSTEM DESCRIPTION	QUAN.	UNIT	MAN-HOURS	COST PER PAIR	
				MAT.	TOTAL
Shutters, exterior blinds, aluminum, louvered, 1'-4" wide, 3'-0" long	1.000	Set	.800	35.00	78.00
4'-0" long	1.000	Set	.800	38.00	82.00
5'-4" long	1.000	Set	.800	41.00	89.00
6'-8" long	1.000	Set	.889	54.00	110.00
Wood, louvered, 1'-2" wide, 3'-3" long	1.000	Set	.800	47.00	96.00
4'-7" long	1.000	Set	.800	65.00	125.00
5'-3" long	1.000	Set	.800	58.00	110.00
1'-6" wide, 3'-3" long	1.000	Set	.800	54.00	110.00
4'-7" long	1.000	Set	.800	74.00	135.00
Polystryrene, solid raised panel, 3'-3" wide, 3'-0" long	1.000	Set	.800	70.00	130.00
3'-11" long	1.000	Set	.800	81.00	150.00
5'-3" long	1.000	Set	.800	97.00	170.00
6'-8" long	1.000	Set	.889	130.00	225.00
Polystyrene, louvered, 1'-2" wide, 3'-3" long	1.000	Set	.800	29.00	78.00
4'-7" long	1.000	Set	.800	38.00	82.00
5'-3" long	1.000	Set	.800	42.00	90.00
6'-8" long	1.000	Set	.889	56.00	115.00
Vinyl, louvered, 1'-2" wide, 4'-7" long	1.000	Set	.720	33.00	72.00
1'-4" wide, 6'-8" long	1.000	Set	.889	54.00	110.00

Be sure to read pages 155–157 for proper use of this section.

Insulation

DESCRIPTION	QUAN.	UNIT	MAN-HOURS	COST PER S.F. MAT.	COST PER S.F. TOTAL
Poured insulation, cellulose fiber, R3.8 per inch	1.000	S.F.	.003	.04	.18
Fiberglass, R4.0 per inch	1.000	S.F.	.003	.03	.15
Mineral wool, R3.0 per inch	1.000	S.F.	.003	.08	.24
Polystyrene, R4.0 per inch	1.000	S.F.	.003	.17	.36
Vermiculite, R2.7 per inch	1.000	S.F.	.003	.18	.38
Perlite, R2.7 per inch	1.000	S.F.	.003	.18	.38
Reflective, aluminum foil on kraft paper, foil one side, R9	1.000	S.F.	.004	.03	.19
Multilayered with air spaces, 2 ply, R14	1.000	S.F.	.004	.19	.41
3 ply, R17	1.000	S.F.	.005	.23	.52
5 ply, R22	1.000	S.F.	.005	.34	.68
Rigid insulation, fiberglass, unfaced,					
1-1/2" thick, R6.2	1.000	S.F.	.008	.47	.96
2" thick, R8.3	1.000	S.F.	.009	.61	1.17
2-1/2" thick, R10.3	1.000	S.F.	.010	.95	1.75
3" thick, R12.4	1.000	S.F.	.010	.95	1.75
Foil faced, 1" thick, R4.3	1.000	S.F.	.008	1.29	2.18
1-1/2" thick, R6.2	1.000	S.F.	.009	1.62	2.68
2" thick, R8.7	1.000	S.F.	.009	1.96	3.21
2-1/2" thick, R10.9	1.000	S.F.	.010	2.30	3.74
3" thick, R13.0	1.000	S.F.	.011	3.70	5.80
Foam glass, 1-1/2" thick, R2.64	1.000	S.F.	.011	1.84	3.06
2" thick, R5.26	1.000	S.F.	.011	2.61	4.23
Perlite, 1" thick, R2.77	1.000	S.F.	.011	.47	1.04
2" thick, R5.55	1.000	S.F.	.011	.88	1.67
Polystyrene, extruded, blue, 2.2#/C.F., 3/4" thick, R4	1.000	S.F.	.010	.50	1.08
1-1/2" thick, R8.1	1.000	S.F.	.011	.81	1.57
2" thick, R10.8	1.000	S.F.	.011	1.07	1.95
Molded bead board, white, 1" thick, R3.85	1.000	S.F.	.011	.21	.65
1-1/2" thick, R5.6	1.000	S.F.	.011	.33	.86
2" thick, R7.7	1.000	S.F.	.011	.41	.98
Urethane, no backing, 1/2" thick, R2.9	1.000	S.F.	.010	.32	.80
1" thick, R5.8	1.000	S.F.	.011	.57	1.18
1-1/2" thick, R8.7	1.000	S.F.	.011	.80	1.55
2" thick, R11.7	1.000	S.F.	.011	1.07	1.95
Fire resistant, 1/2" thick, R2.9	1.000	S.F.	.010	.37	.89
1" thick, R5.8	1.000	S.F.	.011	.89	1.47
1-1/2" thick, R8.7	1.000	S.F.	.011	.98	1.82
2" thick, R11.7	1.000	S.F.	.011	1.31	2.31
Non-rigid insulation, batts					
Fiberglass, kraft faced, 3-1/2" thick, R11, 11" wide	1.000	S.F.	.005	.26	.56
15" wide	1.000	S.F.	.005	.26	.56
23" wide	1.000	S.F.	.005	.26	.56
6" thick, R19, 11" wide	1.000	S.F.	.006	.44	.84
15" wide	1.000	S.F.	.006	.44	.84
23" wide	1.000	S.F.	.006	.44	.84
9" thick, R30, 15" wide	1.000	S.F.	.006	.61	1.11
23" wide	1.000	S.F.	.006	.61	1.11
12" thick, R38, 15" wide	1.000	S.F.	.006	.87	1.49
23" wide	1.000	S.F.	.006	.87	1.49
Fiberglass, foil faced, 3-1/2" thick, R11, 15" wide	1.000	S.F.	.005	.33	.65
23" wide	1.000	S.F.	.005	.33	.65
6" thick, R19, 15" thick	1.000	S.F.	.005	.47	.86
23" wide	1.000	S.F.	.005	.47	.86
9" thick, R30, 15" wide	1.000	S.F.	.006	.68	1.20
23" wide	1.000	S.F.	.006	.68	1.20

Be sure to read pages 155–157 for proper use of this section.

DIVISION 5 ROOFING

Gable End Roofing System

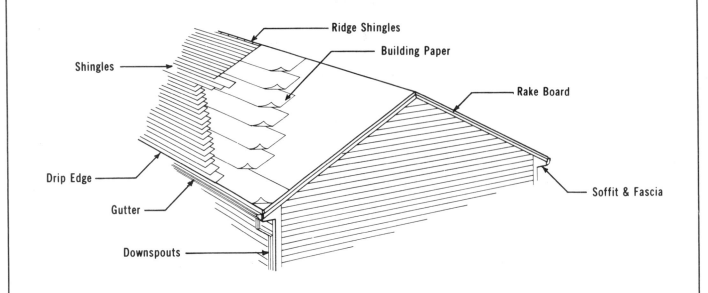

SYSTEM DESCRIPTION	QUAN.	UNIT	MAN-HOURS	MAT. COST	COST PER SQUARE FOOT
ASPHALT, ROOF SHINGLES, CLASS A					
Shingles, asphalt standard, inorganic class A, 210-235 lb./sq.	1.160	S.F.	.017	.44	
Drip edge, metal, 5" girth	.150	L.F.	.003	.04	
Building paper, #15 felt	1.300	S.F.	.001	.04	
Ridge shingles, asphalt	.042	L.F.	.001	.03	
Soffit & fascia, white painted aluminum, 1' overhang	.083	L.F.	.012	.14	
Rake trim, painted, 1" x 6"	.040	L.F.	.002	.03	
Gutter, seamless, aluminum, painted	.083	L.F.	.005	.09	Contractor's Fee
Downspouts, aluminum, painted	.035	L.F.	.001	.02	
TOTAL			.042	.83	**2.81**
WOOD, CEDAR SHINGLES, NO. 1 PERFECTIONS					
Shingles, wood, cedar, No. 1 perfections, 5" exposure, 4/12 pitch	1.160	S.F.	.034	1.67	
Drip edge, metal, 5" girth	.150	L.F.	.003	.04	
Building paper, #15 felt	1.300	S.F.	.001	.04	
Ridge shingles, cedar	.042	L.F.	.001	.06	
Soffit & fascia, white painted aluminum, 1' overhang	.083	L.F.	.012	.14	
Rake trim, painted, 1" x 6"	.040	L.F.	.002	.03	
Gutter, seamless, aluminum, painted	.083	L.F.	.005	.09	Contractor's Fee
Downspouts, aluminum, painted	.035	L.F.	.001	.02	
TOTAL			.059	2.09	**5.35**

Be sure to read pages 155–157 for proper use of this section.

Hip Roof Roofing System

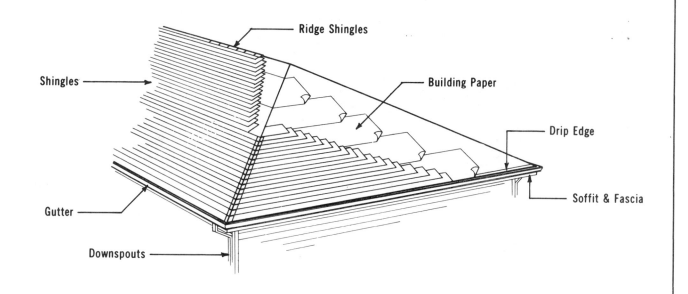

SYSTEM DESCRIPTION	QUAN.	UNIT	MAN-HOURS	MAT. COST	COST PER SQUARE FOOT
ASPHALT, ROOF SHINGLES, CLASS A					
Shingles, asphalt standard, class A, 210-235 lb./sq. 4/12 pitch	1.570	S.F.	.023	.58	
Drip edge, metal, 5" girth	.122	L.F.	.002	.03	
Building paper, #15 asphalt felt	1.800	S.F.	.002	.07	
Ridge shingles, asphalt	.075	L.F.	.001	.06	
Soffit & fascia, white painted aluminum, 1' overhang	.120	L.F.	.017	.20	
Gutter, seamless, aluminum, painted	.120	L.F.	.008	.13	
Downspouts, aluminum, painted	.035	L.F.	.001	.02	Contractor's Fee
TOTAL			.054	1.09	**3.61**
WOOD, CEDAR SHINGLES, NO. 1 PERFECTIONS					
Shingles, wood, cedar, No. 1 perfections, 5" exposure, 4/12 pitch	1.570	S.F.	.046	2.22	
Drip edge, metal, 5" girth	.122	L.F.	.002	.03	
Building paper, #15 asphalt felt	1.800	S.F.	.002	.07	
Ridge shingles, wood, cedar	.075	L.F.	.002	.10	
Soffit & fascia, white painted aluminum, 1' overhang	.120	L.F.	.017	.20	
Gutter, seamless, aluminum, painted	.120	L.F.	.008	.13	
Downspouts, aluminum, painted	.035	L.F.	.001	.02	Contractor's Fee
TOTAL			.078	2.77	**6.95**

Be sure to read pages 155–157 for proper use of this section.

Gambrel Roofing System

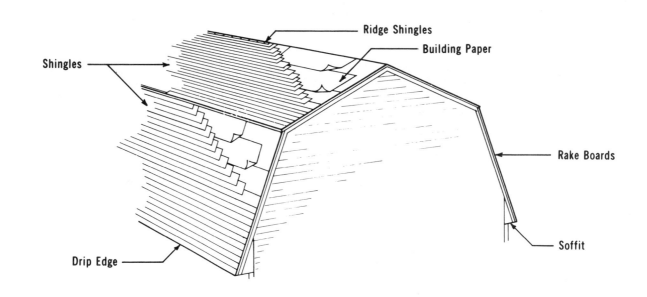

Ridge Shingles
Building Paper
Shingles
Rake Boards
Soffit
Drip Edge

SYSTEM DESCRIPTION	QUAN.	UNIT	MAN-HOURS	MAT. COST	COST PER SQUARE FOOT
ASPHALT, ROOF SHINGLES, CLASS A					
Shingles, asphalt standard, inorganic class A, 210-235 lb./sq.	1.450	S.F.	.021	.55	
Drip edge, metal, 5" girth	.146	L.F.	.002	.04	
Building paper, #15 asphalt felt	1.500	S.F.	.002	.06	
Ridge shingles, asphalt	.042	L.F.	.001	.03	
Soffit & fascia, painted aluminum, 1' overhang	.083	L.F.	.012	.14	
Rake, trim, painted, 1" x 6"	.063	L.F.	.005	.06	
Gutter, seamless, aluminum, painted	.083	L.F.	.005	.09	
Downspouts, aluminum, painted	.042	L.F.	.001	.03	Contractor's Fee
TOTAL			.049	1.00	**3.26**
WOOD, CEDAR SHINGLES, NO. 1 PERFECTIONS					
Shingles, wood, cedar, No. 1 perfections, 5" exposure	1.450	S.F.	.043	2.09	
Drip edge, metal, 5" girth	.146	L.F.	.002	.04	
Building paper, #15 asphalt felt	1.500	S.F.	.002	.06	
Ridge shingles, wood	.042	L.F.	.001	.06	
Soffit & fascia, white painted aluminum, 1' overhang	.083	L.F.	.012	.14	
Rake, trim, painted, 1" x 6"	.063	L.F.	.005	.06	
Gutter, seamless, aluminum, painted	.083	L.F.	.005	.09	
Downspouts, aluminum, painted	.042	L.F.	.001	.03	Contractor's Fee
TOTAL			.071	2.57	**6.40**

Be sure to read pages 155–157 for proper use of this section.

Mansard Roofing System

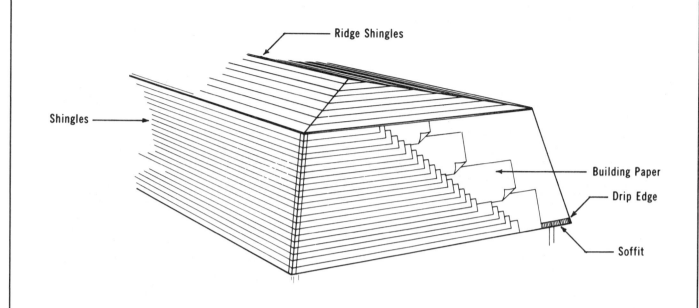

- Ridge Shingles
- Shingles
- Building Paper
- Drip Edge
- Soffit

SYSTEM DESCRIPTION	QUAN.	UNIT	MAN-HOURS	MAT. COST	COST PER SQUARE FOOT
ASPHALT, ROOF SHINGLES, CLASS A					
Shingles, asphalt standard, inorganic class A, 210-235 lb./sq.	2.210	S.F.	.031	.80	
Drip edge, metal, 5" girth	.122	L.F.	.002	.03	
Building paper, #15 asphalt felt	2.300	S.F.	.003	.08	
Ridge shingles, asphalt	.090	L.F.	.002	.07	
Soffit & fascia, white painted aluminum, 1' overhang	.122	L.F.	.017	.21	
Gutter, seamless, aluminum, painted	.122	L.F.	.008	.13	
Downspouts, aluminum, painted	.042	L.F.	.001	.03	Contractor's Fee
TOTAL			.064	1.35	**4.32**
WOOD, CEDAR SHINGLES, NO. 1 PERFECTIONS					
Shingles, wood, cedar, No. 1 perfections, 5" exposure	2.210	S.F.	.064	3.06	
Drip edge, metal, 5" girth	.122	L.F.	.002	.03	
Building paper, #15 asphalt felt	2.300	S.F.	.003	.08	
Ridge shingles, wood	.090	L.F.	.002	.12	
Soffit & fascia, white painted aluminum, 1' overhang	.122	L.F.	.017	.21	
Gutter, seamless, aluminum, painted	.122	L.F.	.008	.13	
Downspouts, aluminum, painted	.042	L.F.	.001	.03	Contractor's Fee
TOTAL			.097	3.66	**8.90**

Be sure to read pages 155–157 for proper use of this section.

Shed Roofing System

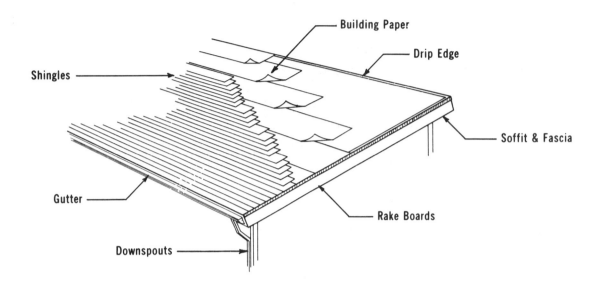

SYSTEM DESCRIPTION	QUAN.	UNIT	MAN-HOURS	MAT. COST	COST PER SQUARE FOOT
ASPHALT, ROOF SHINGLES, CLASS A					
Shingles, asphalt standard, inorganic class A, 210-235 lb./sq.	1.230	S.F.	.018	.47	
Drip edge, metal, 5" girth	.100	L.F.	.002	.02	
Building paper, #15 asphalt felt	1.300	S.F.	.001	.04	
Soffit & fascia, white painted aluminum, 1' overhang	.080	L.F.	.011	.13	
Rake trim, painted, 1" x 6"	.043	L.F.	.003	.04	
Gutter, seamless, aluminum, painted	.040	L.F.	.002	.04	
Downspouts, aluminum, painted	.020	L.F.		.01	Contractor's Fee
TOTAL			.037	.75	**2.55**
WOOD, CEDAR SHINGLES, NO. 1 PERFECTIONS					
Shingles, wood, cedar, No. 1 perfections, 5" exposure	1.230	S.F.	.034	1.67	
Drip edge, metal, 5" girth	.100	L.F.	.002	.02	
Building paper, #15 asphalt felt	1.300	S.F.	.001	.04	
Soffit & fascia, white painted aluminum, 1' overhang	.080	L.F.	.011	.13	
Rake trim, painted, 1" x 6	.043	L.F.	.003	.04	
Gutter, seamless, aluminum, painted	.040	L.F.	.002	.04	
Downspouts, aluminum, painted	.020	L.F.		.01	Contractor's Fee
TOTAL			.053	1.95	**4.90**

Be sure to read pages 155–157 for proper use of this section.

Gable Dormer Roofing System

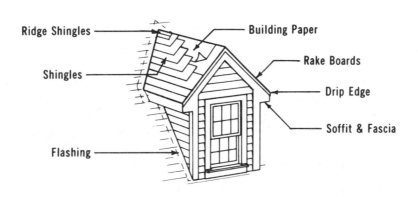

SYSTEM DESCRIPTION	QUAN.	UNIT	MAN-HOURS	MAT. COST	COST PER SQUARE FOOT
ASPHALT, ROOF SHINGLES, CLASS A					
Shingles, asphalt standard, inorganic class A, 210-235 lb./sq.	1.400	S.F.	.020	.51	
Drip edge, metal, 5″ girth	.220	L.F.	.004	.06	
Building paper, #15 asphalt felt	1.500	S.F.	.002	.06	
Ridge shingles, asphalt	.280	L.F.	.006	.22	
Soffit & fascia, aluminum, vented	.220	L.F.	.031	.37	Contractor's Fee
Flashing, aluminum, mill finish, .013″ thick	1.500	S.F.	.082	.52	
TOTAL			.145	1.74	**7.95**
WOOD, CEDAR, NO. 1 PERFECTIONS					
Shingles, wood, No. 1 perfections, 16″ long, 5″ exposure	1.400	S.F.	.040	1.95	
Drip edge, metal, 5″ girth	.220	L.F.	.004	.06	
Building paper, #15 asphalt felt	1.500	S.F.	.002	.06	
Ridge shingles, wood	.280	L.F.	.008	.37	
Soffit & fascia, aluminum, vented	.220	L.F.	.031	.37	Contractor's Fee
Flashing, aluminum, mill finish, .013″ thick	1.500	S.F.	.082	.52	
TOTAL			.167	3.33	**11.10**
SLATE, BUCKINGHAM, BLACK					
Shingles, Buckingham, Virginia, black	1.400	S.F.	.063	5.68	
Drip edge, metal, 5″ girth	.220	L.F.	.004	.06	
Building paper, #15 asphalt felt	1.500	S.F.	.002	.06	
Ridge shingles, slate	.280	L.F.	.011	1.29	
Soffit & fascia, aluminum, vented	.220	L.F.	.031	.37	Contractor's Fee
Flashing, copper, 16 oz.	1.500	S.F.	.105	4.72	
TOTAL			.216	12.18	**26.00**

Be sure to read pages 155–157 for proper use of this section.

Shed Dormer Roofing System

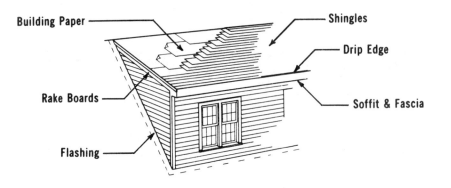

SYSTEM DESCRIPTION	QUAN.	UNIT	MAN-HOURS	MAT. COST	COST PER SQUARE FOOT
ASPHALT, ROOF SHINGLES, CLASS A					
Shingles, asphalt standard, inorganic class A, 210-235 lb./sq.	1.100	S.F.	.015	.40	
Drip edge, aluminum, 5" girth	.250	L.F.	.005	.04	
Building paper, #15 asphalt felt	1.200	S.F.	.001	.04	
Soffit & fascia, aluminum, vented, 1' overhang	.250	L.F.	.036	.43	Contractor's Fee
Flashing, aluminum, mill finish, .013" thick	.800	L.F.	.044	.28	
TOTAL			.101	1.19	**5.50**
WOOD, CEDAR, NO. 1 PERFECTIONS					
Shingles, wood, cedar No. 1 perfections, 5" exposure	1.100	S.F.	.032	1.53	
Drip edge, aluminum, 5" girth	.250	L.F.	.005	.04	
Building paper, #15 asphalt felt	1.200	S.F.	.001	.04	
Soffit & fascia, aluminum, vented, 1' overhang	.250	L.F.	.036	.43	Contractor's Fee
Flashing, aluminum, mill finish, .013" thick	.800	L.F.	.044	.28	
TOTAL			.118	2.32	**7.75**
SLATE, BUCKINGHAM, BLACK					
Shingles, slate, Buckingham, black	1.100	S.F.	.050	4.46	
Drip edge, aluminum, 5" girth	.250	L.F.	.005	.04	
Building paper, #15 asphalt felt	1.200	S.F.	.001	.04	
Soffit & fascia, aluminum, vented, 1' overhang	.250	L.F.	.036	.43	Contractor's Fee
Flashing, copper, 16 oz.	.800	L.F.	.056	2.52	
TOTAL			.148	7.49	**16.45**

Be sure to read pages 155–157 for proper use of this section.

Built-up Roofing System

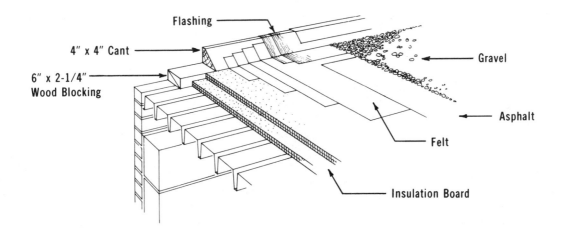

SYSTEM DESCRIPTION	QUAN.	UNIT	MAN-HOURS	MAT. COST	COST PER SQUARE FOOT
ASPHALT, ORGANIC, 4-PLY, INSULATED DECK					
Membrane, asphalt, 4-plies #15 felt, gravel surfacing	1.000	S.F.	.025	.47	
Insulation board, 2-layers of 1-1/16" glass fiber	2.000	S.F.	.016	1.21	
Wood blocking, treated, 6" x 2-1/4" & 4" x 4" cant	.040	L.F.	.005	.11	Contractor's Fee
Flashing, aluminum, 0.040" thick	.050	S.F.	.002	.08	
TOTAL			.048	1.87	**4.40**
ASPHALT, INORGANIC, 3-PLY, INSULATED DECK					
Membrane, asphalt, 3-plies type IV glass felt, gravel surfacing	1.000	S.F.	.025	.51	
Insulation board, 2-layers of 1-1/16" glass fiber	2.000	S.F.	.016	1.21	
Wood blocking, treated, 6" x 2-1/4" & 4" x 4" cant	.040	L.F.	.005	.11	Contractor's Fee
Flashing, aluminum, 0.040" thick	.050	S.F.	.002	.08	
TOTAL			.048	1.91	**4.53**
COAL TAR, ORGANIC, 4-PLY, INSULATED DECK					
Membrane, coal tar, 4-plies #15 felt, gravel surfacing	1.000	S.F.	.025	.78	
Insulation board, 2-layers of 1-1/16" glass fiber	2.000	S.F.	.016	1.21	
Wood blocking, treated, 6" x 2-1/4" & 4" x 4" cant	.040	L.F.	.005	.11	Contractor's Fee
Flashing, aluminum, 0.040" thick	.050	S.F.	.002	.08	
TOTAL			.048	2.18	**4.93**
COAL TAR, INORGANIC, 3-PLY, INSULATED DECK					
Membrane, coal tar, 3-plies type IV glass felt, gravel surfacing	1.000	S.F.	.028	.62	
Insulation board, 2-layers of 1-1/16" glass fiber	2.000	S.F.	.016	1.21	
Wood blocking, treated, 6" x 2-1/4" & 4" x 4" cant	.040	L.F.	.005	.11	Contractor's Fee
Flashing, aluminum, 0.040" thick	.050	S.F.	.002	.08	
TOTAL			.051	2.02	**4.63**

Be sure to read pages 155–157 for proper use of this section.

Single-ply Roofing System

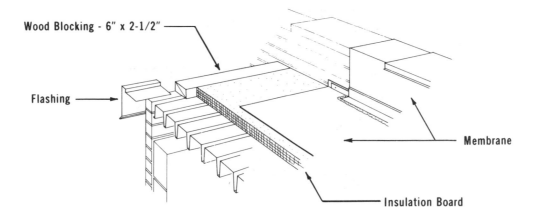

Wood Blocking - 6" x 2-1/2"

Flashing

Membrane

Insulation Board

SYSTEM DESCRIPTION	QUAN.	UNIT	MAN-HOURS	MAT. COST	COST PER SQUARE FOOT
CHLOROSULFONATED POLYETHYLENE - HYPALON (CSPE)					
Membrane, 35 mil CSPE, fully adhered	1.000	S.F.	.011	1.69	
Insulation board, 2-1/2" perlite/urethane composite	1.000	S.F.	.011	1.08	
Wood blocking, treated, 6" x 2-1/2"	.040	L.F.	.002	.05	Contractor's Fee
Flashing, aluminum, 0.040" thick	.080	S.F.	.002	.08	
TOTAL			.026	2.90	**5.10**
ETHYLENE PROPYLENE DIENE MONUMER (EPDM)					
Membrane, 45 mil EPDM, loose-laid & ballasted w/stone (10 psf)	1.000	S.F.	.006	.77	
Insulation board, 2-1/2" perlite/urethane composite	1.000	S.F.	.011	1.08	
Wood blocking, treated, 6" x 2-1/2"	.040	L.F.	.002	.05	Contractor's Fee
Flashing, aluminum, 0.040" thick	.080	S.F.	.002	.08	
TOTAL			.021	1.98	**3.60**
MODIFIED BITUMEN					
Membrane, 160 mil mod, bitumen w/asphalt emulsion coating	1.000	S.F.	.020	1.00	
Insulation board, 2 layers of 2-1/4" glass fiber	2.000	S.F.	.020	1.82	
Wood blocking, treated, 6" x 4-1/2" & 4" x 4" cant	.040	L.F.	.005	.10	Contractor's Fee
Flashing, aluminum, 0.040" thick	.080	S.F.	.002	.08	
TOTAL			.047	3.00	**5.90**
REINFORCED POLYVINYL CHLORIDE (PVC)					
Membrane, 48 mil reinforced PVC, partially attached	1.000	S.F.	.008	2.90	
Insulation board, 2-1/2" perlite/urethane composite	1.000	S.F.	.011	1.08	
Wood blocking, treated, 6" x 2-1/2"	.040	L.F.	.002	.05	Contractor's Fee
Flashing, aluminum, 0.040" thick	.080	S.F.	.002	.08	
TOTAL			.023	4.11	**6.80**

Be sure to read pages 155–157 for proper use of this section.

DIVISION 6
INTERIORS

Drywall & Thincoat Wall System

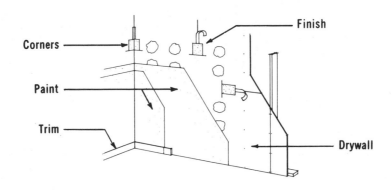

SYSTEM DESCRIPTION	QUAN.	UNIT	MAN-HOURS	MAT. COST	COST PER SQUARE FOOT
1/2" SHEETROCK, TAPED & FINISHED					
Drywall, 1/2" thick, standard	1.000	S.F.	.009	.24	
Finish, taped & finished joints	1.000	S.F.	.008	.07	
Corners, taped & finished, 32 L.F. per 12' x 12' room	.083	L.F.	.001	.01	
Paint, primer & 2 coats	1.000	S.F.	.009	.11	Contractor's Fee
Trim, baseboard, painted	.125	L.F.	.008	.14	**1.94**
TOTAL			.034	.57	

Drywall & Thincoat Ceiling System

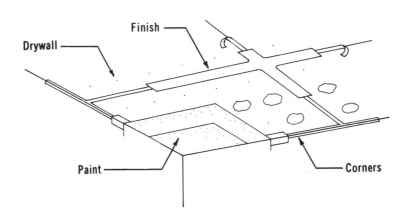

SYSTEM DESCRIPTION	QUAN.	UNIT	MAN-HOURS	MAT. COST	COST PER SQUARE FOOT
1/2" SHEETROCK, TAPED & FINISHED					
Drywall, 1/2" thick, standard	1.000	S.F.	.009	.24	
Finish, taped & finished	1.000	S.F.	.008	.07	
Corners, taped & finished, 12' x 12' room	.330	L.F.	.004	.02	Contractor's Fee
Paint, primer & 2 coats	1.000	S.F.	.009	.11	**1.61**
TOTAL			.029	.44	

Be sure to read pages 155–157 for proper use of this section.

Plaster & Stucco Wall System

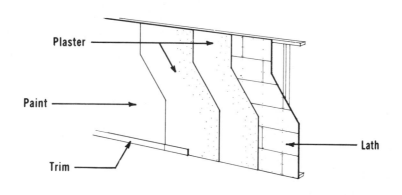

SYSTEM DESCRIPTION	QUAN.	UNIT	MAN-HOURS	MAT. COST	COST PER SQUARE FOOT
PLASTER ON GYPSUM LATH					
Plaster, gypsum or perlite, 2 coats	1.000	S.F.	.042	.39	
Lath, 3/8" gypsum	1.000	S.F.	.010	.44	
Corners, expanded metal, 32 L.F. per 12' x 12' room	.083	L.F.	.002	.01	
Painting, primer & 2 coats	1.000	S.F.	.009	.11	Contractor's Fee
Trim, baseboard, painted	.125	L.F.	.008	.14	
TOTAL			.071	1.09	**3.92**

Plaster & Stucco Ceiling System

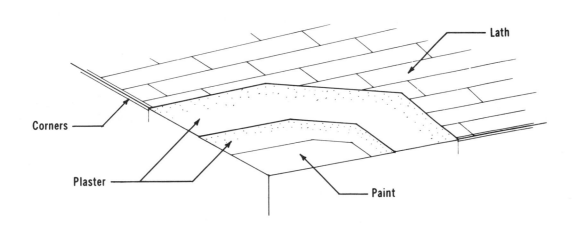

SYSTEM DESCRIPTION	QUAN.	UNIT	MAN-HOURS	MAT. COST	COST PER SQUARE FOOT
PLASTER ON GYPSUM LATH					
Plaster, gypsum or perlite	1.000	S.F.	.048	.39	
Lath, 3/8" gypsum	1.000	S.F.	.014	.44	
Corners, expanded metal, 12' x 12' room	.330	L.F.	.009	.03	
Painting, primer & 2 coats	1.000	S.F.	.009	.11	Contractor's Fee
TOTAL			.080	.97	**4.06**

Be sure to read pages 155–157 for proper use of this section.

Suspended Ceiling System

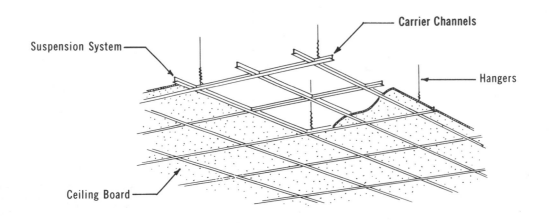

SYSTEM DESCRIPTION	QUAN.	UNIT	MAN-HOURS	MAT. COST	COST PER SQUARE FOOT
2′ X 2′ GRID, FILM FACED FIBERGLASS, 5/8″ THICK					
Suspension system, 2′ x 2′ grid, T bar	1.000	S.F.	.012	.51	
Ceiling board, film faced fiberglass, 5/8″ thick	1.000	S.F.	.013	.43	
Carrier channels, 1-1/2″ x 3/4″	1.000	S.F.	.017	.17	
Hangers, #12 wire	1.000	S.F.	.001	.02	Contractor's Fee
TOTAL			.043	1.13	**3.17**
2′ X 4′ GRID, FILM FACED FIBERGLASS, 5/8″ THICK					
Suspension system, 2′ x 4′ grid, T bar	1.000	S.F.	.010	.46	
Ceiling board, film faced fiberglass, 5/8″ thick	1.000	S.F.	.013	.43	
Carrier channels, 1-1/2″ x 3/4″	1.000	S.F.	.017	.19	
Hangers, #12 wire	1.000	S.F.	.001	.02	Contractor's Fee
TOTAL			.041	1.10	**3.02**
2′ X 2′ GRID, MINERAL FIBER, REVEAL EDGE, 1″ THICK					
Suspension system, 2′ x 2′ grid, T bar	1.000	S.F.	.012	.51	
Ceiling board, mineral fiber, reveal edge, 1″ thick	1.000	S.F.	.013	.91	
Carrier channels, 1-1/2″ x 3/4″	1.000	S.F.	.017	.19	
Hangers, #12 wire	1.000	S.F.	.001	.02	Contractor's Fee
TOTAL			.043	1.63	**3.89**
2′ X 4′ GRID, MINERAL FIBER, REVEAL EDGE, 1″ THICK					
Suspension system, 2′ x 4′ grid, T bar	1.000	S.F.	.010	.46	
Ceiling board, mineral fiber, reveal edge, 1″ thick	1.000	S.F.	.013	.91	
Carrier channels, 1-1/2″ x 3/4″	1.000	S.F.	.017	.19	
Hangers, #12 wire	1.000	S.F.	.001	.02	Contractor's Fee
TOTAL			.041	1.58	**3.74**

Be sure to read pages 155–157 for proper use of this section.

Interior Door System

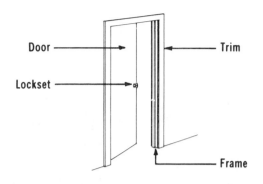

SYSTEM DESCRIPTION	QUAN.	UNIT	MAN-HOURS	MAT. COST	COST EACH
LAUAN, FLUSH DOOR, HOLLOW CORE					
Door, flush, lauan, hollow core, 2'-8" wide x 6'-8" high	1.000	Ea.	.889	23.00	
Frame, pine, 4-5/8" jamb	17.000	L.F.	.731	41.00	
Trim, casing, painted	34.000	L.F.	1.938	26.00	
Butt hinges, chrome, 3-1/2" x 3-1/2"	1.500	Pr.		32.00	
Lockset, passage	1.000	Ea.	.500	10.90	
Paint, door & frame, primer & 2 coats	2.000	Face	3.282	9.10	Contractor's Fee
TOTAL			7.340	142.00	**450.00**
BIRCH, FLUSH DOOR, HOLLOW CORE					
Door, flush, birch, hollow core, 2'-8" wide x 6'-8" high	1.000	Ea.	.889	30.00	
Frame, pine, 4-5/8" jamb	17.000	L.F.	.731	41.00	
Trim, casing, painted	34.000	L.F.	1.938	26.00	
Butt hinges, chrome, 3-1/2" x 3-1/2"	1.500	Pr.		32.00	
Lockset, passage	1.000	Ea.	.500	10.90	
Paint, door & frame, primer & 2 coats	2.000	Face	3.282	9.10	Contractor's Fee
TOTAL			7.340	149.00	**460.00**
RAISED PANEL, SOLID, PINE DOOR					
Door, pine, raised panel, 2'-8" wide x 6'-8" high	1.000	Ea.	.889	110.00	
Frame, pine, 4-5/8" jamb	17.000	L.F.	.731	41.00	
Trim, casing, painted	34.000	L.F.	1.938	26.00	
Butt hinges, bronze, 3-1/2" x 3-1/2"	1.500	Pr.		66.00	
Lockset, passage	1.000	Ea.	.500	10.90	
Paint, door & frame, primer & 2 coats	2.000	Face	4.800	9.45	Contractor's Fee
TOTAL			8.858	263.35	**675.00**

Be sure to read pages 155–157 for proper use of this section.

Closet Door System

SYSTEM DESCRIPTION	QUAN.	UNIT	MAN-HOURS	MAT. COST	COST EACH
BI-PASSING, FLUSH, LAUAN, HOLLOW CORE, 4'-0" X 6'-8"					
Door, flush, lauan, hollow core, 4'-0" x 6'-8" opening	1.000	Ea.	1.330	85.00	
Frame, pine, 4-5/8" jamb	18.000	L.F.	.774	44.00	
Trim, both sides, casing, painted	36.000	L.F.	1.836	27.00	Contractor's Fee
Paint, door & frame, primer & 2 coats	2.000	Face	3.282	9.10	
TOTAL			7.222	165.10	**480.00**
BI-PASSING, FLUSH, BIRCH, HOLLOW CORE, 6'-0" X 6'-8"					
Door, flush, birch, hollow core, 6'-0" x 6'-8" opening	1.000	Ea.	1.600	120.00	
Frame, pine, 4-5/8" jamb	19.000	L.F.	.817	46.00	
Trim, both sides, casing, painted	38.000	L.F.	1.938	28.00	Contractor's Fee
Paint, door & frame, primer & 2 coats	2.000	Face	4.102	11.35	
TOTAL			8.457	205.35	**575.00**
BI-FOLD, PINE, PANELED, 3'-0" X 6'-8"					
Door, pine, paneled, 3'-0" x 6'-8" opening	1.000	Ea.	1.230	85.00	
Frame, pine, 4-5/8" jamb	17.000	L.F.	.731	41.00	
Trim, both sides, casing, painted	34.000	L.F.	1.734	25.00	Contractor's Fee
Paint, door & frame, primer & 2 coats	2.000	Face	4.800	9.45	
TOTAL			8.495	160.45	**515.00**
BI-FOLD, PINE, LOUVERED, 6'-0" X 6'-8"					
Door, pine, louvered, 6'-0" x 6'-8" opening	1.000	Ea.	1.600	170.00	
Frame, pine, 4-5/8" jamb	19.000	L.F.	.817	46.00	
Trim, both sides, casing, painted	38.000	L.F.	1.938	28.00	Contractor's Fee
Paint, door & frame, primer & 2 coats	2.000	Face	6.000	11.85	
TOTAL			10.355	255.85	**715.00**

Be sure to read pages 155–157 for proper use of this section.

Stairway

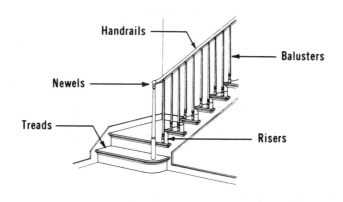

SYSTEM DESCRIPTION	QUAN.	UNIT	MAN-HOURS	MAT. COST	COST EACH
7 RISERS, OAK TREADS, BOX STAIRS					
Treads, oak, 9-1/2" x 1-1/16" thick	6.000	Ea.	2.664	120.00	
Risers, 3/4" thick, beech	6.000	Ea.	2.625	103.00	
Balusters, birch, 30" high	12.000	Ea.	3.432	73.00	
Newels, 3-1/4" wide	2.000	Ea.	2.280	73.00	
Handrails, oak laminated	7.000	L.F.	.931	36.00	Contractor's Fee
Stringers, 2" x 10", 3 each	21.000	L.F.	2.583	19.90	
TOTAL			14.515	424.90	**1120.00**
14 RISERS, OAK TREADS, BOX STAIRS					
Treads, oak, 9-1/2" x 1-1/16" thick	13.000	Ea.	5.772	260.00	
Risers, 3/4" thick, beech	13.000	Ea.	5.250	205.00	
Balusters, birch, 30" high	26.000	Ea.	7.436	158.00	
Newels, 3-1/4" wide	2.000	Ea.	2.280	73.00	
Handrails, oak, laminated	14.000	L.F.	1.862	72.00	Contractor's Fee
Stringers, 2" x 10", 3 each	42.000	L.F.	5.166	40.00	
TOTAL			27.766	808.00	**2125.00**
14 RISERS, PINE TREADS, BOX STAIRS					
Treads, pine, 9-1/2" x 3/4" thick	13.000	Ea.	5.772	49.00	
Risers, 3/4" thick, pine	13.000	Ea.	5.082	56.00	
Balusters, pine, 30" high	26.000	Ea.	7.436	110.00	
Newels, 3-1/4" wide	2.000	Ea.	2.280	73.00	
Handrails, oak, laminated	14.000	L.F.	1.862	72.00	Contractor's Fee
Stringers, 2" x 10", 3 each	42.000	L.F.	5.166	40.00	
TOTAL			27.598	400.00	**1500.00**

Be sure to read pages 155–157 for proper use of this section.

Carpets

SYSTEM DESCRIPTION	QUAN.	UNIT	MAN-HOURS	COST PER S.F.	
				MAT.	INST.
Carpet, direct glue-down, nylon, level loop, 26 oz.	1.000	S.F.	.018	2.08	3.67
32 oz.	1.000	S.F.	.018	2.34	4.06
40 oz.	1.000	S.F.	.018	3.17	5.30
Nylon, plush, 20 oz.	1.000	S.F.	.018	1.29	2.49
24 oz.	1.000	S.F.	.018	1.41	2.66
30 oz.	1.000	S.F.	.018	1.78	3.21
36 oz.	1.000	S.F.	.018	2.06	3.64
42 oz.	1.000	S.F.	.022	2.34	4.17
48 oz.	1.000	S.F.	.022	2.82	4.88
54 oz.	1.000	S.F.	.022	3.42	5.75
Needle bonded, 20 oz.	1.000	S.F.	.018	1.44	2.96
Olefin, 15 oz.	1.000	S.F.	.018	.67	1.57
22 oz.	1.000	S.F.	.018	.85	1.85
Scrim installed nylon spongeback carpet, 20 oz.	1.000	S.F.	.018	2.02	3.57
60 oz.	1.000	S.F.	.018	2.82	4.77
Tile, foam backed, needle punch	1.000	S.F.	.017	2.42	4.14
Tufted loop or shag	1.000	S.F.	.017	2.12	3.70
Wool, 36 oz., level loop	1.000	S.F.	.018	3.97	6.45
32 oz., patterned	1.000	S.F.	.020	3.53	5.90
48 oz., patterned	1.000	S.F.	.020	4.96	8.00
Padded, sponge rubber cushion, minimum	1.000	S.F.	.006	.31	.65
Maximum	1.000	S.F.	.006	.80	1.38
Felt, 32 oz. to 56 oz., minimum	1.000	S.F.	.006	.34	.70
Maximum	1.000	S.F.	.006	.53	.98
Bonded urethane, 3/8" thick, minimum	1.000	S.F.	.006	.37	.74
Maximum	1.000	S.F.	.006	.64	1.14
Prime urethane, 1/4" thick, minimum	1.000	S.F.	.006	.23	.53
Maximum	1.000	S.F.	.006	.40	.78
Stairs, for stairs, add to above carpet prices	1.000	Riser	.267		8.75
Underlayment plywood, 3/8" thick	1.000	S.F.	.011	.50	1.12
1/2" thick	1.000	S.F.	.011	.56	1.21
5/8" thick	1.000	S.F.	.011	.69	1.42
3/4" thick	1.000	S.F.	.012	.80	1.61
Particle board, 3/8" thick	1.000	S.F.	.011	.29	.81
1/2" thick	1.000	S.F.	.011	.34	.89
5/8" thick	1.000	S.F.	.011	.37	.95
3/4" thick	1.000	S.F.	.012	.48	1.14
Hardboard, 4' x 4', 0.215" thick	1.000	S.F.	.011	.34	.89

Be sure to read pages 155–157 for proper use of this section.

Flooring

SYSTEM DESCRIPTION	QUAN.	UNIT	MAN-HOURS	COST PER S.F. MAT.	COST PER S.F. TOTAL
Resilient flooring, asphalt tile on concrete, 1/8" thick					
Color group B	1.000	S.F.	.020	.85	1.91
Color group C & D	1.000	S.F.	.020	.91	2.00
Asphalt tile on wood subfloor, 1/8" thick					
Color group B	1.000	S.F.	.020	1.03	2.18
Color group C & D	1.000	S.F.	.020	1.10	2.28
Vinyl composition tile, 12" x 12", 1/16" thick	1.000	S.F.	.025	.61	1.73
Embossed	1.000	S.F.	.025	.79	2.00
Marbleized	1.000	S.F.	.025	.79	2.00
Plain	1.000	S.F.	.025	.91	2.18
.080" thick, embossed	1.000	S.F.	.025	.88	2.13
Marbleized	1.000	S.F.	.025	1.07	2.41
Plain	1.000	S.F.	.025	1.44	2.96
1/8" thick, marbleized	1.000	S.F.	.025	.97	2.26
Plain	1.000	S.F.	.025	1.64	3.26
Vinyl tile, 12" x 12", .050" thick, minimum	1.000	S.F.	.025	1.21	2.62
Maximum	1.000	S.F.	.025	3.03	5.30
1/8" thick, minimum	1.000	S.F.	.025	1.82	3.52
Maximum	1.000	S.F.	.025	2.42	4.41
1/8" thick, solid colors	1.000	S.F.	.025	3.03	5.30
Florentine pattern	1.000	S.F.	.025	3.63	6.20
Marbleized or travertine pattern	1.000	S.F.	.025	8.75	13.85
Vinyl sheet goods, backed, .070" thick, minimum	1.000	S.F.	.032	1.21	2.84
Maximum	1.000	S.F.	.040	2.42	4.88
.093" thick, minimum	1.000	S.F.	.035	1.52	3.37
Maximum	1.000	S.F.	.040	2.85	5.50
.125" thick, minimum	1.000	S.F.	.035	1.76	3.73
Maximum	1.000	S.F.	.040	3.94	7.10
.250" thick, minimum	1.000	S.F.	.035	2.73	5.20
Maximum	1.000	S.F.	.040	5.25	9.05
Wood, oak, finished in place, 25/32" x 2-1/2" clear	1.000	S.F.	.074	2.61	6.40
Select	1.000	S.F.	.074	4.24	8.80
No. 1 common	1.000	S.F.	.070	3.87	8.10
Prefinished, oak, 2-1/2" wide	1.000	S.F.	.047	6.05	10.60
3-1/4" wide	1.000	S.F.	.043	7.25	12.20
Ranch plank, oak, random width	1.000	S.F.	.055	7.25	12.60
Parquet, 5/16" thick, finished in place, oak, minimum	1.000	S.F.	.077	2.12	5.75
Maximum	1.000	S.F.	.107	6.05	12.60
Teak, minimum	1.000	S.F.	.077	3.58	7.90
Maximum	1.000	S.F.	.107	6.90	13.85
Sleepers, treated, 16" O.C., 1" x 2"	1.000	S.F.	.007	.11	.40
1" x 3"	1.000	S.F.	.008	.17	.53
2" x 4"	1.000	S.F.	.011	.41	.99
2" x 6"	1.000	S.F.	.012	.62	1.35
Subfloor, plywood, 1/2" thick	1.000	S.F.	.011	.50	1.12
5/8" thick	1.000	S.F.	.012	.53	1.20
3/4" thick	1.000	S.F.	.013	.63	1.39
Ceramic tile, color group 2, 1" x 1"	1.000	S.F.	.087	3.75	8.15
2" x 2" or 2" x 1"	1.000	S.F.	.087	4.06	8.55

Be sure to read pages 155–157 for proper use of this section.

DIVISION 7
SPECIALTIES

Kitchen System

Soffit Drywall

Countertop

Soffit Framing

Top Cabinets

Bottom Cabinets

SYSTEM DESCRIPTION	QUAN.	UNIT	MAN-HOURS	MAT. COST	COST PER LINEAR FOOT
KITCHEN, ECONOMY GRADE					
Top cabinets, economy grade	1.000	L.F.	.170	48.00	
Bottom cabinets, economy grade	1.000	L.F.	.255	73.00	
Countertop, laminated plastics, post formed	1.000	L.F.	.267	9.45	
Blocking, wood, 2" x 4"	1.000	L.F.	.032	.32	
Soffit, framing, wood, 2" x 4"	4.000	L.F.	.072	1.28	Contractor's Fee
Soffit drywall, painted	2.000	S.F.	.062	.95	
TOTAL			.858	133.00	**225.00**
AVERAGE GRADE					
Top cabinets, average grade	1.000	L.F.	.213	61.00	
Bottom cabinets, average grade	1.000	L.F.	.319	90.00	
Countertop, laminated plastic, square edge, incl. backsplash	1.000	L.F.	.267	30.00	
Blocking, wood, 2" x 4"	1.000	L.F.	.032	.32	
Soffit framing, wood, 2" x 4"	4.000	L.F.	.072	1.28	Contractor's Fee
Soffit drywall, painted	2.000	S.F.	.062	.95	
TOTAL			.965	183.55	**305.00**
CUSTOM GRADE					
Top cabinets, custom grade	1.000	L.F.	.256	91.00	
Bottom cabinets, custom grade	1.000	L.F.	.384	121.00	
Countertop, laminated plastic, square edge, incl. backsplash	1.000	L.F.	.267	30.00	
Blocking, wood, 2" x 4"	1.000	L.F.	.032	.32	
Soffit framing, wood, 2" x 4"	4.000	L.F.	.072	1.28	Contractor's Fee
Soffit drywall, painted	2.000	S.F.	.062	.95	
TOTAL			1.073	244.55	**395.00**

Be sure to read pages 155–157 for proper use of this section.

Wood Deck System

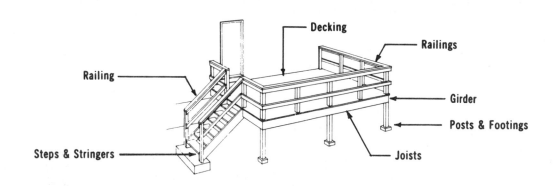

SYSTEM DESCRIPTION	QUAN.	UNIT	MAN-HOURS	MAT. COST	COST PER SQUARE FOOT
8' X 12' DECK, PRESSURE TREATED LUMBER, JOISTS 16" O.C.					
Decking, 2" x 6" lumber	2.080	L.F.	.027	1.25	
Joists, 2" x 8", 16" O.C.	1.000	L.F.	.017	.87	
Girder, 2" x 10"	.125	L.F.	.002	.15	
Posts, 4" x 4", including concrete footing	.250	L.F.	.020	.47	
Stairs, 2" x 10" stringers, 2" x 10" steps	1.000	Set	.020	.48	
Railings, 2" x 4"	1.000	L.F.	.026	.41	Contractor's Fee
TOTAL			.112	3.63	**9.30**
12' X 16' DECK, PRESSURE TREATED LUMBER, JOISTS 24" O.C.					
Decking, 2" x 6"	2.080	L.F.	.027	1.25	
Joists, 2" x 10", 24" O.C.	.800	L.F.	.014	.94	
Girder, 2" x 10"	.083	L.F.	.001	.10	
Posts, 4" x 4", including concrete footing	.122	L.F.	.015	.33	
Stairs, 2" x 10" stringers, 2" x 10" steps	1.000	Set	.012	.29	
Railings, 2" x 4"	.670	L.F.	.017	.26	Contractor's Fee
TOTAL			.086	3.17	**7.70**
12' X 24' DECK, REDWOOD OR CEDAR, JOISTS 16" O.C.					
Deckings, 2" x 6" redwood	2.080	L.F.	.027	2.18	
Joists, 2" x 10", 16" O.C.	1.000	L.F.	.018	1.83	
Girder, 2" x 10"	.083	L.F.	.001	.15	
Post, 4" x 4", including concrete footing	.111	L.F.	.018	.89	
Stairs, 2" x 10" stringers, 2" x 10" steps	1.000	Set	.012	1.40	
Railings, 2" x 4"	.540	L.F.	.004	.37	Contractor's Fee
TOTAL			.080	6.82	**12.95**

Be sure to read pages 155–157 for proper use of this section.

Greenhouse System

SYSTEM DESCRIPTION	QUAN.	UNIT	MAN-HOURS	COST EACH MAT.	COST EACH TOTAL
Economy, lean to, shell only, not incl. 2' stub wall, foundation, floors, or heat, 4' x 10'	1.000	Ea.	18.840	1450.00	2800.00
4' x 16'	1.000	Ea.	26.234	2025.00	3900.00
4' x 24'	1.000	Ea.	30.285	2325.00	4500.00
6' x 10'	1.000	Ea.	16.560	1675.00	3075.00
6' x 16'	1.000	Ea.	23.046	2325.00	4250.00
6' x 24'	1.000	Ea.	29.808	3000.00	5500.00
8' x 10'	1.000	Ea.	22.080	2225.00	4100.00
8' x 16'	1.000	Ea.	38.419	3875.00	7100.00
8' x 24'	1.000	Ea.	46.680	5000.00	9200.00
Free standing, 8' x 8'	1.000	Ea.	17.344	2550.00	4400.00
8' x 16'	1.000	Ea.	30.189	4450.00	7675.00
8' x 24'	1.000	Ea.	39.024	5750.00	9950.00
10' x 10'	1.000	Ea.	18.800	3150.00	5300.00
10' x 16'	1.000	Ea.	24.064	4025.00	6800.00
10' x 24'	1.000	Ea.	31.584	5275.00	8900.00
14' x 10'	1.000	Ea.	20.720	3900.00	6525.00
14' x 16'	1.000	Ea.	24.864	4675.00	7850.00
14' x 24'	1.000	Ea.	33.314	6275.00	10,500.00
Standard, lean to, shell only, not incl. 2' stub wall, foundation, floors, or heat, 4' x 10'	1.000	Ea.	28.260	2175.00	4200.00
4' x 16'	1.000	Ea.	39.375	3025.00	5850.00
4' x 24'	1.000	Ea.	45.451	3500.00	6750.00
6' x 10'	1.000	Ea.	24.840	2500.00	4600.00
6' x 16'	1.000	Ea.	34.555	3475.00	6400.00
6' x 24'	1.000	Ea.	44.712	4500.00	8275.00
8' x 10'	1.000	Ea.	33.120	3350.00	6150.00
8' x 16'	1.000	Ea.	57.628	5800.00	10,700.00
8' x 24'	1.000	Ea.	74.520	7500.00	13,800.00
Free standing, 8' x 8'	1.000	Ea.	26.016	3825.00	6625.00
8' x 16'	1.000	Ea.	45.284	6675.00	11,500.00
8' x 24'	1.000	Ea.	58.536	8625.00	14,900.00
10' x 10'	1.000	Ea.	28.200	4725.00	7950.00
10' x 16'	1.000	Ea.	36.096	6050.00	10,200.00
10' x 24'	1.000	Ea.	47.376	7925.00	13,400.00
14' x 10'	1.000	Ea.	31.080	5850.00	9800.00
14' x 16'	1.000	Ea.	37.296	7000.00	11,800.00
14' x 24'	1.000	Ea.	49.979	9400.00	15,800.00
Deluxe, lean to, shell only, not incl. 2' stub wall, foundation, floors, or heat, 4' x 10'	1.000	Ea.	20.640	3675.00	6125.00
4' x 16'	1.000	Ea.	33.024	5875.00	9800.00
4' x 24'	1.000	Ea.	49.536	8825.00	14,700.00
6' x 10'	1.000	Ea.	30.960	5525.00	9175.00
6' x 16'	1.000	Ea.	49.536	8825.00	14,700.00
6' x 24'	1.000	Ea.	74.304	13,200.00	22.000.00
8' x 10'	1.000	Ea.	41.280	7350.00	12,200.00
8' x 16'	1.000	Ea.	66.048	11,800.00	19,600.00
8' x 24'	1.000	Ea.	99.072	17,700.00	29,400.00
Free standing, 8' x 8'	1.000	Ea.	18.624	5100.00	8175.00
8' x 16'	1.000	Ea.	37.248	10,200.00	16,400.00
8' x 24'	1.000	Ea.	55.872	15,300.00	24,500.00
10' x 10'	1.000	Ea.	29.100	7975.00	12,800.00
10' x 16'	1.000	Ea.	46.560	12,800.00	20,400.00
10' x 24'	1.000	Ea.	69.840	19,200.00	30,700.00
14' x 10'	1.000	Ea.	40.740	11,200.00	17,900.00
14' x 16'	1.000	Ea.	65.184	17,900.00	28,600.00
14' x 24'	1.000	Ea.	97.776	26,800.00	42,900

Be sure to read pages 155–157 for proper use of this section.

DIVISION 8
MECHANICAL

Two Fixture Lavatory System

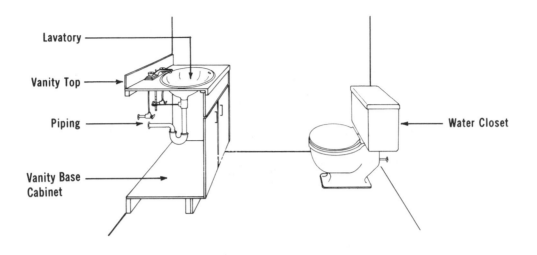

Lavatory

Vanity Top

Piping

Vanity Base Cabinet

Water Closet

SYSTEM DESCRIPTION	QUAN.	UNIT	MAN-HOURS	MAT. COST	COST EACH
LAVATORY INSTALLED WITH VANITY, PLUMBING IN 2 WALLS					
Water closet, floor mounted, 2 piece, close coupled, white	1.000	Ea.	3.020	140.00	
Rough-in supply, waste and vent for water closet	1.000	Ea.	2.860	37.00	
Lavatory, 20" x 18", P.E. cast iron, white	1.000	Ea.	2.500	140.00	
Rough-in supply, waste and vent for lavatory	1.000	Ea.	3.542	36.00	
Piping, supply, 1/2" copper	10.000	L.F.	1.510	10.00	
Waste, 4" cast iron, no-hub	7.000	L.F.	2.114	42.00	
Vent, 2" cast iron	12.000	L.F.	3.144	40.00	
Vanity base cabinet, 2 door, 30" wide	1.000	Ea.	1.630	200.00	Contractor's Fee
Vanity top, plastic & laminated, square edge	2.670	L.F.	.712	81.00	
TOTAL			21.032	726.00	**1725.00**
LAVATORY WITH WALL-HUNG LAVATORY, PLUMBING IN 2 WALLS					
Water closet, floor mounted, 2 piece, close coupled, white	1.000	Ea.	3.020	140.00	
Rough-in supply, waste and vent for water closet	1.000	Ea.	2.860	37.00	
Lavatory, 20" x 18", P.E. cast iron, wall hung, white	1.000	Ea.	2.000	155.00	
Rough-in supply, waste and vent for lavatory	1.000	Ea.	3.542	36.00	
Piping, supply, 1/2" copper	10.000	L.F.	1.510	10.00	
Waste, 4" cast iron, no-hub	7.000	L.F.	2.114	42.00	
Vent, 2" cast iron	12.000	L.F.	3.144	40.00	
Carrier, steel, for studs, no arms	1.000	Ea.	1.140	14.85	Contractor's Fee
TOTAL			19.330	474.85	**1300.00**

Be sure to read pages 155–157 for proper use of this section.

Two Fixture Lavatory System

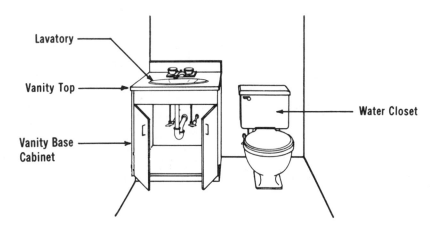

Lavatory

Vanity Top

Vanity Base Cabinet

Water Closet

SYSTEM DESCRIPTION	QUAN.	UNIT	MAN-HOURS	MAT. COST	COST EACH
LAVATORY INSTALLED WITH VANITY, PLUMBING IN 1 WALL					
Water closet, floor mounted, 2 piece, close coupled, white	1.000	Ea.	3.020	170.00	
Rough-in supply, waste and vent for water closet	1.000	Ea.	2.860	37.00	
Lavatory, 20″ x 18″ P.E. cast iron, white	1.000	Ea.	2.500	160.00	
Rough-in supply, waste and vent for lavatory	1.000	Ea.	3.542	36.00	
Piping, supply, 1/2″ copper	6.000	L.F.	.906	6.00	
Waste, 4″ cast iron, no-hub	4.000	L.F.	1.208	24.00	
Vent, 2″ cast iron	6.000	L.F.	1.572	19.60	
Vanity base cabinet, 2 door, 30″ wide	1.000	Ea.	1.630	200.00	
Vanity top, plastic & laminated, square edges	2.670	L.F.	.712	81.00	Contractor's Fee
TOTAL			17.950	733.60	**1575.00**
LAVATORY WITH WALL-HUNG LAVATORY, PLUMBING IN 1 WALL					
Water closet, floor mounted, 2 piece close coupled, white	1.000	Ea.	3.020	170.00	
Rough-in supply, waste and vent for water closet	1.000	Ea.	2.860	37.00	
Lavatory, 20″ x 18″, P.E. cast iron, wall hung, white	1.000	Ea.	2.000	125.00	
Rough-in supply, waste and vent for lavatory	1.000	Ea.	3.542	36.00	
Piping, supply, 1/2″ copper	6.000	L.F.	.906	6.00	
Waste, 4″ cast iron, no-hub	4.000	L.F.	1.208	24.00	
Vent, 2″ cast iron	6.000	L.F.	1.572	19.60	
Carrier, steel, for studs, no arms	1.000	Ea.	1.330	97.00	Contractor's Fee
TOTAL			16.438	514.60	**1275.00**

Be sure to read pages 155–157 for proper use of this section.

Three Fixture Bathroom System

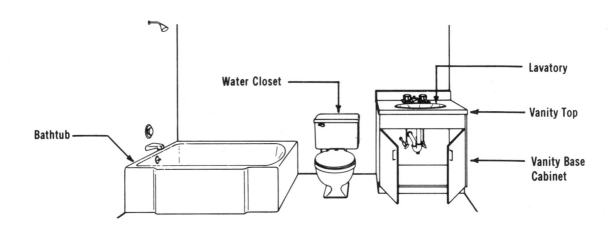

SYSTEM DESCRIPTION	QUAN.	UNIT	MAN-HOURS	MAT. COST	COST EACH
BATHROOM INSTALLED WITH VANITY					
Water closet, floor mounted, 2 piece, close coupled, white	1.000	Ea.	3.020	140.00	
Rough-in supply, waste and vent for water closet	1.000	Ea.	2.378	37.00	
Lavatory, 20" x 18", P.E. cast iron with accessories, white	1.000	Ea.	2.500	140.00	
Rough-in supply, waste and vent for lavatory	1.000	Ea.	2.790	35.00	
Bathtub, P.E. cast iron, 5' long with accessories, white	1.000	Ea.	3.640	320.00	
Rough-in supply, waste and vent for bathtub	1.000	Ea.	2.410	39.00	
Piping, supply, 1/2" copper	20.000	L.F.	1.980	20.00	
Waste, 4" cast iron, no-hub	9.000	L.F.	2.484	53.00	
Vent, 2" galvanized steel	6.000	L.F.	1.500	20.00	
Vanity base cabinet, 2 door, 30" wide	1.000	Ea.	1.630	200.00	
Vanity top, plastic laminated square edge	2.670	L.F.	.712	60.00	Contractor's Fee
TOTAL			25.044	1064.00	**2450.00**
BATHROOM WITH WALL-HUNG LAVATORY					
Water closet, floor mounted, 2 piece, close coupled, white	1.000	Ea.	3.020	140.00	
Rough-in supply, waste and vent for water closet	1.000	Ea.	2.378	37.00	
Lavatory, 20" x 18" P.E. cast iron, wall hung, white	1.000	Ea.	2.000	155.00	
Rough-in supply, waste and vent for lavatory	1.000	Ea.	2.790	35.00	
Bathtub, P.E. cast iron, 5' long with accessories, white	1.000	Ea.	3.640	320.00	
Rough-in supply, waste and vent for bathtub	1.000	Ea.	4.778	84.00	
Piping, supply, 1/2" copper	20.000	L.F.	1.980	20.00	
Waste, 4" cast iron, no-hub	9.000	L.F.	2.484	53.00	
Vent, 2" galvanized steel	6.000	L.F.	1.500	20.00	
Carrier, steel, for studs, no arms	1.000	Ea.	1.140	14.85	Contractor's Fee
TOTAL			25.710	878.85	**2150.00**

Be sure to read pages 155–157 for proper use of this section.

Three Fixture Bathroom System

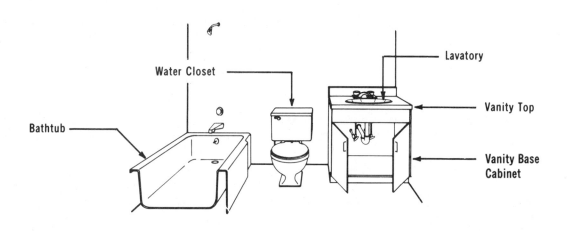

SYSTEM DESCRIPTION	QUAN.	UNIT	MAN-HOURS	MAT. COST	COST EACH
BATHROOM WITH LAVATORY INSTALLED IN VANITY					
Water closet, floor mounted, 2 piece, close coupled, white	1.000	Ea.	3.020	140.00	
Rough-in supply, waste and vent for water closet	1.000	Ea.	2.378	37.00	
Lavatory, 20″ x 18″, P.E. cast iron with accessories, white	1.000	Ea.	2.500	140.00	
Rough-in supply, waste and vent for lavatory	1.000	Ea.	2.790	35.00	
Bathtub, P.E. cast iron, 5′ long with accessories, white	1.000	Ea.	3.640	320.00	
Rough-in supply, waste and vent for bathtub	1.000	Ea.	2.410	39.00	
Piping, supply, 1/2″ copper	10.000	L.F.	.990	10.00	
Waste, 4″ cast iron, no-hub	6.000	L.F.	1.656	36.00	
Vent, 2″ galvanized steel	6.000	L.F.	1.500	20.00	
Vanity base cabinet, 2 door, 30″ wide	1.000	Ea.	1.630	200.00	
Vanity top, plastic laminated square edge	2.670	L.F.	.712	60.00	Contractor's Fee
TOTAL			23.226	1037.00	**2350.00**
BATHROOM WITH WALL-HUNG LAVATORY					
Water closet, floor mounted, 2 piece, close coupled, white	1.000	Ea.	3.020	140.00	
Rough-in supply, waste and vent for water closet	1.000	Ea.	2.378	37.00	
Lavatory, 20″ x 18″ P.E. cast iron, wall hung, white	1.000	Ea.	2.000	155.00	
Rough-in supply, waste and vent for lavatory	1.000	Ea.	2.790	35.00	
Bathtub, P.E. cast iron, 5′ long with accessories, white	1.000	Ea.	3.640	320.00	
Rough-in supply, waste and vent for bathtub	1.000	Ea.	2.410	39.00	
Piping, supply, 1/2″ copper	10.000	L.F.	.990	10.00	
Waste, 4″ cast iron, no-hub	6.000	L.F.	1.656	36.00	
Vent, 2″ galvanized steel	6.000	L.F.	1.500	20.00	
Carrier, steel, for studs, no arms	1.000	Ea.	1.140	14.85	Contractor's Fee
TOTAL			21.524	806.85	**1975.00**

Be sure to read pages 155–157 for proper use of this section.

Three Fixture Bathroom System

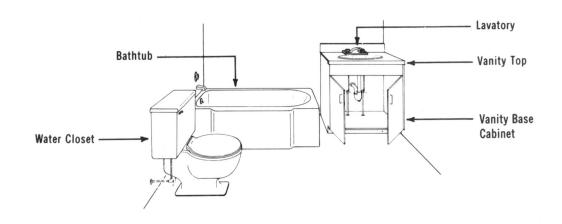

SYSTEM DESCRIPTION	QUAN.	UNIT	MAN-HOURS	MAT. COST	COST EACH
BATHROOM WITH LAVATORY INSTALLED IN VANITY					
Water closet, floor mounted, 2 piece, close coupled, white	1.000	Ea.	3.020	140.00	
Rough-in supply, waste and vent for water closet	1.000	Ea.	2.378	37.00	
Lavatory, 20" x 18", P.E. cast iron with accessories, white	1.000	Ea.	2.500	140.00	
Rough-in supply, waste and vent for lavatory	1.000	Ea.	2.790	35.00	
Bathtub, P.E. cast iron, 5' long with accessories, white	1.000	Ea.	3.640	320.00	
Rough-in supply, waste and vent for bathtub	1.000	Ea.	2.410	39.00	
Piping, supply, 1/2" copper	32.000	L.F.	3.168	32.00	
Waste, 4" cast iron, no-hub	12.000	L.F.	3.312	71.00	
Vent, 2" steel, galvanized	6.000	L.F.	1.500	20.00	
Vanity base cabinet, 2 door, 30" wide	1.000	Ea.	1.630	200.00	Contractor's Fee
Vanity top, plastic laminated square edge	2.670	L.F.	.712	60.00	
TOTAL			27.060	1094.00	**2575.00**
BATHROOM WITH WALL-HUNG LAVATORY					
Water closet, floor mounted, 2 piece, close coupled, white	1.000	Ea.	3.020	140.00	
Rough-in supply, waste and vent for water closet	1.000	Ea.	2.378	37.00	
Lavatory, 20" x 18" P.E. cast iron, wall hung, white	1.000	Ea.	2.000	155.00	
Rough-in supply, waste and vent for lavatory	1.000	Ea.	2.790	35.00	
Bathtub, P.E. cast iron, 5' long with accessories, white	1.000	Ea.	3.640	320.00	
Rough-in supply, waste and vent for bathtub	1.000	Ea.	2.410	39.00	
Piping, supply, 1/2" copper	32.000	L.F.	3.168	32.00	
Waste, 4" cast iron, no-hub	12.000	L.F.	3.312	71.00	
Vent, 2" steel, galvanized	6.000	L.F.	1.500	20.00	
Carrier, steel, for studs, no arms	1.000	Ea.	1.140	14.85	Contractor's Fee
TOTAL			25.358	863.85	**2175.00**

Be sure to read pages 155–157 for proper use of this section.

Three Fixture Bathroom System

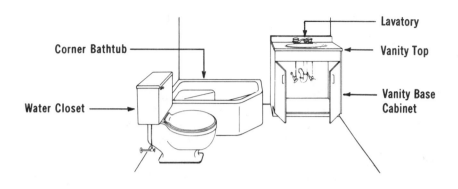

Corner Bathtub

Water Closet

Lavatory

Vanity Top

Vanity Base Cabinet

SYSTEM DESCRIPTION	QUAN.	UNIT	MAN-HOURS	MAT. COST	COST EACH
BATHROOM WITH LAVATORY INSTALLED IN VANITY					
Water closet, floor mounted, 2 piece, close coupled, white	1.000	Ea.	3.020	140.00	
Rough-in supply, waste and vent for water closet	1.000	Ea.	2.378	37.00	
Lavatory, 20" x 18", P.E. cast iron with fittings, white	1.000	Ea.	2.500	140.00	
Rough-in supply, waste and vent for lavatory	1.000	Ea.	2.790	35.00	
Bathtub, P.E. cast iron, 5' long corner, with fittings, white	1.000	Ea.	3.640	1025.00	
Rough-in supply, waste and vent for bathtub	1.000	Ea.	2.410	39.00	
Piping, supply, 1/2" copper	32.000	L.F.	3.168	32.00	
Waste, 4" cast iron, no-hub	12.000	L.F.	3.312	71.00	
Vent, 2" steel, galvanized	6.000	L.F.	1.500	20.00	
Vanity base cabinet, 2 door, 30" wide	1.000	Ea.	1.630	200.00	
Vanity top, plastic laminated, square edge	2.670	L.F.	.712	81.00	Contractor's Fee
TOTAL			27.060	1820.00	**3650.00**
BATHROOM WITH WALL-HUNG LAVATORY					
Water closet, floor mounted, 2 piece, close coupled, white	1.000	Ea.	3.020	140.00	
Rough-in supply, waste and vent for water closet	1.000	Ea.	2.378	37.00	
Lavatory, 20" x 18", P.E. cast iron, with fittings, white	1.000	Ea.	2.000	155.00	
Rough-in supply, waste and vent, for lavatory	1.000	Ea.	2.790	35.00	
Bathtub, P.E. cast iron, 5' long corner, with fittings, white	1.000	Ea.	3.640	1025.00	
Rough-in supply, waste and vent, bathtub	1.000	Ea.	2.410	39.00	
Piping, supply, 1/2" copper	32.000	L.F.	3.168	32.00	
Waste, 4" cast iron, no-hub	12.000	L.F.	3.312	71.00	
Vent, 2" steel, galvanized	6.000	L.F.	1.500	20.00	
Carrier, steel, for studs, no arms	1.000	Ea.	1.140	14.85	Contractor's Fee
TOTAL			25.358	1568.85	**3225.00**

Be sure to read pages 155–157 for proper use of this section.

Three Fixture Bathroom System

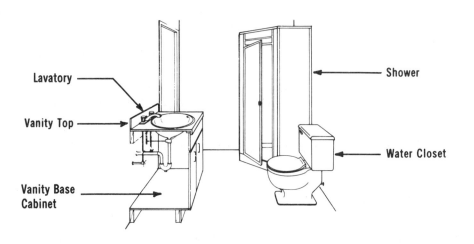

Lavatory

Vanity Top

Vanity Base
Cabinet

Shower

Water Closet

SYSTEM DESCRIPTION	QUAN.	UNIT	MAN-HOURS	MAT. COST	COST EACH
BATHROOM WITH SHOWER, LAVATORY INSTALLED IN VANITY					
Water closet, floor mounted, 2 piece, close coupled, white	1.000	Ea.	3.020	140.00	
Rough-in supply, waste and vent for water closet	1.000	Ea.	2.378	37.00	
Lavatory, 20" x 18", P.E. cast iron with fittings, white	1.000	Ea.	2.500	140.00	
Rough-in supply, waste and vent for lavatory	1.000	Ea.	2.790	35.00	
Shower, steel enameled, stone base, white	1.000	Ea.	8.000	350.00	
Rough-in supply, waste and vent for shower	1.000	Ea.	3.243	39.00	
Piping supply, 1/2" copper	36.000	L.F.	4.158	42.00	
Waste, 4" cast iron, no-hub	7.000	L.F.	2.760	60.00	
Vent, 2" steel galvanized	6.000	L.F.	2.250	30.00	
Vanity base cabinet, 2 door, 30" wide	1.000	Ea.	1.630	200.00	Contractor's Fee
Vanity top, plastic laminated, square edge	2.170	L.F.	.712	63.00	
TOTAL			33.441	1136.00	**2850.00**
BATHROOM WITH SHOWER, WALL-HUNG LAVATORY					
Water closet, floor mounted, 2 piece, close coupled, white	1.000	Ea.	3.020	140.00	
Rough-in supply, waste and vent for water closet	1.000	Ea.	2.378	37.00	
Lavatory, 20" x 18", P.E. cast iron with fittings, white	1.000	Ea.	2.000	155.00	
Rough-in supply, waste and vent for lavatory	1.000	Ea.	2.790	35.00	
Shower, steel enameled, stone base, white	1.000	Ea.	8.000	350.00	
Rough-in supply, waste and vent for shower	1.000	Ea.	3.243	39.00	
Piping supply, 1/2" copper	36.000	L.F.	4.158	42.00	
Waste, 4" cast iron, no-hub	7.000	L.F.	2.760	60.00	
Vent, 2" steel, galvanized	6.000	L.F.	2.250	30.00	
Carrier, steel, for studs, no arms	1.000	Ea.	1.140	14.85	Contractor's Fee
TOTAL			31.739	902.85	**2450.00**

Be sure to read pages 155–157 for proper use of this section.

Three Fixture Bathroom System

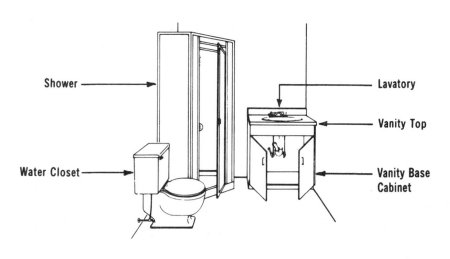

SYSTEM DESCRIPTION	QUAN.	UNIT	MAN-HOURS	MAT. COST	COST EACH
BATHROOM WITH CORNER SHOWER, LAVATORY INSTALLED IN VANITY					
Water closet, floor mounted, 2 piece, close coupled, white	1.000	Ea.	3.020	140.00	
Rough-in supply, waste and vent for water closet	1.000	Ea.	2.378	37.00	
Lavatory, 20″ x 18″, P.E. cast iron with fittings, white	1.000	Ea.	2.500	140.00	
Rough-in supply, waste and vent for lavatory	1.000	Ea.	2.790	35.00	
Shower, steel enameled, stone base, corner, white	1.000	Ea.	8.000	350.00	
Rough-in supply, waste and vent for shower	1.000	Ea.	3.243	39.00	
Piping, supply, 1/2″ copper	36.000	L.F.	3.564	36.00	
Waste, 4″ cast iron, no-hub	7.000	L.F.	1.932	42.00	
Vent, 2″ steel, galvanized	6.000	L.F.	1.500	20.00	
Vanity base cabinet, 2 door, 30″ wide	1.000	Ea.	1.630	200.00	
Vanity top, plastic laminated, square edge	2.670	L.F.	.712	60.00	Contractor's Fee
TOTAL			31.269	1099.00	**2725.00**
BATHROOM, WITH CORNER SHOWER, WITH WALL-HUNG LAVATORY					
Water closet, floor mounted, 2 piece, close coupled, white	1.000	Ea.	3.020	140.00	
Rough-in supply, waste and vent for water closet	1.000	Ea.	2.378	37.00	
Lavatory, wall hung, 20″ x 18″, P.E. cast iron with fittings, white	1.000	Ea.	2.000	155.00	
Rough-in supply, waste and vent for lavatory	1.000	Ea.	2.790	35.00	
Shower, steel enameled, stone base, corner, white	1.000	Ea.	8.000	350.00	
Rough-in supply, waste and vent for shower	1.000	Ea.	3.243	39.00	
Piping, supply, 1/2″ copper	36.000	L.F.	3.564	42.00	
Waste, 4″ cast iron, no-hub	7.000	L.F.	1.932	42.00	
Vent, 2″ steel, galvanized	6.000	L.F.	1.500	20.00	
Carrier, steel, for studs, no arms	1.000	Ea.	1.140	14.85	Contractor's Fee
TOTAL			29.567	868.85	**2325.00**

Be sure to read pages 155–157 for proper use of this section.

Four Fixture Bathroom System

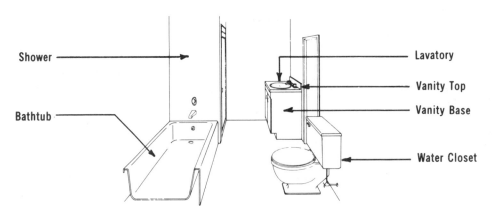

Shower —
Bathtub —

Lavatory
Vanity Top
Vanity Base
Water Closet

SYSTEM DESCRIPTION	QUAN.	UNIT	MAN-HOURS	MAT. COST	COST EACH
BATHROOM WITH LAVATORY INSTALLED IN VANITY					
Water closet, floor mounted, 2 piece, close coupled, white	1.000	Ea.	3.020	140.00	
Rough-in supply, waste and vent for water closet	1.000	Ea.	2.378	37.00	
Lavatory, 20″ x 18″, P.E. cast iron with fittings, white	1.000	Ea.	2.500	140.00	
Shower, steel, enameled, stone base, corner, white	1.000	Ea.	8.890	665.00	
Rough-in supply, waste and vent for lavatory and shower	2.000	Ea.	7.668	95.00	
Bathtub, P.E. cast iron, 5′ long with fittings, white	1.000	Ea.	3.640	320.00	
Rough-in supply, waste and vent for bathtub	1.000	Ea.	2.410	39.00	
Piping, supply, 1/2″ copper	42.000	L.F.	4.158	42.00	
Waste, 4″ cast iron, no-hub	10.000	L.F.	2.760	59.00	
Vent, 2″ steel, galvanized	13.000	L.F.	3.250	43.00	
Vanity base, 2 doors, 30″ wide	1.000	Ea.	1.630	200.00	**Contractor's Fee**
Vanity top, plastic laminated, square edge	2.670	L.F.	.712	60.00	
TOTAL			43.016	1840.00	**4225.00**
BATHROOM WITH WALL-HUNG LAVATORY					
Water closet, floor mounted, 2 piece, close coupled, white	1.000	Ea.	3.020	140.00	
Rough-in supply, waste and vent for water closet	1.000	Ea.	2.378	37.00	
Lavatory, 20″ x 18″, P.E. cast iron with fittings, white	1.000	Ea.	2.000	155.00	
Shower, steel enameled, stone base, corner, white	1.000	Ea.	8.890	665.00	
Rough-in supply, waste and vent for lavatory and shower	2.000	Ea.	7.668	95.00	
Bathtub, P.E. cast iron, 5′ long with fittings, white	1.000	Ea.	3.640	320.00	
Rough-in supply, waste and vent for bathtub	1.000	Ea.	2.410	39.00	
Piping, supply, 1/2″ copper	42.000	L.F.	4.158	42.00	
Waste, 4″ cast iron, no-hub	10.000	L.F.	2.760	59.00	
Vent, 2″ steel, galvanized	13.000	L.F.	3.250	43.00	
Carrier, steel, for studs, no arms	1.000	Ea.	1.140	14.85	**Contractor's Fee**
TOTAL			41.314	1609.85	**3850.00**

Be sure to read pages 155–157 for proper use of this section.

Four Fixture Bathroom System

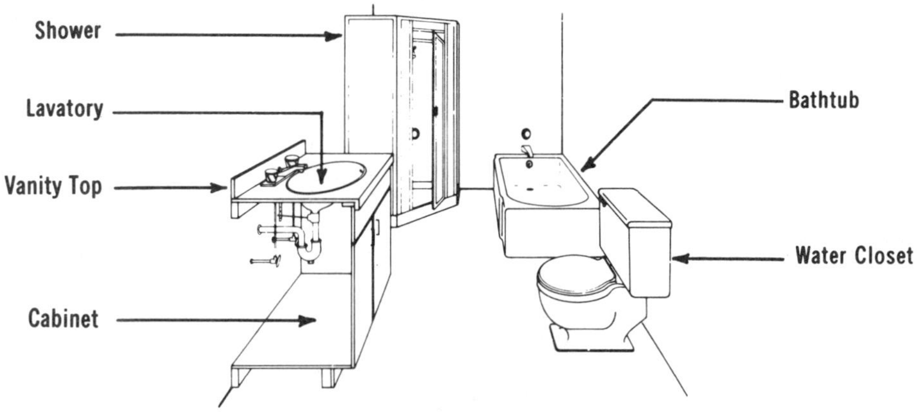

Shower
Lavatory
Vanity Top
Cabinet
Bathtub
Water Closet

SYSTEM DESCRIPTION	QUAN.	UNIT	MAN-HOURS	MAT. COST	COST EACH
BATHROOM WITH LAVATORY INSTALLED IN VANITY					
Water closet, floor mounted, 2 piece, close coupled, white	1.000	Ea.	3.020	140.00	
Rough-in supply, waste and vent for water closet	1.000	Ea.	2.378	37.00	
Lavatory, 20" x 18", P.E. cast iron with fittings, white	1.000	Ea.	2.500	140.00	
Shower, steel, enameled, stone base, corner, white	1.000	Ea.	8.890	665.00	
Rough-in supply waste and vent for lavatory and shower	2.000	Ea.	7.668	95.00	
Bathtub, P.E. cast iron, 5' long with fittings, white	1.000	Ea.	3.640	320.00	
Rough-in supply waste and vent for bathtub	1.000	Ea.	2.410	39.00	
Piping supply, 1/2" copper	42.000	L.F.	4.950	50.00	
Waste, 4" cast iron, no-hub	10.000	L.F.	4.140	89.00	
Vent, 2" steel galvanized	13.000	L.F.	4.500	60.00	
Vanity base, 2 doors, 30" wide	1.000	Ea.	1.630	200.00	
Vanity top, plastic laminated, square edge	2.670	L.F.	.712	62.00	Contractor's Fee
TOTAL			46.438	1897.00	**4450.00**
BATHROOM WITH WALL-HUNG LAVATORY					
Water closet, floor mounted, 2 piece, close coupled, white	1.000	Ea.	3.020	140.00	
Rough-in supply, waste and vent for water closet	1.000	Ea.	2.378	37.00	
Lavatory, 20" x 18", P.E. cast iron with fittings, white	1.000	Ea.	2.000	155.00	
Shower, steel enameled, stone base, corner, white	1.000	Ea.	8.890	665.00	
Rough-in supply, waste and vent for lavatory and shower	2.000	Ea.	7.668	95.00	
Bathtub, P.E. cast iron, 5' long with fittings, white	1.000	Ea.	3.640	320.00	
Rough-in supply, waste and vent for bathtub	1.000	Ea.	2.410	39.00	
Piping, supply, 1/2" copper	42.000	L.F.	4.950	50.00	
Waste, 4" cast iron, no-hub	10.000	L.F.	4.140	89.00	
Vent, 2" steel galvanized	13.000	L.F.	4.500	60.00	
Carrier, steel for studs, no arms	1.000	Ea.	1.140	14.85	Contractor's Fee
TOTAL			44.736	1664.85	**4050.00**

Be sure to read pages 155–157 for proper use of this section.

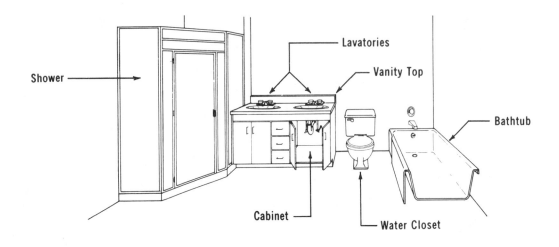

SYSTEM DESCRIPTION	QUAN.	UNIT	MAN-HOURS	MAT. COST	COST EACH
BATHROOM WITH SHOWER, BATHTUB, LAVATORIES IN VANITY					
Water closet, floor mounted, 1 piece combination, white	1.000	Ea.	3.020	780.00	
Rough-in supply, waste and vent for water closet	1.000	Ea.	2.860	37.00	
Lavatory, 20" x 16", vitreous china oval, with fittings, white	2.000	Ea.	5.000	410.00	
Shower, steel enameled, stone base, corner, white	1.000	Ea.	8.890	665.00	
Rough-in supply, waste and vent for lavatory and shower	3.000	Ea.	10.434	105.00	
Bathtub, P.E. cast iron, 5' long with fittings, white	1.000	Ea.	3.640	355.00	
Rough-in supply, waste and vent for bathtub	1.000	Ea.	3.862	45.00	
Piping, supply, 1/2" copper	42.000	L.F.	6.342	42.00	
Waste, 4" cast iron, no-hub	10.000	L.F.	3.020	59.00	
Vent, 2" steel, galvanized	13.000	L.F.	3.250	43.00	
Vanity base, 2 door, 24" x 48"	1.000	Ea.	2.420	255.00	Contractor's
Vanity top, plastic laminated, square edge	4.170	L.F.	1.113	94.00	Fee
TOTAL			53.851	2890.00	**5925.00**

Be sure to read pages 155–157 for proper use of this section.

Gas Heating/Cooling System

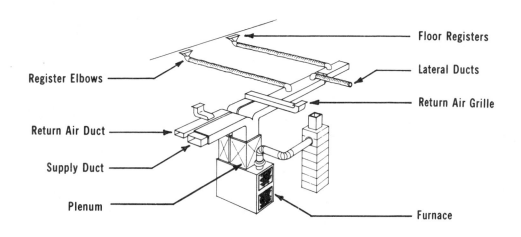

SYSTEM DESCRIPTION	QUAN.	UNIT	MAN-HOURS	MAT. COST	COST EACH
HEATING ONLY, GAS FIRED HOT AIR, ONE ZONE, 1200 S.F. BUILDING					
Furnace, gas, up flow	1.000	Ea.	4.710	565.00	
Intermittent pilot	1.000	Ea.		91.00	
Supply duct, rigid fiberglass	176.000	L.F.	12.144	97.00	
Return duct, sheet metal, galvanized	158.000	Lb.	16.116	245.00	
Lateral ducts, 6" flexible fiberglass	144.000	L.F.	8.928	255.00	
Register, elbows	12.000	Ea.	3.204	120.00	
Floor registers, enameled steel	12.000	Ea.	3.000	140.00	
Floor grille, return air	2.000	Ea.	.728	28.00	
Thermostat	1.000	Ea.	1.000	16.30	
Plenum	1.000	Ea.	1.000	61.00	Contractor's Fee
TOTAL			50.830	1618.30	**4175.00**
HEATING/COOLING, GAS FIRED FORCED AIR, ONE ZONE, 1200 S.F. BUILDING					
Furnace, including plenum, compressor, coil	1.000	Ea.	14.720	2950.00	
Intermittent pilot	1.000	Ea.		91.00	
Supply duct, rigid fiberglass	176.000	L.F.	12.144	97.00	
Return duct, sheet metal, galvanized	158.000	Lb.	16.116	245.00	
Lateral duct, 6" flexible fiberglass	144.000	L.F.	8.928	255.00	
Register elbows	12.000	Ea.	3.204	120.00	
Floor registers, enameled steel	12.000	Ea.	3.000	140.00	
Floor grille, return air	2.000	Ea.	.728	28.00	
Thermostat	1.000	Ea.	1.000	16.30	
Refrigeration piping	25.000	L.F.		145.00	Contractor's Fee
TOTAL			59.840	4087.30	**8150.00**

Be sure to read pages 155–157 for proper use of this section.

Oil Fired Heating/Cooling System

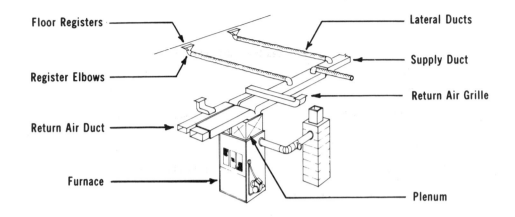

Floor Registers — Lateral Ducts — Supply Duct — Register Elbows — Return Air Grille — Return Air Duct — Furnace — Plenum

SYSTEM DESCRIPTION	QUAN.	UNIT	MAN-HOURS	MAT. COST	COST EACH
HEATING ONLY, OIL FIRED HOT AIR, ONE ZONE, 1200 S.F. BUILDING					
Furnace, oil fired, atomizing gun type burner	1.000	Ea.	4.570	810.00	
Oil piping to furnace	1.000	Ea.	3.181	37.00	
Oil tank, 275 gallon, on legs	1.000	Ea.	3.200	240.00	
Supply duct, rigid fiberglass	176.000	L.F.	12.144	97.00	
Return duct, sheet metal, galvanized	158.000	Lb.	16.116	245.00	
Lateral ducts, 6" flexible fiberglass	144.000	L.F.	8.928	255.00	
Register elbows	12.000	Ea.	3.204	120.00	
Floor register, enameled steel	12.000	Ea.	3.000	140.00	
Floor grille, return air	2.000	Ea.	.728	28.00	
Thermostat	1.000	Ea.	1.000	16.55	Contractor's Fee
TOTAL			56.071	1988.55	**4925.00**
HEATING/COOLING, OIL FIRED, FORCED AIR, ONE ZONE, 1200 S.F. BUILDING					
Furnace, including plenum, compressor, coil	1.000	Ea.	16.000	3350.00	
Oil piping to furnace	1.000	Ea.	3.413	93.00	
Oil tank, 275 gallon on legs	1.000	Ea.	3.200	240.00	
Supply duct, rigid fiberglass	176.000	L.F.	12.144	97.00	
Return duct, sheet metal, galvanized	158.000	Lb.	16.116	245.00	
Lateral ducts, 6" flexible fiberglass	144.000	L.F.	8.928	255.00	
Register elbows	12.000	Ea.	3.204	120.00	
Floor registers, enameled steel	12.000	Ea.	3.000	140.00	
Floor grille, return air	2.000	Ea.	.728	28.00	
Refrigeration piping	25.000	L.F.		145.00	Contractor's Fee
TOTAL			66.733	4713.00	**9325.00**

Be sure to read pages 155–157 for proper use of this section.

Hot Water Heating System

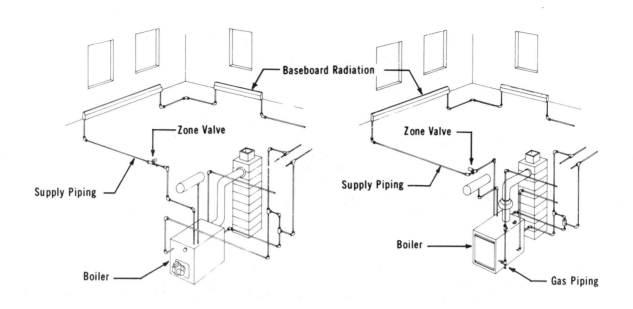

SYSTEM DESCRIPTION	QUAN.	UNIT	MAN-HOURS	MAT. COST	COST PER SYSTEM
OIL FIRED HOT WATER HEATING SYSTEM, AREA TO 1200 S.F. BUILDING					
Boiler package, oil fired, 97 MBH, area to 1200 S.F. building	1.000	Ea.	12.630	1900.00	
Oil piping, 1/4" flexible copper tubing	1.000	Ea.	3.219	45.00	
Oil tank, 275 gallon, with black iron filler pipe	1.000	Ea.	3.200	240.00	
Supply piping, 3/4" copper tubing	176.000	L.F.	18.480	260.00	
Supply fittings, copper 3/4"	36.000	Ea.	15.156	13.85	
Supply valves, 3/4"	2.000	Ea.	.800	38.00	
Baseboard radiation, 3/4"	106.000	L.F.	29.256	870.00	
Zone valve	1.000	Ea.	.400	41.00	Contractor's Fee
TOTAL			83.141	3407.85	**8075.00**
OIL FIRED HOT WATER HEATING SYSTEM, AREA TO 2400 S.F. BUILDING					
Boiler package, oil fired, 225 MBH, area to 2400 S.F. building	1.000	Ea.	17.140	2875.00	
Oil piping, 3/8" flexible copper tubing	1.000	Ea.	3.264	55.00	
Oil tank, 550 gallon, with black iron filler pipe	1.000	Ea.	4.000	1100.00	
Supply piping, 3/4" copper tubing	228.000	L.F.	23.940	340.00	
Supply fittings, copper	46.000	Ea.	19.366	17.70	
Supply valves	2.000	Ea.	.800	38.00	
Baseboard radiation	212.000	L.F.	58.512	1750.00	
Zone valve	1.000	Ea.	.400	41.00	Contractor's Fee
TOTAL			127.422	6216.70	**13,775.00**

Be sure to read pages 155–157 for proper use of this section.

DIVISION 9
ELECTRICAL

Electric Service System

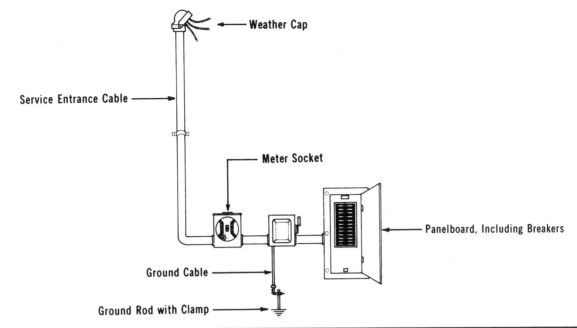

Weather Cap

Service Entrance Cable

Meter Socket

Panelboard, Including Breakers

Ground Cable

Ground Rod with Clamp

SYSTEM DESCRIPTION	QUAN.	UNIT	MAN-HOURS	MAT. COST	COST EACH
100 AMP SERVICE					
Weather cap	1.000	Ea.	.667	4.60	
Service entrance cable	10.000	L.F.	.760	33.00	
Meter socket	1.000	Ea.	2.500	25.00	
Ground rod with clamp	1.000	Ea.	1.510	10.80	
Ground cable	5.000	L.F.	.250	7.25	
Panel board, 12 circuit	1.000	Ea.	6.670	115.00	Contractor's Fee
TOTAL			12.357	195.65	**750.00**
200 AMP SERVICE					
Weather cap	1.000	Ea.	1.000	13.50	
Service entrance cable	10.000	L.F.	1.140	24.00	
Meter socket	1.000	Ea.	4.210	45.00	
Ground rod with clamp	1.000	Ea.	1.820	27.00	
Ground cable	10.000	L.F.	.500	14.50	
3/4" EMT	5.000	L.F.	.310	2.64	
Panel board, 24 circuit	1.000	Ea.	12.310	285.00	Contractor's Fee
TOTAL			21.290	411.64	**1400.00**
400 AMP SERVICE					
Weather cap	2.000	Ea.	12.500	230.00	
Service entrance cable	180.000	L.F.	5.760	245.00	
Meter socket	1.000	Ea.	4.210	45.00	
Ground rod with clamp	1.000	Ea.	2.070	30.00	
Ground cable	20.000	L.F.	.480	18.25	
3/4" greenfield	20.000	L.F.	1.000	7.75	
Current transformer cabinet	1.000	Ea.	6.150	100.00	
Panel board, 42 circuit	1.000	Ea.	33.330	2175.00	Contractor's Fee
TOTAL			65.500	2851.00	**6675.00**

Be sure to read pages 155–157 for proper use of this section.

Electric Heating System

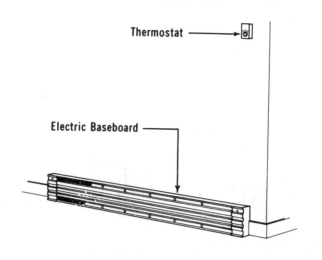

Thermostat

Electric Baseboard

SYSTEM DESCRIPTION	QUAN.	UNIT	MAN-HOURS	MAT. COST	COST EACH
4' BASEBOARD HEATER					
Electric baseboard heater, 4' long	1.000	Ea.	1.190	54.00	
Thermostat, integral	1.000	Ea.	.500	28.00	
Romex, 12-3 with ground	40.000	L.F.	1.600	19.80	
Panel board breaker, 20 Amp	1.000	Ea.	.300	5.70	Contractor's Fee
TOTAL			3.590	107.50	**295.00**
6' BASEBOARD HEATER					
Electric baseboard heater, 6' long	1.000	Ea.	1.600	80.00	
Thermostat, integral	1.000	Ea.	.500	28.00	
Romex, 12-3 with ground	40.000	L.F.	1.600	19.80	
Panel board breaker, 20 Amp	1.000	Ea.	.400	7.60	Contractor's Fee
TOTAL			4.100	135.40	**360.00**
8' BASEBOARD HEATER					
Electric baseboard heater, 8' long	1.000	Ea.	2.000	105.00	
Thermostat, integral	1.000	Ea.	.500	28.00	
Romex, 12-3 with ground	40.000	L.F.	1.600	19.80	
Panel board breaker, 20 Amp	1.000	Ea.	.500	9.55	Contractor's Fee
TOTAL			4.600	162.35	**410.00**
10' BASEBOARD HEATER					
Electric baseboard heater, 10' long	1.000	Ea.	2.420	120.00	
Thermostat, integral	1.000	Ea.	.500	28.00	
Romex, 12-3 with ground	40.000	L.F.	1.600	19.80	
Panel board breaker, 20 Amp	1.000	Ea.	.750	14.30	Contractor's Fee
TOTAL			5.270	182.10	**465.00**

Be sure to read pages 155–157 for proper use of this section.

Wiring Device Systems

The prices in this system are on a cost each basis and include 200 feet of
wire and conduit (as necessary) for each device.

SYSTEM DESCRIPTION	QUAN.	UNIT	MAN-HOURS	COST EACH MAT.	COST EACH TOTAL
Air conditioning receptacles					
Using non-metallic sheathed cable	1.000	Ea.	.800	10.05	44.00
Using BX cable	1.000	Ea.	.964	15.10	58.00
Using EMT conduit	1.000	Ea.	1.190	17.60	70.00
Disposal wiring					
Using non-metallic sheathed cable	1.000	Ea.	.889	8.80	47.00
Using BX cable	1.000	Ea.	1.070	12.60	58.00
Using EMT conduit	1.000	Ea.	1.330	16.35	75.00
Dryer circuit					
Using non-metallic sheathed cable	1.000	Ea.	1.450	25.00	92.00
Using BX cable	1.000	Ea.	1.740	31.00	110.00
Using EMT conduit	1.000	Ea.	2.160	35.00	135.00
Duplex receptacles					
Using non-metallic sheathed cable	1.000	Ea.	.615	10.05	38.00
Using BX cable	1.000	Ea.	.741	15.10	51.00
Using EMT conduit	1.000	Ea.	.920	17.60	60.00
Exhaust fan wiring					
Using non-metallic sheathed cable	1.000	Ea.	.800	10.05	44.00
Using BX cable	1.000	Ea.	.964	15.10	58.00
Using EMT conduit	1.000	Ea.	1.190	18.90	72.00
Furnace circuit & switch					
Using non-metallic sheathed cable	1.000	Ea.	1.330	13.85	70.00
Using BX cable	1.000	Ea.	1.600	17.60	87.00
Using EMT conduit	1.000	Ea.	2.000	23.00	110.00
Ground fault					
Using non-metallic sheathed cable	1.000	Ea.	1.000	45.00	105.00
Using BX cable	1.000	Ea.	1.210	51.00	120.00
Using EMT conduit	1.000	Ea.	1.480	54.00	135.00
Heater circuits					
Using non-metallic sheathed cable	1.000	Ea.	1.000	10.05	52.00
Using BX cable	1.000	Ea.	1.210	13.85	66.00
Using EMT conduit	1.000	Ea.	1.480	17.60	83.00
Lighting wiring					
Using non-metallic sheathed cable	1.000	Ea.	.500	10.05	34.00
Using BX cable	1.000	Ea.	.602	15.10	45.00
Using EMT conduit	1.000	Ea.	.748	18.90	56.00
Range circuits					
Using non-metallic sheathed cable	1.000	Ea.	2.000	38.00	130.00
Using BX cable	1.000	Ea.	2.420	52.00	170.00
Using EMT conduit	1.000	Ea.	2.960	59.00	200.00
Switches, single pole					
Using non-metallic sheathed cable	1.000	Ea.	.500	10.05	34.00
Using BX cable	1.000	Ea.	.602	15.10	45.00
Using EMT conduit	1.000	Ea.	.748	17.60	54.00
Switches, 3-way					
Using non-metallic sheathed cable	1.000	Ea.	.667	12.50	43.00
Using BX cable	1.000	Ea.	.800	18.90	57.00
Using EMT conduit	1.000	Ea.	1.330	30.00	94.00
Water heater					
Using non-metallic sheathed cable	1.000	Ea.	1.600	12.60	79.00
Using BX cable	1.000	Ea.	1.900	17.60	97.00
Using EMT conduit	1.000	Ea.	2.350	21.00	120.00
Weatherproof receptacle					
Using non-metallic sheathed cable	1.000	Ea.	1.330	73.00	160.00
Using BX cable	1.000	Ea.	1.600	77.00	175.00
Using EMT conduit	1.000	Ea.	2.000	82.00	195.00

Be sure to read pages 155–157 for proper use of this section.

Light Fixture Systems

The costs for these fixtures are on an each basis and include installation
of the fixture only. See wiring device systems.

DESCRIPTION	QUAN.	UNIT	MAN-HOURS	COST EACH MAT.	COST EACH TOTAL
Fluorescent strip, 4' long, 1 light, average	1.000	Ea.	.941	28.00	76.00
Deluxe	1.000	Ea.	1.129	33.00	92.00
2 lights, average	1.000	Ea.	1.000	29.00	87.00
Deluxe	1.000	Ea.	1.200	35.00	97.00
8' long, 1 light, average	1.000	Ea.	1.190	46.00	115.00
Deluxe	1.000	Ea.	1.428	55.00	135.00
2 lights, average	1.000	Ea.	1.290	53.00	125.00
Deluxe	1.000	Ea.	1.548	64.00	150.00
Surface mounted, 4' x 1', economy	1.000	Ea.	.912	46.00	100.00
Average	1.000	Ea.	1.140	57.00	130.00
Deluxe	1.000	Ea.	1.368	68.00	155.00
4' x 2', economy	1.000	Ea.	1.208	75.00	160.00
Average	1.000	Ea.	1.510	93.00	200.00
Deluxe	1.000	Ea.	1.812	110.00	235.00
Recessed, 4' x 1', 2 lamps, economy	1.000	Ea.	1.120	41.00	105.00
Average	1.000	Ea.	1.400	51.00	130.00
Deluxe	1.000	Ea.	1.680	61.00	155.00
4' x 2', 4' lamps, economy	1.000	Ea.	1.360	56.00	130.00
Average	1.000	Ea.	1.700	70.00	165.00
Deluxe	1.000	Ea.	2.040	84.00	200.00
Incandescent, exterior, 150W, single spot	1.000	Ea.	.500	19.35	47.00
Double spot	1.000	Ea.	1.167	57.00	130.00
Recessed, 100W, economy	1.000	Ea.	.800	44.00	95.00
Average	1.000	Ea.	1.000	54.00	120.00
Deluxe	1.000	Ea.	1.200	65.00	145.00
150W, economy	1.000	Ea.	.800	45.00	96.00
Average	1.000	Ea.	1.000	56.00	120.00
Deluxe	1.000	Ea.	1.200	67.00	145.00
Surface mounted, 60W, economy	1.000	Ea.	.800	34.00	80.00
Average	1.000	Ea.	1.000	39.00	95.00
Deluxe	1.000	Ea.	1.190	85.00	170.00
Mercury vapor, recessed, 2' x 2' with 250W DX lamp	1.000	Ea.	2.500	295.00	535.00
2' x 2' with 400W DX lamp	1.000	Ea.	2.760	310.00	560.00
Surface mounted, 2' x 2' wtih 250W DX lamp	1.000	Ea.	2.960	270.00	510.00
2' x 2' with 400W DX lamp	1.000	Ea.	3.330	295.00	565.00
High bay, single unit, 400W DX lamp	1.000	Ea.	3.480	285.00	550.00
Twin unit, 400W DX lamp	1.000	Ea.	5.000	570.00	1030.00
Low bay, 250W DX lamp	1.000	Ea.	2.500	350.00	610.00
Metal halide, recessed 2' x 2', 250W	1.000	Ea.	2.500	325.00	575.00
2' x 2', 400W	1.000	Ea.	2.760	370.00	650.00
Surface mounted, 2' x 2', 250W	1.000	Ea.	2.960	300.00	550.00
2' x 2', 400W	1.000	Ea.	3.330	350.00	640.00
High bay, single, unit, 400W	1.000	Ea.	3.480	330.00	621.00
Twin unit, 400W	1.000	Ea.	5.000	655.00	1150.00
Low bay, 250W	1.000	Ea.	2.500	405.00	700.00

Be sure to read pages 155–157 for proper use of this section.

APPENDIX
LOCATION
MULTIPLIERS

LOCATION MULTIPLIERS

Costs shown in *Home Improvement Cost Guide* are based on National Averages for materials and installation. To adjust these costs to a specific location, simply multiply the base cost by the multiplier for that city. The data is arranged alphabetically by state and postal zip code numbers. For a city not listed, use the factor for a nearby city with similar economic characteristics.

STATE/ZIP	CITY	MULTIPLIER
ALABAMA		
350-352	Birmingham	.83
354	Tuscaloosa	.86
355	Jasper	.83
356	Decatur	.85
357, 358	Huntsville	.86
359	Gadsden	.85
360, 361	Montgomery	.87
362	Anniston	.85
363	Dothan	.89
364	Evergreen	.89
365, 366	Mobile	.94
367	Selma	.89
368	Phenix City	.89
369	Butler	.89
ALASKA		
995, 996	Anchorage	1.30
997	Fairbanks	1.30
998	Juneau	1.30
999	Ketchikan	1.30
ARIZONA		
850		
852, 853	Phoenix	.96
855	Globe	.96
856, 857	Tucson	.95
859	Show Low	.96
860	Flagstaff	.96
863	Prescott	.96
864	Kingman	.96
865	Chambers	.96
ARKANSAS		
716	Pine Bluff	.86
717	Camden	.86
718	Texarkana	.86
719	Hot Springs	.86
720-722	Little Rock	.86
723	West Memphis	.90
724	Jonesboro	.90
725	Batesville	.86
726	Harrison	.86
727	Fayetteville	.88
728	Russellville	.88
729	Fort Smith	.88
CALIFORNIA		
900-918	Los Angeles	1.13
920, 921	San Diego	1.13
922	Palm Springs	1.15
923, 924	San Bernardino	1.15
925	Riverside	1.15
926, 927	Santa Ana	1.15
928	Anaheim	1.15
930	Ventura	1.14
931	Santa Barbara	1.15
932, 933	Bakersfield	1.13
934	San Luis Obispo	1.15
935	Mojave	1.12
936, 937	Fresno	1.14
939	Salinas	1.10
940, 941	San Francisco	1.21
943	Palo Alto	1.19
944	San Mateo	1.21
945, 946	Oakland	1.21
947	Berkeley	1.21
948	Richmond	1.21
948	San Rafael	1.19
950, 951	San Jose	1.21
952, 953	Stockton	1.14
954	Santa Rosa	1.13

STATE/ZIP	CITY	MULTIPLIER
CALIFORNIA (Cont.)		
955	Eureka	1.15
956-958	Sacramento	1.15
959	Marysville	1.15
960	Redding	1.15
961	Susanville	1.15
COLORADO		
800-802	Denver	.99
803	Boulder	.99
804	Golden	.99
805	Fort Collins	.95
806	Greeley	.95
807	Fort Morgan	.95
808, 809	Colorado Springs	.96
810	Pueblo	.97
811	Alamosa	.97
812	Salida	.96
813	Durango	.97
814	Montrose	.96
815	Grand Junction	1.00
816	Glenwood Springs	1.00
CONNECTICUT		
060, 061	Hartford	1.02
062	Willimantic	1.02
063	New London	1.02
064, 065	New Haven	1.02
066	Bridgeport	1.01
067	Waterbury	1.01
068, 069	Stamford	1.01
DELAWARE		
197, 198	Wilmington	1.02
199	Dover	1.02
DISTRICT OF COLUMBIA		
200-205	Washington	.94
FLORIDA		
320, 322	Jacksonville	.88
323	Tallahassee	.81
324	Panama City	.81
325	Pensacola	.83
326	Gainesville	.88
327, 328	Orlando	.87
329	Melbourne	.86
330, 331	Miami	.90
333	Fort Lauderdale	.90
334	W. Palm Beach	.93
335, 336	Tampa	.89
337	St. Petersburg	.89
338	Lakeland	.86
339	Fort Myers	.88
GEORGIA		
300-303	Atlanta	.85
304	Statesboro	.85
305	Gainesville	.85
306	Athens	.85
307	Dalton	.89
308, 309	Augusta	.85
310, 312	Macon	.86
313, 314	Savannah	.86
315	Waycross	.83
316	Valdosta	.83
317	Albany	.84
318, 319	Columbus	.83
HAWAII		
967, 968	Honolulu	1.18

LOCATION MULTIPLIERS

STATE/ZIP	CITY	MULTIPLIER
IDAHO		
832	Pocatello	.97
833	Twin Falls	.97
834	Idaho Falls	.97
835	Lewiston	1.05
836, 837	Boise	.96
838	Coeur D'Alene	1.05
ILLINOIS		
600-606	Chicago	1.03
609	Kankakee	1.02
610, 611	Rockford	1.02
612	Rock Island	1.03
613	La Salle	1.02
614	Galesburg	1.02
615, 616	Peoria	1.01
617	Bloomington	1.01
618, 619	Champaign	1.01
620, 622	East St. Louis	1.02
623	Quincy	.99
624	Effingham	1.02
625-627	Springfield	1.01
628	Centralia	1.02
629	Carbondale	1.02
INDIANA		
460-462	Indianapolis	1.00
463, 464	Gary	1.03
465, 466	South Bend	.98
467, 468	Fort Wayne	.94
469	Kokomo	.97
470	Lawrenceburg	1.01
471	New Albany	.95
472	Columbus	1.01
473	Muncie	.96
474	Bloomington	1.01
475	Washington	.98
476, 477	Evansville	.97
478	Terre Haute	.98
479	Lafayette	.96
IOWA		
500-503	Des Moines	.95
504	Mason City	.94
505	Fort Dodge	.94
506, 507	Waterloo	.95
508	Creston	.94
510, 511	Sioux City	.88
512	Sibley	.88
513	Spencer	.88
514	Carroll	.94
515	Council Bluffs	.95
516	Shenandoah	.95
520	Dubuque	.96
521	Decorah	.96
522-524	Cedar Rapids	.99
525	Ottumwa	.99
526	Burlington	1.00
527, 528	Davenport	.96
KANSAS		
660-662	Kansas City	1.01
664-666	Topeka	.93
667	Fort Scott	1.01
668	Emporia	.93
669	Belleville	.93
670-672	Wichita	.91
673	Independence	.91
674	Salina	.91
675	Hutchinson	.91
676	Hays	.91
677	Colby	.91
678	Dodge City	.91
679	Liberal	.91

STATE/ZIP	CITY	MULTIPLIER
KENTUCKY		
400-401	Louisville	.93
403-405	Lexington	.92
406	Frankfort	.94
407-409	Corbin	.94
410	Covington	1.01
411, 412	Ashland	.94
413, 414	Campton	.92
415, 416	Pikeville	.94
417, 418	Hazard	.92
420	Paducah	.94
421, 422	Bowling Green	.94
423	Owensboro	.94
424	Henderson	.94
425, 426	Somerset	.92
427	Elizabethtown	.94
LOUISIANA		
700, 701	New Orleans	.91
703	Thibodaux	.91
704	Hammond	.90
705	Lafayette	.88
706	Lake Charles	.88
707, 708	Baton Rouge	.89
710, 711	Shreveport	.84
712	Monroe	.84
713, 714	Alexandria	.84
MAINE		
039	Kittery	.90
040, 041	Portland	.89
042	Lewiston	.89
043	Augusta	.90
044	Bangor	.90
045	Bath	.90
046	Machias	.90
047	Houlton	.90
048	Rockland	.90
049	Waterville	.91
MARYLAND		
206	Waldorf	.95
207, 208	College Park	.95
209	Silver Spring	.96
210-212	Baltimore	.94
214	Annapolis	.94
215	Cumberland	.91
216	Easton	.94
217	Hagerstown	.94
218	Salisbury	.94
219	Elkton	.94
MASSACHUSETTS		
010, 011	Springfield	1.02
012	Pittsfield	.99
013	Greenfield	1.02
014	Fitchburg	1.10
015, 106	Worcester	1.10
017	Framingham	1.12
018	Lowell	1.07
019	Lynn	1.12
020-022	Boston	1.12
023, 024	Brockton	1.02
025	Buzzards Bay	1.02
026	Hyannis	1.03
027	New Bedford	1.03
MICHIGAN		
480	Royal Oak	1.08
480-482	Detroit	1.08
484, 485	Flint	.97
486, 487	Saginaw	.94
488, 489	Lansing	1.02
490, 491	Kalamazoo	.98
492	Jackson	1.04
493-495	Grand Rapids	.94
496	Traverse City	.94
497	Gaylord	.96
498, 499	Iron Mountain	.97

243

LOCATION MULTIPLIERS

STATE/ZIP	CITY	MULTIPLIER
MINNESOTA		
550, 551	St. Paul	1.01
553, 554	Minneapolis	1.03
556-558	Duluth	.96
559	Rochester	1.00
560	Mankato	1.01
561	Windom	1.01
562	Willmar	1.01
563	St. Cloud	1.01
564	Brainerd	1.01
565	Detroit Lakes	.86
566	Bemidji	.86
567	Thief River Falls	.86
MISSISSIPPI		
386	Clarksdale	.87
387	Greenville	.87
388	Tupelo	.85
389	Greenwood	.87
390-392	Jackson	.87
393	Meridian	.87
394	Laurel	.88
395	Biloxi	.88
396	Mc Comb	.85
397	Columbus	.85
MISSOURI		
630, 631	St. Louis	.99
633	Bowling Green	.99
634	Hannibal	.99
635	Kirksville	.90
636	Flat River	.99
637	Cape Girardeau	.99
638	Sikeston	.99
639	Poplar Bluff	.99
640, 641	Kansas City	1.01
644, 645	Saint Joseph	.90
645	Chillicothe	.90
647	Harrisonville	1.00
648	Joplin	.90
650, 652	Columbia	.99
651	Jefferson City	.99
653	Sedalia	.99
654, 655	Rolla	.99
656-658	Springfield	.90
MONTANA		
590-591	Billings	.95
592	Wolf Point	.95
593	Miles City	.95
594	Great Falls	.95
595	Havre	.95
596	Helena	.95
597	Butte	.95
598	Missoula	.95
599	Kalispell	.95
NEBRASKA		
680, 681	Omaha	.91
683-685	Lincoln	.91
686	Columbus	.91
687	Norfolk	.91
688	Grand Island	.91
689	Hastings	.91
690	Mc Cook	.91
691	North Platte	.91
692	Valentine	.91
693	Alliance	.90
NEVADA		
890, 891	Las Vegas	1.07
893	Ely	1.07
894, 895	Reno	1.04
897	Carson City	1.04
898	Elko	1.04

STATE/ZIP	CITY	MULTIPLIER
NEW HAMPSHIRE		
030, 031	Manchester	.93
032, 033	Concord	.93
034	Keene	.93
035	Littleton	.93
036	Charlestown	.93
037	Claremont	.93
038	Portsmouth	.93
NEW JERSEY		
070, 071	Newark	1.09
072	Elizabeth	1.09
073	Jersey City	1.09
074, 075	Paterson	1.11
076	Hackensack	1.11
077	Long Branch	1.09
078	Dover	1.09
079	Summit	1.09
080, 083	Vineland	1.09
081	Camden	1.09
082, 084	Atlantic City	1.09
085, 086	Trenton	1.09
087	Point Pleasant	1.09
088, 089	New Brunswick	1.09
NEW MEXICO		
870, 871	Albuquerque	.90
873	Gallup	.90
874	Farmington	.90
875	Santa Fe	.90
877	Las Vegas	.90
878	Socorro	.90
879	Truth/Conseq.	.90
880	Las Cruces	.90
881	Clovis	.90
882	Roswell	.90
883	Carrizozo	.90
884	Tucumcari	.90
NEW YORK		
100	Manhattan	1.21
103	Staten Island	1.21
104	Bronx	1.21
105	Mount Vernon	1.20
106	White Plains	1.20
107	Yonkers	1.15
108	New Rochelle	1.15
109	Suffern	1.15
110	Queens	1.21
111	Long Island City	1.21
112	Brooklyn	1.21
113	Flushing	1.21
114	Jamaica	1.21
115, 117, 118	Hicksville	1.21
116	Far Rockaway	1.21
119	Riverhead	1.21
120-122	Albany	.96
123	Schenectady	.97
124	Kingston	1.15
125, 126	Poughkeepsie	1.15
127	Monticello	1.15
128	Glens Falls	.99
129	Plattsburgh	.99
130-132	Syracuse	.99
133-135	Utica	.93
136	Watertown	.93
137-139	Binghamton	.93
140-142	Buffalo	1.08
143	Niagara Falls	1.08
144-146	Rochester	1.01
147	Jamestown	1.08
148, 149	Elmira	.93

LOCATION MULTIPLIERS

STATE/ZIP	CITY	MULTIPLIER
NORTH CAROLINA		
270, 272-274	Greensboro	.80
271	Winston-Salem	.83
275, 276	Raleigh	.83
277	Durham	.81
278	Rocky Mount	.83
279	Elizabeth City	.86
280-282	Charlotte	.82
283	Fayetteville	.83
284	Wilmington	.82
285	Kingston	.83
286	Hickory	.83
287, 288	Asheville	.82
289	Murphy	.83
NORTH DAKOTA		
580, 581	Fargo	.86
582	Grand Forks	.86
583	Devils Lake	.86
584	Jamestown	.86
585	Bismarck	.86
586	Dickinson	.86
587	Minot	.86
588	Williston	.86
OHIO		
430-432	Columbus	1.00
433	Marion	.98
434-436	Toledo	1.04
437, 438	Zanesville	1.00
439	Steubenville	1.01
440, 441	Cleveland	1.15
442-443	Akron	1.05
444, 445	Youngstown	1.02
446, 447	Canton	1.01
448, 449	Mansfield	1.01
450-452	Cincinnati	1.01
453, 454	Dayton	1.00
455	Springfield	.98
456	Chillicothe	1.01
457	Athens	1.00
458	Lima	1.06
OKLAHOMA		
730, 731	Oklahoma City	.89
734	Ardmore	.89
735	Lawton	.89
736	Clinton	.89
737	Enid	.89
738	Woodward	.89
739	Guymon	.89
740, 741	Tulsa	.93
743	Miami	.93
744	Muskogee	.93
745	McAlester	.89
746	Ponca City	.93
747	Durant	.89
748	Shawnee	.89
749	Poteau	.88
OREGON		
970-972	Portland	1.04
973	Salem	1.03
974	Eugene	1.03
975	Medford	1.03
976	Klamath Falls	1.03
977	Bend	1.03
978	Pendleton	.97
979	Vale	.97
PENNSYLVANIA		
150-152	Pittsburgh	1.06
153	Washington	1.06
154	Uniontown	1.06
155	Bedford	1.06
156	Greensburg	1.06
157	Indiana	1.06
158	Du Bois	1.06
159	Johnstown	1.06

STATE/ZIP	CITY	MULTIPLIER
PENNSYLVANIA (Cont.)		
160	Butler	1.06
161	New Castle	1.06
162	Kittanning	1.06
163	Oil City	.98
164, 165	Erie	.98
166	Altoona	1.06
167	Bradford	.98
168	State College	.97
169	Wellsboro	.95
170, 171	Harrisburg	.97
172	Chambersburg	.97
173, 174	York	.97
175, 176	Lancaster	.97
177	Williamsport	.97
178	Sunbury	.97
179	Pottsville	.97
180	Lehigh Valley	1.04
181	Allentown	1.04
182	Hazleton	1.04
183	Stroudsburg	1.04
184, 185	Scranton	.94
186, 187	Wilkes Barre	.94
188	Montrose	.94
189	Doylestown	.94
190, 191	Philadelphia	1.08
193	Westchester	1.08
194	Norristown	1.08
195, 196	Reading	.94
RHODE ISLAND		
028, 029	Providence	.99
SOUTH CAROLINA		
290-292	Columbia	.80
293	Spartanburg	.80
294	Charleston	.81
295	Florence	.80
296	Greenville	.80
297	Rock Hill	.80
298	Aiken	.80
299	Beaufort	.81
SOUTH DAKOTA		
570, 571	Sioux Falls	.91
572	Watertown	.91
573	Mitchell	.91
574	Aberdeen	.91
575	Pierre	.91
576	Mobridge	.92
577	Rapid City	.92
TENNESSEE		
370-372	Nashville	.84
373, 374	Chattanooga	.88
376	Johnson City	.87
377-379	Knoxville	.86
380, 381	Memphis	.89
382	Mc Kenzie	.84
383	Jackson	.81
384	Columbia	.84
385	Cookeville	.84
TEXAS		
750	Mc Kinney	.97
751	Waxahackie	.92
752, 753	Dallas	.90
754	Greenville	.96
755	Texarkana	.96
756	Longview	.96
757	Tyler	.96
758	Palestine	.85
759	Lufkin	.85
760, 761	Fort Worth	.93
762	Denton	.96
763	Wichita Falls	.90
764	Eastland	.93

LOCATION MULTIPLIERS

STATE/ZIP	CITY	MULTIPLIER
TEXAS (Cont.)		
765	Temple	.90
766, 767	Waco	.87
768	Brownwood	.87
769	San Angelo	.87
770-772	Houston	.90
773	Huntsville	.89
774	Wharton	.93
775	Galveston	.93
776, 777	Beaumont	.96
778	Bryan	.90
779	Victoria	.86
780-782	San Antonio	.85
783, 784	Corpus Christi	.86
785	Mc Allen	.86
786, 787	Austin	.90
788	Del Rio	.86
789	Giddings	.90
790, 791	Amarillo	.90
792	Childress	.87
793, 794	Lubbock	.87
795, 796	Abilene	.88
797	Midland	.86
798, 799	El Paso	.83
UTAH		
840, 841	Salt Lake City	.94
843, 844	Ogden	.94
845	Price	.94
846	Provo	.94
VERMONT		
050	White River Jct.	.90
051	Bellows Falls	.90
052	Bennington	.90
053	Brattleboro	.90
054	Burlington	.90
056	Montpelier	.90
057	Rutland	.90
058	St. Johnsbury	.90
059	Guildhall	.90
VIRGINIA		
220, 221	Fairfax	.95
222	Arlington	.95
223	Alexandria	.95
224, 225	Fredericksburg	.95
226	Winchester	.95
227	Culpeper	.95
228	Harrisonburg	.95
229	Charlottesville	.88
230-232	Richmond	.88
233-235	Norfolk	.84
236	Newport News	.85
237	Portsmouth	.84
238	Petersburg	.88
239	Farmville	.88
240, 241	Roanoke	.84
242	Bristol	.85
243	Pulaski	.84
244	Staunton	.88
245	Lynchburg	.86
246	Grundy	.99
WASHINGTON		
980, 981	Seattle	.97
982	Everett	.97
983, 984	Tacoma	1.05
985	Olympia	1.05
986	Vancouver	1.07
988	Wenatchee	.99
989	Yakima	1.05
990-992	Spokane	1.04
993	Richland	1.04
994	Clarkston	1.04

STATE/ZIP	CITY	MULTIPLIER
WEST VIRGINIA		
247, 248	Bluefield	1.00
249	Lewisburg	1.00
250-253	Charleston	1.00
254	Martinsburg	.96
255-257	Huntington	.98
258, 259	Beckley	1.00
260	Wheeling	.98
261	Parkersburg	.98
262	Buckhannon	1.00
263, 264	Clarksburg	1.00
265	Morgantown	1.00
266	Gassaway	1.00
267	Romney	.93
268	Petersburg	1.00
WISCONSIN		
530-532	Milwaukee	.98
534	Racine	1.02
535, 537	Madison	.95
538	Lancaster	.95
539	Portage	.95
540	New Richmond	1.00
541-543	Green Bay	.97
544	Wausau	.95
545	Rhinelander	.95
546	La Crosse	.95
547	Eau Claire	1.00
548	Superior	1.00
549	Oshkosh	.96
WYOMING		
820	Cheyenne	.97
821	Yellowstone Nat'l. Park	.97
822	Wheatland	.97
823	Rawlins	.97
824	Worland	.97
825	Riverton	.97
826	Casper	.97
827	Newcastle	.97
828	Sheridan	.97
829-831	Rock Springs	.97
CANADIAN FACTORS (reflect Canadian currency)		
ALBERTA		
	Calgary	1.05
	Edmonton	1.05
BRITISH COLUMBIA		
	Vancouver	1.08
MANITOBA		
	Winnipeg	1.02
NEW BRUNSWICK		
	Saint John	.95
	Moncton	.95
NEWFOUNDLAND		
	St. John's	.96
NOVA SCOTIA		
	Halifax	.95
ONTARIO		
	Hamilton	1.06
	London	1.04
	Ottawa	1.04
	Sudbury	1.04
	Toronto	1.07
PRINCE EDWARD ISLAND		
	Charlottetown	.96
QUEBEC		
	Montreal	1.05
	Quebec	1.05
SASKATCHEWAN		
	Regina	1.03
	Saskatoon	1.03

INDEX